To the memory of my father

EDWARD HENDERSON
1876-1934

*who played no small part in the
early religious and social life
of the village of Lochore*

ISB Number 0 9513806 0 5

Printed by Allen Litho, Kirkcaldy

II

THE HISTORY OF LOCHORESHIRE

*from the earliest of times
to the first quarter of
the present century*

by
EDWARD HENDERSON, F.S.A. Scot.

1988

ACKNOWLEDGEMENT

During my years in collecting material for this book, I have received much help and encouragement from many quarters. I mention in particular the Historical Department of Register House, Edinburgh, the National Library and the Signet Library, the Dunfermline and Ayr Public Libraries, the Mitchell Library, the Library of Glasgow University and the British Museum. To the staffs of these libraries, for their unfailing courtesy, I tender my grateful thanks.

The following individuals also earn my thanks: John Duncan, Crosshill, Vice President of the Benarty Antiquarian Club who for two seasons gave me continued assistance in excavating Lochore Castle and to the present; Mrs Edith Briggs Constable, Kingussie, for giving me details of the Constable family; Professor A.A.M. Duncan and Dr. I.B. Cowan, Department of History, and William Craw, Department of French, all of Glasgow University; Dr. J.C. Corson, Honorary Librarian of Abbotsford; the Rt. Rev. Monsignor David McRoberts, Keeper of the Catholic Archives; David Smith, Advocate, Sheriff of Kilmarnock, who generously translated a host of latin charters; Harry Blackhall, Troon, who read the book in manuscript and gave me much helpful assistance in compiling the index.

I specially record my indebtedness to the late Mrs Isabella Grindlay, Troon, who gave up so much of her time in typing the book and for her infinite patience throughout. My thanks are also due to David Adams, Crosshill, of the Publication Committee, for his continuous help.

I alone am responsible for views expressed and for any errors, factual or otherwise.

The following have kindly granted me permission to reproduce copyright material and illustrations:
Central Library, Dunfermline, Frontispiece, John Duncan, 3, 5, 45, 47 and 76. Society of Antiquaries of Scotland, 7, 72, 73 and quotation on page 219. David Westwater, 10. Milne, Tannahill & Methven Ltd., 12, 29 and quotation on page 39. "Old Glasgow" Museum, 19. Captain Keith Adam, 21 and 38. Eneas Mackay, 29. Glasgow Art Gallery and Museum, 36. Elizabeth W. Grierson, Allan Stewart and A. & C. Black, Ltd., 37. Scottish Record Office, 43. Mrs Jenny Dawson, 44. The Kinross-shire Advertiser Ltd., 52. From the Abbotsford Collection, 54. Natural Portrait Gallery, 55, 77 and 88. T. & A. Constable, 59. Pittencrieff House Museum, 66. National Coal Board, 69. Hector Charles Cameron and William Heinemann, 79, 80 and 81. The late Miss Jessie Drysdale, 83. The Earl of Rosebery, 87. John Smith & Son, 93. The late Walter Wilson, Appendix III. William Beck, 22. National Library, 84 and Appendix IV.

The following line drawings are my own, 6, 8, 13, 14, 16, 18, 26, 27, 28, 30, 33, 40, 41, 46, 48, 49, 50, 51, 53, 57, 60, 61, 64, 65, 67, 89, 92 and 94.

FOREWORD

This book gives a well researched and detailed resumé of the Social and Economic History of that part of Fife Region which was a "shire" in its own right until combined with the neighbouring "shires" to form the County of Fife.

The area has long been regarded as having medieval and pre-historic settlements as well as evidence of Roman occupation.

This work, however, brings together these fragments of knowledge into a cohesive and easily readable form and for the first time the history of the area is drawn together from pre-history through the Roman occupation of Britain into the times leading up to and beyond the Industrial Revolution until the present.

I would commend this lifetime's work to both academics and also those who simply enjoy a historical book, remembering that this is "fact" not fiction. It is a "must" for those who are concerned with the study of environment and the social and economic changes in this important and ancient part of what is now Fife Region.

Thomas M. Dair, J.P.
Chairman
Fife Regional Council Education Committee

CONTENTS

LIST OF ILLUSTRATIONS

Page

PREFACE

One lovely summer's afternoon over seventy years ago a small boy was standing on the Clune Hill in the parish of Ballingry within the remains of an Iron Age "hut circle" in the company of two learned gentlemen. He was too young to take part in their conversation, but what they were discussing was of great interest to him.

As he stood on the windswept summit of the hill he edged round to the leeward side of the nearest gentleman and standing there almost knee-deep among the bracken and bluebells he heard, between the cries of the curlews overhead, a voice proclaim from a point somewhere above his head "someone aught to write a history of the parish". This met with a ready response from his companion, and as the small boy looked down at the bluebells, he became conscious of being a witness to a solemn undertaking that one of the gentlemen would write the secular history of the parish and the other its ecclesiastical history. They had, however, not reckoned with the uncertainties of the times. The guns of war were soon to be sounding in France and the parish history was never written; — the present writer was the small boy.

Although many years have passed since the writer left Ballingry, he still has an interest in the parish. He has until now withheld writing a history of the locality, always hoping that a resident with a nimbler pen than his own would undertake the task. Advancing years, however, have a way of compelling one to make a decision. The results of his research are given here under the title *The History of Lochoreshire*.

Like many others before him, the writer accepted without question much of what had been said by the eighteenth century writers on the early history of Lochoreshire. He had, however, not gone far in his story when he found it increasingly difficult to reconcile certain statements with what he was now discovering.

This led him to the decision to consult all the available information at its source, including for the most part the public records. As a result, much of his account of the early history of the region had to be re-written in the light of the new evidence. His research has been most profitable, as it has revealed many facts of which he had hitherto been entirely unaware.

Not surprisingly, much is said that runs contrary to accepted local belief. The writer hopes his book will appeal not only to those who reside in the area, but to those who come to Lochore to enjoy the recreational facilities at the Meadows Country Park and who wish to know something of its past history, and also to those abroad whose roots are in Lochoreshire.

Edward Henderson

'Benarty', Troon, Ayrshire
1988

INTRODUCTION

A century has almost passed since the Rev. David Jamie wrote his *Old Church Life in Ballingry* and his book has since been the chief source of information about the past life of the parish.

As Mr Jamie wrote chiefly on matters concerning the ecclesiastical life of the parish, what he wrote about the lairds is related mainly to their connection with the church. The present writer has endeavoured to present the history of the locality on broader lines, and to emphasise its secular history. He has, however, included what is now known of the early history of Ballingry church and the chapel of Inchall, and other matters concerning local church history which have hitherto received only a brief notice.

Great changes have taken place since Mr Jamie's time, and with the introduction of deep-seam coal mining at the turn of the present century, "Bonnie Bingry" lost much of its rural charm. The contrast between olden times and the present day is emphasised by an entry in Sir Walter Scott's journal under June 1830. Sir Walter writes: "we settled this morning to go to church at Lochore, that is, at Ballingray; but when we came to the earthly paradise so called ...". One wonders what Sir Walter would have written had it been possible for him to have seen the new township where in his day there stood stooks of corn and hay ricks, and in the whole parish, according to his friend the Rev. James Greig, one could count only "seventy reekin lums".

Lochore and district has been much maligned in the past, and to some extent still is. Although coal mining had been carried on in the area since 1560, the small "howkings" of former days did not protrude on the landscape.

It was not until recent years, following the closing-down of the collieries, that suppurating sores in the form of coal slurry-ponds, and ever increasing colliery refuse tips were removed in an effort to restore the countryside to something resembling its former self. It would be wrong, however, to assume that Lochore has no history beyond that connected with mining. A writer in 1875 refers to the "short and simple annals of Ballingry". Had he lived a century later, he may have written otherwise, for time and chance have unlocked many of the secrets of the past.

In recording these "annals", the writer has had to travel beyond the confines of the neighbourhood, and to recall some of the tragic figures in our national history, Lady Macbeth, Rizzio, Darnley and Mary Queen of Scots. For does a fourteenth century document not speak of a well situated in Ballingry called Gruoch's Well, and is it not so clearly described that one knows exactly where it is! The well is still there, but our modern town-planners have taken the water from it and conveyed it underground, so that a place of learning is now built on top of the stream. The writer hopes that the fact of the well, and other circumstances relating to the derivation of the name Ballingry, will stimulate an interest in others to study the early history of the neighbourhood, not least the pupils of Benarty School. Furthermore, was a laird of Lochore's son-in-law not involved in the murder of Rizzio, and was a son of the laird of Capeldrae, being the Queen's usher, not required to give evidence concerning the murder of Lord Darnley?

Few have not heard of the Queen's "Four Marys", but it is not so well known that there were in fact five ladies of the Queen's bedchamber, and that a local laird's daughter was one of that number. She is, of course, not enshrined in the song, *The Four Marys* as her name was not Mary, but Nicholas.

It goes without question that the imprisonment of the Queen in Lochleven Castle must have been a subject for local discussion on many occasions. It is not surprising, therefore, to find that Nicholas's uncle sided with the Queen in her adversity, and that he, and another local kinsman, took part in the plot to effect the Queen's escape.

The north-going route by way of Loch Ore, Kirkness and the Gullet Bridge over the old course of the River Leven, has been open to travellers since the dawn of history, and one can only guess what strange companies must have passed this way, from the days of the Roman legionaries and all the centuries that lie between then and now. It is said to have been used by troops during the Wars of Independence but, apart from an account of a company of Jacobites who passed this way in 1715, and also what is about to be said, history is regrettably silent as to those who took the road through "Bonnie Bingry". There is a tradition, which is repeated by several writers, that one person well-known in history passed through the neighbourhood.

The battle of Inverkeithing had been fought, and the victor was on his way to Perth. The year was 1651, and Oliver Cromwell, so tradition has it, decided to divide his forces, one half going north by the west side of Loch Leven, and the other half, under his own command, to take the east route by way of the Gullet Bridge. So it was that, in the afternoon of a hot July day, after leaving the cluster of houses of easter and wester Lochgillie, the Protector began to descend into the Or valley, where to the north lay Loch Or set against the wooded heights of Benarty Hill and Blaircushnie. He had now entered wester Lochquhorschir.

By consulting the records of the period, it is possible to get some idea of what the neighbourhood looked like when Cromwell's column made its way through the parish, and as the writer has already given the old form of place-names he will continue to do so.

Passing between the lands of Cairthmoir and Wester Cowquelis, the column reached a few thatched houses grouped beside the river Fitty, called Quontill, where the horsemen crossed the Clochrat ford and headed for the rising ground, passing the entrance to Cluneycraig House. On the east side of the road was the Coalheugh of Inchgaw and a little further east, Inchgaw Mill, with Shirram Brae in the distance. To the west were the lands of Cluneycraig, with a wisp of smoke rising from a few sheilins called Clerkwhig, and beyond these the remains of the Chapel of Bothedlech overlooking the Commonty of Lumfynnens, lying south of the river Fitty. The column was now ascending the rising ground and passed on its right the Spail Inn, a place of rest for travellers. To the west lay the loch with a few fishing boats upon it, and the roofless castle on the island of Inchgaw owned then by the Earl of Rothes.

Here, the ford was crossed at the mouth of the loch, also the mill lades that fed the meal mill of Lochor, situated in the Templin, and the waulk mills at the Milntoun of Inchgaw. Having crossed the ford, they were now in the Burgh of Corsehill. In the Milntoun to the east, could be seen the gaunt, double-storey, crow-stepped gabled house called Castlerags, and beside it, the Parliament Stane, and beyond it, the Maynes lands, which in past years had provided food for the people of the castle. Situated also in the Milntoun were the Smiddy lands, and not far way was the Fuller's and the Litster's barn where cloth was bleached and dyed. In the middle distance stood the lands of the Waulkmill of Balbegie and beyond that, Harelaw.

On the west side of the road were the lands of Corsehill, with the thatched and turfed roofs of the brewer's premises, and the booth belonging to Johne Budgall, the flesher, who, along with Robert Meldrum, the miller, was a constable of the parish. Nearby stood the croft where the Serjand of the castle lived, until, with the departure of the Wardlaw family, the office fell into disuse. Also in Corsehill, stood the croft that once belonged to James Dave, whose worldly possessions, amounting to "thre ky, ane hors, ane mair, cornis and ane heddar stak", were seized when he was outlawed for his part in the slaughter of David Balfour of Urquhile.

Beyond the scatter of biggins that made up the toun of Corsehill, the ruins of the chapel of Inchgaw could be seen away to the west, and farther still, the woods of Gilquhomy, and on the horizon the lands of Blaircramplbee. A little to the north of the ruined chapel could be seen the Bowhous of Inchgaw dominating the Harran Hill. Soon the cavalcade was approaching the Mercat Croce of Corsehill, which stood on an eminence on the west side of the road, and today is within earshot of the laughter of school children. To the left and right lay the lands of Wester and Easter Corsehill and on the horizon to the east could be seen the Commonty of the Miltoun Moss of Inchgaw, part of which, in later years, was to be known as "The Old Loan".

By the time the rear-guard had crossed the mill lades, the vanguard had reached the Hynds of Inchgaw with its house and steading. To the west, between the steading and the road, lay a small lochan, fed with water no doubt, from the near-by Rose well. A bowling green now occupies the site of the little loch. Beyond this point, to the west, lay the lands of Ladath, while to the east were the Kirklands of Corsehill.

Ahead midway up the rising ground lay crossroads. The road to the west led to the Kirkton of Bingry, and that to the east, to the Common. Beyond the crossroads to the west lay the Glebe lands of Bingry, while to the east, lay the lands of Flockhous, part of which at a later date became known as Rosewell. After the sweating teams of horses had dragged their heavy loads up the rough water-rutted road, they eased off on the level ground, by which time the vanguard could see to the south-west, the ancient House and steading of Ladath, and nearby the Bowhous of Kildounie, and farther west the Commonty of Bunertiehills, while to the north-west stood Bingry House and steading, situated on the slope of Bunertiehills. On the rising ground a little to the west of the house could be seen a ribbon of water cascading over the rocks as it issued from Gruoch's well, and on the comparatively level ground below the hill stood the kirk of Bingry, dominating a cluster of thatched houses.

Lochore House had not yet been built. Five years were to pass before the same Cromwell was to sign a charter granting John Malcolm of Balbedie the barony of Inchgaw. The column by this time was about to descend the hill leading to the Lochty Burn. Before doing so, it passed on its right, at the road leading to the toun and lands of Cappilldrae, a large house known as the Flockhous of Inchgaw. Having passed the Butter well on its right situated in the parish of Auchtirdoun, and the Munshock moss on

4

its left, it was now approaching the kirklands of Bingry, while straight ahead could be seen a cluster of biggins and an aleshouse, which marked the site of the "staney ford of Navetay". After men and horses had manoeuvred the guns over the ford, the leading horseman began to ascend the Shank of Navetay. To the west lay the kirklands, and to the east the lands of Kirkness, with Boglochty occupying the low ground, known as the Commonty of Strathrudie.

The House and village of Kirkness with its chapel, lay straight ahead.

Using an entrance which led through an avenue of ancient trees, long since abandoned, the Protector halted, and stayed overnight as the guest of Sir William Douglas. The soldiers found shelter in the village, and the horses were allowed to graze on the luscious pasture of "The Greens."

THE EXTENT OF THE SHIRE

Lochoreshire in ancient times included within its bounds that part of modern Fife which today forms part of the west boundary of the new Fife Region with Kinross-shire. Westward, it was dominated by the Benarty Hill upon whose heights stood the oppidum of a Pictish tribe, which in very early times probably possessed the neighbourhood under the leadership of its chieftain called Gedhor. From there, it stretched eastward halfway to the sea as far as Dogton in the parish of Kinglassie, where stands the armless cross said to mark the inroads of the Danes in the ninth century, beyond which lay the vale which still retains its name Strathor. To the north it was bounded by the river Leven. The lands there, consisting of Balbedie and part of Kinglassie, were separated from the southern portion of Lochoreshire by Kirkness, which was, and still is, in Portmoak parish. This intervening wedge of land stretched from Loch Leven to a point more than halfway towards the eastward limits of Lochoreshire. Its southern boundary with Lochoreshire was on more than one occasion a matter of dispute. From the accumulative evidence so far obtained, it would appear that the ancient estate of Ballingry in early times lay outwith Lochoreshire, although it was included at a much later date. Lochoresburn near Loch Gelly, in the parish of Auchtertool, marked its extent southward.

2 *Dogton Cross, Kinglassie (as it was)*

In short, it embraced the parishes of Ballingry, Auchterderran and Kinglassie, a small portion of the parish of Auchtertool, part of the parish of Cleish, and probably a small part of Portmoak parish. At a later date, it included by annexation, certain lands in the parish of Markinch and property in Cupar.

By virtue of its geographical position, Lochoreshire in early times, with the neighbouring shires of Bishopshire, Gaitmilkshire and Kirkcaldyshire, lay not in Fife proper, but within the equally ancient province of Fothreve or Fothrif which extended westward as far as the Ochil Hills. These shires in many cases were the visible outcome of the sharing of the land in Celtic times, and were originally the tracks of land belonging to the feudal lord, which in course of time became parishes with, in many cases, the baron's private chapel becoming the church for the parish, so that Lochoreshire may possibly mean in simple terms, Lochore's share.

THE PRE-HISTORIC PERIOD

Contained in a rock basin lying between Benarty Hill and the upthrust of igneous rock of the Clune, is the loch (now much reduced in size) which gave its name to the shire. Its origin takes us back far beyond the fringe of recorded history to a period when the land was locked in the grip of a great icefield, when slow-moving glaciers travelled from the west and carved out the land masses, and sculptured the local landscape much as we see it today. Benarty Hill stood as a bastion withstanding the force of the ice as it moved slowly eastward to the sea. The precipitous rock on the west face of the hill split the icefield in two. One half moved along the north side of the hill and ground out a great hollow and gave us the Leven valley, likewise the icefield to the south of the hill pushed all before it and, leaving only the lower mass of igneous rock at the Clune, gouged out a great hollow and gave us the Ore valley.

With the change to a more temperate climate, the icefield melted and dropped its load of clay, gravel and sand, and as it receded it left behind ice-worn rock surfaces and erratic boulders such as the "Capel Stone" at Capeldrae, and many others. It also produced many morainic mounds such as those to be seen at Craigie-Malcolm and the small one on which Ballingry Church is built. So it was, when the climate became more genial, two rivers followed in the wake of the receding ice, and meltwaters moulded the contours of our neighbourhood. Where ribs of rock straddled the course of the rivers they broadened out, each forming a loch on either side of the hill. The one to the south gave its name to the shire.

3   *The "Capel Stone"*

The advantages to be had by living near a loch must have appealed to men from the earliest of times. As water attracts wildlife of all kinds, game would be plentiful and they could more easily provide for themselves and their families. The banks of the loch

8

would provide pasture for their flocks and on the higher ground, after clearing and digging the soil with their stone implements, they would grow their cereals. The earliest people who lived beside the loch of which we have any evidence, belonged to the Bronze Age (1800-500 BC) and are known by the presence of their burial cairns and isolated urn-burials which have come to light from time to time. There is also evidence that a community of Iron Age People (500 BC-100 AD) settled beside the loch on what is now known as the Clune.

An eighteenth century writer remarks on the number of burial cairns which were to be seen on the plain to the east of the loch in his day. There was a Bronze Age cairn situated about a mile north of the loch. From a description of the site, the cairn probably stood on the high ground in what is now the public park at Lochore, and stood within some form of defensive earthwork. The cairn was opened in 1820 when a stone cist was found and several urns containing bones.

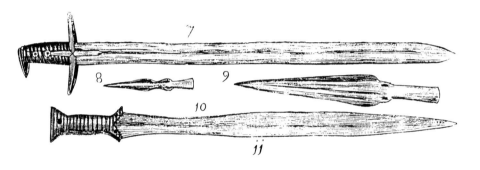

4 *Swords and spear-heads of bronze found near Loch Ore about the year 1615.*

Several Bronze Age swords and spearheads were found beside the loch about the year 1615*, and many more were found in the bed of the loch during draining operations towards the end of the eighteenth century. Stone axe heads of the same period were found at Craigie-Malcolm within the first quarter of the present century. A little further afield at Tollie Hill near Lumphinnans, while workmen were engaged in constructing a green on Cowdenbeath golf course in 1927, they unearthed three Bronze Age urns, and in the following year a further two urns were found at the same place, all belonging to the late Bronze Age period. Sometime prior to 1854 several stone cists were found near Powguild Farm, a little north of Loch Gelly, and in a moss near the same loch, there was found in 1886 a bronze flagon. The latest discovery of relics of the Bronze Age occurred in 1970 at Gairneybridge while the M90 motorway was being constructed. Five stone cists were unearthed: three were inhumation burials and two were cremation burials. Two cinerary urns were found along with a bronze spearhead and the blade of a bronze knife. The burials dated from around 1500 BC.

* Some of these were placed in Sir Andrew Balfour's private museum.

5 *Harelaw Cairn*

By far the most imposing monument belonging to this period is the cairn which crowns Harelaw, a mile and a half distant to the east of Lochore. It commands a conspicuous site on the horizon overlooking the loch and it is no doubt the resting place of a Bronze Age chief and also his kinsfolk who lie buried around him. The smaller cairns which were to be seen on the intervening plain between Harelaw and the loch, no doubt marked the graves of the humbler folk. Although Harelaw cairn has been partially excavated, there is reason to believe that a thorough excavation would reveal more burials.

The cairn was opened by several members of the Ballingry Antiquarian Club during the years 1890 and 1891*. It was described in 1850 as being about two hundred and twenty five feet in circumference and attaining a height of over twenty feet and surrounded by a low wall which stood about twelve feet from its base, the foundations of which were exposed during the early part of the work. The excavators drove a trench into the west side of the cairn and, after reaching a distance of twenty-one feet, they uncovered a stone cist composed of roughly dressed slabs of freestone set on edge with a freestone cover. The cist contained a food vessel "highly ornamental with zig-zags and notches". The food vessel stood five and a half inches in height and was twenty inches in circumference at its greatest girth. The cist also contained the remains of several teeth and bones.

No sooner had the excavators left the site than the news spread throughout the village, and on the following day hundreds of people trekked to the cairn to view its contents; some, encouraged by the belief of hidden treasure, smashed the stones of the cist and dug down to a depth of three to four feet and left the excavation in a disgraceful condition. After the lapse of a week the excavators returned and with the aid of an experienced antiquary in the person of Alexander Hutcheson, an architect from Broughty Ferry, they drove a trench simultaneously from both sides of the cairn. On

---

* These included Mr Constable of Glencraig, Rev. Mr Jamie of Ballingry, Rev. Mr Dewar of Lochgelly, Rev. Mr Houston of Auchterderran, Mr Drysdale of Inchgall Farm and Mr Begg of Kinross.

reaching the centre, a second and larger cist was found having all its joints and crevices luted with tough yellow clay. This cist contained decayed bones and teeth and a strip of metal so oxidised as to be unidentifiable.

Work was resumed the following year when the cairn was cut into from the north and a third, the smallest cist exposed. It contained a food vessel having the usual crude ornamentation. It stood four inches in height and sixteen inches round the lip and eight inches at the base and had five lug handles or eyelets about three quarters of an inch below the lip. Close to the base of the food vessel was an indentation caused by the potter's thumb on the soft clay. The food vessel was found crammed with bones to the weight of twelve pounds. This was clearly a cremation burial. The second cist, from its position in the centre of the cairn and the deepest, appears to have been the primary deposit. It was an inhumation burial. The excavators noted that the body had been laid on its side in the usual crouched-up position. The food vessels were re-interred.*

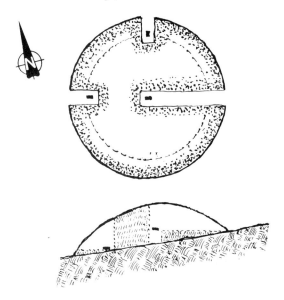

6 *Plan and Section of Excavation at Harelaw Cairn*

Belonging to the Iron Age is a large hillfort or oppidum situated on the west shoulder of Benarty Hill. This defensive enclosure occupies the summit of the hill immediately above the precipitous rocks on its west face, bounded to the north by steep cliffs, and by a deep gulley to the east. An early seventeenth century description of it refers to vestiges of a double trench which were by then very fragmentary. In order to provide a defended enclosure, a massive wall had been built along the south edge of the summit, extending in length to four hundred and fifty yards and included stones of prodigious proportions. The area enclosed extended to five acres.

---

* The cairn is scheduled as an ancient monument and it is to be hoped that it will be restored to its original height, the surrounding wall exposed and become a place of interest in the local nature trail.

11

7   Food vessels from Harelaw Cairn

Other types of structures of this period were the circular timber-framed house and the lake-dwelling or crannog. On the Clune Hill, the elevated ground to the south of Loch Ore, are to be seen the remains of several circular houses. They are scattered over a wide area, in groups of two and three and are in some cases so close to one another that their walls almost touch. The diameters of these houses vary from thirty feet to almost fifty feet. The walls are represented by two concentric circles of stones averaging four feet apart. These little settlements were probably the homes of small peasant farmers who grazed their stock on the rough pasturage on the hill, who tilled the small plots of ground enclosed by earthen banks in the moorland beside their dwellings and who eked out an existence by hunting and fishing in the loch.

The houses are clearly not all of the same period. The earliest of those, whose remains can be detected, probably date from the first century BC, and are those which display two concentric circles of earthfast stones, the space between the circles being the thickness of the walls. The walls probably consisted of two series of upright stakes set at regular intervals, in a circular base of stones and earth. Light branches or stout reeds were interlaced between the upright stakes to produce two wattle screens, thus forming the inner and outer faces of the walls which probably rose to a height of three or four feet. As these screens were plastered over with clay and the intervening space filled with heather or grass the whole would thus be rendered fairly draught-proof. It will be seen that cavity-wall insulation is nothing new! The lower end of the rafters of a low-pitched conical roof rested on top of the stout upright stakes which supported the outer wattle screen. The apex of the roof was supported by a stout post set into a deep socket in the centre of the floor: in the case of very large dwellings two or more supporting posts were used. The roof was covered either with a thatch of reeds and turf or animal skins. Near the centre of the floor would be a flat stone to serve as a hearth, or there may have been a fire-pit. The smoke from the fire escaped through a hole in the apex of the roof. Excavations have shown that, in some instances, a porch or baffle screen was erected at the entrance to the house. A flap of skin probably served as a door.

The remains of a group of circular houses to seen to the south-east of the hill are of a much later date. The walls are largely composed of stone and now appear as well-defined rings of stone and earth. Also to this later period belongs the remains of a single dwelling of rectangular shape, having slightly rounded ends. This house is situated to the north of the hill and has associated with it slight indications of cultivation terraces. It now appears as a slightly oval mound of stones with a pronounced hollowed centre.

These people of the Iron Age also made provision for their safety in times of stress. Amid the various groups of remains of houses is an earthwork which occupies the summit of an isolated stump of rock. It has a diameter of fifty feet, and its walls, though fragmentary, are four feet thick. The site is precipitous on three sides and on the remaining side where there is the only logical approach, there are indications of rough walling forming an entry to the site. It is not improbable that this site was used as a place of retreat. When danger was expected, the inhabitants of this Iron Age village driving their flocks before them, ensuring the safety of themselves and their animals, would converge on this defensive enclosure.

Due west from this enclosure and on the rising ground immediately up from the edge of the loch are the remains of what may have been a homestead of the late Iron Age period. The layout suggests living quarters and enclosures for domestic animals. The whole was surrounded by a stone wall which is now represented only by the outer and inner faces of earth-fast stones. The entrance faced east where the wall appears to be of considerable thickness. Tentative excavations were carried out on the site by the proprietor of the ground in 1890. Not far from this homestead, and probably associated with it, were to be seen the remains of a crannog or lake-dwelling, and at the same spot were found in 1926, the blackened oak remains of a dug-out canoe.

In choosing to live on the Clune Hill, these people of the Iron Age would be safe from the dangers of marsh and swamp and periodical floods. Here, they would till their small fields and tend their flocks in comparative safety. This small community of pastoral people would hear of the coming of the Roman legions in the first century AD; and their descendants would live to see the departure of the Romans in the fifth century. During these four hundred years, they would no doubt be under the watchful eye of the legionary patrols as they marched to and from their coastal fort of Horrea on the south shore of the Tay, identified with the modern Carpow. In return for Roman "protection" they would give up a quota of their yearly crop to help to fill the Roman granaries at Horrea.

8 *Dug-out canoe found in Loch Ore*

13

The little hill of Clune not only attracted men from the dawn of history, it also drew to itself people of a much later date. It was here, in the thirteenth century that the monks of Inchcolm grazed their cattle, and built their chapel of Bothedlech. Only a stone-throw from the site of the chapel, amid the ruins of ancient buildings and the refreshing waters of the Butter Well, stood a cottar's house, the last of a long line of habitations, still occupied as late as the first quarter of the present century.

When the present bridge was built over the river Fitty at Cluneycraig (Glencraig) in 1671 to replace a ford there, it was given the name of Clochrat Bridge, evidently recalling an appellation borne by the place at a much earlier date; Cloch=stone, rat= rath, "the stone rath or fort", this may refer to the defensive enclosure on the Clune Hill.

What may afford a glimpse into the beliefs of these Iron Age people is to be found in the local name Navitie. They lived in a mystical age when everything around them was permeated by the unseen. Every stone, stream and cave would be haunted by some mystic deity, and on festive days ancient rites would be observed and Beltane fires lit on the neighbouring hills. One can imagine these people following the Druid priests as they ascended Navitie Hill to watch the sunrise.

Nevy, nevity, navity are aspirated forms of the pre-christian word Nemed or Nemet, (the "M" becoming "V") denoting a Druid's holy place or place of judgment, and popularly associated with earthen mounds, stone circles or Druidal stones. The name in course of time was transferred to early Christian churches, as is the case in early Ireland. In many cases, land bearing the name became church property, and we find this to be the case at Ballingry. Navitie is known to have remained part of the ecclesiastical lands of Ballingry as late as the last decade of the fourteenth century. The name therefore appears to bear witness to the beliefs of a long-since vanished race.

THE FINDING OF ROMAN COINS

There are no known Roman antiquities in Lochoreshire. The site at Chapel Farm which has long been claimed as a Roman fort, is now known to belong to a later period. There have been, however, several Roman coins found in the Lochore district, and while these do not necessarily imply the presence of the Romans, it may be of interest to record their find-spots.

The earliest account of the finding of Roman coins at Lochore was about the year 1760, when a coin of Pertinax was found within an early medieval site, a little to the east of Inchgall farm. It was long thought that the site which could not be identified, lay within the parish of Auchterderran. The writer has however identified the site and while it is but a short distance from the boundary of Auchterderran parish, it is without doubt within the parish of Ballingry. This was the only known coin of Pertinax to be found in Scotland until 1951 when a schoolboy found another coin of the same Emperor at Cardenden, and about the year 1810 two ancient coins were found a little west of Harelaw, but it is not known if these were Roman.

The next occurrence of Roman coins coming to light was in 1851, but as no one knows exactly where the coins were found, and as there are varying accounts as to the "find-spot" and the number of coins found, it may be of interest to recount the source of information.

The "find", which was the largest hitherto found in Scotland, is described in a letter by Sir Daniel Wilson, of the Society of Antiquaries of Scotland, to a friend, dated January 1852, in which he states "a hoard of fine Roman silver, upwards of 600 in number, was dug up last month at Kinross, including a complete series, with many varieties, from Nero to Severus. I have secured a portion for the museum, but thanks to our wise Treasure Trove laws, we dare not make so interesting a fact public, or let any notice of it appear in the reports of our meetings". The fact that the concealment of treasure trove was a crime in Scotland may account why the report of a meeting of the Society in March 1852, at which the coins were exhibited and an account given of how they were found, did not appear in print until 1855.

The report gives "an account of a remarkable discovery of Roman coins and other remains in the parish of Portmoak, Fifeshire. The field where they were found was formerly a deep bog, which by draining and burning, has been brought into cultivation and is now good corn land". The date of the "find" is then given as October 1851, and we are told that "a boy, while reaping, turned up a Roman coin with the point of his hook. This led to a further search and upwards of 600 Roman denarii were found, all lying close together, as if they had been enclosed in a bag, and at a depth of only three or four inches from the surface. There were also found at the same spot an iron sword and a beautiful ornament, thought to have formed the crest of a helmet".

In 1859, the author of *View of the Coinage of Scotland* also gives the foregoing account, but before doing so he states that "in 1851 in a moss near Kinross was found a hoard of from 700 to 800 Roman denarii".

Apart from the possibility of some confusion as to the exact location of the "find", the number of the coins has not in any way diminished. To add to the confusion, Sir Daniel, in his second edition of his *Prehistoric Annals of Scotland*, states that "a valuable hoard amounting to about 700 Roman coins, dug up in the vicinity of Kinross, towards the close of 1857, belongs apparently to the latter (Severus) expedition". Sir Daniel thus brings the date of the "find" foward by six years, and also adds one hundred coins to his original number. This discrepancy can be accounted for, by the fact that Sir Daniel wrote the second edition of his *Annals* while in Canada, and was therefore far removed from the source of his information.

From the date of Sir Daniel's second reference to the "find", there is a lapse of twenty-five years before another writer takes up the story. The writer is the Rev. Charles Ross. He has the advantage of a more intimate knowledge of the district and brings us nearer to the location of the "find". After referring to the supposed Roman camp at Chapel farm, he states that "a few years ago the conduct of a woman hoeing potatoes, near the camp of Lochore, attracted attention. Though ever busy, her labours were confined to one spot. Next day her brother came to her aid, still, except at the approach of a stranger, they confined themselves to the same spot. When neighbours investigated the cause of this singular conduct, it was discovered that they had collected about three hundred silver Roman coins. Those we inspected were in a state of excellent preservation".

Interesting though this account may be, the coins are now believed to have been found in Fife, and the number is the lowest yet recorded.

*9 Coin of Septimius Serverus Pertinax
found at Cardenden in 1951*

In the year 1890 further light is thrown on the matter as the Rev. David Jamie, minister of Ballingry, on the testimony of many of his parishioners informs us that "three hundred Roman coins were discovered a few years ago in a potato field. Since the camp was at Lochore, it was immediately supposed by those who did not know the facts, and it is now widely believed that the coins were found in Lochore. There are those among us who as children played with the coins, and who can take us at this moment to the very spot where they were found, but as North Bogside is in Portmoak parish, the coins do not belong to us at all!"

It will be readily seen that the foregoing account enables us to arrive at a possible explanation for the varying accounts of the "find". The probability of the coins having been found at Lochore is immediately disposed of and it is further pointed out that the parish of Portmoak is not in Fife. North Bogside, which is part of Kirkness estate lies in a portion of Kinross-shire which extends in a narrow neck well into Fife. There is no tradition of Roman coins having been found at Kinross. The possibility therefore, of

Kinross being referred to instead of Kinross-shire is very strong. Indeed, this is not surprising, for as late as 1939, a writer, endeavouring to clear up the matter once and for all, and who was obviously not acquainted with the locality, refers to Kirkness as being at Kinross.

There is a tradition that coins were found near the Gullet Bridge over the river Leven during the making of the "cutting" for the partial drainage of the loch. This, however, would take place some twenty years after the "find" at North Bogside, and although mention is made of the finding of antiquities at that time, no reference is made of many coins having been found.

Most of the coins found their way into different hands. One hundred and three were sent to Edinburgh, and as late as 1932 a collection of twenty-six of the coins came to light. They belonged to Mr Henry Flockhart of Annacroich, the Kinross-shire Antiquary, who was one of those on the scene shortly after the discovery. A note preserved along with the coins, said that they had been "found at Kirkness in 1851, in a moss". In 1933, a further seven coins were sent to Edinburgh for identification. These belonged to Mr Young of Wester Balgedie Farm, Kinross-shire, who along with Mr Flockhart, had helped in the search.

Although many of the coins were used by children as playthings, it is strange that from the entire hoard, whatever its number may have been, not a single coin is now to be found among the residents of Ballingry.

EARLY BEGINNINGS

As is to be expected when dealing with ancient land divisions, no one can say with certainty when Lochoreshire came into being. However, as the castle of Lochore stood on the north shore of the loch of that name, it can be assumed that the land in the immediate vicinity of this early residence formed the nucleus of Lochoreshire. It is now believed that the original grant of land, no doubt consisting of a knight's fief, was made in the reign of Alexander I or even earlier, but in order to understand the early beginnings of land-ownership in this neighbourhood, we shall go back to a period before Lochore appears on record.

Our knowledge of the district at the beginning of the twelfth century is, not surprisingly very fragmentary. If we accept the writings of those who appear to have had access to information no longer available, we are to conclude that by the year 1115 there was already in being a loosely defined region including in it Loch Ore, having as its centre a place called Balbechie which was situated in the vicinity of Kirkness. Little else is known of the region except the legend of the crusading knight.

The name Kirkness is said to be of teutonic origin and means "the ness or promontory belonging to the church"; it appears in our earliest recorded royal grant to the church, the gift made by Macbeth and his Queen Gruoch to the Culdees of St. Serfs in Lochleven. The name is hardly descriptive of the land situated to the east of the loch: it was therefore probably given by the church following the royal gift and was similar in name to places already belonging to the church situated on the coast at Crail and Balmerino. Kirkness, and the name possibly of even earlier origin, the gaelic "Balbechie" appear together in early writings. The "Vil of Balbechie" it is clear, was in the neighbourhood of Kirkness. In the thirteenth century it is written "Balbethy" and by the mid-fifteenth century it appears in the more recognisable form "Balbeth" which may mean "the house of Beth". The name is retained in "Balbedie" the estate which now constitutes the detached portion of the parish of Ballingry, and was, and still is, contiguous with the lands of Kirkness. It was identified at a much later date by a manor house of that name, long since in ruins.

It is noteworthy that the latter part of the name is to be found elsewhere in association with Macbeth. The traditional site of Macbeth's castle in the parish of St. Martin is known as "Carn Beddie" or "Carn beth", the rock or fort of Macbeth. Kirkness and Balbedie are undoubtedly very ancient "places" and as places of residence pre-date Lochore Castle and Inchgall Castle. Strange tales come from Kirkness. The earliest relates how one of the boundaries marking the limits of the estate became known as the "Irishmen's Stone". During the reign of Malcolm Canmore a company of Irishmen came to the house of one Mochan by name who lived there. The Irishmen took possession of the house in Mochan's absence by overpowering the womenfolk of the house. Mochan, on hearing of the affair, hastened home and made repeated entreaties to his mother to come out of the house. But she refused as she wished to protect the Irishmen, whereupon Mochan who looked upon the Irishmen as sacrilegious men and barbarians, set fire to the house. All the occupants perished including his own mother.

The ancient story concludes by stating that for this reason that place is called the Irishmen's stone.

Returning to Balbechie, perhaps there is something behind the legend of the crusading knight. There are those who assert that the land-holder of the period was a non-survivor of the first crusade. Be that as it may, it cannot be doubted that the old records tell of one, Robert the Burgundian who took the cross in 1096 and who had a third son called Robert, but it is not known if the crusader returned to his patrimony. It is known however that a Robert of Burgundy was Lord of Lochore in about the year 1128, but while the evidence is strong, there is as yet no conclusive evidence to link the son of the crusader with the person who held Lochore.

LOCHORE: THE PLACE NAME

Scholars are not all agreed in their interpretation of the second element in the name Lochore. Many interpretations have been given, some of which are less etymologically satisfying than others, such as the suggestion that "Ore" is imply "over" and that the river derived its name because it is the overflow from the loch.

Some hold the "Ore" comes from the Gaelic word "Odhar" meaning grey and that the name means the "Grey Loch", but as any loch will reflect the prevailing conditions, one wonders what unusual qualities were to be found in Loch Ore to give it this particular epithet. Perhaps the people of long ago viewed the loch under very different surroundings and gave it what was to them an apt description. Others hold that the name is derived from the Gaelic "Uar" or "Fuar" meaning "cold", or in its widest sense simply "water".

Again, those who have made a study of place-names believe that river-names, such as "Ore" and "Ayr" go back to a period before the Celtic-speaking people arrived in Scotland. They tell us that river-names are among the oldest in our language and that many are derived from a language which goes back into pre-history and of course before the Gaelic language was spoken. "Ore", may mean something akin to "flowing water".

If this derivation is correct, one wonders why the river is so often referred to in the old records as "Ore water" or the "water of Or". To speak of the "water of the flowing water" does not somehow sound convincing, nonetheless, let us spare a thought for its antiquity the next time we contemplate the flow of the water as it splashes and gurgles among the stones east of the Templelands on its way to Inchgall farm, and remind ourselves that it may be anything upwards of three thousand years ago since this little burn got its name, possibly from the people whose remains lie beneath the Bronze-Age cairn that crowns the nearby Harelaw.

All this sounds very romantic and one is over-awed by the sheer probability of such a remote origin. The present writer, however, is inclined to a more practical approach to the subject, and, although he is conscious of adding yet another to the list of interpretations, he would draw attention to certain facts which hitherto appear to have been overlooked.

In order to arrive at a probable interpretation, it is necessary to examine the earliest form of the name. When it appears in 1160 in the person of Constantine de Lochor and those who hold that name in the following century, there is no final "e". The name consists of two elements Loch + Or, sometimes Lachor. The more fanciful forms such as Lowchqwor, Louchquhor and a host of others equally fanciful, appear at a much later date. If the earlier writings can be relied upon, the name appears in the reign of Edgar (1097-1107). Here again the name "Strathor" bears the second element "Or".

Now, "Or" is a common element in the Gaelic language and denotes gold, so that the name could mean "the loch of the gold". If, as is suggested, the second part contains the gold element, it is a fair assumption that gold was to be found locally as early as the first half of the twelfth century. If the same can be said of the "Or" in the other local names such as Gedor, Inchgedor, not to mention Bellochor which may, or may not have had a local connection, then the presence of gold may have been known at a much earlier date. This is not so improbable as it would first appear.

What seems to lend a certain plausibility to this interpretation is the fact that gold is known to have been found in certain parts of Fife in ancient times, and what reinforces this belief is a grant made to the Monastery of Dunfermline by King David I wherein he bestows on the Monastery, a tenth of all the huntings between Lammermuir and Tay, a tenth of all his wild mares in Fife and Forthriff, a tenth of all the salt and iron brought to Dunfermline for his own use, and a tenth of all the gold which might come to him from Fife and Fothriff.

The monks, in addition to being the coal-mining experts of their day, may also have known how to "pan" for gold, for they are said to have had a gift in 1136 of a gold mine from the King, which they continued to work for almost two hundred years, but as the yield was never of much account the mine was abandoned in 1333.

What in some measure appears to establish this etymology is the fact that a document of about the year 1550, recounting from an earlier source, states that gold was known to have been found in Benarty Hill and that the find-spot or place where it had been worked was known as *Sarus Arrius*. This may be a medieval latinisation of two local names; Sarran, a monk who testified to the boundaries of Kirkness and Lochore in 1128 and Harran a name contained in Harran Hill and Harran Wood. Harran Hill forms the lower slopes of Benarty and was in bygone days washed by the waters of Loch Ore.

It is of special interest to learn that gold-bearing rock was found in the old coalmine at Benarty. As late as the last century a young miner found two small nuggets of gold.

In the heart of the Harran wood there is to be seen an ancient stone bridge spanning a stream which was, according to tradition known to the Constable family, used by the monks of old, but whether the bridge is a relic of the early coal-mining era or belongs to the far-off period when monks searched for and found a mineral exceedingly more valuable than coal, no one can say.

It is equally uncertain how far back in the history of Lochore the finding of gold would take us. It is tempting to see in the name an allusion to the early exploitation of the natural resources of the district. The finding of gold ornaments in association with pre-historic cultures postulates the search for gold going back to very early times, and it is natural that the finding of a metal so much sought after should be reflected in the placename.

The presence of gold is made known in certain placenames elsewhere. At Balliean-Or (the town of the gold) in Sutherland, the derivation of the placename was confirmed dramatically in 1818 by the finding of a nugget of gold, and in 1869 a considerable quantity of gold was found in the river gravel in the same neighbourhood.

The gold from Benarty was probably obtained by panning the water in the hill streams which flowed into the loch. What could be more natural than, in order to identify the loch at a period before fixed placenames came into use, that people should describe it as Loch Or — the loch of the gold.

The early twelfth century saw an influx of Anglo-Normans during the reigns of Alexander I and David I and the setting up of the Norman feudal system of land tenure. During this period many Normans received grants of land from the Crown and in return

21

they set up their motte-and-bailey castles to administer their newly acquired estates. The land-holding class at this period spoke Norman French in preference to the native Gaelic. It will be seen later on in our story that the first known person to possess the lands of Lochore was a Frenchman.

So far, we have assumed that the name was coined by the local Gaelic-speaking inhabitants. It may be asked, however, is it not more likely that the overlord of the estate would establish the name. The probability is that the place was known by this name long before the Norman knight came to possess it. No one can say with certainty until further evidence is forthcoming as "Or" in the French language also means gold.

BALLINGRY: THE PLACE NAME

The fact that all place names have a meaning and were coined at some remote time by people who perhaps wished to describe their natural surroundings, or perhaps record an unusual event or the fact that someone of note was associated with the place, has been used as a starting-off point by all those who have made a study of place names and their meaning.

The majority of place names belong to a language no longer spoken, and with the passage of time many have become so obscured that their present-day form bears little resemblance to the original, and where this occurs, very often it is the second element that suffers.

There have been many interpretations of the name Ballingry, some rather fanciful, others less so, but none very convincing. The first element presents no difficulty, "Ball" is the very common Gaelic prefix "Baile", meaning town, farm or residence. It has been suggested that in some instances it may also mean a portion (of land). "In", in this case is no doubt the Gaelic article "an", meaning "the" or "of". However, it is the third element which is of special interest to the student of place names.

Mr W. J. N. Liddell of Navitie, Advocate, who wrote his *Place Names of Fife and Kinross* in 1896, believed that Ballingry was derived from Baile-an-gharaidh, meaning the "the town of the garden". In support of this interpretation, it is to be said that as early as 1388, the lands of East Ballingry were considered to be very fertile by the people who lived in the east part of Fife.

More recent scholars have stated that the name may have come from Baile-an-greigh, meaning "the farm of the flock". Some credence is given to this interpretation by the presence of the Flockhouse which appears on record in 1605 onwards, but unless it existed at a very much earlier date it could not possibly have been the farm-town which gave rise to the Gaelic "Baile". This form implies the presence of sheep, but apart from the name there is nothing to suggest that the locality merited this distinction any more than any other place where sheep were being reared. The name is variously spelt down through the centuries, and upwards of thirty-five forms are known to the writer. An examination of all the early forms shows that the letters "gr" in the third element are constant, so that the latter part undoubtedly commenced with these letters.

Whatever the appeal either of these interpretations may have, there is nonetheless a strong probability that the earliest form of the name was Baile-an-Gruoch, signifying "the farm-town or residence of Gruoch", or simply "Gruoch's portion". Gruoch, the reader will recall, was a grand-daughter of Kenneth the III, the wife of Gillacomgain, mormaer of Moray, by whom she had a son, Lulach. Following the death of Gillacomgain, Gruoch married Macbeth. Gruoch, we are told, belonged to the family of Boite or Bodhe. A well-known authority has stated that, as Gruoch's name is united with Macbeth's in their gift of the lands of Kirkness to the Culdees, it points to the family of Bodhe being particularly connected with Fife. The name bears a close resemblance to Buidhe a family name belonging to an earlier period. The descendants of Eachach Buidhe and Eochaid Buidhe were traditionally those who made up the sovereignty of

Fife, an allusion to the remote period when a Kingdom of the Scots was established in the province of "Fib" or Fife.

We shall have more to say about Kirkness and Ballingry later on. Meanwhile, there arises the interesting question as to whether Gruoch's family name is contained in Bothedlech, the name given to the land immediately south-west of the Clune and adjoining the river Fitty and which was for a long time in the possession of the monastery of Inchcolm. A tiny chapel of this name was situated on the Clune on the rising ground above the river. Bothedlech may mean "Bodhe's stone", although another interpretation is possible.

It would appear that at the period when land divisions were being formed and the parochial system was taking shape, the name of the chief residence in the area, Baile-an-Gruoch, was adopted as the name of the parish.* This seems to be borne out by the early inhabitants who, when speaking of Ballingry, thought primarily of the feudal holding, the estate of Ballingry on Benarty Hill, not the parish. This recognition by the Gaelic-speaking inhabitants of the original Baile-an-Gruoch obviously led to the frequent transpositioning of the first syllable of each of these names in everyday speech, and gave rise to their appearing from time to time in the records of the period as Beningry and Balnarty.

10 *Gruoch's Well*

---

* The writer is referring to the period prior to the coming of the Anglo-Norman landholder and before the castles of Lochore and Inchgall were built.

We would place the Baile-an-Gruoch on the site of the present Ballingry farm which no doubt was the caput of the estate of that name and probably was at a much later date the site of the house of Ricardo-de-Ballingry, who appears in 1395. The view from Ballingry is indeed very fine and is well chosen for a dwelling place. From its elevated position, the whole of the Ore Valley can be seen, and almost the full extent of what was once Lochoreshire. It is sheltered on the north by Benarty Hill and most of the land belonging to the estate lies on a gentle slope with a southern exposure. It probably presents the finest situation in the whole of the parish and as such would undoubtedly be chosen at a very early period.

Dunmore, under whose shadow Ballingry farm stands, bears witness to a period when Gaelic was spoken in the neighbourhood. The name may mean the large or strong fort or enclosure and probably alludes to an early fortified enclosure, or "Dun" which stood in its vicinity, the "Baile-an-Gruoch".

What adds considerable weight to this interpretation is the presence of Gruoch's well situated a little southwest of Ballingry farm. It is referred to in the old records by name, being the source of the Lochty Burn and the division between Lochore and Kirkness. The well remains as a constant reminder to the people of Ballingry, of Macbeth's Queen and, if this interpretation is correct, of one whose presence gave rise to the place name.

ROBERT THE BURGUNDIAN: THE FIRST LAIRD

A new name appeared among the many witnesses to charters during the early years of the reign of David I. It concerned a Burgundian knight who had not as yet received a fixed surname so that he was variously described by the Latin scribes as Robertus Burguine, Robertus Burg, Robertus Burguillun and Robertus Burgeis. He was known to the clergy of St. Serfs island in Lochleven as Robertus Burgonensis Miles — Sir Robert the Burgundian. Sir Robert, who is believed to have taken part in the first crusade, is said to have been knighted by David I in 1124 and to have married a sister of Constantine Macduff, Earl of Fife. He probably received the estate of Lochore in about the beginning of the twelfth century, an estate which in the opinion of scholars may have constituted a knight's fee as early as Edgar or Alexander I. On receiving his grant of land, Sir Robert erected a castle in order to overawe the serfs, and to establish himself as Lord of the region. His period of ownership was probably of short duration. It was certainly not without incident.

Sir Robert was in the eyes of the Culdees "a fire and furnace of iniquity" who, in the "heat of his rapacity and unbridled tyranny, wickedly and maliciously harassed them with oppression and injustice", and deprived them of a quarter of Kirkness. An account of the dispute was originally recorded in a book, written in Gaelic, belonging to the Culdees of St. Serfs Isle, which contained records of gifts of land and other memoranda concerning the Priory. This book is lost, but an abstract of it written in Latin is contained in the Register of the Priory of St. Andrews.

11 *Page from the Register of the Priory of St. Andrews*

As there is no record of Sir Robert's side of the case, we have no way of knowing how far the Culdees were justified in denouncing their neighbour in such strong terms. Remembering the old saying, "there are two sides to every story", we should perhaps accept with some reservation the Culdees' description of the Baron of Lochore as it seems unlikely, even in those days, that Sir Robert would seize part of his neighbour's lands, especially when these belonged to a religious community, without believing that he had some ground for having a claim on them. That the case for the Culdees was not altogether as clear cut as they seemed to have believed, is shown by the fact that it went to trial.

The Culdees had been in peaceful possession of Kirkness since it was granted to them by Macbeth and his Queen nearly three quarters of a century earlier, so on the advice of the Augustinians of St. Andrews, they appealed to King David for protection from the inroads of their neighbour. The King at length ordered a trial which took place about the year 1128. He sent his messengers through the provinces of Fife and Fothrif summoning a great number of men. The place of assembly is not known, Cupar has been suggested, but the number of persons present in two armies implies that the meeting place was in the open country probably in sight of the disputed lands.

The trial probably took place at Kirkness, as was the case a little over two and half centuries later when the boundaries of Kirkness and Lochore were again the subject of a dispute. It is possible that after the trial a formal perambulation of the marches took place to establish afresh the boundaries as lawfully determined by the court. In any case, to the assembly point came Constantine, Earl of Fife, a "discreet and eloquent man", along with his bodyguard and the army of Fife. The bishop of St. Andrews, if he did not appear in person, at least sent his army under its leaders, Budadh and Slogadadh. Macbeth, Thane of Falkland and other leading men of the province including Soan, the general with his household, also came. Along with Earl Constantine came Dufgal son of Motche and Meldoineth, son of Machedath.

12 *The Priory Chapel on St. Serf's Island on Loch Leven as it appeared about 1900 when it was used as a fishing bothy*

27

When all the leading men of the province had assembled, three arbiters were appointed to try the case before Constantine, "High Judge in Scotland", Dufgal, "an aged man venerable and upright" and Meldoineth, "a good judge and prudent". The clergy who gave evidence on behalf of the Culdees, by stating on oath what they knew of the boundaries of Kirkness were, Duftah or Dustah, "priest and abbot", probably a Culdee Abbot of St. Serfs, Sarran, son of Sodelne, Eugene, a monk, Dovenald, grandson of Leod, Merrchat, an Irishman of venerable age, and the aged Cathan. It is regrettable that no notice whatever is given of the evidence put forward by Sir Robert, as such evidence may have revealed some interesting facts about early Lochoreshire.

After hearing the evidence of those who attested the boundaries of Kirkness, Dufgal gave his verdict in favour of the Culdees. The other two arbiters, Earl Constantine and Meldoineth, acknowledging Dufgal's experience and knowledge of the law, yielded to his judgment and so the disputed lands were restored to the Culdees.

Sir Robert's encounter with the Culdees turned out to be his undoing. He fell into disfavour in high places and after a short period of declining influence he crossed the border into England.

The account of the dispute is of more than passing interest as it probably arose out of an earlier change of ownership following the royal gift to the Culdees of the lands of Kirkness. In seeking to discover the portion of Kirkness over which the quarrel arose, cognizance must be taken of the fact that there is no evidence that the small estate of Ballingry lay within Lochoreshire at this period. It is noteworthy that the name does not appear in any of the writings dealing with the barony of Lochore at this date. The estate of Ballingry, as distinct from the parish, was church property as late as the close of the fourteenth century, and only appears to have been annexed to the barony of Inchgall along with the small estate of Navitie, which is known to have been part of Kirkness, after the coming of the Wardlaws in the early fifteenth century. The evidence is strong that the estate of Ballingry went over to the Culdees along with Kirkness, of which it probably was a part, in the gift of Macbeth and his Queen Gruoch. This may account for Gruoch's name appearing in the grant as the estate of Ballingry appears to have been her part of the gift.

It is clear that the boundary between the lands of Lochore and those of Kirkness was the Lochty Burn from its source at Gruoch's well in Benarty Hill to where it crossed the public road at the Shank of Navitie and continued eastward till it entered Bog Lochty. As the estate of Ballingry lies on the Kirkness side of the burn and is adjacent to the lands of Lochore this and the foregoing evidence points to the estate of Ballingry as having been in all likelihood the lands in question.

LOCHORE CASTLE

Ask anyone in the village of Crosshill the whereabouts of Lochore Castle and he will immediately point to the husk of broken masonry standing a little to the east of the Meadows and probably say "Over there". Although generations of local usage have established this belief and is accepted by almost everyone, it is clear to the historian that this is not so. This is not to say that a castle of this name never existed, indeed, such a castle did exist but not on this site.

What has been said may surprise the reader, but in order to avoid possible confusion, it is necessary to explain that the ruined tower, which today is known as Lochore Castle, was not known as such throughout its history. The Castle took its name from the island on which it was built, and was called from beginning to end, Inchgall Castle. It was only after the coming of the Malcolm family in the second half of the seventeenth century, by which time the Castle stood unroofed, that the ruin received its present name.

Following the sub-division of the estate, probably in the thirteenth century, the owner of the western part built his residence on the island, to which the local people were quick to apply the name Inchgall — "Isle of the Foreigner". It was thus that the Castle received its name and from this time onward Wester Lochoreshire became known as the barony of Inchgall.

All trace of the Castle of Lochore has vanished, but as it pre-dated Inchgall Castle, and was in its second phase probably the caput of the Lochore family, we shall deal with it first. The ancient Castle of Lochore, for such we may call it, stood on the north side of the loch. It was not a castle as the name is understood today, for it was the work of carpenters and ditchers rather than stone-masons. It was the age of serfdom. The unskilled work of digging the ditches and making the ramparts would probably be done by forced labour drawn from the feudal tenants in the newly formed estate. Long after it had been abandoned, the earthworks associated with it were still traceable on the ground. These earthworks gave rise to much speculation among antiquaries when first examined in the eighteenth century, when sites of this nature were all too readily attributed to the Romans.

Apart from a brief reference by Sir Robert Sibbald in 1707, the site was first seriously discussed by the same author in his *History of Fife* in 1710.* From this time onward till 1950 the site had attracted a host of writers, antiquaries and archaeologists. Some viewed it from the height of the nearby Harran Hill, while others walked along the line of the ditches. Many stepped out the length and breadth of the earthworks and gave the distances in so many paces. Others more meticulously took measurements with a Gunter's chain and measuring tape, and gave the resultant measurements in feet, taking note also the position of the causeway entrances that bridged the gaps over the ditches. Many had no doubt at all as to its Roman origin, others were more cautious, some non-committal.

* Sibbald believed it to be Roman.

By the beginning of the present century grave doubts were being expressed as to its Roman origin as the site did not fit into any known pattern of Roman military strategy. By the middle of the century the site was being seriously engulfed by industrial waste and flooding. With a large part of the site irretrievably lost, it fell to the writer to make a last hour attempt to establish, if possible, the nature and origin of the site. With the assistance of a few willing helpers the task of excavating the site was carried out during the years 1950 and 1951*. Superficially, it bore some resemblance to a small Roman military post, but the presence of what appeared to have been a motte hill along with the factual evidence of a medieval chapel warranted further examination. The discovery of flatbottomed ditches soon confirmed the belief that the site was medieval. As a result of these excavations the site has now been assigned to a much later period than has hitherto been accepted.

From the evidence obtained from the excavation work coupled with the accounts of those who had previously examined the site, it is possible to obtain some idea of the main features of what was undoubtedly a motte-and-bailey castle. This, we can be assured, would not be so unusual as may be at first imagined. In the neighbouring barony of Cleish mention is made of a motte in 1471, and nearer still at Blaircrammy (now Blairadam) a charter makes reference to a motte there as late as 1499. Although these motte-hill castles must have been abandoned long before these dates, these references point to the prevalence at one time of this type of castle in the neighbourhood.

The earliest part of the Castle of Lochore was situated to the east and typologically dated from the twelfth century. As castle-building was an essential element to feudal tenure, one of the first things Sir Robert of Burgundy† would do on being granted the lands of Lochore would be to erect a strong defensive enclosure or castle after the fashion of his Norman forebears at a suitable place on his estate. He would therefore select a naturally defensive site requiring a minimum of adaptation for his purpose. This we know he found on the north side of the loch, choosing a slightly elevated site which was defended by the loch on its south side and by marshy ground to the east and north. Where the ground jutted slightly into the loch, he built his motte-hill which was about 60 feet in diameter and on top of it he erected a strongly framed wooden tower, cross-braced and strutted for strength, and reached by means of a ladder-like stair. The motte-hill was surrounded by a broad and deep ditch. Adjoining the motte-hill to the north he constructed a bailey or base court to accommodate the subsidiary wooden buildings to house his retainers. The bailey court measured about 500 feet from east to west and 350 feet from north to south. The east side was defended by two ditches and two ramparts, while the north and west sides were defended by three ditches and as many ramparts. The innermost rampart was surmounted with a timber palisade which may also have surrounded the base of the motte-hill. The ditches varied from 12 feet to 15 feet in width and ranged from 5 feet to 7 feet in depth. They appear to have been dug to a given level throughout and not to have followed the contours of the ground, so that

---

* The team of helpers formed the nucleus of an Antiquarian Club, an idea which the writer had long cherished and did much to stimulate a like interest in others. His efforts culminated in the formation of the Benarty Antiquarian Club, a club which he was privileged to name and to become its first secretary.
† His name appears in various forms.

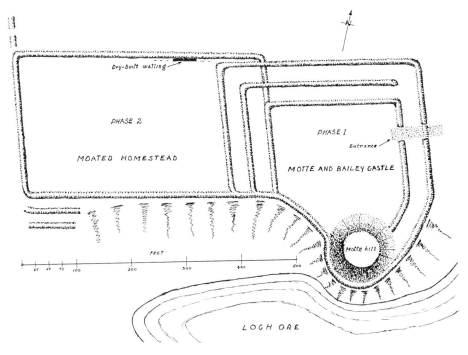

13 *Lochore Castle*

where the ground rose in height towards the west it was at this point that the ditches attained their greatest depth. It may be assumed therefore, that the water from the loch filled the ditches. There were at least two causeyed entrances to the bailey court, one on the east and another on the north side. This then, was probably the residence of the first known laird of Lochore, and although dark and damp his castle may have been and lacking in almost every comfort, it was nonetheless the outward symbol of his feudal authority.

We do not know how long the motte-and-bailey castle continued in use, but as Robert of Burgundy witnessed a charter in about the year 1138, it is assumed that the castle was still being occupied at this period. Sometime during the second half of the twelfth century a change of ownership took place and with it a change of residence. As the Macduff family were natives of Fife, it is not surprising that they should build their residence in a different manner. The motte-hill residence was abandoned and the bailey court was extended some 450 feet further west to take in slightly higher and therefore drier ground. The outer defences of the new extension consisted of one ditch only and a stockaded rampart. The excavators had little difficulty in detecting the junction of the new extension with the old bailey court, as the single ditch of the former lay 12 feet north from the outmost ditch of the latter, nor did the extension lie on the same alignment but was inclined 3 degrees to the north. The change in the character of the earthworks was emphasised in the depth of the ditches. Where the ditches reached their greatest depth

31

at the north-west corner of the bailey court, the depth of the ditch of the new extension was by comparison not much more than half.

The whole complex appears to have taken the form of a moated Grange or Homestead. The ditch enclosing the extension was flat-bottomed and 12 feet to 15 feet in width and remained almost constant in depth at 3½ feet. It exceeded this depth at the extreme west side where it took an almost right angle turn southward and continued for 350 feet. Where the ground reached its greatest height, the ditch reached a depth of 6 feet. The rampart consisted of wrought clay interspersed with stones and had a stone revetment resting on the inner lip of the ditch*. Where the site had not been denuded by agricultural work, this walling stood to a height of 2 courses at a depth of 3 feet. A nineteenth century map shows a large enclosure attached to the north side of the second phase of the castle. This proved to have been a ditched enclosure and probably had been used for grazing animals or the cultivation of crops. A much smaller enclosure of the same character lay to the south west and near the edge of the loch.

The new laird in the person of Hugo de Lochor, the second eldest son of Gillimichael Macduff, lived within this moated Homestead which was to be from now on the home of the Lochores until the coming of the Vallance family. His home was probably of the hall-house type built of timber or timber and wattle, with subsidiary buildings in which his retainers lived. In addition, there would probably be a barn, granary and stable. It is known that the subsidiary buildings included a chapel, the ruins of which, in a late eighteenth century account, are described as standing on the "height at the south over the circular part" from which it may be inferred that the chapel stood on the old motte-hill, which according to an earlier description stood to a height of approximately 10 feet.

The date of the chapel of Lochore is not known for certain, but it was in existence in 1188 when it belonged to the abbey of Scone. This second residence, which is shown to have incorporated the earlier motte-and-bailey castle, was the Castle of Lochore for which two dates have been given — 1160 and 1180.

Very little is known of the castle, apart from its being referred to in its second phase as "the oppidum" so that the history of the site can be briefly told. The "Chapel of Louchor" was dedicated to St. Andrew and in a charter of about 1245 *John* was its rector. If "ecclisia de Louchorn" can be accepted as referring to Lochore, then it figured in Bagimond's Roll of 1275 when it was taxed to the amount of 6 merks.

The castle continued in use until the building of Inchgall Castle. From this time onward the chapel was called Inchgall Chapel and continued in use for centuries after Lochore Castle went out of use. Although it is mentioned in the Malcolm charter of 1662 it probably ceased as a place of worship following the departure of the Wardlaw family in 1632. It was a ruin in 1682. In 1726 Alexander Gordon came to Lochore and surveyed the site, but because of its dilapidated condition he was unable to produce a sufficiently complete plan for inclusion in his book *Itinerarium Septentrionale*. However in about the year 1770 the castle aroused the interest of a prominent antiquary in the person of John Clerk of Eldin who repeatedly visited the site accompanied by his

---

* The lower jawbone of an animal found in one of the ditches and sent to the Royal Scottish Museum was identified as belonging to a small horse.

nephew William Adam of Blairadam, the future friend of Sir Walter Scott. They measured it accurately, we are told, and produced a very correct drawing of it. They were often visited by Sir Michael Malcolm the laird, and many local people came to look on at their operations. Unfortunately all enquiries have failed to produce Clerk's drawing.

With the departure of Clerk and his young nephew, silence again descends on the place. The silence of the next forty years is broken only by an occasional visit made by some ardent antiquary, sometimes in the person of a churchman, a soldier, a traveller or historian. It was not until Mr Syme in 1811 built a farm steading on the site, that the place once more claimed attention. It was found necessary to have a farm here in order to work the ground which had lately been reclaimed following the draining of the loch. In preparing the site for the building of the farm steading, workmen came across several articles of domestic use belonging to the medieval period. They also found the remains of many of the wooden stakes that had formed the palisade and the remains of what were probably wooden buildings. The position of the steading was such that it was built on top of the 3 ditches and ramparts that formed the west side of the original bailey court. It is conjectured from the description given at this time that the castle was destroyed by fire — further evidence perhaps of the unsettled state of the country towards the end of the thirteenth century.

The farm was appropriately named Chapel Farm. Sir Walter Scott in 1825 refers to it as the Steading of Chapel, while doctor Charles Rogers, an author and antiquary of some repute who lodged at the farm in 1850, retained the old appellation and called it Chapel of Lochore. With the return of the waters of the loch by the middle of the present century, the acreage of farm land was greatly reduced so that the steading gradually fell into disuse. The site of the castle was easily identified until 1970. In this year the ruined farm buildings were demolished and overlaid with debris as part of the land reclamation scheme then in progress. Not a vestige of the castle now remains.

The determining of the real nature of the site as being that of the Castle of Lochore dismisses for good the claim made respecting the great antiquity of the stone-built Castle of Inchgall as dating from the twelfth century, a claim doubted by many in the past. It also disposes of the long-held belief of the presence of a Roman camp.

The Castle of Lochore was not the only site in the neighbourhood defended by a bank and ditch. Future research into the early feudal land-holders at Lochore should include an exploratory excavation of the site known as Balbeggie (the home of the lesser man) which lies a little to the east of Inchgall farm and near the boundary of the parish of Ballingry with that of Auchterderran. It contains what was described in 1812 as a bank-and-ditch rectilineal enclosure. It appears to have had a causeyed entrance on its west side. On the authority of General Melville, a silver coin of the Roman Emperor Pertinax was found there about the year 1760. The site is probably coeval with the second phase of the Castle of Lochore.

THE LOCHORE FAMILY: ITS ORIGIN AND DESCENT

14

As the lands of Lochore, following the departure of Sir Robert of Burgundy reverted to the Macduff family, we shall follow the descent of the Macduffs in order to see how a junior branch became known as "of Lochore".

During the first half of the twelfth century, part at least if not the whole of Lochoreshire, was held by the Macduff family, the old Celtic chiefs or Mormaers of Fife. There are varying accounts of the origin of the family and its connection with Fife. One is, that the family was descended from one Macduff who is said to have assisted Kenneth MacAlpine in his wars against the Picts and, following his final subjugation of these people in 840, the King bestowed on Macduff the lands of Othelinar, and subsequently made him Mormaer of the territory, for the most part included in modern Fife and extending westward as far as Clackmannan. As to the family's connection with the royal house, it is believed that it is traceable to Cinaed MacDubh of the House of Constantine who flourished in the late tenth century. Evidence points to the family having its roots in Banffshire. It is noteworthy that the Earls of Fife, who represented the senior branch of the family, owned large tracts of land in that region.

Others hold that the family's connection with Fife came at a much later date and refer to the tradition that, among those who followed Macbeth southward from the Mormaership of Moray when he asserted his claim to the throne, were some members of the clan Duff, and that their chief quarrelled with Macbeth and thereafter supported the cause of Malcolm Canmore.

Whatever the circumstances that led to the family coming southward, there can be little doubt that the Macduff of Shakespeare was a real person. Traditionally, he was Duncan Macduff, and it is said he served the youthful Malcolm by leading a revolt against Macbeth. This enabled Malcolm Canmore to leave England where he had gone following the slaying of his father by Macbeth. Assisted by his kinsman Siward, Earl of Northumbria, the forces of Malcolm, now a rival claimant to the throne, met Macbeth in 1054, when Macbeth was defeated. Macbeth, however, had considerable followers and it was not until 1057 that Malcolm slew Macbeth in battle at Lumphannan in Aberdeenshire.

In recognition of his services, Malcolm is said to have bestowed on Macduff and his heirs certain privileges, altogether 3 in number. He and his successors, as Mormaers of Fife were henceforth to have the right of leading the van in battle, of placing the monarch on the Stone of Destiny at the coronation ceremony, and the right of sanctuary should any person within the 9th degree of the Mormaer commit unpremeditated slaughter. Remission was to be had by the payment of money and kin. Evidence of this peculiar "girth" or asylum was to be found in Macduff's Cross which stood near Newburgh. The first case of a claim for amnesty under this privilege occurred in 1391 when Sir Alexander Moray was tried for the slaughter of William de Spaldyne. A later case concerned the slaughter of a person with the local name of Kinninmonth. The last case on record of a person tried under the law of the clan Macduff was in 1548.

These privileges were perhaps not so much an innovation as restoring an ancient right enjoyed by the head of the clan Macduff. Traditionally, Duff was the Oir-righ or King of Fife, and as the Lyon Rampant — the arms of the Macduffs — was similar to those of the King, it suggests that even at that late period the family still retained something of its former regal status.

The title frequently used by the Macduffs, "by the grace of God, Earl of Fife", shows that they held the title as being bestowed not by the king merely, but by divine right. A further proof of the connection between the Macduffs and the royal House is the frequency with which royal names occur in the family, i.e. Constantine, Duncan and Malcolm. It is worth noting that the ancient genealogies given for Macbeth and his son-in-law Lulach are headed "Genealogies of Clan Duff".

Shakespeare calls Macduff the Thane of Fife. Although there is no historical evidence of a Thane of Fife, nonetheless thaneages are known to have existed in Scotland at a later date. Kinross was a thaneage and one Macbeth is referred to as Thane of Falkland in a document relating to the boundaries of Kirkness and Lochore.

15 *Seal of the Earl of Fife*

There is some doubt as to the early holder of the title, consequently the succession of the earldom is obscure. Earl Constantine is generally considered to have been the 3rd Earl. He is described as Magnus judex in Scotia — chief judge in the lands north of the Forth — and is known to have had an interest in the lands of Kirkcaldy, as it is on record that he forcibly withheld these lands from the Abbey of Dunfermline. He died about the year 1129 and was buried in Dunfermline Abbey.

It may be asked, from whom did the Lochore family descend and how did they come to acquire the estate? To find an answer to these questions it is necessary to go back to Constantine. It will have been seen that Sir Robert of Burgundy may have acquired part of Lochoreshire through marriage. Whether this was the case or not, it is certain that Lochoreshire was included in the extensive estates held by the Macduff family. As several places in the east of Fife are traditionally associated with the family, it is fairly certain that the seat of the earldom lay somewhere in that region. On the death of Earl Constantine, Gillimichael Macduff, who was probably his son, succeeded him as 4th Earl of Fife and heir to his estates. It is probable that the earldom for the first time became hereditary in him and his heirs. Gillimichael, who witnessed the foundation charter of the Abbey of Holyrood in 1128, left at least 2 sons, Duncan and Hugo; he may have had a third son named Adam. He also had a daughter Ete who married Gartnait, Earl of Buchan. Gillimichael, with the consent of his eldest son Duncan, is known to have bestowed on Hugo, his second son, some lands in Lochoreshire, also the lands of Wemyss-shire and certain lands in the parish of Kennoway. Hugo also obtained from his brother, Duncan, certain lands in the parish of Markinch all of which were contiguous to one another. The lands situated in Lochoreshire were probably those which constituted the eastern part of the estate and would include the parish of Auchterderran and possibly Kinglassie.

Not all of the old writers agree in their account of the Macduff family or of the families who claimed descent from them. Much of the evidence is fragmentary and obscure. Some state that Gillimichael died in 1136, others that he was present at the battle of the Standard in 1138 and died the following year, while Duncan (in whom we have a special interest) if not present at the battle as some writers affirm, was sent to England, along with other four heirs of the Scottish nobility, as a hostage by King David I to Stephen of England, that the terms of the truce following the battle would be observed.

It is not known when Hugo Macduff received the lands from his father, but it must have taken place some time between 1129 and 1139. This Hugo, who died in 1157 or 1158, is witness to several charters when he appears as "Hugo son of Gillimichael". Some writers, however, affirm that he also took the seigniorial name of Hugo de Lochor and that his son, Hugo or Eugenius, who succeeded him also styled himself "de Lochor". There is no reason to doubt that father and son assumed this territorial designation. We see then in Hugo, son of Gillimichael Macduff, or perhaps more correctly in his son Hugo, the progenitor of the Lochore family. Hugo had a second son, Orm, who was the ancestor of the Abernethy family.

Hugo or Eugenius confirmed to the Canons of St. Andrews the church of Markinch sometime before 1171. He died after 1200. The Rev. Henry Malcolm, minister of Ballingry (1684-1701), considered Hugo the younger to be the ancestor of the Wemyss family, however, as the earliest known ancestor of the family, of which there is documentary proof, was John of Methkill (Methill), who was also known as John of Wemyss, he is generally considered the first to have taken the name of Wemyss*.

---

* Henry Malcolm's Commonplace Book, which was of considerable antiquarian value, was last known to have been in the possession of Robert Chalmers, the well known historian.

From the eastern part of Lochoreshire and the neighbouring lands included in Gillimichael's gift to his son, we return to the portion of Lochoreshire which was held by Sir Robert of Burgundy. We have seen that following his dispute with the Culdees, Sir Robert fell into disfavour. It is said he shortly afterwards returned to England, leaving his estate in the hands of his brother-in-law, Earl Constantine, but this could hardly have been so, as Sir Robert's name appears as a witness to a charter along with that of Earl Gillimichael. It is more probable that Sir Robert gave up his estate sometime after Constantine's death, as Gillimichael, shortly before his death in 1139, is believed to have left this portion of the lands of Lochore in the safe-keeping of his second son Hugo, in the absence of his eldest son Duncan, who, at this period was held as a hostage at the court of Stephen of England.

Following the death of his father, Duncan was allowed to return home to succeed to the earldom and would no doubt reside at the chief seat of the Earls of Fife, probably at Cupar. It therefore seems unlikely that Duncan Macduff would have had a personal interest in Lochore. Sir Robert Sibbald in his *History of Fife* (1710) is the earliest writer to refer to Duncan de Lochor. It is probable that the Rev. Henry Malcolm who was no doubt the source of his information, had evidence that is no longer available.* The assertion that Duncan built the Castle of Lochore in 1160 (he died in 1154) is of comparatively recent date being first made by Cardonnel in 1793. Be that as it may, if there was up till now some uncertainty as to who first took the seigniorial name Lochore, it cannot be doubted that Duncan's brother Hugo, gave to his son Hugo the lands of Lochore, and the son in styling himself "Hugo de Lochore" had by then established the family name.

The native Earls of Fife are known to have given valuable service to their country, not as outstanding soldiers so much as capable statesmen holding high office, and by their constant loyal support to the Crown. The frequency with which royal Christian names occur in the family suggests that there was a blood-connection with the Royal House, possibly going back to Celtic times. The high esteem in which the Earls of Fife were held by David I, is clearly seen in the fact that when the king resolved on the death of his son Henry that his grandson Malcolm should succeed him, it was Earl Duncan whom he appointed to take the boy through the kingdom and show him to the people as the heir to the throne.

King David died the following year (1153) and Earl Duncan, who is said to have been tutor to Malcolm, was, according to Andrew Wyntoun, Prior of Loch Leven, made Regent of Scotland and in accordance with the privileges of the Clan Macduff he had the honour of placing the young king on the throne. Duncan died in 1154 and was survived by 2 sons and a daughter. Duncan, the elder son, succeeded his father in the earldom. He is said to have married Ada a niece of the king sometime between 1160 and 1162†, when he received from the king as his bride's tocher the lands of Strathmiglo,

---

* Sir Robert Sibbald in his "History of Fife" refers to Mr Malcolm as "the learned antiquary and historian", and in his preface he acknowledges the help he had received from him — "but above all I am obliged to the Rev. Mr Malcolm, parson of Bingray, who furnished me both with descriptions and extracts out of charters and monastic books".

† It is doubtful if the King had a niece of marriageable age at this period, furthermore, Earl Duncan II's wife's name is known to have been Ella or Hela.

Falkland, Rathillet and Kingskettle in Fife and Strathbran in Perthshire. He was also granted at a later date, from William the Lion, Malcolm's brother and successor, Strathleven in Fife after it had been surrendered by Hugo, grandson of Gillimichael Macduff sometime before 1178. Duncan II does not appear to have held any lands in Lochoreshire.

Previous to this, King William in 1173 was taken prisoner at the siege of Alnwick by an English force and was taken to Normandy and eventually imprisoned at Falaise. So it was that in the following year we hear of Earl Duncan II, along with Philip de Vallance (whom we will meet later on) and the king's brother David and many others, being delivered as hostages to Henry II of England for the liberation of the king. Earl Duncan II died in 1203.

Earl Duncan I's second son, Adam, was known as Adam of Ceres. This Adam had a son called Duncan who, on succeeding his father, was known as Duncan of Ceres. Another Adam, a grandson of Earl Duncan I, possibly a second son of Adam of Ceres, was almost certainly the Adam of Kilconquhar who married Marjorie, Countess of Carrick before 1269; and their daughter whose name may have been Isabel, became half-sister to King Robert the Bruce, and mother of Thomas Randolph who was appointed Governor of Scotland on the death of Bruce. Following the death of Adam of Kilconquhar in the second crusade in 1270, his widow married Robert Bruce, Lord of Annandale. The eldest son of her second marriage was King Robert I. As a possible connection, it is noteworthy that the name of Matilda de Louchore appears among the relations of King Robert who received payments out of the Royal Exchequer.

Earl Duncan I's daughter who was named Affreka or Affrica, became the wife of Harold, Earl of Orkney, in 1139; but for reasons unknown Harold put Affreka away and married secondly a daughter of Malcolm MacHeth. Although King William did not approve of Harold's action, he was unsuccessful in persuading him to take back his first wife.

Earl Duncan II had a least one son and one daughter. To illustrate the customs of the period, we would remark that Earl Duncan paid 500 merks to become the guardian of Rodger de Merlay, Lord of Morpeth while in his minority, on the understanding that Rodger, when he became of age in 1194 would marry his daughter.

Duncan's son Malcolm became 7th Earl of Fife on the death of his father. He married Maud, daughter of Gilbert, Earl of Strathearn sometime between 1194-98 and received from Earl Gilbert the lands of Glendevon, Carnbo, Aldie, Fossoway, Dalkeith and Pitfar, all lying in the parishes of Glendevon and Fossoway. He founded the Abbey of Culross in 1217 and when he died in 1229 he was buried in the church of St. Serf there. We mention this as one can only guess the circumstances which gave rise to the strange story that links Ballingry with Culross, how 2 stone coffins were removed from Ballingry Church and taken to Culross Abbey. When this unusual occurrence took place — if it actually did — no one now can tell.

Constantine I of Lochore

Constantine, whose relationship to Hugo of Lochore is not known, but whose Christian name undoubtedly suggests a close connection with the Macduff family, signed himself "Costentin de Lochor" when he witnessed a charter by Arnold, Bishop of St. Andrews between 1160-62. He also witnessed a gift by Duncan, 6th Earl of Fife to the nuns of North Berwick before 1177, and he was witness to a charter granted in the time of Bishop Rodger of St. Andrews (1188-1202).

In addition to the Lochore estate, he had an interest in part of the lands of Pitfirrane near Dunfermline. Constantine had at least one brother whose name is not known. He also had a nephew, David de Lochor and, as there are more members of the family bearing this Christian name we shall, for the sake of clarity, designate him David I of Lochore.

Constantine was survived by three sons at least; Philip his heir, Andrew and William. He may have had a fourth son called Adam.

William I of Lochore

William had received as a gift from his father, the third part of the lands of Pitfirrane, and in a charter made towards the end of the reign of William the Lion, probably about 1210, he confirmed the grant of these lands which he had made to his cousin, Sir David Louchquhor.

It was as Willelmo de Louchor, Sheriff of Perth, that he witnessed a mandate by King Alexander III in 1251 concerning royal gifts made to the church of the Blackfriars there.

Adam I of Lochore

Nothing is known of Adam de Lochor beyond the fact that he preceded William de Lochor as Sheriff of Perth in the reign of Alexander II (1214-49).

Andreas of Lochore

Andreas de Lochor is witness to a charter in 1235 by Constantine, his nephew, acknowledging that he had no longer any rights over the lands of Kinglassie.

Philip I of Lochore

Philip de Louchor appears in 1230 when he is one of an assize which determined certain lands in Fife. In an obligation of Philip dated 1235, there appears the name of Adam de Bosville of Oxmuir in Berwickshire whose great-great-grandson Rodger de Bosville, a hundred years later, was to marry a daughter of a laird of Lochore.

Philip is witness to three undated charters probably belonging to the period between 1179 and 1231. The first deals with tofts and crofts situated at a place called Clerleandeftun. He also is witness to a charter of confirmation concerning Gafkirrie-nunf, another place no longer identifiable. The third charter deals with 3 acres of land at Cramond gifted to Dunfermline Abbey.

Hugh I of Lochore

We have already seen that Hugo of Lochore received from his brother Constantine II in about the year 1245 certain lands in Pitfirrane. As Hugone de Lochor his name appears in the Register of the Abbey of Arbroath when he witnessed a charter concerning the mill of Possey in about the year 1260. As Hugh de Louchor he was appointed Sheriff of Fife in 1289 and probably held this office for a little over one year. As Sheriff, he witnessed 2 charters by David of Wemyss, in one of which the mill of Lochore is mentioned for the first time. He followed his nephew Constantine III of Lochore as Sheriff in 1293 when he appears on record as Hughone de Lochor. In the absence of any evidence to the contrary, it is to be assumed that Hugh held this office till April 1296 when he is known to have been taken prisoner at the battle of Dunbar.

Fife troops were chosen to garrison the Castle of Berwick following John Balliol's renunciation of his allegiance to Edward of England. The Scottish King had tried unsuccessfully in the month previous to Dunbar, to hold out against the English troops; this resulted in the massacre of the people of Berwick on the orders of Edward. The wanton destruction of the town and the violence towards its people so horrified the Scots that, from then onwards, the whole character of the war changed. As Sheriff of Fife, it may be assumed that Hugh of Lochor was present among the men of Fife when they held the Castle of Berwick. On the garrison being allowed to depart with the honours of war, they shortly joined up with the Scottish army near Dunbar when again the English army was victorious. On the surrender of the Castle following the engagement, 3 earls, 70 knights and many others were taken prisoner. The more notable, we are told, were laden with fetters and sent to different castles in England. In a list drawn up at Roxburgh Castle on 16th May, almost 3 weeks after the battle, the Sheriff's name appears as Hugh de Loughore, by which time he was imprisoned in Chester Castle near the Welsh border. Various writs issued from time to time to the justiciary of Chester show that Hugh of Lochore was still a prisoner in the castle there in September 1300. It is not certain when he was released. He was, like many others who were committed to prison, of a rank which automatically put him in the ransomable class. His duration in prison would therefore depend on how soon the ransom money could be paid. He appears, however, to have returned to Fife by 1304.

Philip II of Lochore

Philip de Lochor was one of the witnesses to the Kinglassie Charter of 1235. It was probably this same Philip who witnessed an undated charter concerning the lands of Balwearie.

Constantine II of Lochore

Constantine II in 1231 was one of a jury mentioned in a deed of perambulation of the lands belonging to the Abbey of Dunfermline and those of David Durward of Dunduff. Constantine's bondsman Gillecostentin was also a witness to the deed. In the same year he and his brother Philip are witnesses to a similar deed concerning the lands of Cleish belonging to Gilbert, the son of Robert, the laird of the neighbouring estate of Crambeth. In 1235 Constantine renounced his claim to the lands of Kinglassin (Kinglassie) and Pitbachly near Dunfermline in favour of the Abbey of Dunfermline. David, his son and heir, Philip his brother, and Andrew his uncle, were witnesses to the charter. From this time onward Kinglassie ceased to be part of Lochoreshire. Constantine II also made a gift of the lands of Lumfilan (Lumphinnans) to his son Adam, which was confirmed in a charter by King Alexander II in 1242. The charter is extant and has the Great Seal of Scotland appended to it. The following is an abstract from a translation of the Latin Charter.

> *"Alexander King of Scots makes known that he confirmed that gift which Constantine of Louchor made to Adam his son of the lands of Lumfilan for his homage and service: To be held by the said Adam and his heirs of the said Constantine and his heirs in feu and heritage by its right marches and with all liberties and easements justly pertaining to it or which may at any time pertain thereto freely and quietly as his charter to the said Adam testifies, saving the King's service. Witnesses — Alexander Cumyn, William de Mar, John de Vallibus, Robert de Meyners, Robert Byset, Robert Cumyn, at Forfar."*

In 1244 we find Constantine in straightened circumstances, and in order to make ends meet he granted the Abbot and Canons of Inchcolm Abbey a 15 years' lease of the Clon (Clune Hill) which marched with the lands of Bothedlech belonging to the Abbey. The Chapel of Bothedlech appears in a list of the possessions of the Abbey, and if a sixteenth century map can be relied upon, it stood on the slightly elevated ground at the south-east end of the hill, up from the marshes on the north bank of the river Fitty. Constantine received 15 years' rent in advance and agreed to half a merk yearly after the 15 years period. Things did improve for Constantine, for it was probably in the following year that he gave to his brother Hugh, a third part of his lands of Pitfuren (Pitfirrane). The charter is witnessed by Constantine's sons Sir David and Adam and Philip his brother. John, rector of the church of Louchor, is also a witness. Constantine II died between 1260-70 and had at least 4 sons, Sir David II his heir, Constantine III, Adam II, known as Adam of Lumphinnans and sometimes Adam of Lochgelly, and William II.

David II of Lochore

We know a little more about Sir David than the other members of the family. We have already seen that he witnessed a charter by his father in the year 1245 and in that year he also witnessed a charter by William of Brechin concerning lands which he, William, had resigned in favour of the church of Rathmuriel. William, in an earlier charter refers to Sir David as "my knight", by which we are to assume that Sir David discharged the military service which was due by William of Brechin in respect of the lands held by him.

In 1253 he witnessed a charter by King Alexander III when he appears as David de Louthore. In 1255, when he was Sheriff of Perth, he sought from the Abbot and Monastery of Dunfermline 4 merks for their default of suit to the sheriff court of Perth from certain lands belonging to the Monastery. The Abbot refused payment and appealed to the Crown. In order that the case could be heard, the King commanded the Earl of Buchan then Justiciary of Scotland to hold an inquest. This was held at Holyrood when the verdict was given in favour of the Abbot. It was stated that, while men from the lands belonging to the Monastery were sometimes seen at court, they did not come there as suitors. On account of the verdict the king in full council entirely quitclaimed the Abbot and his men from attending court in respect of the lands which had been in dispute.

Sir David was much involved in national affairs and was a member of the Scottish Council. During the period of the king's minority he attached himself to the powerful Cumyn party which was opposed to King Henry III of England (King Alexander's father-in-law) interfering in Scottish affairs. Henry, taking advantage of the youthfulness of Alexander (he married when he was 10 years of age), tried to assume control over the Royal Court and the affairs of the country through certain pro-English councillors who, it is said, were in the pay of Henry. The existence of the pro-English and anti-English parties gave rise to rivalries within the council, and Henry exerted pressure on the young king to put down those who went against his (Henry's) authority. All those who did so were to be regarded as rebels.

Following an unsuccessful plot by Alan Durward and many others of the "noblest men" of the kingdom, including Sir David, to kidnap the king, Alexander, in September 1255, wrote to his father-in-law telling him that he had removed from the council the anti-English party which included many of the Cumyn family and their accomplices and sympathisers. Two years later, feelings against the English faction of the king's advisors became so strong that many of the lords who had been removed from office in 1255 resolved on further action. So it was that, fearing "the dishonour of the king and the kingdom" they abducted the king and queen from Lochleven Castle during the hours of darkness and took them to Stirling Castle. They also took possession of the king's Great Seal. Their object was to alienate the monarch from the influence of his pro-English advisors and thus lessen the power of his father-in-law in matters dealing with the realm. Those in revolt mustered their arms in readiness to oppose the rival faction. They also entered into an alliance with the Welsh lords who likewise were opposed to Henry III, and were struggling for their independence. Their action evoked the censure of the church and not long after, we are told, all those who took part in the Kinross episode, including Sir David de Louchor and many who bore the name of Cumyn, were put under the dreaded sentence of ex-communication by the Bishop of Dunblane.

Be that as it may, we next meet with Sir David three years later in 1260 when he witnessed a deed along with John de Kinross and the neighbouring laird, Duncan de Crambeth. With the king taking over control of the nation's affairs on his becoming of age in 1262 it appears that the laird of Lochor had become sufficiently reconciled to the monarch to warrant his being appointed to the office of Sheriff of Gowrie in that year.

Two years later, in 1264, he became Sheriff of Fife and in his capacity as Sheriff, he is mentioned in a Papal letter of that year as being one of those who charged John Russell and his wife with the poisoning of Walter Cumyn, Earl of Menteith. For the following two years the sums of money collected by Sir David as "vicecomitis de Fyfe" are recorded in the Exchequer Rolls.

He was probably no longer Sheriff when he witnessed a charter in 1269 along with one Symon Vallance. He appears again in 1277 when he appends his name to an agreement made between the Abbot of Inchcolm and Thomas de Philiberto, concerning the lands of Cullelo in the neighbourhood of Aberdour; Duncan de Crambeth is also a witness, as also David's uncle Hugh de Lochor. During the following two years Sir David's name appears as a witness to charters signed at Cupar and at nearby Orrock, and lastly at Roxburgh in 1279. He is last heard of in 1294 when John Balliol appointed him as Great Chamberlain in that year. In addition to Lochore, he owned Ardargie in Perthshire and Westerdron in Fife.

Sir David probably died in 1295 without a male heir. It is certain that by 1296 his two daughters between them possessed the greater portion of the lordship of Lochore; that is, the lands attached to the mill of Lochore. We shall not discuss the new owners at the moment but rather have something to say about Sir David Lochore's brothers.

It was in the same year 1296 that John Balliol and the Scottish nobles finally broke with Edward I of England by renouncing their fealty and allegiance to him. Edward's retaliation in destroying Berwick and his defeat of the Scottish army afterwards near Dunbar and his regaining possession of the castle there, were the first acts in a long drawn out struggle which stiffened the Scottish people in their resolve to fight for the freedom of their country whatever the cost. It was not until after Bannockburn that English domination was finally broken. Meanwhile, Edward's policy of total subjugation affected men of all ranks. In continuing our narrative, we shall now and then catch a brief glimpse of our local lairds as they took part in the stirring events of the period.

Constantine III of Lochore

This Constantine first appears on record in 1266 when he is tutor to one John Blair. As tutor he gives his consent, as does John's mother Helen Ramsay, to John allowing the priory of St. Andrews to use his mill which is situated on his lands of Nyden. It is stated that the priory is to have the use of the mill only during John's minority. At a later date both John and his tutor consent to changing the situation of the mill on condition that John receives one pound of pepper annually.

John was the son of Alexander Blair and grandson of Sir William de Blair Steward of Fife, but what we find more interesting is that the youthful John was the Fife-born John Blair who was educated along with William Wallace at Dundee, and who, after studying in Paris, entered the Monastery of Dunfermline. With the rise of Wallace in 1297, he was called out of the Monastery at Wallace's request to be his Chaplain. After seeing at first-hand most of Wallace's exploits, he returned to the Monastery on the death of his master, when he is said to have changed his name to Arnald in order to avoid detection. He devoted his remaining years in the Monastery to writing a history of Wallace's life.

We next hear of Constantine in 1268. In a charter of this date he mentions among others two persons who, if not already related to him, were soon to be so; William of the family of Vallance and Michael of the family of Wemyss. He also witnessed charters in 1281, 1289 and 1293. In a charter by his relative David of Wemyss of a date about 1290-96, he is referred to as one of two free tenants in the barony of Lochore.

Constantine followed his uncle, Hugh of Lochore, as Sheriff of Fife in 1290, and in his capacity as Sheriff he swore fealty to Edward I at Dunfermline in the Abbey there in July of the following year, when he signed his name as Constantine de Loghor on the Roll of Homage, acknowledging Edward as overlord of Scotland. As the number of men of rank summoned to do homage was considerable, the act of homage was carried out simultaneously at the high altar in the Abbey and in the Chapter House of the Monastery.

Constantine was Sheriff for a year following his submission to Edward I for, as we have already seen, his uncle once more became Sheriff in 1293. It is probable that the change in the holder of the office on this occasion coincided with John Balliol attaining to the Scottish throne. Constantine may not have remained Edward's man for long. Like many arms-bearing men of the period he would no doubt maintain that an oath taken under duress was not binding. When King John revolted under the studied insults of Edward, Constantine probably took the opportunity to renounce his allegiance to the English monarch and strike a blow for independence.

Like his uncle, he was present at the battle of Dunbar and was taken prisoner on the surrender of the castle. In a list of prisoners his name appears as Dominus Constantine de Loghore, along with a fellow Scot, Dominus Michael de Scot, Lord of Balwearie. Both were sent to Wallingford in the county of Berkshire, not far from Oxford where they were imprisoned in the castle there, a stronghold on the banks of the river Thames. A writ of 1296 to the Sheriff of Oxford and Berkshire, refers to certain sums of money for the keep and maintenance of the two Scots prisoners and also for the two warders who were responsible for their security. Like Hugh of Lochore, it is not clear when the two prisoners were released. Michael Scot may have been released in 1297 after agreeing to serve in Edward's foreign service; he was back in Fife by the end of the year. It has been said that Constantine was present at the battle of Blackearnside (June 12th, 1298) but the evidence for this is not clear. If he indeed took part in this engagement he probably left Wallingford Castle at the same time as his fellow prisoner. In any case, Constantine must have again come into Edward's peace soon after, and had so far gained his confidence as to be appointed Sheriff of Fife by the Parliament held at Westminster in February, 1305. The official entry reads as follows, Monsire Constantyn de Loghore Viscunt. In May of that year he conducted an inquest at Perth relating to the barony of Crail and later on in the same year he headed an inquiry concerning a certain Michael de Miggel (Meigle), who had been in prison in Nottingham Castle following Dunbar, and who in 1299 was exchanged for one James de Lindsay whom the Scots held in Bothwell Castle. He appealed to Edward to have his goods and chattels returned to him. Michael, who had joined Sir William Wallace and had been captured by the English about the same time as his leader, gave evidence to show how strict the measures were that Wallace had to enforce in order to maintain discipline in his band of followers. Michael had tried on two occasions to escape from Wallace. In his first attempt he had travelled two leagues, and on his second he succeeded in getting away for a distance of over three leagues, but had on both occasions been brought back by force and violence by Wallace's armed accomplices. He was thereafter warned that if he made a further attempt to escape he would lose his life. Michael succeeded in convincing Constantine and his panel of enquiry that his continuing to be with Wallace was not of his own free-will but arose out of a fear of death. The chamberlain was accordingly commanded to return to Michael his belongings with the king's special grace. Constantine had a sister who it appears married a Halkelt of Pitfirrane. Their son Philip came to possess the third part of Pitfirrane, once held by the Lochore family.

Adam II of Lochore

We have already seen that Adam received a gift of the lands of Lumphinnans from his father in 1242. In a charter about the year 1290-6 he is referred to as Adam of Lochgelly, and along with his brother Constantine III of Lochore, he is stated to be a free tenant of the barony. Adam does not apear to have been survived by any offspring, as this is the only instance of Lochgelly being used as a personal appellation. Unlike Lochore, "Lochgelly" was not destined to become a family name.

We have still to record the actions of other persons bearing the name of Lochore, and while it may seem strange that their relationship one to the other has not yet been established, there can be no doubt that they were all in some way blood-related. The first of these is Sir Thomas of Lochore.

Sir Thomas of Lochore

To those who may have more than a passing interest in the history of this ancient family, we would suggest a visit to the old banqueting hall in Edinburgh Castle, for there you will see displayed beside the Arms of Robert the Bruce, the Armorial bearings of Sir Thomas of Lochore. Like most of the early Coats of Arms, Sir Thomas's shield carries quite a simple device:— Argent, three piles issuing from the Chief, their points conjoining in base, Sable. Like many other Scots during this period, Sir Thomas appeared for a while to have gone along with Edward's policy of subjugating Scotland to English rule, but was only waiting till an opportunity arose to defend his country. With the rise of Wallace, he attached himself to the National cause and latterly became a trusted associate of The Bruce.

It can be assumed from the records of the period that Sir Thomas had received a good education. Edward I, who was no mean judge of a man's abilities, appointed Sir Thomas to the post of Clerk to the Parliament. In a mandate despatched from Montrose and dated July 10th, 1296, Edward ordered the Chancellor of England and eight others to proceed to Berwick to meet him the following month so that he would receive the homages of a great number of Scottish freeholders, and thereafter to hold a Parliament to draw up an ordinance for the government of Scotland. The mandate contains two names and possibly a third, of those who, no doubt would be looked upon by their countrymen as degenerate Scots. The clerk who wrote the document gives Sir Thomas's name in the form, Thomam de Lugore.

Sir Thomas was still an English partisan two years after the Berwick Parliament. He continued in the post of one of the clerks to the Parliament and is referred to in a writ of summons from Sandwycum as Magiftro Thome de Lughore. It could not have been long after this before he took up arms in defence of his country. He is said to have fought alongside Sir William Wallace against a contingent of the English army at the battle of Blackearnside, near Newburgh in 1298 and was one of several Scottish knights who were wounded. After the death of Wallace he continued his adherance to the cause of Scottish Independence under the leadership of Bruce, and is last heard of in April 1315 when he was present at a Parliament held in the Church of St. John in Ayr to consider "the condition, defence and perpetual security of the kingdom of Scotland". It was agreed that, failing a male heir of King Robert, the succession of the crown should go to his brother, Edward Bruce. Thomas de Lochor, militis, witnessed the Act also, among many others, Dominus Michael de Wemyss.

Hugh II of Lochore

This Hugh of Lochore is to be distinguished from the previous Hugh in so far that his name appears on the Ragman Roll of those who rendered homage to Edward I at Berwick on August 28th, 1296, while his namesake was a prisoner in Chester Castle and is known to have remained there until after September, 1300.

As Huwe de Logore his name appears on the Roll beside those of his relatives through marriage, Adam and William de Valoyns and David de Wemyss. For the reasons already stated it was probably this Hugh who witnessed a charter confirming the lands of Carslogie on John Clephane in about the year 1300 and probably the same person, who as Hugone de Locwor, witnessed the homage of Duncan, Earl of Fife to Robert de Crail the Abbot of Dunfermline, for the lands of Cluny in 1316. In the following year he was witness to two charters, one concerning a gift by John de Graham of the church of Newlands to the Abbey of Dunfermline, and another which dealt with the Commonty of Gaitmilk, in the parish of Kinglassie. We last hear of Hugh de Lochore when he witnessed along with Michael and David de Wemyss, a charter by Duncan the last Earl of Fife shortly before 1346.

William II of Lochore

William of Lochore was possibly the youngest son of Constantine II and, if so, a brother of Sir David of Lochore. He was witness to a charter by Michael Scot, Lord of

Balwearie, about the year 1300. His name also appears in an inquest which was held on his behalf during the reign of Robert the Bruce concerning the lands of Balmuto wherein the names Alexander III, John Balliol and William Wallace appear. Sir William was survived by two daughters. Mariotte, one of the co-heiresses, married Roger Boswell, second son of Richard Boswell of Oxmuir, in Berwickshire about the year 1330.

Philip III of Lochore

Philip of Lochore is known only for a brief entry in an English document of July 8th, 1312. He was a horseman of the first rank who was in the pay of Edward II. In 1312 he was one of a large garrison with a high proportion of Scots which held St. Johnstone (Perth) for Edward II under the command of the Perthshire Knight, Sir William Oliphant, one time Constable of Stirling Castle, who had spent four years in an English prison and released in 1308 on condition that he would oppose Bruce. In 1312, Philippes de Loghouere, according to the record, was paid £10. Perth at this period was surrounded on three sides by a high wall and a ditch filled with water; the fourth side was protected by the river Tay. The year 1312 saw the garrison in a condition scarcely able to hold out for any considerable time. In January 1313 the Scottish Army under Bruce made a night attack on the town by scaling the wall by means of rope ladders after negotiating the water-filled ditch; the King himself was the second man to scale the wall. With the surrender of the town the English troops were allowed to go free, but a few of the leading Scots were slain as an example to the rest. Philip of Lochore is believed to have been dead by 1315. One wonders if he was one of those who paid the supreme penalty.

David III of Lochore

He may have been the David de Lochor who is described in a charter about the year 1330 as a cousin of Sir David of Wemyss, and the "David" whom we know from another source, to have been the son of Hugh of Lochore, but whose identity beyond this is not clear. Like most of the freeholders of land in Scotland, he rendered fealty to Edward I at Berwick in 1296. He probably was the David de Louchore who received an annuity from Inverkeithing from 1327-1331.

Philip IV of Lochore

Lastly, we learn of a Philip of Lowchquor late lord of the third part of Pitfirrane. The other two-thirds of Pitfirrane were held by the Scotts of Balwearie and the Abbey of Dunfermline. Philip may have been alive about the year 1400, but was certainly dead before 1435.

47

During the second half of the fourteenth century, by which time the whole of Lochoreshire had gone over to other families through marriage, the French "de" in the family name was increasingly being dropped. The name continued to flourish however, well into the seventeenth century, as the burgh records of Dunfermline show. Today it is to be found but rarely in Fife, although it still appears in Ayrshire and surprisingly as far away as New Zealand. No one of the name is known in later times to have distinguished himself in public life, with perhaps one exception, that of Robert Lochore (1762-1852), one of Scotland's minor poets whose literary tastes brought him into contact with Robert Burns, and who composed an elegiac pastoral on the death of the national bard.

THE WEMYSS FAMILY

16

The Wemyss family and the Lochore family were closely related, each having a common ancestor in the person of Hugo, son of Gillimichael, Earl of Fife. Later on, the common bond was strengthened by the marriage of Sir Michael Wemyss and the younger daughter of Sir David Lochore. Their son, Sir David Wemyss inherited his mother's portion of Lochoreshire.

Sir Michael Wemyss

The lineage in the early part of the family's history is not clear, but Sir Michael, father of Sir John was probably fourth in succession from "Big John of the Cave" also known as John of Methil. Sir Michael was one of the auditors for John Balliol in his claim to the Scottish throne, and was present when Balliol did homage to Edward I at Norham in 1292. He swore allegiance to the English king at Stirling in June 1296 and as "Sire Michel de Wymes del counte de Fyf", his name appears again on the Roll of Allegiance drawn up at Berwick-on-Tweed in August of the same year. In May of the following year we find Sir Michael and his son David among several knights to whom Edward I addressed a letter announcing his intention to cross over to France, and stating how certain matters affecting Scotland should be dealt with in his absence. Sir David swore fealty to Edward I for a second time at the Parliament held at St. Andrews in March 1304. Following his act of homage, Edward issued a writ from Kinghorn on the 11th of the following month, ordering that his wife's dower-land situated near Berwick, be restored to Sir David and Margaret, his wife.

It was probably during the winter of 1303-4 when Edward resided at Dunfermline monastery for a period of over three months, that Sir Michael hospitably entertained the king at Wemyss Castle.

It is from a Roll of the war horses of the period which belonged to those who were actively supporting the English king, that we find that Sir Michael owned a reddish-brown horse — a bay — which the steward of the royal household valued at £10. In the year following the execution of Sir William Wallace, Sir Michael renounced his fealty to Edward and again became active in the cause of Scottish Independence under the leadership of Bruce. By so doing, he forfeited his estate and no sooner had his defection become known, than Edward was petitioned by Sir Alexander Cheveroill and Sir Giles Dare to have his lands and those of Sir David Wemyss. Edward's reply of 16th June, 1306 was that their request would require to remain in abeyance until he came to Scotland. Edward however, wasted no time, as three days later he ordered the destruction of all Sir Michael's property, stating, "we have not found in Sir Michael either good word or service and he has now shown in deed that he is a traitor and our enemy".

Edward's harsh treatment had the effect of intensifying Sir Michael's efforts in support of the new king, and in 1315 he was present at Bruce's Parliament held at Ayr when he witnessed the Act of Settlement of the Crown. Both Sir Michael's and Sir Thomas Lochore's seal is appended to the Act. In 1316 Sir Michael is witness along with his son Sir David, to a charter granted by Duncan, Earl of Fife to John Clephane of Carslogie. In 1319, the year before his death, we find Sir Michael and his son among a company of persons chosen to perambulate the marches of certain lands belonging to the monastery of Dunfermline.

Sir David Wemyss

Andrew of Wyntoun, the Prior of the monastery of St. Serfs, writing his "Cronykil" in the nearby Inch in Lochleven in about the year 1420 at the request of Sir John Wemyss, great, great-grandson of Sir David Wemyss, tells us that in 1290 Sir David was chosen as an ambassador to cross over to Norway to bring back the child princess Margaret, because "he of the language weile couth ken". Sir David's fellow-ambassador was Sir Michael Scott who had studied astrology and necromancy and whose predictions so impressed his contemporaries that he is known in local history as the "Wizard of Balwearie". Sir Michael Scott was another of John Balliol's auditors.

When Sir Michael accompanied Sir David Wemyss as ambassador to Norway he is reckoned to have been in his seventies. If we allow for Sir David nearing middle-age when called upon to cross "over the water", it places his parents' marriage somewhere about the middle of the thirteenth century. To mark the occasion of his visit, Sir David received from the King of Norway a silver basin which is still preserved in Wemyss Castle. With the death of the Maid of Norway, Scotland was soon to be plunged into the Wars of Indpendence.

Soon after the death of Sir David of Lochore, Sir David Wemyss received from his mother the lands which constituted her portion of Lochoreshire. The following list, if not complete, contains at least most of the lands included in his mother's inheritance. Wester Raith, Powguild, Glennistoun, Balbethy (Balbedie), Capildrayth (Capeldrae) Pitkinnie and Strathrudie in Lochoreshire, and Ardargy and Westerdron in Perthshire and half of Eglisdikin in the earldom of Menteith. It will be seen that the lands situated in Lochoreshire, with the exception of Wester Raith, are those in the parish of Auchterderran which lie adjacent to the eastern boundary of Ballingry parish. These lands, along with Ballingry parish constituted the mill-lands of Lochore.

Sir David, on receiving these lands styled himself "Lord of the lands of Sir David, formerly Lord of Lochore" referring of course, to his grandfather. The mill of Lochore at this period (C.1296) was the common property of Sir Adam de Vallance and himself. It was in 1296 that Sir David swore fealty to Edward I. This of course, is not the first instance of the Wemyss family holding lands in Lochoreshire, by this time they had in their possession by descent, the extreme eastern portion of the Lochore estate, that is, the portion of the parish of Auchterderran which lay contiguous to the lands of Markinch and Wemyss-shire and, as referred to earlier on, constitutioned part of the lands gifted by Gillimichael Macduff, with the consent of his eldest son Duncan to his second son Hugo, the progenitor of the Wemyss family.

17 *Seal of Michael of Methil and Wemyss*

Sir David very soon shared his newly acquired possessions with his relatives. He gave to his wife, Annabella St. Clair, widow of Sir John Bisset, the lands of Balbedie, Capeldrae, Pitkinnie and Strathruddie, also his lands in Perthshire and Menteith. It is expressly stated in the charter conveying these lands to his wife that Constantine of Lochore and Adam of Lochgelly are free tenants in the barony of Lochore. No doubt the privileges enjoyed by Constantine and Adam included free multure in the mill of Lochore. Reference is also made to the fishings of Balbedie and Capeldrae, an allusion no doubt to the river Leven and Boglochty, from which Annabella received an annual rent of 10/8d. By 1304 Sir David had married for the second time. Sometime previous to this he had conveyed by charter the lands of Raith to his uncle, John Wemyss and, no doubt with the consent of Adam de Vallance, he allowed his uncle to grind his corn at the mill of Lochore without payment, on condition that he rendered to him a pair of gilt spurs, the symbol of knighthood, or six pennies. The charter is witnessed by Sir David's father also Matthew of Crambeth Bishop of Dunkeld, Constantine and Hugh of Lochore and Walter de Ramsay who was by then Sir David's father-in-law. In addition, Sir David allowed his uncle and his men dwelling on the lands of Raith to take sufficient fuel, both in heather and peat from his moor of Mcleofgarmunth and his lands of Polqulde (Powguild) near Lochgelly for an annual payment of two pennies. Sir David may have been the *David Wemyss* who appears as one of the signatories to the Declaration of Arbroath which was sent to Pope John XXII in 1320. Sir David died about 1330 and was succeeded by his son, Sir Michael.

51

Sir Michael Wemyss II

Sir Michael was with the Scottish army at the battle of Halidon Hill in 1333 when he was taken prisoner and afterwards released on swearing fealty to Edward III. In the same year he obtained a charter from the Earl of Fife of the lands of Easter Munichie and Westerdron. In continuing his adherence to the Engish king, he and his son David along with the neighbouring laird of Arnot, joined a joint force of English troops and the supporters of Edward Balliol, the son of John Balliol, in besieging Lochleven Castle in 1335 which was being held for King David II by Sir Alan de Vipont of Aberdour. After a period of many months in which repeated attempts to besiege the Castle from a fort which had been constructed in the kirkyard of Kinross had failed, the garrison in the Castle seized a suitable opportunity of a counter-attack, when it became known that most of the besiegers had gone off to Dunfermline to attend the festival held on St. Margaret's day. Sir Alan Vipont's men made a sudden sally from the Castle and attacked the few besiegers who had been left to guard the fort. After a brief engagement the Castle garrison returned with all the spoils of war and sufficient supplies of food to continue the defence of the Castle from the blockade.

Following this encounter, the attackers, so it is said, transferred their military operations to the east end of the loch, where they hit on the idea of damming up the outlet of the loch at a point called Leven Mouth, in an effort to drown the garrison in the Castle. Once again, so the story goes, the defenders attacked the Englishmen and the Balliol supporters, and by breaking down the dam the pent-up waters swept away horses, baggage, tents and men. It is said that the laird of Arnot was among those who lost their lives. Some credence is given to the latter part of the story by the fact that there is still to be seen at the east end of the loch a ditch and rampart of considerable proportions, the purpose for which has not been satisfactorily explained. Some three months after this event in March 1336 Edward III ordered £40 to be paid to Sir Michael Wemyss in recognition of his efforts.

Sir Michael's son John pre-deceased him so that when Sir Michael died in 1342, his estate passed to his two daughters whose husbands, Sir John of Inchmartin and John Livingstone of Drumry came to possess Wemyss-shire, Methil and Cameron. Sir Michael may have had a third daughter who it is said married a Boswell, thought to have been Roger, second son of Richard de Boswell, but, the manuscript account of that family states that Roger married Mariota, daughter of William of Lochore in about the year 1330, some twelve years before the disposal of Sir Michael's estate. It is possible therefore, that Roger de Boswell was twice married and Sir Michael's third daughter was his second wife. It is certain that by the end of the fourteenth century, the families of Livingstone and Boswell possessed between them the lands of Easter Lochoreshire and part of Wester Lochoreshire with the Boswells holding the greater portion. Sir John Boswell and Sir Robert Livingstone are referred to as "Lords of the Barony of Lochore" in the year 1395.

The Boswell lands at this period comprised Bowhill, Balgreggie, Balgony, Dundonald, Spittal, Glassmount, Muircames, Muirtoun, Strathruddie, Easter Balbedie, Easter Capeldrae and Cartmore. They had also the superiority of the lands of

Little Raith, Powguild, Glennistoun, Balmungie, Colquhally, Pitkinnie and Lochgelly. Of these Spittal and Cartmore are in the parish of Ballingry.

There is evidence that the lands in Wemyss-shire were recovered by the Wemyss family during the second quarter of the seventeenth century and that several lands in Lochoreshire also returned to that family about the same period. That the Wemyss family did not lose all their connections with Lochoreshire on the death of Sir Michael, is shown by the fact that a Sir John Wemyss of the period was in possession of the lands lying a little to the north of Inchgall Mill in 1482 and that he was ordered to return to David Wemyss who was his tenant there, a number of oxen and sheep and a horse which he had wrongfully taken from his kinsman. In respect of certain lands held by the Wemyss family, the Wemyss lairds had the right of a seat in Ballingry church.

THE VALLANCE FAMILY

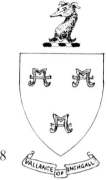

18

Following the death of Sir David of Lochore about the year 1295 (perhaps the last laird of the Lochore family to occupy Lochore Castle), the western portion of Lochoreshire was divided between his two daughters as co-heiresses. As the two ladies were already married, their respective husbands became the new lairds in right of their wives. In the case of Wemyss however, it appears that, following closely on the death of Sir David, his daughter (probably the younger) who had married Sir Michael Wemyss, made a gift of her portion of the estate to their eldest son Sir David Wemyss. Adam de Vallance, who had married the other co-heiress came to possess the remaining and larger portion of the western part of the estate.

From the point of view of family descent the new lairds could not have been more dissimilar. Sir David Wemyss could claim, through both his parents, descent from the old Celtic Mormaers of Fife through the House of Macduff, the hereditary Earls of Fife, his father and mother having a common ancestor in Hugo Macduff. His family had taken its name from the many caves or weems to be found along the foreshore on their estate. The first of the family being known as "Eoin Mor Na Vamb" — Big John of the Cave. Sir David was in a very real sense a native of Fife.

Adam de Vallance on the other hand was by descent an Anglo-Norman. His great-grandfather, the first of the family to come north, had settled in Scotland not more than 130 years before and had been dead only some 80 years. Indeed, it may not be too much to say that Adam may have in many ways shown a strong tendency to French or English ways in his every day relationship with his contemporaries, and at a time when the French language was being used often at court and in ordinary intercourse, Adam may very well have spoken in French. This would undoubtedly emphasize still further the difference which must have existed between the newly established feudal lord and his Gaelic-speaking vassals.

The family name appears in various forms in early writings. Sometime during the latter part of the reign of Malcolm IV, Philip de Valoniis and his younger brother Roger, sons of Roger de Valoniis of England, came north to Scotland. Their grandfather, Pierre de Valoniis, who took his name from Valones or Valoignis in Normandy, was prominent among the followers of William the Conqueror, from whom it is said he obtained 57 lordships in 6 counties in England. He was appointed High Sheriff of Essex in 1087 and built for himself a castle in Suffolk. He and his wife Abreda, daughter of Hubert, Lord of Rie, founded the Priory of Binham in Northfolk and amply endowed it. He was succeeded in all his possessions by his son, Roger, who by his wife Agnes had six sons, of whom Philip was the fifth and Roger the sixth.

Roger de Valoniis

It was not long before the two brothers began to receive royal favours. Roger was created lord of the manor of East Kilbride by William the Lion in recognition of services to the Crown and lived in the Castle of Kilbride. His name appears in many of the chartularies of the religious houses of the period. The register of the Bishopric of Glasgow records his donation to the church there sometime between 1175 and 1189, of his Chapel of Kilbride. The Deed is witnessed by his brother Philip. He was survived by his son William, and his daughter Isabella who eventually succeeded to her father's estate. Isabella married early in the thirteenth century Sir David Comyn one of the "Magnates Scotiae" who was appointed to maintain peaceful relations with England in 1237. Sir David was the son of Richard Comyn, Earl of Buchan and brother of Sir John, the Red Comyn, Lord of Badenoch and grand-uncle of John, the Red Comyn who was murdered by Robert the Bruce in the church of the Minorite Friars of Dumfries in 1306. Sir David pre-deceased his wife and was buried in the crypt of Glasgow Cathedral, to which Isabella had been by far the most generous benefactor. It is believed that the face of a woman and a man which are to be seen carved on two vault-bosses in the north aisle of the Cathedral are the protraits of Isabella and her husband.

19 *Isabella de Valoniis and her husband, Sir David Comyn*

In 1250, Isabella gifted to the church of Glasgow her fifteen pounds lands situated in Kirkpatrick, called the Forrest of Dalkarne. The charter conveying the gift was confirmed by John of Balliol and Alexander III. Among the witnesses was Sir William de Valoniis, Isabella's brother, who appears to have pre-deceased her. Isabella was succeeded by her elder son, William in 1253 and when he died sometime after 1280, the manor of Kilbride devolved on John Comyn, his younger brother. John was involved in the struggles of the period and was taken prisoner by the English in 1296, probably at Dunbar. Not long afterwards the family's possessions passed to Edward Comyn who, along with his kinsman, opposed the rise of Bruce and fought in support of John Balliol. Edward eventually lost his life, and on Bruce gaining the throne he stripped the family of their possessions and in this manner the lands of Kilbride became the dowry-lands of Bruce's daughter Marjory when she married Walter the Steward.

Philip de Valoniis

Philip appears to have been not long settled in Scotland before he joined the King's service. He was the King's Chamberlain in 1166 and it is probable that he was appointed to the office when William the Lion became King the year before. His surname appears in many forms; e.g. Vallon, Valunnes, Valun, Valoin, Valuin, Wailons, Waloines and greatly exceeds his brother in the many occasions in which his name appears in the records of the period. The king sometimes refers to him as "My Chamberlain". What is perhaps one of the earliest Deeds witnessed by Philip is a charter by William the Lion, granted between 1165 and 1178 wherein he gives and confirms a grant of land and certain privileges to the burgesses of Inverkeithing.

Following the convention of Falaise in 1174, Philip, along with many others including the king's brother David and Duncan, Earl of Fife, was sent to Henry of England as a hostage in token of the fulfilment of an agreement arrived at for the release of William the Lion. In recompense for his faithful services, the king, on being released, granted Philip the lands of Panmure, Benvie and Balrundry in the vicinity of Arbroath. As is to be expected, Philip was much at Court and was often to be found in the entourage of the king. During this period tournaments were a frequent amusement in which knights jousted with one another to display their skill in the weapons of war. There is an account of a tournament held in France in which the King of Scotland was present along with a large company of knights. Although Sir Philip de Valoniis was defeated, he is described by the chronicler as the best equipped and most notable of the Scottish party that accompanied the King.

Philip again succeeded to the office of Lord High Chamberlain in 1190, and in 1206 he was sent as the king's ambassador to treat with King John of England. Three years later he witnessed at Durham an agreement between William the Lion and King John, and in 1212 he was at Carlisle on matters of importance, when a payment of 30/- was made to his clerk, Master Matthew to defray the cost of food and the stabling of his master's horse.

On the death of William the Lion in 1215 his son, Alexander II, appointed Philip as his High Chamberlain, but by the end of the year Philip de Valoniis was dead. The old writers tell us that Philip, Lord of Panmure, was interred with great solemnity in the

Chapter House at Melrose Abbey and that at the time of his death he had, in addition to his manors in Forfarshire, many lands in the west and south of Scotland and several lordships in England. He also held some lands in Fife, but it is not disclosed where the Fife lands were situated. He was survived by a son William and two daughters, Sibilla and Lora.

20 *Seal of Philip de Valoniis*

Sibilla de Valoniis

This lady married Robert de Stuteville, Lord of Liddel in Cumberland. Her father gave her the lordship of Torpenhow in that county in free marriage. They had one son, Robert.

Lora de Valoniis

Lora married Sir Henry de Balliol, Chamberlain of Scotland, and grand-uncle of John Balliol, King of Scotland. Her father gave her the lands of Panlathy and Balbenie in Forfarshire which lay contiguous to his own estate of Panmure.

Philip may have had a third daughter Alice, who was the wife of Walter Corbet, Lord of Makerston. Their daughter Christina married William, son of Earl Patrick of Dunbar.

William de Valoniis

William, who was much at the court of England, returned to Scotland towards the end of the reign of William the Lion. In 1202 he, along with his father, witnessed a charter whereby the town of Ayr was erected into a free burgh, and in 1217 his name appears as a witness to a charter by Malcolm, Earl of Fife, to the monks of Culross for the foundation of their Abbey. On the death of his father he received from Alexander

II the office of High Chamberlain and succeeded to the manor of Panmure along with the lands of Benvie and Balrudry in Perthshire. In 1218 he acted as guardian to his nephew Robert de Stuteville, Lord of Liddel, who was at this period under age. His name appears frequently in the chartulary of the abbey of Melrose along with that of his father and his uncle Roger. William died at Kelso in 1219 and, contrary to the wishes of the monks there, he was taken to Melrose and buried in the Chapter House beside his father. He was succeeded in his estates by his daughter Christian.

Christian de Valoniis

Christian married before the year 1215, Sir Peter who was of the Anglo-Norman family of Maule, who had settled in the Lothians and who afterwards held lands in Perthshire. Robert de Maule, the first of the family to appear in Scotland, claimed descent from Guarian de Maule who accompanied William of Normandy in his invasion of England in 1066. The marriage of Sir Peter de Maule to Christian de Valoniis brought great possessions to his family. Following the death of William de Valoniis the lands of Benvie and Balrudry, although situated in Perthshire, were united and annexed to Panmure and the whole erected into a barony known as the barony of Panmure.

On the death of the Countess of Essex who died without issue in 1234, Christian de Valoniis along with her aunt Lora Balliol and her father's cousin Isabella Comyn, received an equal portion of the de Valoniis possessions in the counties of Cambridge, Essex, Hertford, Northfolk and Suffolk. Christian brought further possessions to her husband on the death of her aunt Sibilla, the widow of Robert de Stutville, when she succeeded to her inheritance.

In 1254, shortly before the death of her husband, Christian and Sir Peter gave in free alms to the monks of Arbroath, the lands of Brakis in the barony of Panmure. Meanwhile, her aunt Lora and her husband Henry Balliol had exhanged their lands of Panlathy and Balbenie for others belonging to Christian and her husband. Shortly after 1254 Christian, who was now a widow, gave these lands by charter to John Liddel. The charter is of interest in that the conditions or limitation set down show Christian to have had her dislikes. John Liddel could dispose of these lands freely to anyone, but he was on no account to sell them to monks or jews!

In 1280, by which time Christian must have been a very old lady, she was finding that the management of her affairs, especially in relation to her extensive possessions in England was beginning to cause her concern. She accordingly appealed to Edward of England stating that she was finding difficulty in making arrangements for paying her debts due to the Exchequer, and asking for an extension of time. Her request was granted by the king, who on 7th June 1281 agreed that "Christina de Valoines be given a respite till the octaves of Trinity next". In a charter about the year 1250 Christian's seal is shown, and has been described as "very large in red wax showing a gentle woman with a goose hawk on her hand and her right hand on her own breast a little above the belt with this circumscription, Sigillum Christianae de Valouns". Christian was survived by her two sons Sir William and Sir Thomas de Maule.

Valoniis of Inchgall

It is a matter of surprise that while there were six sons of Roger de Valoniis of England, it was in the person of William de Valoniis the son of Philip the Chamberlain that the continuation of the branch of the family in Scotland depended. Three of Roger's sons died without issue and one was survived by an only daughter. Roger of Kilbride's son William, pre-deceased his sister and died without issue, and, as already seen, William de Valoniis of Panmure was succeeded by his daughter Christian. In view of the foregoing the question may be asked, from whom was the family of Valoniis of Inchgall descended. The answer probably lies in the little-known fact that William had a son named Roger. Now, this Roger seems to have been illegitimate: otherwise he would have succeeded to his father's estates instead of his half-sister Christian who, as all the old writers affirm, succeeded to her father's possessions, being his lawful heir. It is to be said however, that Christian's name does not appear in connection with any lands situated in Fife. The absence of any reference to these lands being among Christian's possessions may be that they, the lesser lands, were given to Roger. Families with the name of Valoniis are known by the end of the thirteenth century to have had interests in the lands of Torry, Lochore and Rosyth, while at a later date their name appears in connection with Peteddie, Lindors and Rossie. There is a tradition that a Vallance fought alongside Wallace and was present at the battle of Blackironside which took place in the neighbourhood of Lindors Abbey in 1298.

Coming to Adam de Valoniis of Inchgall, Sir Robert Sibbald in his *History of Fife* states that Adam was "the son of a gentlemen". If we accept this in its purely heraldic sense, it means that Adam's father belonged to the class in society below that of an esquire and above the common people, and was entitled by inheritance or otherwise to bear arms. Adam, we are told, was of the family of Torry an estate a little to the west of Dunfermline. The old writers speak of "Valange of Torry", whose son "married one of the co-heiresses of the Lord Loquhoir". Torry, which may have been one of the Fife lands belonging at one time to Philip de Valoniis, continued to be the chief seat of the family, while Inchgall was held by the eldest son.

We do not know for certain when Adam de Valoniis married the co-heiress of Lochore. It is only after the death of Sir David Lochore, his father-in-law that his name appears on his coming into possession of half of the barony of Lochore. A family named Vallance appears to have settled in Dalginch, in the parish of Markinch at a period a little earlier than that in which the Valoniis's of Inchgall emerged. In 1254 a "Sir William de Valoynes" appears in connection with a complaint by the Prior and chapter of St. Andrews that certain knights, including Sir William, had erected chapels in parishes within their bounds without their consent. On the matter being resolved the relationship between the Prior and Sir William seems to have grown quite amicable. Sir William and his wife Margaret gave to the priory in 1284 the gift of a meadow at Markinch along with pastorage for two cows and their calves. It is revealed in the charter that Sir William had a son and heir named William and a daughter Mary. In a transumpt of a charter of 1400, William de Valoniis of the period 1288-96, is described as the son and heir of the late William de Valoniis knight lord of Dalginch. This William was contemporary with Adam de Valoniis of Inchgall. Both men did homage to Edward I at Berwick on 28th August, 1296. It is very probable that they were related, the more so, as it is known that the lands of Dalginch at a later date were annexed to Western Lochoreshire during the time of the Valoniis's of Inchgall.

Adam de Valoniis of Inchgall

Of the two daughters of Sir David of Lochore, it can be assumed that Adam married the elder, as it was a point in feudal law that the eldest of co-heiresses re-eived with her share the caput of the family, Adam therefore, may have lived for some time in the Castle of Lochore following the death of his father-in-law. The castle was probably destroyed in 1298 shortly after the battle of Falkirk. Fife and Fothrif were singled out for special reprisal by Edward for the support which the Earl of Fife and his men had given Wallace at Falkirk. The Earl's son was among those who fell that day fighting along with the "gentlemen of Fife". Part of Edward's army marched from Stirling and avenged themselves by leaving a trail of devastation behind them. All the castles built of timber were burnt to the ground and the more substantial ones of stone were destroyed. There is evidence to suggest that the Castle of Lochore was destroyed by fire.

Although Adam's submission to Edward at Berwick made him nominally Edward's man, it can hardly be expected that he would be granted permission to build a castle until he had proved his loyalty to the English side. In this there seems to have been some doubt, for his name appears again among those who did homage at the Parliament held at St. Andrews in March 1304. Adam shortly afterwards was openly supporting Bruce in his bid for the Crown, and three months after Bruce's coronation in 1306, Edward, in retaliation, forfeited all the landowners who had helped Bruce, so that Adam, in the eyes of Edward, had become a "false traitor". There were many in the English army who looked forward to obtaining forfeited lands north of the border. It is not surprising therefore, to find that Adam's lands were given to an English partisan, although there is no evidence to show that the lands of Wester Lochoreshire were in fact ever held by one of Edward's minions. To be given a grant of land by a Deed signed in Newport Pagnell, in far away Buckinghamshire was one thing, to obtain actual possession was quite another matter. In a document dated 27th June, 1306, written in old French, we learn that one John de Autry, squire of Lord Nicole, petitioned Edward I for the lands belonging to a Thomas de Boys, probably the Thomas de Boys of Edinburghshire who did homage in 1296 and was beheaded in September 1306. Edward immediately granted John de Autry his request and, in addition gave him the lands belonging to Adam de Valoygnes who, he remarked was with the Lord Carrick (Bruce). Adam's lands it is stated, were valued at £40.

Whether the need for a new residence arose from the destruction of the Castle of Lochore by the English, or with the advance in military art and the consequent development in castle-building, the old castle with its ditches and ramparts had become obsolete: there is as yet no way of knowing. In any case, Adam about this period must have set about building a more comfortable and commodious residence for his family on the island in the loch in the improved style of a stone-built Keep. If Adam had not already done so, he probably commenced the work after attending Bruce's first Parliament held at St. Andrews in 1309, by which time the threat of having his lands taken from him had become less probable, providing he continued to support the new king. When Adam moved into his new residence, his gaelic-speaking vassals were probably slow to accept him as their new overlord. He was not of their blood, his name spoke of foreign descent (Adam probably spoke more French than Scots). To them he was a stranger and a foreigner and accordingly they spoke of the "Island of the Foreigner". From henceforth the earlier appellation was dropped and the barony was known as Inchgall and the Chapel of Lochore became the Chapel of Inchgall. This remained so until the abandonment of Inchgall Castle as a place of residence. The Malcolm family built Inchgall House to replace the castle as the seat of the family.

We have already referred to Adam de Valoniis doing homage to Edward I. As he was a Fife landowner he was chosen by Edward to sit on an Inquest to decide the succession to the Fife lands of the late Elena la Zousche. The Inquest was held at Berwick on the 24th of the month, four days before the appointed day for the English king to receive the homage of Scottish landowners.

On looking over the list of names of Scotsmen as they appear on the Ragman Roll, one can obtain some idea of how it must have looked on that day in August, 1296. Every free holder of land in Scotland of any standing and those holding high offices in the country were required to swear fealty to Edward as overlord of Scotland. We may be sure that in such a gathering ranging from Earls downwards, Adam de Valoniis of Inchgall would be regarded as small fry. If homage was done in person and not by proxy as has been suggested, there seems to have been quite a company of the Fife gentry present at Berwick. Of those of our neighbourhood, the Lord of Inchgall comes first. One can imagine him as moving slowly forward in a long line of notables, when at last he reaches the trestle-table behind which a clerk is sitting he repeats after him the oath of allegiance and thereafter signs his name as "Adam de Valoynes". Another ten persons take the oath, then the next person having sworn fealty writes "Huwe de Loghor". He is followed in like manner by "Willolmo de Valynes" (presumably of Dalginch), the fourth person behind him repeats the oath of allegiance and signs his name "David de Wymes", no doubt as Lord of the eastern half of Lochoreshire. A little later on "Henrius de Crambath" (now part of Blair Adam estate) swears fealty for his office of Dean of Dunkeld.

Probably related to Sir Adam, was John de Valoniis whose name appears about this time. He was Sheriff of Fife, although not all writers are agreed as to when he held that office. He is said to have been Sheriff during the reign of John Balliol, although 1298 has also been given. One writer states he was "of Inchgall". It is probable, however, that John belonged to the Torry branch of the family. After a period of indecision, he came out in support of Sir William Wallace after the latter had successfully routed the English forces at Perth. It is not known how long Sir Adam was in possession of Inchgall. He was probably dead by 1345 by which time there appears to have been a change in ownership.

61

Sir Andrew de Vallance

The next person to claim our attention is Sir Andrew de Vallance of Inchgall. An earlier Andrew de Vallance occurs about the year 1200 when, along with Michael and David de Wemyss and Michael Scott, he is witness to a charter of Duncan II, Earl of Fife. Although this Andrew is believed to have been domiciled in Fife, his relationship if any, to Sir Andrew de Vallance is not known. Likewise the relationship of Sir Andrew to Sir Adam de Vallance of Inchgall is not known for certain, but as Sir Andrew succeeded to the barony, there is a strong assumption that he was a son of Sir Adam.

Sir Andrew first appears about the year 1300, when as "Sir Andrew of Vallans" he witnessed a quit claim by Michael of Wemyss to John of Inglis, Lord of Inglis, Tarbet. His name occurs again in 1306 when, along with one surnamed Louchor and many others, he was witness to a charter. Again in 1330 his name appears along with Henrico de Vallonia, no doubt a relative. Between the years 1346-57 Sir Andrew received from John Earl of Carrick one third of the Barony of Rosyth, which lands by inheritance passed in due course to the Wardlaw family along with those of Inchgall. Sir Andrew appears again about the year 1350 as witness to a charter of Duncan Earl of Fife. It is also known that by 1354 Sir Andrew held the superiority of certain lands in Lochgelly.

In the agreement drawn up at Newcastle-upon-Tyne, dated 13th July, 1354, between the English and Scottish Commissioners for the ransom of King David II, upwards of 20 hostages were to be given for the payment of 90,000 merks within a period of 9 years. The hostages were to include the sons and heirs of the Scottish nobility, among them being the heirs of the Earls of Sutherland, March and Wigton. The list of hostages to be drawn from families of lesser rank included the son and heir of Sir Andrew de Vallance and David, son and heir of Sir David de Wemyss. Three years afterwards in a memorandum of Edward III dated October 3rd, 1357, it is stated that John Fleming, heir to the Earl of Wigton and John, son of Sir Andre de Valoniis were delivered to one Alewn de Strother. The clerk who wrote the memorandum is careful to point out, however, that Alewn received the hostages not in his capacity as sheriff.

In 1361 Sir Andrew held the post of "Senescallus" (steward) of Fife. How long he continued in this office is not known. In the following year he is witness to a charter as "Andreas de Valonise militibus". On 17th April, 1365 he appears in Perth and four years afterwards he is witness to a charter at Falkland. In 1368 he witnessed a charter of Isabella Countess of Fife.

The succession of the Vallance family up to this point is still not clear. It cannot be said with certainty that Sir Andrew was the son of Sir Adam. Nothing more is heard of John de Vallance the hostage. Many of the hostages are known to have died in England and it is likely that John shared the same fate. It has been suggested that there were two Sir Andrews, father and son, and that the Sir Andrew of whom we are to speak was a younger brother of John de Vallance. On the assumption that the foregoing is correct, Sir Andrew on the death of his elder brother became heir to his father. He probably succeeded to his father's estate sometime before 1372. On 5th November of that year he had a charter of confirmation from King Robert II of a grant of half of the mill of Lochore from Sir John Wemyss of Kincaldrum, Rires and Wemyss. As is already known Sir Adam de Vallance owned half the mill of Lochore, the Wemyss family the other half. It is probable that by now Sir Andrew was in possession of the whole of the mill-lands of Lochore, consisting of the parish of Ballingry which in the main constituted the barony of Inchgall otherwise known as Wester Lochoreshire. It is about this period that Sir Andrew resigned into the King's hands his lands of Byniane in the barony of Methven, whereupon the King granted them to John McKelly.

Sir Andrew was present at the Parliament held at Scone in April of the following year, when he appended his name to the second Act of Settlement by King Robert II whereby the order of succession in the male line to the Crown was agreed upon. He accordingly took the oath that day for himself and his heirs.

Sir James de Vallance I

Sir James was the son of Andrew de Vallance. Shortly before 1354 he married Agnes, the widowed daughter and one of the heiresses of Duncan de Crambeth a neighbouring laird who lived in Crambeth Castle situated a little to the west of Benarty Hill in the parish of Cleish. William Lindsay of Logie married the daughter and heiress of Agnes de Crambeth and Sir James de Vallance. It was in this way that early in the 16th century the then representatives of the family changed the name of their residence from Crambeth Castle to that of Dowhill Castle, calling it after lands belonging to them in the north. Perhaps the most prominent member of the Crambeth family was Matthew de Crambeth. Although Matthew was not appointed one of the Guardians of the realm in 1286, he nonetheless gave valuable help in matters concerning the weal of the realm. It was while he held the office of Dean of Aberdeen that he was appointed Bishop of Dunkeld in 1288 with the approval of the Guardians. The office of Dean was filled by his kinsman Master Hervey of Crambeth and in 1296 Hervey followed Matthew to become Dean of Dunkeld.

Matthew was much to the fore in the dealings with Edward of England during the troublesome times leading up to Edward's pronouncement on the claims by the many competitors to the throne. Matthew supported Bruce in 1292 and was one of the 40 auditors nominated by Bruce to support his claim to the Crown.

Following the Parliament held at Stirling in 1295 when the government of the realm was taken out of the hands of John Balliol, Matthew was elected to a council consisting of 12 drawn from bishops, earls and barons to manage the affairs of the country. In the same year he was sent to France along with the Bishop of St. Andrews and 2 noblemen to treat with King Philip on behalf of John Balliol for an offensive and defensive alliance against their common enemy the King of England. Matthew was still in France when the sack of Berwick took place following the defeat of Balliol and the submission to Edward of over 2,000 freeholders.

In the Scottish submission of 1304 certain conditions were negotiated including an amnesty and the restoration of the lands of those who had fought against Edward. In the

21 *Crambeth Castle: Re-named Dowhill Castle by the Lindsay Family*

Parliament held at St. Andrews in that year, Edward received the homage of most of the leading landowners in Fife and the neighbouring counties, but Matthew, who had been ill for some time was unable to travel to St. Andrews, nevertheless Edward restored to him the temporalities of his See and his estate of Crambeth, and also the other lands which had belonged to him — Bogie, Cockairney and Dalqueich in Kinross. Matthew had sufficiently recovered in health to enable him to journey to London the following year to be present at the Parliament held at Westminster. Probably the Bishop's last appearance in public was at St. Andrews in order to attend Bruce's first Parliament held there in 1309.

To return to Sir James de Vallance, as already stated, he married shortly before 1354. In that year David II confirmed a charter by his wife Agnes in his favour, granting to him and his heirs, her portion of the lands of Crambeth and Cleish which she held of the king, also her portion of the lands of Lochgelly which she held of Sir Andrew de Vallance who was by then her father-in-law. She also conveyed to Sir James and their heirs to be, her portion of the lands of Balverdie, held of the late Sir William de Monteith, also her lands of Authfring in Angus held of Sir John de Kinross together with her right over certain feus in Kinross. Sir James and Agnes had two daughters, Elizabeth and Christian and a son, James. In 1381, following the death of Sir James, his portion of the lands of Rosyth were by Robert II gifted in ward to Sir Thomas Erskine until such time that the heirs of Christian de Vallance became of age. Christian's sister Elizabeth appears to have married William Lindsay of Logie who became afterwards as "of Crambeth". It was thus that the family of Lindsay of Dowhill became established. This family also came into possession of the lands of Rossie, which formerly belonged to Elizabeth's father.

Sir James de Vallance II

Sir James de Vallance was succeeded in the Barony by his son Sir James, whom we first meet with in 1384 when he signs a document in Inchgall Castle as "James the Valons, knight Lord of Inchgall". In the following year, Sir James and Christine Erskine, daughter of Sir Thomas Erskine, declared themselves man and wife in the presence of friends. Sir James however, was to find that a former indiscretion was to have its effect later on. It was revealed that Christine Erskine and a servant girl with whom Sir James had had an improper relationship were related within the third degree of common kindred. Under these circumstances the marriage was forbidden by the church and they were accordingly excommunicated for contracting an unlawful marriage. However, in 1386 Sir James obtained the help of the Abbot of Holyrood in forwarding a petition to the Pope wherein he explained the impediment to his marriage and stated that he and Christine had lived together as man and wife for a year without obtaining a dispensation. Nothing more is heard of the matter and it is assumed that Sir James obtained his dispensation.

We next meet with Sir James in 1393 when he had what appears to have been a dispute with a kinsman over the boundary of his lands of Wester Gartmore (Cartmore) and the lands of Lumphenen (Lumphinnans) belonging to his cousin Philip Halkett. It will be remembered that Philip was the nephew and heir of Philip de Lochore, late lord of one third part of the lands of Pitfirrane. In the brieve of perambulation the two proprietors are thus described "James of Wallance knight Lord of Inchegalle and Philip Haket, Lord of Lumphenen". In this same year 1393, Sir James had a charter from Robert III, granting to him a quarter of the Barony of Crambeth on the resignation of Allan de Erskine and Alexander de Crambeth. Two years afterwards he signed himself "Jacobus de Valance" when he witnessed a charter by Robert, Earl of Fife and Menteith to Sir John Wemyss of the lands of Innerleven and Westhaugh of Scoonie. In the charter it is stated by the earl that he and Sir James are blood-related.

It is about this time that Sir James' wife Christine died. In July 1396 there is a mandate addressed to the Bishop of St. Andrews to grant dispensation for the marriage of James de Valens, knight and Elizabeth de Lyndesay, both being related in the fourth degree of consanguinity and in the fourth degree of affinity. In the mandate Sir James and Elizabeth are called "noble". Two years afterwards, Sir James was one of the witnesses to a charter by the Regent Albany to William de Ramsay of Culuthy, signed at the manor-place of Falkland.

The year of Sir James's death is not known for certain. He is last heard of when he witnessed a charter at Perth in 1406. He was probably dead by the following year as his name does not appear among the witnesses to a charter signed at Inchgall in 1407. Elizabeth Lyndsay survived her husband for a good many years. In 1432 she is designated "Elizabeth of Valans, lady of Inchgall". As superior of the third part of the lands of Lochhead near Lochgelly, she ratified a charter of this date in favour of John of Lumsden, Sheriff of Fife, granting that her lands be held by the Sheriff, reserving for herself and her heirs the services "due and want". Sir James is not known to have had a son, he was survived however, by at least two daughters, Christian and Euphane. Sir

Robert Sibbald in his *History of Fife,* states that "Jacobus de Valoniis leaving three daughters, the eldest married Sir Andrew Wardlaw of Torry and with her he got Wester-Lochoreshire, or the parish of Ballingry. The second daughter was married to Roger Boisvill pre-decessor to Balmuto, and her portion was the half of Auchterderrani, with Glassmount and Muircambus. His third daughter was married to Livingstone of East-Weems, who got with her the other half of Auchterdirane parish". It will be seen that the lands which came to Boswell and Livingstone were situated in Easter Lochoreshire. As the extent of the Vallance family's interest in Lochoreshire was confined to the barony of Inchgall, it is clear that Sibbald has mistaken two heiresses of an earlier period with those of the Vallance family. We have already seen that Roger de Boswell married a daughter of Sir William Lochore about the year 1330 and it is almost certain that John Livingstone of Drumry and East Wemyss married a daughter of Sir Michael of Wemyss who died about the year 1342; indeed, John de Boisvill knight, and Sir John de Livingstone knight, are described as "lords of the barony of Lochore" in 1395 and this was while Sir James de Vallance was still alive.

Christian de Vallance, as stated by Sibbald, married Andrew Wardlaw. Many writers have followed Sibbald in stating that Andrew was "of Torry". It is known, however, from evidence from more than one source, that Christian's forebear Sir Adam de Vallance was of the family who owned Torry. It is clear therefore, that Torry came to the Wardlaws only after Sir Andrew married into the Vallance family. Euphane de Vallance married John Sibbald about the beginning of the year 1413 as appears from a charter by Robert, Duke of Albany "to John Sibbald of Balgony of all and sindrie the half of the third of the barony of Rosyth and Crambeth lyan within the sheriffdom of Fyfe formerly belonging to Euphane Vallange and now resigned by her to hold of the king by the said John and Euphane and the longer liver and their heirs lawfully begot, which failing, her heirs".

Christian and Euphane may have had a sister who married William Scott, Lord of Balweary, cousin of Philip Halket Lord of Limphinnans. The evidence is rather uncertain.

It is not known if the Barns of Inchgall had the right of pit and gallows, but it is fairly certain that they held courts at Inchgall. There was identifiable, as late as the end of last century, a certain stone situated at the Milton, known as the Parliament Stone. This stone appears to have been part of the outcrop of rock which is to be seen a little to the west of Mains farm, and was about 2 feet high. As the name of the stone implies, the site was the venue of the local Barns court, at which all matters concerning the locality came under the jurisdiction of the laird.

Nearby stood a two-storey house of spacious dimensions, and of uncertain age, but dating at least from the mid-seventeenth century, with the unusual name of Castlerags. The name is a corruption of Castle Rigs, a name which is to be found elsewhere in association with medieval residences. It refers to the cultivation of the soil by the owner of the castle. We have a further allusion to this fact in the name Mains farm. The land in close proximity to the laird's house was usually reserved for the laird's personal use to provide produce for the table. It was usually the best land on the laird's domain or "mains". The "mains lands of Inchgall" are frequently mentioned in old charters. Long after the Barons of Inchgall had departed and Castlerags had been pulled down, an ancient and much respected inhabitant of the Milton, in the person of old Jenny Dick who lived in the "Wee white house" (formerly Captain Park's workmens' houff) when abroad during the summer months, used the Parliament Stone as her favourite seat.

THE MILL OF LOCHORE

This mill is not to be confused with Inchgall mill which appears on record at a much later date. The mill was situated on the south bank of the river Ore some three hundred yards east of the public road in what was to be known later as the Templelands. It was quite a small building, not much more than twenty feet in length and probably half this measurement in width, with its long axis lying parallel to the river and built partly into the riverbank. The ruins some fifty years ago stood to a height of two storeys but it is obvious that the mill had originally consisted of three compartments. The top floor would no doubt be used for the storage of grain and would house a wooden hopper and chute down through which the grain would be fed on to the millstones. The middle compartment had contained the millstones and the timber gear-wheels whereby the water-wheel turned the uppermost millstone.

The basement would contain wooden boxes or trays for catching the flour as it came from the millstones above. Owing to the slope on the river bank, the entrance to the uppermost compartment was probably reached by means of a timber gantry with a protecting handrail. Entrance to each compartment would be reached by means of an interior timber stair or ladder set in one corner of the building and passing through the top and middle compartment floors to reach the basement. Water for driving the mill was obtained from the loch by means of a mill lade. The track of the lade was, until recent years, still discernible and was for many a year a convenient dumping ground for the people who lived at the Templelands. A kiln for drying the grain prior to grinding was situated some eighty yards on the higher ground to the south of the mill. The mill is shown on several old maps and may have been in use until the draining of the loch in 1792.

In the early phase of the setting up of the barony, the mill obviously stood some distance from the castle but it was in fact the nearest site where an ample and continuous supply of water could be had. In this case the loch served the purpose of a mill pond. The baronial mill was a valuable piece of property to the feudal lord and was always a sure source of income. The neighbouring vassals were compelled to have their corn ground at the mill for which they paid; all too often the charge was excessive.

We do not know when the mill of Lochore was built, but in all probability it followed on shortly after the building of the notte-and-bailey castle, for a mill was a valuable adjunct just as a chapel was a spiritual necessity to a barony. These three, castle, mill and chapel were the chief elements in the layout of early feudal days and in many cases were the origin of early burghs. Along with the land gifted by the crown they formed the parochial origins of Anglo-Norman times.

The grinding stones for the mills in the neighbourhood were hewn from an out crop of rock on the Crambeth estate known of old, and up to the nineteenth century by which time it was no longer in use, as the Millstone Quarry.

Bringing home the millstones was always an important event in the life of the village, calling for the help of most of the male inhabitants. The stones were usually man-handled all the way. Owing to their enormous weight and size, the most efficient mode

68

of transport was to pass a treetrunk through the hole in the centre of the stone by which means it was brought to an upright position. After the tree-trunk had been firmly wedged in place the stone was rolled forward on its edge by a team of men working in relays.

The lands in the immediate vicinity of the mill of Lochore were known of old and are still known today as the Templelands. Although these lands are mentioned in 1439 it is not known when the Knights Templars first came to possess lands in the lordship of Lochoreshire. It is evident however that the Order feued out their land to the lairds of Inchgall up to the time of the Reformation.

Remembering the story of the crusading knight, it is perhaps not surprising that there should be lands belonging to the Knights Templars, albeit close to the laird's residence at the heart of the barony. This military Order, "The Order of the Temple of Solomon", was founded in the early twelfth century and soon developed into a powerful international organisation arising out of the military expeditions known as the Crusades. With the loss of the Holy Lands in 1291 the Order received a crushing blow from which it never recovered. Meanwhile it had become very wealthy, its discipline had become relaxed and the brethren had succumbed to the pleasures of the world. "To drink like a Templar" had by then become a common-place reproach. Its final demise came in 1324 when its possessions went over to the Order of the Hospital of St. John of Jerusalem, commonly known as the Hospitallers.

The Preceptor of the Order in Scotland at the Reformation was Sir James Sandilands of Calder. As his position was insecure he resigned in 1564 all the lands and property belonging to the Order of St. John to the Crown and received in return a Royal Charter granting them to himself and his heirs with the title of Lord of Torphichen, on the payment of ten thousand crowns and an annual feu duty of five hundred merks. It was thus that the Templelands of Inchgall became part of the lordship of Torphichen and for a short period afterwards all the Templelands in Fife were made over to George Lauder of Bass who probably held them in feu ferm.

The barony of Torphichen passed to Sir James Sandilands' grand-nephew who parted with a large portion of his estate. It was about this time that the remaining Templelands were sold to Sir Thomas Hamilton, afterwards Lord Binning and Byrie and Earl of Haddington. It is clear that by the year 1614 the Templelands of Inchgall belonged to Sir Thomas who by now held the office of Secretary of State. In 1645 John Hamilton, Earl of Haddington, was retoured heir to his father in the Templelands of Fife by which process the Templelands of Inchgall were now part of the barony and regality of Drem and remained so as late as 1670 when Charles fifth Earl of Haddington was the proprietor.

The Hospitallers were the founders of a great many of the medieval hospitals and the name through the wear and tear of the centuries has given us the many place-names containing the usual abbreviation "Spittal", denoting that a hosptial or hospice once stood in the neighbourhood. This name is to be found a mile or so to the east of Lochgelly. One can only guess at the reason and significance, if any, for the lands and mill of Spittal, surrounded as they are on all sides by Auchterderran parish, remaining part of Ballingry parish and in the barony of Inchgall.

22　*The remains of the miller's house on the Templelands of Lochore c.1900*

There was in the olden times a resting place for travellers situated in the Templelands known as Spail Inn. One is tempted to ask, was this a contraction of Spittal Inn. More interesting perhaps is the fact that a hospital or hospice in the burgh of Cupar was in medieval times annexed to the barony of Inchgall.

LOCH ORE: INCHGALL ISLAND AND CASTLE

The extent of Loch Ore, as described by eighteenth century writers, varied from 150 to over 200 acres. The reason for the difference in acreage can to some extent be accountable by the fact that the loch would vary in size according to the seasons of the year. The margin of the loch was well defined to the east, but its western extremity merged into marsh land and this part tended to be very shallow. Considerable additional ground was submerged during exceptionally wet weather. The average depth of the water was four feet. At the cessation of coal-mining the bed of the loch had dropped in places to ten times this depth.

The loch was fed from three sources. The chief of these was Piery's Burn or, to give it its modern name, Kelty Burn, which rises in the Cleish Hills, some 3 miles west of Kelty, and flowed into the loch at its west end. The second source was the Ladath Burn which rises in the lower slopes of Benarty Hill, and discharged into the loch on its north side below the Bowhouse bank. The third source was a stream which issued from a lochan in the vicinity of Tushielaw, and thereafter skirted the east and south side of the rising ground now occupied by Montrose Crescent, Lochore and, after a circuitous course, which at a later period was marked by a mineral railway, it entered the loch at a point which is identified by the ruins of a row of houses once known as Peveril Place. The loch afforded many kinds of fish, and during the seventeenth century the fishing rights were let out by the lairds. In addition to trout, perch and pike, there was salmon to be had in the river Ore.

The highway running north passed within a very short distance of the east end of the loch, where its outlet was, and from whence it was known as the river Ore. The outlet was, in ancient times, situated some fifty yards further north than at present. The modern road has been heightened considerably at this point, and makes it difficult to realise that for centuries all traffic crossed the river by means of a shallow ford. It is during the last quarter of the seventeenth century that mention is made of a timber bridge spanning the river.

INCHGALL ISLAND

The island on which Inchgall Castle stood was roughly pear-shaped measuring approximately one hundred yards in length and between fifty and sixty yards at its greatest width. It rose to a height of ten feet above water level, and according to the old writers, it extended eight paces beyond the barmkin wall of the Castle on three sides. On the south-west side of the Castle, the island extended to a greater distance.

The long axis of the island lay parallel to the south-east edge of the loch and sixty yards from it. It was reached by means of a stone causeway eight feet broad, the remains of which can still be seen. There was also a landing place for boats on the north side of the loch at a point opposite the island.

The story of the island in Loch Ore probably takes us back to a period before surnames came into use and when the earliest form of personal names appeared.

The parish historian has to gather his material from many sources; from large tomes containing public records to vellum parchments bearing the signatures of those who knew the place many centuries ago; from handwritten genealogies to estate maps: the list is almost endless.

These are the quarry from which the antiquary has to dig out the facts, many of which are very obscure but always interesting. Sometimes an isolated name, such as the one we are about to discuss, immediately arrests his attention often because of its possible association with things already known.

Just as tradition connects Condal, King of the Picts with the Castle-island in Lochleven and Brude with St. Serf's Isle, so it is possible that Gedheor, of whom we have already spoken, may have had a connection with Loch Ore.

It is in these early personal names, like Brude of Lochleven and Gedhe of the Or, that the mind conjures up visions of the long ago. When we view the ruins of Inchgall Castle, it is difficult not to reflect on what sort of primitive structure stood on the island before the coming of the Norman-French settlers and of the possibility that a local land-name takes us back to this almost forgotten period.

Historical allusions associated with certain local names such as Balor, Strathor, Bellochor and Gedheor or Gedor all having "or" as their second element suggest that the place-name was coined at a fairly early date. There is also the local land-name Inchgeber. The form here given may have arisen from a copyist's error or from the name having gone through several mutations, as it seems likely to have appeared originally as Inchgedor.

The name Inchgall in the light of certain circumstances, cannot at most, date much earlier than the last quarter of the thirteenth century, and it is reasonable to suppose that the island bore a name before this period, as it is almost certain to have had a dwelling of some sort built upon it from the earliest of times. It is possible therefore that the island was known by the name Inchgeber or by its more likely form Inchgedor with its allusion to the early Pictish Chief.

It is also noteworthy that the two syllables Loch-Or constitute the second and the final element in a compound name which was in use during the reign of Donald Bane and relates to the royal palace. James Wilkie refers to the island of Inchgall in his *History of Fife* and suggests with certain reservations, that the "Bellochor" mentioned in an ancient chronicle of the kings of Scotland may have been situated on the island in Loch Ore. Bellochor is said to have been a royal seat of the Scottish kings and the place where Donald, the brother of Kenneth MacAlpine, died. Donald is a name not unknown in Lochoreshire, but beyond the name nothing is known, for history is silent as to the identity of the "Donald" who built his "Dun" or stone-built enclosure on the high ground overlooking the river Ore near Cardenden.

It is probably safe to assume that "Bell" in this instance takes the place of the Gaelic prefix "Baile" meaning among other derivations "residence" and that the name may mean "the residence in or beside Loch Or". Without going into the question as to where Donald Bane died, the name Bellochor points to the possibility of a site of this name having been near Loch Ore or at a place situated in Fife as yet unidentified.

One nineteenth century authority while acknowledging that the site lay somewhere in Fife, transcribed the name as Bal-Lochor and sought to identify it with Leuchars the earlier form being "Locres", probably on the site of the old castle there, however, on the evidence of the place-name alone, it would be difficult to deny the strength of the claim in favour of the Loch Ore site. Meanwhile, the island keeps its secret and will do so until further research enables the whole story to be told.

INCHGALL CASTLE

James de Vallance, whose family built the Castle is referred to as "of Inchgall", not Lochore, and when the Tower is mentioned in the Wardlaw charters, it is always in the context of the barony of Inchgall, and it continued to be so in the Malcolm charters. The mansion-house built by John Malcolm was known as Inchgall House before it became Lochore House. It is not clear when the Castle and mansion-house became known by their present names, but it undoubtedly took place during the time of the Malcolms. Although the Castle is very ruinous, it is still possible to trace the outline of the buildings and arrive at some idea of the plan. The principal Tower-House or Keep is built of sandstone random rubble. There are many traditions relating to the building of old castles and Inchgall is no exception. The story handed down is to the effect that, as the Castle was being built, in order to keep the stone masons with a ready supply of materials, the "wee men" formed a line from the quarry to the Castle, each man standing an arm's length from his neighbour. Each stone as it left the quarry was handed from one man to another until it arrived at the Castle.

The nearest spot where sandstone was to be had was at a quarry on the north side of the River Fitty south of the Clune Hill, near what was known as the Cadgers' ford.

The Tower measures thirty-four and a half feet from north to south and thirty-five and a quarter feet from east to west and has two external offset courses in its height. The walls at their greatest thickness measure over nine feet. The Tower had four floors and rose to a height of forty feet. The ground floor is now inaccessible but it appears to have a vaulted roof.* An entrance to this apartment is situated at the north corner of the west wall but it does not appear to be original. The entrance to the first floor was originally situated in the east wall and was reached no doubt by means of a timber fore-stair. It led through a mural chamber fourteen feet by eight feet into a hall which measured seventeen and a half feet by fifteen and a quarter feet. There was a mural chamber in the south wall measuring twelve feet by six feet with a window beyond and a corresponding chamber six feet by four feet in the north wall with no window. A fireplace occupied the greater part of the west wall, that is the wall furthest away from the entrance to the apartment.

The earliest account of the internal arrangement states that a narrow timber stair occupied the north-east corner of the hall and gave access to the second floor. There can still be seen in the north wall a putlog hole which had received the end of the bridle joist which formed the opening through which the timber stair gave access to the apartment above. This floor consisted of a single apartment measuring seventeen feet by fourteen feet with a mural chamber which measured eleven feet by ten feet, with a window. There was also a small recess in the north wall which may have had a window. The east wall contained a mural chamber approximately twelve feet by seven feet which partially projected beyond the external wall of the Tower. As this chamber contained a vent, and as it adjoined what was obviously the principal sleeping apartment, it may have been in

---

* Here, as in most tower-houses, the ground floor would be reached by means of a trap door set in the floor of the hall above, probably in the wide embrasure of the south window where the vault has been breeched.

74

part at least, a garderobe. There were two windows in the west wall of the second floor, one gave light directly into the apartment, the other lit a stair built in the thickness of the wall in the south-west corner of the Tower and also gave light to the second floor through a pointed arch. This narrow winding stair led to the third floor apartment which was situated partly in the roof and terminated in a cap-house which gave access to an embattled wall-walk at the top of the Tower.

An interesting feature of the second floor was a "spy-hole" which was placed in the west wall of the sleeping apartment and opened into the chimney of the fireplace in the hall below. These are known to have existed elsewhere and were called "luggies"*. Walls had ears at Inchgall! No doubt the laird would, as the occasion demanded, find it not amiss to listen to what was being discussed by his retainers as they sat by the fire in the hall.

The Tower was surrounded by a stout stone barmkin wall over ten feet in height and between three feet and four feet thick. The wall was roughly oval on plan measuring about one hundred and four feet from north to south and one hundred and twenty-four feet from east to west and enclosed a barmkin or courtyard. The Castle was approached from the south-east by means of a causeway, and contrary to what has often been said, its remains have not entirely disappeared. A small but well-defined portion which had obviously escaped the dyke-builders of the eighteenth century, is to be seen one hundred yards or so south-east of the Castle on what at one time was the approach to the edge of the loch. The remains show that the causeway had been substantially built of large whinstones carefully laid to a width of about eight feet.

23 *Inchgall Castle as it appeared in Cardonnel's*
"Picturesque Antiquities of Scotland" in 1793

* A somewhat similar device at Castle Fraser was known as "the Laird's Lug".

These then were the main structural elements of the Castle as built by the Vallance family. The whole period of the Vallance occupation was a troublous one. The Wars of Independence had broken out and were to continue almost until the Castle went to the Wardlaws through marriage. In 1306 Sir Adam de Vallance renounced his allegiance to Edward I and gave Bruce his support, and was subsequently joined by his son, Andrew. Sir Adam and his son therefore were "marked men" and it is possible, that, in accordance with Bruce's scorched-earth policy, the Castle was deliberately rendered uninhabitable in case it should fall into English hands. On the other hand Sir Michael Wemyss, to whom Sir Adam was related, had become in that year "a traitor and an enemy" in the eyes of Edward I and was singled out for special punishment. The English King commanded Aymer de Vallance, his lieutenant in Scotland, to "burn down Sir Michael's manor where he stayed and all his other manors, to destroy his lands and goods and to strip his gardens clean so that nothing is left for an example to others like him". As the Wemyss family possessed the lands contiguous to the lands of Inchgall, whose owner was also a "traitor" and his lands forfeited, one wonders if Inchgall Castle escaped the general destruction which must have followed the issuing of these orders.

Although the precise reason for doing so is not clear and can only be guessed at, it is known that Sir Andrew de Vallance and his lady found it necessary to live for a period at Inchgall Mill. Whether arising out of decay and neglect or the ravages of war or simply a desire for a greater measure of domestic comfort, it is clear that the Castle received an extensive overhaul including several improvements and embellishments and it is equally clear that the work was carried out during the period of the Wardlaws. The name "Robertus Wardlaw" appeared above a new and improved entrance to the Tower and was still to be seen as late as 1875. There were several members of the Wardlaw family bearing the name Robert, but the one most likely to have been the improver of the Castle was the son of Sir Henry Wardlaw the seventh laird. In 1511 King James IV granted Sir Henry power to make his "toun of Corsehill into a burgh of barony", and on the strength of this he is generally believed to have been the laird who rebuilt the Castle. However, as Sir Henry died in September two years afterwards (the month and year of Flodden): it is possible that he bit the dust on Flodden Field and that his son Robert completed the work on the Castle.

The main structural alteration to the Castle was the round-about-turn in its general layout. The old entrance in the east wall of the Tower was partly built up and a window inserted, while a new entrance was made in the west wall. The making of this entrance no doubt presented some difficulties as the fireplace in the hall occupied the greater portion of the west wall, the remaining space being taken up by the lower part of the mural staircase. It is believed that this staircase originally led from the hall to the second floor and thus to the top of the Tower and in this respect the Castle was similar to Lochleven Castle, as having only one staircase leading to all the floors. In order to obtain sufficient space, the new entrance was cut through the lower part of the mural staircase. This, plus a slight curtailment in the width of the fireplace by the erection of a relatively light partition-wall, enabled the improvers to construct the new entrance. To replace the part of the mural staircase thus removed, a narrow timber stair already described as occupying the north-east corner of the hall was constructed to give access to the second floor. A seven feet vertical joint in the stonework of the interior face of the south wall probably indicates where alterations had been carried out, as the new stonework had not been bonded to the old. While many external alterations and improvements would be carried out on the Tower of which no evidence now remains, we can be sure that the "pepper-box" turrets on the roof would be added during this period.

24   *Inchgall Castle as it appeared in Grose's*
"The Antiquities of Scotland" in 1797

    What appears to have been domestic premises were attached to the west wall of the Tower. These were contained in one building which extended from the Tower to the barmkin wall, being some forty-five feet in length and twenty feet in width. The building consisted of two storeys and was so placed that its roof was directly above the new entrance, and as such it provided additional shelter from the prevailing west wind. This building had a fireplace situated in its west gable wall. The main advantage derived from this arrangement, was that the fireplace in the hall of the Tower would no longer be used for cooking purposes, as the preparation of food and cooking would be done in the new premises, the hall would therefore be used as a sitting room and dining room. The upper floor of the kitchen premises would no doubt be used as sleeping apartments for the domestics. A further building was built on the ground north of the Tower and extended to the barmkin wall. This building, which was also of two storeys and which may have had three separate compartments, measured about twenty-five feet in length and nineteen feet in width. From the arrangement of the drain leading from this building it is probable that it was in part at least, a wash-house and laundry. The gable wall to the north contained a fireplace.

77

From the Tower and outbuildings the improvers probably turned their attention to the barmkin wall. This they reinforced by building round towers at strategic points. One tower stood at the south-east corner of the wall and thus commanded the causeway. Another was placed at the north-east corner and incorporated in it a postern gate. A third faced north-west and was so placed as to guard the main entrance through the wall. Each tower was about twelve feet in diameter and probably had two levels from which observations could be made. The towers were pierced with gunports and were crowned with conical roofs. The gunports were of the "inverted key-hole" type which came into use about the year 1400. These were merely the old arrow-slits adapted to take the barrel of a gun by inserting a circular aperture at their base. The vertical slit above would be of use in sighting the gun. Those at Inchgall were two feet two inches in height, the circular aperture was seven inches in diameter and the slot above two inches wide. The postern or side-gate to the Castle which was incorporated in the north-east tower, was a small aperture in the wall and not more than two feet across. A flight of stone steps gave access to the courtyard, but in order to do so it was necessary to enter the tower and at this point the entrance became very narrow indeed. By this means only one person at a time could enter the courtyard and it was thus more easily defended.

Directly opposite the new entrance to the Tower, a new strongly defended portal was constructed in the barmkin wall with moulded jambs and a semi-circular arch. Above this a machicolated jutty was built so that the defenders above could discharge muskets through the space between the stone corbals. No doubt the portal would incorporate a stout wooden door or a drawbridge as some suggest, and behind this an iron "yett". In the courtyard on the south side of the portal, situated behind it and adjoining the range of domestic premises, was a small building probably a guard house. Outside the Castle between the barmkin wall and the water's edge, was a seven feet wide paved mooring for boats and a flight of stone steps led from the water to the foot of the barmkin wall.

One cannot conclude a description of the Castle without mentioning a feature which has interested and sometimes puzzled antiquaries. It is what has been described as a "speaking-tube". It consisted of a horizontal aperture in the thickness of the barmkin wall which appears to have extended in length from the main entrance in the wall to the round tower which stood a little to the north of it. The aperture which can still be seen, is four inches square in section and extends to approximately four yards. There is no reason to doubt that it was a means whereby orders could be given to the guard at the entrance to the courtyard by those stationed in the barmkin tower and vice versa. So-called speaking tubes are known elsewhere. At Winchester Castle the King was able to communicate by this means from his royal apartment to those in the great hall below. A "speaking tube" at Bindon Tower House was analogous with the one at Inchgall Castle in that it communicated with those stationed at the entrance to the Tower.

The names of many people appear from time to time in connection with matters dealing with the barony; in many instances it is almost certain they visited the Castle and no doubt received the laird's hospitality. Many charters were signed at Inchgall and the names of the witnesses show that they came from varied stations in life and were not always people near at hand. The earliest charter known to have been signed in the

25 *Inchgall Castle as it appeared in MacGibbon and Ross's "Castellated and Domestic Architecture of Scotland" in 1889*

Castle is dated 8th November, 1384 and concerns certain lands in the barony of Rosyth. In the words of the charter, it was witnessed "at Inchgall the aucht day of the monath of Novembir the yher of our Lord a thwsand thre hundir fourscor and four" and is witnessed by "a worthyman and a noble schir Jamis the Valons Knycht lord of Inchgal, Jhon Multrar lord of Markynch beforsayd, Wat the Valons, William of Allirdes, schir Thomas of Kingorn vicar of Innirkethyng befor nemmyt and Henry Malvyn with othir sindry to this thing callit and specialy reyuirit".

"Wat the Valons" was probably a son of Sir James, while William of Allirdes is known to have had an interest in part of the nearby barony of Crambeth. It is not known where Henry Malvyn hailed from nor the "othir sindry" who had been specially called to witness the charter. Perhaps the most distinguished person to append his name to a charter at Inchgall took place in 1407, when Robert, Duke of Albany, third son of Robert II, Regent of Scotland visited the Castle. In another instance two ministers, the Rev. William Scott from Cupar and the Rev. John Chalmers from Auchterderran, append their names. On another occasion John Tod of Capeldrae and James Smyth a burgess in Cupar oblige. Edward Edgar an Edinburgh merchant, John Halliday, Advocate, Henry Law of Kirkness, Adam Lindsay son of the laird of Dowhill and many others all testify to various charters and sign their names in the hall of the Castle. Then for reasons not now known charters were not witnessed at Inchgall, they were stated to have been dated and witnessed at Ballingry or Kirkness. Of the many visitors to the

Castle mention must be made of Archbishop Beaton who visited his sister and brother-in-law at Inchgall. As far as records go, the Castle appears only once in the history of the country. The period is the mid-sixteenth century and the connection is very slight. Before going into this however, we would correct a statement which has often been made to the effect that, following the battle of Methven in 1306, Sir Christopher Seton was taken prisoner in Lochore Castle for his part in the murder of the Red Comyn. The Castle in question was of course Loch Doon in Ayrshire (written in the old records Lochdor). What is more convincing proof that the incident did not take place at Lochore is, what has been said earlier, that Lochore Castle (so-called) was known from beginning to end as Inchgall Castle.

26 *Inchgall Castle (Restored)*

Referring to our previous remark, the incident in history in which Inchgall Castle is mentioned (written Inchgaw) relates to the Earl of Hertford's invasion of Scotland in 1545. The English fleet had appeared in the Firth of Forth in the summer of the previous year, when Leith and Edinburgh were plundered and burned. When Hertford's soldiers crossed the border in the following year and commenced the devastation of towns and villages, Archbishop Beaton wrote to John Wardlaw, his brother-in-law, urging him to put the Castle in a state of readiness against attack. It was thus that the good men of Crosshill manned the Castle walls. How many times this took place before or after 1545 no one can tell for history is silent. We know however, that on this occasion the laird was re-imbursed to the amount of £8 to meet the expense of providing meal for feeding the garrison.

Although Hertford's troops did not enter Fife in 1545, it appears that not everyone was happy, for in 1547 when they returned by sea and seized the ferry boat at North Queensferry and set fire to the town, a James Henrisone, no doubt a Fife man, wrote to the Earl stating that he knew someone who "for a small reward would help his Grace to get hold of the four strongest castles in Fife". We do not know the secret of the intended stratagem, but the Castle of Inchgall headed the list.

We have been unable to discover when the Castle became uninhabitable. The last of the Wardlaw lairds, a mere boy of 11 years, because of increasing financial difficulties was compelled to sell the barony, and through this means it went to John Leslie, Earl of Rothes, in 1632. The Castle is mentioned in the Rothes charter as the chief messuage and it is presumed therefore that it was still habitable. With the building of Inchgall House (Lochore House) by the Malcolms sometime between 1656 and 1662, probably in 1658, the Castle was by this time no longer in use and was unroofed. This was some thirty years before its sister castle on Lochleven shared the same fate.

As the Castle became ruinous and trees began to grow in the courtyard and shrubs on the broken walls and battlements, it took on an air of antiquity and a certain picturesqueness which caught the eye of the artist. Three sketches have survived. The first was made by John Clerk of Eldin about the year 1770. Clerk married a daughter of Adam of Blairdam in 1753. He was a frequent visitor to Blairdam and made many sketches of local scenes. His sketch of the Castle was reproduced in Cardonnel's *Picturesque Antiquities of Scotland* in 1793. This was followed by a sketch by Lieutenant-General Henry Hutton which he made in 1781 and appeared in Grose's *The Antiquities of Scotland* in 1797. The sketches (slightly altered) as they appeared in Cardonnel's and Grose's works under their respective dates were misleading, as the loch had by then been drained. The third sketch was made by MacGibbon and Ross architects, and appeared in their *Castellated and Domestic Architecture of Scotland* in 1889. All these sketches were taken from a point looking south-east. Coming to more recent times an English firm produced decorative ceramic plates showing a line drawing of the Castle in about the year 1890. Twenty years afterwards the first of the picture postcards of the Castle appeared and a little later the Castle was the subject for two paintings by the Dunfermline artist, Adam Westwood.

Following the draining of the loch in 1792 the Castle became an easy quarry for building stones. The first person to rob the Castle appears to have been the laird himself. He required stone for building the retaining walls on either side of the main water course for draining the loch and to obtain this he demolished the round towers and most of the barmkin wall to the south, much to the annoyance of his neighbour William Adam, who states that he destroyed the Castle by taking away the semi-circular arch-stones from the entrance gate and the stones from the windows, and called him a barbarian for doing so. The barmkin wall received further destruction in the mid-nineteenth century by the removal of most of the earth which at one time formed the island. Hundreds of tons of soil were taken away and the operations came so close to the wall that in many places it collapsed.

The Castle, such as it is, was scheduled as an Ancient Monument in 1933 and in 1939 a modified restoration was carried out under the writer's supervision. The present

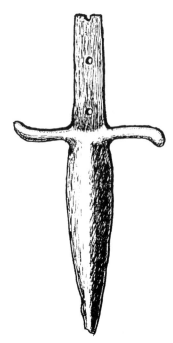

27 Blade of Dagger found at Inchgall Castle

custodian is the Fife Regional Council. The superiority remains with Lieutenant Colonel Gayre of Gayre and Nigg, the present Baron of Lochore.* The hereditary keeper of the Castle was until lately Major General C. T. Beckett of London. His son is the present keeper. The late Colonel William Briggs Constable of Benarty, was keeper depute. The Baron-Officer of the barony of Lochore is Mr Raymond S. Morris of Cupar.

The ruined Castle has the stillness of age upon it. Above the rustling of knee-deep nettles and thistles that shade its walls, it tells a tale of bygone days; of stirring days when men struggled to maintain national independence; of halcyon days when notables assembled within its walls to discuss matters affecting church and state; of days when misfortune befell the lairds and it was sold to others and returned again and again to the lairds as often as their financial affairs allowed; of its gradual decay, tenantless and shorn of its roof; and finally the mournful tale of the departure of the waters followed by mutilation and neglect. Huge rents have split its walls from top to bottom and the ancient hall is the playground of the four winds. Through indifference and wanton destruction the limits of the island can no longer be defined. The waters have returned to the loch but have forsaken and disowned the Castle. Unlike the mill of Lochore, the ruins of which disappeared some years ago, Inchgall Castle has somehow escaped total destruction. It can, however, only be a matter of time before this last link with an age that has long since passed will have gone for ever unless steps are taken soon to preserve and protect the little that now remains.

* Perhaps more correctly "Barn of Inchgall".

THE BOSWELL FAMILY

28

The following brief account of the Boswell family has been collected from various sources including notes compiled by the Rev. Charles Rogers, assistant minister at Ballingry in 1850. The family is of French origin and is said to have taken its name from Beuzeville near Bolbee in France. The first of the name on record was a Sieur de Bosville who came to England in the army of William of Normandy and is believed to have held a command at the battle of Hastings. His descendants came north during the reign of David I, and in the reign of William the Lion they were given the lands of Oxmuir in Berwickshire. Robert Bosville, the head of the family at this period is witness to many charters. His son, Adam de Bosville, has already been noted as appearing in an obligation of Philip de Lochore in 1235. This Adam was succeeded in the Boswell lands by his son Roger, whose son William de Bosville swore fealty to Edward I in 1296 and ultimately came into possession of Oxmuir. It was also in this same year that Walter de Bosville along with the Lochores was taken prisoner at Dunbar.

Another Roger de Bosville, second son of the foregoing William de Bosville, obtained from Robert the Bruce lands near Ardrossan in Ayrshire and was confirmed in the family's estate in Berwickshire. As has been noted elsewhere, he married the daughter of Sir William of Lochore and in right of his wife he became laird of half of Easter Lochoreshire. He was succeeded in these lands by his son John de Bosville who obtained from Edward III a safe conduct to go to England in 1365. He returned the following year and married Margaret, daughter of Sir Robert Melville of Carnbee. In 1367 he received by charter from David II the lands of Balgregie, Strathruddie, Muirtoun, Dundonald, Cartmore, Pitkinny, Capeldrae and Balbedie. He died in the reign of Robert II and was succeeded by his son Sir William Boswell who was designated "of Balgregie". He married Mariote, daughter of Sir John Glen of Balmuto who brought to him a third part of the barony of Balmuto. He and Sir Robert Livingstone were judges in a perambulation of the marches between the barony of Kirkness and the barony of Lochore which took place in 1395. He died in 1430 and was succeeded by his son David.

David Boswell acquired by excambion and purchase, the remaining two thirds of Balmuto between 1458 and 1477. Balmuto was thereafter annexed to the barony of Glassmont although the family continued to be designated "of Balmuto".

David married firstly Elizabeth, daughter of Sir John Melville of Raith. Their younger son Robert became a prominent churchman and no mean scholar. He was born about the year 1458 and was sent to St. Andrews University where he obtained his Bachelor of Arts Degree in 1475 and became Master of Arts in 1477. In November of the following year, he was chosen Dean of the Faculty of Arts while holding the office of Rector of Auchterderran. In May 1479 he was elected Rector of the University when he is styled "Vernerabilis Et Noblilis Vir Magister Robertus Boswel". He had as one of his assistants John Tyrie who had been Rector of Ballingry in 1478. John Tyrie was by this time one of the masters in the University. Robert Boswell was again elected Rector in 1490. He was also Precentor of Dunkeld Cathedral sometime before 1500 when in January of that year he resigned that office for the Deanery of Restalrig. In 1507 he is styled "Canon of Dunkeld". He gave up the Deanery of Restalrig in 1511. Nothing more is known of him beyond the fact that, with advancing years he became more and more esteemed for his piety and learning and when he died he had reached his hundredth year.

David Boswell married secondly Isabel, daughter of Sir Thomas Wemyss of Rires, widow of David Haigh of Naughton. He was succeeded by his eldest son David, who married firstly Grizel, daughter of Sir John Wemyss of Wemyss and secondly in 1480, Lady Margaret Sinclair daughter of William, Earl of Orkney and Caithness. David Boswell was succeeded by Alexander his second son by his first wife. Both he and his half brother Thomas, the eldest son of the marriage, and progenitor of the Boswells of Auchinleck, fell at the Battle of Flodden in 1513.

Sir John Boswell, the great grandson of Alexander Boswell who, succeeded to the estate in 1582 was a favourite of James VI. In a charter of 1587 it is revealed that the Castle of Balmuto was destroyed during his minority. Sir John's great-great-grandson, Andrew Boswell sold the estate in 1722 to John Boswell a cadet of the Auchinleck branch of the family. This John Boswell was the uncle of Alexander Boswell, Lord of Session and Justiciary, who took the title of Lord Auchinleck in 1756.

We come now to the two members of the family who are perhaps best known in history, at least, whose doings seem to have caught the popular imagination. They are James Boswell son of Lord Auchinleck, and his son Sir Alexander Boswell.

James Boswell in early life studied civil law at the Universities of Edinburgh and Glasgow and thereafter in London where he met Doctor Johnson. In order to complete his education he made a tour of Europe, and after passing through several countries he visited the Island of Corsica where he formed an intimate acquaintance with General Pasquale de Paoli in whose palace he resided for some time. Corsica was at this period struggling for independence and among Boswell's publications of the period there appeared his *Account of Corsica with Memoirs of General Paoli*. In 1773 James Boswell and Doctor Johnson made their long-projected tour of the Hebrides and there appeared after a period of twelve years Boswell's *Journal of a Tour of the Hebrides and the Western Isles*. In 1790 he published his *Life of Samuel Johnson*. After the death of

Johnson in 1784 Boswell practised at the Scottish Bar while continuing his literary work and two years afterwards having been called to the English Bar, he moved to London where he produced many publications and enjoyed the acquaintance of many eminent people. He died in 1795.

His father, old Lord Auchinleck, is said to have looked on doctor Johnson and other companions of his son with unmeasured contempt. "There's nae hope for Jamie, man" he said to a friend. "Jamie is gaen clean gyte". "What do ye think, man, he's dune wi' Paoli? He's off wi' the land-louping scoundrel of a Corsican; and whose tail do you think he has pinned himself to now, man? "A dominie, man — an auld dominie. He kept a schule, an' called it an academy".

The Rev. Charles Rogers of Ballingry, drawing on the reminiscences of his father, quotes him as saying "when I entered St. Andrews University, I found that the visit of doctor Samuel Johnson to that ancient seat of learning was still a theme of conversation though seven years had passed since the English sage walked under the porch of St. Salvator. During his visit Johnson indulged to the full in his combativeness of talk, and the professors, while unwilling to speak harshly of one so noted, remembered his visit with distaste!

Sir Alexander Boswell

Sir Alexander, the eldest son of James Boswell, was born in 1775 and succeeded his father in the Auchinleck estate. While at Oxford he was given to composing satirical pieces in verse which received some measure of commendation. In 1803 he published his *Songs, Chiefly in the Scottish Dialect,* several of which have survived such as *Auld Gudeman ye're a Drucken Carle, Jenny's Bawbee, Jenny Dang the Weaver* and *Good Night and Joy be wi' you a'.* In 1810 he published under the name of Simon Grey an excellent poem entitled *Edinburgh or the Ancient Royalty,* and in the following year there appeared his poetical work *Clan-Alpin's Vow.* He afterwards set up a printing press at Auchinleck from which he sent out many pieces both in verse and prose. In recognition of his works he was knighted in 1821. Sir Alexander was the possessor of the famous Auchinleck Library which contained many rare and valuable volumes collected by his ancestors, including at one time the Auchinleck manuscript which contained upwards of forty English romances and fragmentary poems. The MS; was presented to the Advocates Library by Lord Auchinleck in 1744 where it lay for many years unnoticed. It contained a Scottish version of the famous thirteenth century metrical romance, *Sir Tristram* which was attributed to the "Seer of Ercildoune", Thomas the Rhymer. Following its re-discovery, Sir Walter Scott published an edited edition of the poem in 1804.

Sir Alexander was high spirited and of a genial disposition. His death in 1822 profoundly shocked his friends and was no doubt the subject of conversation throughout the Lochgelly neighbourhood for many a day, for the circumstances which occasioned his death were unusual and also unfortunate as they arose out of his own doing. The story has been told before, but it is perhaps not so well known that it can be repeated here. The period around 1822 was one of high political tension when Tory and Whig each strove to mould the administration of the day according to his beliefs. Boswell was an ardent Tory, one of the contributors to an Edinburgh newspaper called *The Beacon*. His article gave great offence to the leading men of the Whig side and political animosity ran high. It was, however, several letters and pieces of satirical poetry that had appeared in a Glasgow newspaper styled *The Sentinel* which in particular offended James Stuart of Dunearn, the younger son of the laird of a small estate near Burntisland. Mr Stuart, who was a Writer to the Signet and a descendant of the Earl of Moray, had been personally attacked. It was not long before he took steps to find out the author of the offending pieces and through an unfortunate disagreement among the editors of the *The Sentinel* a manuscript which had come to light revealed Boswell as the author. Stuart, who held no animosity against Boswell other than the offence which his writings had incurred, would have considered his honour upheld had he received an apology from his political opponent, but as no apology was offered he could see no alternative but to challenge Boswell to a duel according to the fashion of the day. The choice of weapons was pistols; Boswell accepted the challenge and after completing the final arrangements for his duel he dined with Sir Walter Scott at his house in Castle Street, Edinburgh. Lockhart says, "That evening, was I think, the gayest I ever spent in Castle Street; and though Charles Mathews was present and in his best force, poor Boswell's songs, jokes and anecdotes, had exhibited no symptom of eclipse". Boswell had not divulged to his friends his acceptance of Stuart's challenge. The protagonists met at a spot near Auchtertool, not far from Balmuto House on 26th March, each to go through which by now was hoped to be a formality without injury on either side. Mr Stuart had as his second the Earl of Roslin and Sir Alexander, the Honourable John Douglas. Each had his Surgeon. Mr Stuart and Sir Alexander took up their positions at an intervening distance of twelve paces, each with his pistol loaded. At the word of command from the Earl of Roslin the combatants wheeled round and fired. Sir Alexander fired into the air. He had already told his friends he would do so. Mr Stuart fired without taking aim — Sir Alexander fell. Distressed at what had happened Mr Stuart made to run towards Boswell but was restrained by the Earl of Roslin who feared that the shot had been fatal. The surgeons confirmed that Sir Alexander was mortally wounded, the shot had shattered his collar bone. He was taken to Balmuto House and carried into the library where he died the following day. During his periods of consciousness he repeated the words of the Psalms.

The foregoing is an account of the duel as it has hitherto appeared, but there is the almost unknown account by an eyewitness as told to a gamekeeper on the Balmuto estate. He strongly asserts that the quarrel arose out of a remark made by Sir Alexander Boswell concerning a breed of oxen belonging to James Stuart for which the laird of Dunearn had become famous. Stuart took exception to Sir Alexander dubbing him as "The Dunearn Ox", and was encouraged by Lord Rosslyn in seeking his revenge. He accordingly challenged the baronet to a duel.

The odds were all in Boswell's favour. He was known to be a good shot and could snuff a candle at twenty yards twenty times running, while Stuart had a miserable aim. He never raised his gun to his shoulder and could not hit a bucket at five yards distance.

The usual rules were to be observed. Both contestants stood back to back and at a given signal were to walk twelve paces and turn to fire, but Stuart, instead of walking as he was honour-bound to do, ran eight or nine paces and turned and fired his pistol, holding it with both hands. The shot struck Boswell in the back and the baronet fell. Stuart flung his weapon into Auchtertool Loch and made for a post-chaise which was waiting for him. He fled to Belgium and did not return home until a year had passed. This account, although differing from others, gives a possible explanation as to how Stuart succeeded in overcoming the superior skill of his opponent.

29 *Sir Alexander Boswell*

One would hardly expect to gather information at so late a date be it ever so trifling, nonetheless, many years ago a great grandchild of one of the retainers of James Stuart, who had accompanied his master to Auchtertool, repeated a tradition to the writer how a wooden shutter was hurriedly removed from a window in Balmuto House and on this improvised stretcher Sir Alexander was laid. The retainer from Dunearn was one of those who carried the wounded Boswell back to Balmuto House.

Mr Stuart was afterwards tried by the High Court for murder but was acquitted following which he emigrated to America.

The death of Sir Alexander and that of his brother James which had occurred only a fortnight or so before, was keenly felt by Sir Walter Scott. Writing to Miss Edgeworth a month later he says "I feel the loneliness of age when my companions and friends are taken from me. The sudden death of both the Boswells and the bloody end of the last, have given me great pain".

In his novel *St. Roman's Well,* which came out in the following year Scott introduced in the duel scene several circumstances very similar to those of Boswell's death.

It is many years since we visited the one time home of the Boswells. At the time of our visit the ancient place seemed to have been abandoned to the ravages of time. We can still recall the sense of utter neglect when looking through the partly shuttered window of the library we saw ferns and fungi growing between the rows of books which remained on the shelves.

THE WARDLAW FAMILY

30

Andrew Wardlaw, who married Christian de Vallance about the beginning of the fifteenth century, was the fourth laird of Wilton, a barony in the borderlands of Roxburghshire. Traditionally the family entered Scotland in the reign of Malcolm Canmore. The Wardlaws of that ilk are said to have settled in Galloway bordering Dumfries where there were lands of that name. If tradition can be relied on, the head of the family of the period married a daughter of McDowell, Lord of Galloway, whose mother was a sister of John Comyn, one of the competitors for the crown of Scotland. The family is said to have supported Balliol and to have lost their lands during the Wars of Independence. It appears, however, with the abdication of Balliol the family adhered to Bruce and it was during Bruce's reign that the Wardlaws were given half the barony of Wilton.

Robert Dene, Rector of Wilton, swore fealty to Edward I at Berwick in 1296. Shortly afterwards the barony was divided on the orders of the English king who gave it to two valets, William de Charteris and Wellis de Pertchay, each receiving one half. Following Bannockburn, when the independence of the country was secured, Bruce made awards of land to those who had supported him. Henry Wardlaw was given the west half of the barony for a reddendo of the fifth part of the service of one soldier and three suits yearly at the king's court at Roxburgh. The eastern half was awarded to Gilbert Maxwell. The Wardlaw family was without doubt, especially in its earlier history, one of the most distinguished families in the country. A younger son of Henry, the first laird of Wilton, was Walter Wardlaw who, in 1345 was Rector of the University of Paris and subsequently secretary to King David II and Bishop of Glasgow. After a life in dealing with the highest matters concerning church and state he was made the first Scottish Cardinal. Walter Wardlaw's nephew Henry Wardlaw, a younger son of the second laird of Wilton became Bishop of St. Andrews in 1403. He has been described from time to time as a son of Andrew Wardlaw and Christian de Vallance of Inchgall. Unfortunately, Ballingry parish cannot claim this connection with the Bishop. When Sir Andrew and Christian were married, the Vallance family had long been in possession of Torrie, and Sir Andrew was the laird of Wilton. As Henry Wardlaw was born about the year 1365 it is clear that he was not a son of this marriage. Henry

Wardlaw is of course best remembered as being the founder of the University of St. Andrews in 1411, although teaching had begun the year before. In 1420 the Bishop refers to David Hackett, son of Philip Hackett of Lumphinnans, as his cousin.

Andrew Wardlaw of Wilton, Torrie and Inchgall

Andrew Wardlaw was the elder son of Sir William Wardlaw the laird of Wilton and his wife Margaret. Through his marriage to Christian de Vallance, Andrew Wardlaw brought many possessions to his family. In addition to his barony of Wilton he became, in right of his wife, Laird of Torrie and Inchgall. Christian also possessed through inheritance from her Aunt, one half of one third of the lands of Rosyth, part of the barony of Crambeth, and the Vallance lands of Brunton and Dalginch in the parish of Markinch.

We have already seen that the Rosyth lands came to the Vallance family through a gift by the Earl of Carrick to Sir Andrew de Vallance about the middle of the fourteenth century and that they descended to his son Sir James at whose death before 1381 King Robert II gifted them in ward to Sir Thomas Erskine the father of Christine Erskine and future father-in-law of Sir James de Vallance II. The lands at this period appear to have been held by Christian de Vallance, Aunt of the future wife of Andrew Wardlaw. Sometime before 1413 the lands were divided and as we have seen, Christian and her sister Euphane each received a half of one third. Arising out of circumstances not disclosed, we find that early in the year 1436 Christian was in possession of the third part of the barony of Rosyth, by which time she may have inherited or acquired her sister's portion.

Andrew Wardlaw and Christian de Vallance had at least two sons, Henry and George. There may have been a third son and possibly two daughters of the marriage but the evidence is uncertain. Christian was widowed about the year 1430 and by 1433 she had remarried. The following Deed shows who her second husband was. "Be it kent tyl al men be thir present letteris me Jone of Kokburne of Torrie wyth the consent and afsent of Cristyane my wyfe til hafe ratyfyit and affermyt for us and ony of our ayris for evirmar the departysone made be the kingis brefe throw Fynlaw Jonesone schyrrave deput of Fyfe at the Top crag the Lang crag and the Hors Inche lyand in the barony of Rofsyth in the qwhylk departying the Hors Inche is fallyn to Schyr David Stewart the Top crag tyl me and the sayd Cristyane my wyfe and the Lange crag tyl Wylyam of Spyttale the quhylk departysone was done wyth our consent and we are fully content thar of in wytnes of the qwhylk thyngis I hafe put to my seyle and I the sayd Cristyane in wytness of my consent has put to my seyl to thir present letteris at Torrie the fyrst day of the moneth of December the yher of our Lord a thowsand four hundreth thretty and three yher". The William Spittal referred to was a burgess of Inverkeithing, and David Stewart was the eldest son of Robert Stewart of Durisdeer, a descendant of Alexander IV High Stewart of Scotland.

Sir John Cockburn was one of the Scottish Commissioners appointed in 1429 to keep order in the borderlands with England. He was also an arbiter in a dispute between

David Halkett of Lumphinnans and the monastery of Dunfermline in 1437 and his name appears as a witness to two royal charters. He was Sheriff of Kinross in 1450 and is last heard of in 1457. Christian de Vallance had by Sir John Cockburn a son Henry Cockburn who was created Bishop of Ross by Pope Pius II in 1461. In that year the Bishop's parents are referred to as the lay patrons of the rectory of the church of Balhyngram (Ballingry).

Sir Henry Wardlaw of Wilton, Torrie and Inchgall

Henry Wardlaw the elder son of the first marriage succeeded his father in the estate of Wilton and later on came into possession of his mother's estates. In an Indenture dated 1435 we read the following "Christian of Vallance lady of Torrie with the consent of John of Cokburne her spouse on the one part and Henry of Wardlaw of Wilton son and heir apparent to said Christian on the other part whereby said Christian grants to said Henry of Wardlaw all lands pertaining heritable to her with presentation to kirks and all other dues reserving to herself her life rent therefrom in return for which said Henry grants to said John Cokburne and said Christian his spouse in conjunct fee the town of Dalgynche and the Bruntoun in the earldom of Fife on payment of thirty-two merks Scots rent yearly".*

In this same year (1435) Henry Wardlaw was one of the inquest that served James Kynninmont heir to the deceased Sir Elizens Kynninmont, knight, his father, in his lands and also witnessed his doing homage to the Prior of St. Andrews for the same. This took place in the hall of the Priory on the 19th January, 1434. In the following year Henry Wardlaw is given the lands of Pitreavie and part of Fordell in exchange for the third part of the lands of Rosyth in the following Deed, "David Stewart knight Lord of the barony of Rofsyth grants to Henry of Wardlaw Lord of Wilton, the lands of Pitrawy and third part of Fordale in the barony of Rofsyth and sheriffdom of Fyffe, in excambion for the third part of the lands which belonged to Christian the mother of said Henry and which she with consent of John of Cokburn her husband resigned. To be held by the said Henry and the heris of his body whom failing George Wardlaw his brother and the heirs of his body whom failing, said John Cokburn's heirs male begotten betwixt him and said Christian whom failing, to revert to said Christian's heirs whomsoever, of the barony of Rofsyth. Rendering three suits at the three head Courts of said barony. Reserving said Christian's liferent. If the lands shall be judicially evicted from the said Henry or his heirs the said part of Rofsyth shall revert to them". The Deed was signed at Dunfermline.

In this year Sir Henry is mentioned as one of those who accompanied Margaret, daughter of King James I, to France when she whent to marry the Dauphin. It is presumed that Henry Wardlaw was knighted about this time. In 1438 "Sir Henry of Wardlaw Lord of Torrie knight" was one of the "noblemen" present at the settlement of a dispute between the Prior and the monastery of St. Andrews, and Sir James of Kynninmont of that ilk. Sir Henry's seal which bears his family's Coat of Arms, quartered with those of Valoniis, appears appended to various charters of this period.

---

* We have handled this document. It is written in Latin on a piece of velum not larger than an ordinary postcard.

In 1439 we hear of the Templelands of Lochore for the first time in a discharge by "John of Cockburn and Cristayne his spouse daughter and heiress of umquhile Sir James the Valandis to David Halkate laird of Petfuran for £10 for the ward of the Templeland of Lochor". It was also in this year that Sir Henry, as Sheriff Depute of Fife, conducted a retour of the burgh lands of Cupar, and in 1444 he is one of the witnesses to Bishop Kennedy's agreement entered into between the people of St. Andrews and the University.

From now on we find him often in the company of the Bishop of St. Andrews. In July of the same year he accompanied the Bishop to the Kennedy lands of Cassillis in Ayrshire and in 1449 he is one of a company of noblemen, including the Bishop who had a safe conduct for three years, to go on a pilgrimage to the Apostolic thresholds with a retinue of sixty attendants. On his return in 1452 he is witness to a charter of James II in Edinburgh. We hear of him again in 1454 when he grants certain lands in the barony of Wilton to one David Scott and later on in the same year he held a court at St. Andrews when he is designated "Justis and Stewart" to the Bishop of St. Andrews. He died before 1458.

Sir Henry Wardlaw married Christian Lauder, daughter of John Lauder, and granddaughter of Sir Robert Lauder of the Bass. There were four sons of the marriage. Henry, the eldest son and heir, followed his father in his estates. John, the youngest, was a Canon of Holyrood and Chaplain to King James II.

Henry Wardlaw II of Wilton, Torrie and Inchgall

Henry Wardlaw's name appears in a Deed of May 1451 when he is designated son and heir of the Lord of Torrie. Following the death of his father, there was a retour in favour of "Henry Wardlaw as heir to his father deceased Henry Wardlaw knight in the lands of Ynchgall lying in the west part of Louchquherschyr, lands of Dalgynch and a fourth part of the lands of Blaircrambeth lying in the barony of Crambeth". He does not appear however to have had sasine until 1465 when we read "Henrici Wardlaw had sasine of the lands of Inchga, Blaircrombeth and the tenth part of Bin, Drumlochirnock and Dalginch". In May 1468 the laird of Lochore acknowledged having received from Walter Ker the sum of 2040 merks scots in payment for his lands in Hownam in Roxburghshire. In July of the same year William Halkett, laird of Dumfulan refers to Henry Wardlaw as his superior, and in November Henry is witness to a charter of his brother-in-law Laurence first Lord Oliphant. In 1471 Henry received sasine of the tenth part of the lands of Leven.

It is about this period that we again hear of Lord Oliphant. He was appointed oversman by the arbiters representing William Livingstone of Drumry in Dunbartonshire on the one part and David Boswell of Balmuto and his kinsman David Boswell of Glassmount on the other, concerning debates and controversies relating to the lands of "Polraine, Colqueles and Pilkenny and the tenancies of Raith, Glenneseone and Polqudde and the two tenancies of Lochgilly and Balmungy and the patronage of the church of Ochterderay". All these had been the subject of dispute between the parties

91

parties for some time past. Although in 1475 the king had granted a charter of confirmation on certain evidence given by Lord Oliphant in a decree-arbitral, it was not until the following century that the dispute was finally settled and the Boswells of Balmuto received the patronage of the church of Auchterderran.

Henry Wardlaw died before July 1475. By his wife, Margaret Oliphant, he had four sons, Henry the eldest, John, Alexander and William who was "chappelin of St. Andrew's chapel of Loch Gaw" (Inchgaw). He had at least two daughters.

Sir Henry Wardlaw III of Wilton, Torrie and Inchgall

In 1473, the year of Henry Wardlaw's marriage, he and his wife Margaret Lindsay had sasine of the lands of Dalginch and in 1477 he had sasine of the lands of Blair, Byn, Lochynmurtoun, Lochgelly and Clunane. Following the death of his father in that year, he formally resigned into the king's hands the lands of Inchgall. Before the year was out, he had a royal charter of the lands of Blarequhisse, Ladach, Hiltoun, Ballingre, Navody and the Mylntoun of Inchgall. For some unknown reason the mill of Inchgall was expressly excluded.

In 1479, two years after his father's death he had sasine of the barony of Wilton. Five years afterwards he held the family's lands of Burnetoun in the parish of Markinch, and in 1490 he granted in fee and heritage, his lands in Forfarshire to Sir Alexander Home, Great Chamberlain of Scotland.

In 1494 a quarrel arose between the laird and William Halkett of Pitfirrane respecting the Temple houses belonging to the latter which had been destroyed by the laird of Torrie's men. In the year which followed Henry Wardlaw was given sasine of the Templelands of Lochore. He was not a well man and in 1498 he was granted a licence extending to forty days for his "passing owre the sey for the hele of his person". The "licence of protection and respit" was renewed in 1503, allowing him to travel abroad as often as his health required.

It was about this time that he parted with his lands in Forfarshire and also the old Wardlaw lands of Wilton in Roxburghshire. He was now incapable of attending to his affairs and in order to protect his son and heir's interests, he was interdicted from alienating any of his lands. The laird's brother John was appointed his factor, who in the laird's absence dealt with his affairs in a high-handed manner. Henry Wardlaw was knighted in 1503.

In 1506, the year in which his wife was murdered, Sir Henry was "furth of Scotland". Suspicion fell on Sir Henry's brother John but the matter was never satisfactorily cleared up. Sir Henry married secondly Margaret Gourlay by whom he had no family.

In 1511, arising out of irregularities in law whereby many lands in Markinch belonging to the Wardlaw family had been alienated without the king's consent, Sir Henry was obliged to make a formal return of these to the king who granted the lands to him anew along with his legal rights to the same. The king in recognition of the good services of Sir Henry, united these with the lands of Wester Lochoreshire into one barony.

In this same year, Sir Henry was also granted the patronage of the chapel of Inchgall and was given authority to erect the village of Crosshill into a free burgh of barony with a cross and market place daily, along with a special weekly market and a fair twice in the year with power to buy and sell and to appoint baillies provided that they shall not use any authority other than such as is given to them by Sir Henry and his heirs. He was also given licence to feu his lands to tenants. It is generally believed that it was a little before this period that the laird commenced carrying out extensive alterations on Inchgall Castle, work which he was destined not to complete but which was obviously completed by his son Robert. It is a little surprising to find that, although the territorial designation of the Wardlaw's is usually given as "of Torrie", the family's principle residence was at Inchgall Castle. The Houses at Torrie and Brunton were occupied only when varying circumstances made it more suitable to do so. It was about this time that Sir Henry granted to James Wardlaw of Edinburgh and his wife, Margaret Hunter, a charter of the lands of Cartmore and Ballingry, an action which brought to the family considerable trouble in later years.

In 1512 there is one of the all-too-few allusions to Ballingry Church. In this year the Lord High Treasurer recorded the payment of £10 in part payment of the rectory of Ballingry. As recorded earlier, Sir Henry died in the year and month of the battle of Flodden, but whether like his kinsman John Wardlaw of Kilbaberton he died on Flodden's fatal field or not is still to be discovered.

By his first marriage he had at least three sons John, his heir, William (who treated Nicholas Wardlaw shamefully by occupying in his absence his lands of Ballingry, ill-treating his cattle and destroying his goods on his farm), and Robert. The following may also have been his children: Andrew, James rector of Ballingry, Nicholas, who had a lease of the lands of Ballingry, Herbert, a burgess of Edinburgh, and Isabel.

John Wardlaw of Torrie and Inchgall

We first hear of John Wardlaw in 1507 when he, along with his uncle Lord Lindsay of the Byres, accused John Wardlaw, his father's brother, of the murder of his mother.

John Wardlaw married Elizabeth Beaton, daughter of David Beaton of Balfour, about the year 1512. In 1518 he and his wife received in conjunct fee the lands of Brunton and Dalginch along with the mill and the pertinents all lying within the barony of Lochoreshire.

In 1516 James Wardlaw complained that after receiving notice from John Wardlaw baron of Inchgall to proceed to St. Giles kirk in Edinburgh to receive the sum of 1820 merks for the redemption of the lands of Cartmore and Ballingry, he had waited at St. James's altar in the said kirk and that John Wardlaw failed to appear or to produce his reversion. The above lands were probably wadset to James Wardlaw by John's father.

He appears again in 1527 when with John Beaton and many others he is indicted for an assault upon the Sheriff of Fife when bail is imposed. He was fortunate, however, in having his brother-in-law, David Beaton, Abbot of Arbroath (afterwards Cardinal), standing surety and relieving him of his obligation.

The malady which had affected Sir Henry became increasingly apparent in his son, and in 1530 he craved that the King would place him in a position that he may be unable to alienate any of his lands "for certain reasonabill cause moving me and specially for favour and affection I bear to my sone and heir apparand and for the weill of my house and heritage". The King acceded to his request the following day, signing with his own hand.

31

Copies of signatures taken from a manuscript genealogy of the Wardlaw family in the possession of the Author

By the following year John Wardlaw had recovered sufficiently to enable him to attend to his affairs, and in March of that year the King confirmed a charter by him granting to his son Henry and his wife Alison Hume in conjunct fee the lands of Ballingry, Navitie and Byn extending to £5 of old valuation. John Wardlaw's recovery was of short duration. In 1532 "not having power nor witt to gyde himself bot furious and furth of his mind", the King appointed four curators to look after his affairs. These included the Abbots of Arbroath and Dunfermline. Should the need arise they were empowered "to put hands on the said John Wardlaw of Torrie and take and put him in sicker place when they shall think expedient and which taking and halding of him to be no crime". Earlier in the year he gave his nephew John Wardlaw of Dubhouse sasine of the lands of Lumphinnans which lands were still held by this family in 1571.

94

The restrictions now placed on him were proving an embarrassment as he found himself unable to meet his debts or pay his servants. He therefore petitioned to be released from the interdict of 1530, as in order to obtain ready cash he proposed to wadset his Mains lands of Inchgall to William Rynd of Edinburgh in the hope that as his financial position improved he would be able to redeem them.

By all accounts Henry Wardlaw was a dutiful son and acted responsibly towards his father during his period of indisposition. In return we find John Wardlaw conferring on Henry and his wife in return for the goodness shown towards him, the lands of Inchgall consisting of the "Mains lands, the lands of Corshill, Balbeghe, Contill, Clune, Tempilland, Smedyland of Myltoun, Brewland of Miltoun and the Serjandcroft and other lands in the lordship of Inchgall also the right of advocation to the church of Ballingry and to the chapel of the chaplainary of St. Andrew (chapel of Inchgall), also the lands of Brunton and Dalginch, both parts of Easter Newtoun with the manor house, mills and orchard also the lands of Torrie with the mansion, mill and coal pit, to be held of John Wardlaw reserving to himself the free tenancy of the lands of Torrie, accepting two white roses in name of blench ferm".

The charter was confirmed by Queen Mary in 1546. Among the witnesses was John Knox the reformer. The effect of the foregoing was that most of the lands belonging to John Wardlaw were now settled on Henry his heir, fiar of Torrie. John Wardlaw was appointed to the office of "Mair of Fee" for the west quarter of the Sheriffdom of the kingdom of Fife when the office became vacant following the death of David Lindsay.

We find Henry Wardlaw in 1543 granting to David Ramsay in freehold for a sum of money paid to him, the lands of Ballingry and Navitie along with the tofts and crofts and the Common situated on Benarty Hill. In 1549 this was extended to include David Ramsay's son James who, following his father, was to hold these lands in fee.

In this year and on several occasions during the previous twelve years the laird of Inchgall accompanied David Beaton, Abbot of Arbroath, on his several journeys into England and "the partis bezound the sey" (France). David Beaton took with him on these occasions a large number of "freindis and servandis", seldom under two dozen persons, oftener fifty and on each occasion a good proportion of these were either Beatons or Wardlaws. On more than one occasion his sister Elizabeth Beaton accompanied her husband John Wardlaw. The first of these journeys to France was in 1537 when the cardinal went there to arrange the marriage between Mary of Guise and King James V. We last hear of Elizabeth Beaton in 1558 when she journeyed with her nephew the Archbishop of Glasgow who as ambassador had gone there on "effariss concerning the commoun wele of the realme".

John Wardlaw was very much under the domination of his brother William who took advantage of the fact that he could not read or write. When he signed his name it is always "wit my hand to ye pen". He complained to the Lords of Council that his brother had made many writings in his name and had used his seal without his knowledge. On other occasions his brother had brought certain charters to him and had caused him to append his seal but as he could not read he was ignorant of their contents. He therefore revoked all the said writings.

Probably because of his state of health, a document was drawn up in 1546 between

John Wardlaw, Elizabeth Beaton and their son Henry. It affirmed that most of the lands had been settled on their son, although some provision was made for safeguarding the interest of William Wardlaw, John Wardlaw's brother. One of the arbiters in the transaction was Robert Douglas of Lochleven.

John Wardlaw died in 1557. He and Elizabeth Beaton are said to have had twelve sons and four daughters. The following are known to have been their offspring: Henry, their heir, Andrew, Alexander, rector of Ballingry of whom we will speak later, Nicholus, John who in succession was vicar of Peebles, rector of Moffat and perpetual chaplain of St. Andrew's chapel in the barony of Brunton, and canon of the cathedral church in Glasgow, James, Mariota and Margaret.

Henry Wardlaw IV of Torrie and Inchgall

Henry Wardlaw was twice contracted to marry. Firstly, in 1529 to Grisell Leslie of the Rothes family and secondly to Margaret Murray of Blackbarony. For reasons unknown both matrimonial affairs fell through. Henry married Alison Hume, daughter of the third Lord Hume in March 1531.

We followed Henry up to the year 1546 when dealing with his father's affairs in the previous chapter. The only two occasions worthy of note during this period were when he and his wife were granted permission in 1543 to "pass to the realm of France". This coincides with the journeying there of Cardinal Beaton and in all probability Henry was with his uncle on that occasion. The other occasion was his "treacherous going against the Lord Governor for the purpose of killing him". This refers to Henry Wardlaw attaching himself to the faction headed by the Earls of Glencairn and Lennox who opposed the Earl of Arran during the period known as the "rough wooing". Henry Wardlaw was one of five hundred spearmen who, under the Earl of Glencairn, opposed the Earl of Arran on the moor of Glasgow in 1544. For this, and his remaining at home from the armies and ridings he was denounced rebel. He did not obtain a remission of his misdeeds until 1552.

Henry Wardlaw married secondly in 1546 Catherine Lundy, daughter of James Lundy of Balgony. Queen Mary confirmed a charter fulfilling the marriage contract. Probably in order to mark the occasion Henry gave his future father-in-law in life rent, sasine of his lands of Crosshill including the granary, house, castle and lake of Inchgall, also the Templelands, Brewlands and Smiddyland for a yearly rent of one penny. This act of generosity did not however reflect the true position of the family's estate. The difficulties experienced by John Wardlaw in financial affairs did not improve any with the management of the estate by his son. Henry continued to feu the various lands where possible and when he required ready cash he wadset portions of the estate which he redeemed from time to time as his financial position allowed. His father had passed to him a number of reversions dealing with portions of the barony including the lands of Spittal lying east of Lochgelly all of which he had not been able to redeem.

In 1549 Henry Wardlaw gave the east and west Mains lands of Inchgall in conjunct fee to Sir David Murray of Arangask and Janet Lindsay, his wife. The memorandum dealing with this transaction alludes to the ancient and picturesque ceremony of giving sasine. It describes how the Laird of Inchgall gave sasine of the east half of the Mains lands by placing in Sir David's hands earth and stone and in like manner, sasine was given of the west half by Sir David receiving thatch and turf. We may infer from this that the west half of the Mains lands contained houses.

James Lundy appears not to have held the lands of Crosshill for any length of time. In 1549 Henry Wardlaw, with the consent of his wife, gave these lands to the Prior Provincial and Convent of the brother preachers of the burgh of Edinburgh in free blench ferm for the annual sum of one penny.

In this same year Henry Wardlaw redeemed the lands of Navitie from David Ramsay by making a payment to him of one hundred merks Scots, in pure gold and silver.

Things did not always run smoothly among the members of the family. In 1550 Dame Margaret Gourlay took legal action against John Wardlaw her stepson and his wife "for the violent or wrangus occupatioun of the lands of Countill, Cluyn and Tempilland" after they ought to have removed. As Margaret had since fallen foul of the law, having been denounced rebel and put to the horn and therefore without standing in court, her claim for redress was considered null and void. Be this as it may, this was not the only case of this nature which involved the laird of Inchgall and his wife. On a previous occasion which included their son James, they were accused of the violent occupation and withholding of the land and steading of Ladath.

The year 1550 also saw the Laird of Inchgall arrested in Edinburgh. The reason for this unusual affair is not disclosed but it probably had something to do with money matters as Henry Wardlaw, while still in prison, obtained from Sir David Murray a loan of one hundred and forty gold crowns which he acknowledged having received "in his necessity".

It would appear that the barony of Inchgall had been wadset on a previous occasion, to whom is not known. With the loss of rents and profits from the estate the laird's financial position was now very low, but with the help of friends he succeeded in overcoming his difficulties for the time being at least. In 1552 he entered into a contract with Grisel Semple, daughter of Lord Semple and William and John Hamilton her natural sons, from whom he received two thousand five hundred and twenty-six merks and 5/-d in order to redeem the lands of Inchgall. At a later date he received a further one thousand four hundred and seventy-two merks 8/-d and 3d making a total of four thousand merks in all. As security Henry Wardlaw wadset half of his barony of Torrie to William Hamilton on condition that when his financial position improved he could redeem it on payment of two thousand merks. Between 1552 and the year 1563 he wadset the remaining half of Torrie to William Hamilton. In 1563 he set about having his lands redeemed and accordingly warned Grisel Semple to appear in the kirk of St. Giles to receive the redemption of Torrie. She failed to appear and Henry Wardlaw was obliged to go to Grisel's house in Edinburgh where he "knocked six tymes at the foir yett" but failed to get a response.

To return to 1555. In this year Henry Wardlaw decided to sell part of Inchgall. In return for a sum of money already paid to him, he sold to George Forrester of Strathenry, the husband of Margaret Beaton of Capeldrae, half of his lands of

Crosshill. This was the first of the lands to be sold. With this policy being adopted by subsequent lairds the whole of the barony had gone from the Wardlaw family within the space of a life span.

In 1560 reference is made to two charters by Henry Wardlaw to John Wardlaw in North Lumphinnans and Margaret Annand his wife. The first relates to the lands of Ladath; the second, which is of special interest, contains the earliest allusion to coal-mining in the parish of Ballingry. John and Margaret are given in conjunct fee all the lands of Blair with the coals and coal mines of the same and their pertinents, also the western part of the wood of Blair called in the vernacular Gilquhomy, with their pertinents, four acres of part of Kers lying at the western boundary of the same, a quarter of the mill of Inchgall with its pertinents along with the pasture and the liberty of pasturing "ten scoir scheip" and also "ane bow of ky" with their followers and "twentie foure yeild nolt" and six horses on the hill of Benarty.

In 1560 reference is made to Henry Wardlaw's lands of northern and southern Lumphinnans. These lands had been held for generations by the family of Halkett as vassals of the lairds of Inchgall and were to continue to be held for generations to come. Henry Wardlaw, as a free baron sat in parliament in 1560 and in 1565 Queen Mary and Darnley appointed him keeper of the havens of Culross and Torryburn.

Henry Wardlaw's son and heir, Andrew Wardlaw, married Janet Durie in March 1562, and in May of that year his father resigned certain lands in the barony of Inchgall and elsewhere into the Queen's hands. These the Queen incorporated in a new charter in favour of Andrew Wardlaw. In this Royal charter he obtained possession of the following, all of which were situated in Western Lochoreshire. The lands of Brunton and Dalginch with the loch of Balquharg, the advocation of the chapel of Inchgall, the lands of Tretoun with the march, easter and wester Newtoun, over and nether Markinch with the mills and acres of the same, Bychty, Petten Haglis in the lordship of Dalginch, a quarter of Balircrambeth and Kinnaird, half of Drumlochernoch and the Byn with the village of Crosshill above Inchgall with the privileges and liberties of the same, with the tower, fortalices, manors and gardens, orchards, loch, mills, fishings, tenants etc. which the said Henry resigned, and the Queen wished that one sasine should be taken for all of the dominical lands of Inchgall to be held by the said Andrew and the heirs of his body.

From the nature of this charter and the fact that Henry Wardlaw was once more in possession of the barony of Torrie, it is very likely that the father now resided at Torrie House and his son with his newly wedded wife occupied Inchgall Castle. Janet Durie received from her husband the life rent of the whole of the dominical lands of Inchgall with the tower and loch which amounted to thirty merks per annum. This she received in two portions i.e. Whitsunday and Martinmas. She continued to receive her annual rent until 1573 when, at the request of her husband, she resigned her rights. This was followed by a receipt of sasine directed to one Joan Anderson.

Henry Wardlaw supported Mary Queen of Scots in her troubles. His brother was probably the James Wardlaw who along with his kinsman John Beaton of Capledrae helped in the plot to free the Queen from Lochleven Castle. After the Queen's escape the laird of Torrie and his son Andrew of Inchgall joined the Queen's forces and were present at the battle of Langside. For this they were forfeited for treason but escaped the consequences through the intervention of the Lord Regent Moray. Henry Wardlaw did not act kindly towards his brother Alexander the parson of Ballingry. In 1574 he broke open his brother's cattle fauld in the Kirklands of Ballingry and chased his cattle. He ignored several summons to appear in court and was in consequence put to the horn and ordered to restore his brother's cattle. He died towards the end of the year 1580. By his first wife he had Andrew and a daughter named Nicholas. By his second wife he had Henry of Contil, Robert, William, Alexander and Elizabeth.

Nicholas Wardlaw as has been said elsewhere was one of the Queen's Maids of Honour. The others being according to the records of the period, Mary Fleming, Mary Beaton, Mary Seaton and Mary Livingstone. It would appear from the Lord High Treasurer's accounts that Nicholas was with the Queen in France and returned to Scotland with the Queen following the death of her husband Francis, the Dauphin of France. In November 1561 the court mourning was somewhat modified from unrelieved black and the Maids of Honour were given their second mourning dress. We find under this date an entry in the Lord High Treasurer's accounts of payments being made to Jacques de Soulis, tailor to the Queen for making dresses for the Queen's four Maries at a cost of £9 each and a dress for Nicholas Wardlaw costing £10 7/-d. We also learn from an entry in the accounts that Nicholas shared her chamber with one Janet Seaton and that Peir Martyne, tapester received in 1562 the sum of £17 15 10d for making their new bed.

32 *Torrie House (now demolished)*

Following the shock of Rizzio's murder the Queen began to dread the approaching birth of her child. Being haunted by the fear that her confinement would prove fatal she drew up inventories of her personal effects which were to be gifted to her devoted attendants in the event of her death. The Queen's four Maries were foremost in the distribution of her gifts. There is evidence however that Nicholas Wardlaw did receive a gift from the Queen. It consisted of two chains which were probably of similar design. Each was intended to be worn as a belt or band around the waist and consisted of fifty-six gold links embellished with black enamel-work with a large link and a small link alternately. Hanging from each chain was a "Vase", a kind of drop probably for containing a religious relic.

In 1566 Nicholas married Patrick Wood of Bonnyton in Angus. He, along with Alexander Wardlaw of Riccarton (a distant relative of Nicholas), was accused of the murder of Riccio, but a month before his marriage he managed to obtain a remission for his part in the plot, probably through the influence of the Earl of Moray as no doubt Wood was a man of his own faction.

Shortly before the marriage the Earl wrote to the Lord High Treasurer "My Lord Thesaurare efter hertlie commendacionis. Vpon tysday Nicholas Wardlaw beis maryt ye knaw she hes bene ane auld servand and is sic a gentlewoman as is worthie to be furtherit. Their restis to be had to her abilyementis alsmekle purpos veluos as to be hir goon sum pasmentis of gold and uther tryffillis of na greit valu quhilkis mon be heir the morne be Xij houris at the farthest. Quhairfoir I pra you for my saik and for the gentilwomannis awin sail (althocht the Quenis Maiestie had nocht commandit). That ye will not faillwith all possible diligence to answer the thingis contenit in the memoriall Thet it may be heir in convenient tyme. As ye will do me a speciall gude turne and plesour. And sa I bid you hertle fair weill. At Striveling the last day of August 1566. Your gude friend. James Stewart".

The Lord Treasurer acted quickly. The laird of Inchgall's daughter got her wedding gown consisting of thirteen and three quarter elnis of violet coloured velvet which depleted the Treasury to the amount of £68. 15/- and the Treasurer's clerk — surely by not knowing the correct date — entered his expenses under the 30th August, 1566 the day before his Lord received the letter from the Earl! Nicholas Wardlaw stood high in the Queen's favour and as a token of the regard in which she was held, the Queen made her and her future husband a gift of extensive lands in Aberdeenshire. The gift was absolute and free from all restrictions and incumbencies.

Nicholas Wardlaw and her husband had not their troubles to seek. The Master of Gray and others were responsible for instigating a hatred in the sons towards their parents resulting in their eldest son James being beheaded in 1601 for carrying out an act of violence on his father's estate.

Andrew Wardlaw II of Torrie and Inchgall

We have seen that Andrew Wardlaw, during his father's lifetime, had sasine of the barony of Inchgall which by now included the Wardlaw lands in the parish of Markinch. Following the death of his father, Andrew was retoured heir to the lands of Torrie. From this time onwards he probably lived at Torrie House. He had been not unaware of his father's financial difficulties, but it was only after he had come into his inheritance that he realised the full extent of the burden of debt for which he was now responsible. For him the clouds were gathering fast over the family and the demands of his creditors were an increasing embarrassment to him.

Early on, Andrew Wardlaw succeeded in redeeming the lands of Binn (lands which had been wadset by his father) on payment to John Law in Spittal of the sum of eight hundred merks. He also succeeded in redeeming his lands of Ballingry from Walter Arnott of that ilk on payment of one thousand merks, but the debt clouds were thickening fast on his horizon. To add to his troubles his eldest son died suddenly and he himself contracted a bodily ailment which he states made him "corpulent and grown in body wt divers seikness and infirmitee in his body and legges and is na mayor abill to travel to ustis (hosts) wards armours, nor zit upon inquests assyiss, except ye greit danger and haisart of his life".

In consideration of his infirmities the King granted him exemption from these duties and gave him special licence to "remain and byde at hame", provided he always sent his servants to the hosts sufficiently armed.

Andrew Wardlaw's creditors were many, for the most part Edinburgh merchants. The sums of money which he owed to individuals ranged from two thousand to ten thousand merks. The first of those to put him to the horn was his tenant Henry Dick of the Milton of Inchgall and Sarah Beverage his wife, for the non-payment of three thousand merks and £400 expenses. Also during this period Andrew Arnott, minister of Scotlandwell, was seeking payment of the sum of four thousand merks and £200 expenses. For these and monies which were due to two persons in Kirkcaldy the Privy Council ordered that the laird of Inchgall be apprehended by the captain of the guard.

Despite his many troubles Andrew Wardlaw had his moments of Royal favours. James VI in 1596 sent a boy from Edinburgh with a letter requesting him to send venison and wild fowl for the feast that was to follow the baptism of his daughter, princess Elizabeth. The laird also had an invitation to come and take part in the celebrations.

Probably in an effort to clear off his debts the laird entered into a contract in 1604 with Edward Edgar, an Edinburgh merchant and his son, Clement, who were suppliers of wine to Holyrood House. On the payment of twelve thousand five hundred merks, Edward Edgar was granted in feuferm the lands and barony of Inchgall with the Castle, manor, mills, loch and fishings under the right of reversion. The contract was signed in Inchgall Castle. Five years later he entered into a somewhat similar contract with another Edinburgh merchant, Richard Dobie from whom he received a loan of £10,000. By way of interest, Andrew Wardlaw undertook to pay Dobie an annual rent of £1,000 out of his lands of Torrie and Dalginch until such time that he could redeem the loan.

Andrew Wardlaw's troubles included those of a more domestic nature. His eldest surviving son, Andrew, did not behave in a very kindly manner towards his father, so much so that his father took out a summons against him in March 1610. We learn from the father's petition that his son had begun to "molest trouble and oppress him" in his possession of the lands of Techmure in the barony of Inchgall, that he had entered his father's farm yard and taken away most of the corn which was stored in the barn. He also drove away twenty-four young oxen that were grazing in the lands of Techmure. When the father heard of the damage done by his son he locked the doors of his barn in order to preserve the remaining corn but his "unnaturall and unkindlie sone heiping wrang upoun wrang" returned and broke open the barn and took away the remaining corn and disposed of it.

As a result of the many hornings taken out against the Laird of Inchgall his belongings were for a period forfeit, but fortunately his kinsman Henry Wardlaw of Balmule had a gift of the escheat of his lands and goods and thus saved them from falling into the hands of outsiders.

Andrew Wardlaw's troubles, physical, financial and domestic, probably hardened his attitude to people in general. He quarrelled with David Russell in Torryburn, assaulted his wife, took away his horse and destroyed his agricultural implements. Also John Blackadder of Inzevar, who had reason to apprehend danger from Andrew Wardlaw and his sons, took out letters of lawburrows which compelled the Wardlaws to give him security that they would not harm him. Andrew Wardlaw's financial position was such that he was unable to give security, but Sir James Scott of Balweary, his son-in-law, came to his aid. He not only provided two thousand merks required of Andrew Wardlaw but also stood surety for his sons.

Andrew Wardlaw died shortly after 1618. By his wife Janet Durie he had the following children: Henry who died during his father's lifetime, Andrew who succeeded his father as heir to his estate, Patrick of Pitgormo, James of Wester Inzevar, Elizabeth, who married Sir James Scott of Balweary, Janet who married Robert Bruce of Clackmannan, Agnes who married Alexander Colville of Blair (Benarty estate) and Margaret who married David Beaton of Balfour.

Andrew Wardlaw III of Torrie and Inchgall

Andrew Wardlaw became heir apparent to his father on the death of his elder brother Henry. In 1605 he married Agnes Leslie, grand-daughter of Andrew, Earl of Rothes. She brought to him a tocher of ten thousand merks.

In August, 1605 he received from the King a confirmation charter of the barony of Wester Lochoreshire, consisting of the lands of Brunton and Dalginch with the loch of Balfarg, the advocation of the chapel of Inchgall, the lands of Tritoun with the myre, Easter and Wester Newtoun, Over and Neather Markinch with the mills and acres belonging to them, Bichtie and Pitinhagillis in the lordship of Inchgall, a quarter of the lands of Blaircrambeth and Kinnard, half of Drumlochornoch and Byn with the village of Crosshill above Inchgall with the fortalices, manors, lochs, mills, fishings, tenants etc. which Andrew Wardlaw senior of Torrie had resigned, also the dominical lands of Flockhouse and Bowhouse of Inchgall with their mills, the lands of Balbegie, Clune, Cartmore, Lumphinnans, north and south, the lands of Lochhead, Spittal, Ballingry, Navitie and Contill, the hill of Benarty, the advocation of the rectory and vicarage of Ballingry, the lands of Balfarg, the lands of Brunton-moss with the woods and coal heughs, incorporating them all anew in the free barony of Inchgall with the Castle of Inchgall as the principal seat of the barony.

Weighed down with family debts Andrew Wardlaw saw no way out other than that he should part with a portion of his estate. To add to his troubles his wife died in 1609. That he did dispose of part of Inchgall is evident from a charter of 1614. He had however done so without the king's consent, and as this was the second offence of this nature relating to Inchgall, the king stripped him of the barony and gave sasine to William Shaw of Lethangie in Kinross-shire by which he had rights over the Castle, Manors, Loch, Island, the salmon and other fishings, the patronages of churches, benefices and chaplainaries, tenants, mills and coal heughs. The ceremony of sasine took place at the Mains of Inchgall. Andrew Wardlaw married secondly Agnes Colville by whom he had two sons, James and John.

William Shaw resigned the barony of Inchgall into the king's hands after holding it for a year and a half. In return, the king conveyed the barony to Patrick Wardlaw now of Brunton, a brother of Andrew Wardlaw. Patrick received a confirmation charter in March 1616 wherein he was infeft in all the lands of Inchgall and received anew the lands of Brunton. Both lands were to be incorporated as before, into a free barony known as Inchgall.

For a while Andrew Wardlaw strove to exist on the revenue from his barony of Torrie, but in 1622 increasing pecuniary difficulties compelled him to sell the barony to his brother Patrick. From his brother he appears to have received the small estate of Cartmore. Here he was content to live and was known thereafter as "of Cartmore". This laird, whose whole existence seems to have been one uphill struggle against heavy odds, is last heard of in France where he signed a Deed in 1631 and witnessed by James, Lord Colville of Culross.

Patrick Wardlaw of Torrie and Inchgall

Patrick Wardlaw received a better education than most of his forebears. He attended St. Andrews University where he matriculated in 1597 and graduated in 1601. He married Margaret Forbes, daughter of Arthur Forbes of Rires, probably in 1619. He is spoken of at this period as "a worthy and religious gentleman". He was by the year 1622 in possession of all the Wardlaw lands. Two years after receiving the lands of Inchgall he sold Clunecraig, Contill and the Waird-meadow on the north side of Cars-water to John Betson in Eastertoun of Beath in fulfilment of a contract which he had entered into, and in this same year (1618) he gave sasine to his brother-in-law, Alexander Colville, Justice Depute of Scotland, of the lands of Blaircushnie of which we will speak later.

Patrick Wardlaw was intent on turning his lands into hard cash, and by the end of the year he had sold to James Mitchell, portioner of Balbardie and his wife, Isabel Roland, the lands of Ladath for the sum of six thousand three hundred merks. The contract was heritable and irredeemable. James Mitchell thus came to possess the lands and village of Ladath along with the western meadow of Inchgall which pertained to Ladath from ancient times. He had the right of cutting hay there and taking it to the Hayhill. He also had the right to pasture sixteen cows and one hundred sheep on the Common of Benarty and to cut turf two days in the year in part of the moss of Inchgall.

and to win limestone in the quarries of Navitie and Ballingry which were managed by William Inglis. The charter was signed at Burntisland and Inchgall. Among the witnesses were William Scott, minister of Auchterderran and James Wardlaw senior, in Inchgall.

This sale was followed by another in January 1623 when Patrick Wardlaw disposed of the lands of Ballingry to John Greig in Balquhumrie for the sum of £5,000. The right of pasturing two hundred sheep on the Commonty of Benarty was included in the sale. John Greig was also empowered to dig peats for his own use in the moss of Inchgall with the right of entry by way of the road to Bowhouse. The charter was signed at Falkland and Kirkness.

It was in this year that Patrick Wardlaw was made a Justice of the Peace, a commission which he appears to have taken rather lightly. Instead of preserving the peace within his own bounds, he quarrelled violently with his near neighbour Sir Robert Preston of Valleyfield, so much so that Sir Robert had reason to fear his own safety. The outcome was that Robert Forbes (brother-in-law) stood surety in the sum of five thousand merks for Patrick Wardlaw that he would keep the peace and not harm Sir Robert or any of his servants.

Patrick Wardlaw is last heard of in 1625 when he renounced his claim to the "lands of Lochhead with the Manorplace, coal heughs, limestones, the loch called Lochgellie and the fishings in it, the multures, tenants etc., in the barony of Wester Lochoreshire otherwise known as Inchgall". He died in July 1626 leaving his financial affairs in a sorry condition. By his marriage he had Andrew, his heir, Arthur who died young and Anna, who married Robert Straton.

Andrew Wardlaw IV of Torrie and Inchgall

Andrew Wardlaw was five years of age when his father died, and for the following twelve years or so, his affairs were managed by relatives who acted as his guardians or tutors. He would have been spared much unnecessary hardship had his guardians not served him heir to his father and thereby unknowingly exposed him to the demands from his father's creditors.

Andrew was retoured heir to his father in May 1627 in the lands and barony of Lochereschyre-wester otherwise called Inchgall. That is, the lands called Flockhous and Bowhouis of Inchgall with the loch of Inchgall and the right of patronage of the Chapel of Inchgall; the lands of Myletoun of Inchgall with their mills; the lands of Blaircurschenye, Balbegye, Clun, Cathemoir, Norther and Souther Lumfynnance, Lochhead, Spittell, Ballingrie, Navetyt and Quontill; the hills called Banhartiehills with the right of patronage of the Kirk of Ballingrie; a quarter of the lands of Drumlocherinche; a half of the lands of Byne; the lands of Balquharg with the loch within the said barony of Lochereschyre-Wester.

It was not long before creditors were pressing the boy for the payment of debts incurred by his father. In 1628 the sheriff authorised the apprising of the barony of Inchgall to Michael Ramsay of Forth in satisfaction of a debt of one thousand, six hundred and two merks which had been incurred by the boy's father. Although by law the boy could redeem the barony within seven years it appears that someone had come to his aid shortly afterwards and restored the barony to him. The respite was short. Later on in the year the barony was again in the hands of a creditor in the person of David Aytoun, it having been made over to him in settlement of a debt amounting to £15,040 with power of redemption within seven years.

As the boy had no capital, there was no way of easing the burden of debt which had been placed upon him. Letters written by his guardians to the Lords of the Privy Council revealed the true state of affairs and make sorrowful reading. It is clear that Andrew Wardlaw had inherited an insurmountable burden of debt and was in daily fear of travelling beyond the limits of his estate of Torrie lest he be apprehended by his father's creditors and put in prison.

The question of the boy's education appears to have given his guardians much concern. They appealed to the Privy Council in 1629, when Andrew was about seven years old, that their lordships would take some course of action for the boy's protection so that a portion of the rents and other profits from his estates could be set aside for his education.

Their lordships took a sympathetic view of the case and suspended the execution of all hornings and captions against Andrew until he reached the age of twelve years. In 1632 when Andrew was eleven years old, he sold the barony of Inchgall to John Earl of Rothes and was thereafter only in possession of Torrie. In 1634 there was a further supplication on behalf of the boy when the lords granted him their warrant for the safety of his person until he was fourteen years of age. In June of the same year he craved their lordships' protection saying "out of a vehement and earnest desire to satisfy his creditors and clear himself of debt, he is resolved to dispose of his whole estate, both lands and coal, and content himself with what may remain, but he cannot do so without the advice of lawyers, and dare not come to Edinburgh for this without their Lordships' protection, which he accordingly craves". Andrew succeeded in obtaining the necessary protection. Finally in 1635 the lords granted Andrew a further extension of their protection until 1638 so that he could complete his education.

The final demise was not far off. In 1637 the barony of Torrie was sold to the family of Bruce of Carnock and with it this ancient branch of the Wardlaws became landless, and with the death of Andrew Wardlaw who died unmarried in 1651 the branch of the Torrie and Inchgall Wardlaws came to an end.

THE COLVILLE FAMILY

33

The family is said to have derived its name from a place called Coleville in Normandy. The first to appear in Scotland was Philip de Coleuille who was in possession of the baronies of Oxnam and Heiton in Roxburghshire and who witnessed a general confirmation by Malcolm IV, in about the year 1159 of all the donations which his royal predecessors had given to the monastery of Dunfermline. One of the first of the names to appear north of the Forth was Ada de Coleuyll who in 1241 gave the lands of Kynnard (Kinnaird) in Fife to the Abbey of Newbattle.

Sir James Colville I

James Colville is first mentioned in 1505. In about the year 1518 he was appointed Director of Chancery and was Comptroller under the Earl of Angus in 1526. In 1530 he exchanged his lands of Ochiltree in Ayrshire for those of Easter Wemyss and some lands in Easter Lochoreshire belonging to Sir James Hamilton of Finnart. In the following year he acquired an interest in the four merk lands of Dundonald along with the coal there. He was knighted in 1533. Shortly afterwards he was in possession of lands in the parish of Cleish, which lands consisting of the Dolelands, Haltoun of Cleish and Easter and Wester Nivingstoun, he gave in 1537 to his natural son Robert for an annual rent of ten merks.

In 1538 Sir James's name appears in connection with the lands of Strathruddy and Balgreggie and in 1540, the year of his death, he gave to his legitimate son Robert the lands of Pitkinny and Murtoun of Balgony and in this same year this Robert had an interest in the lands of Balbathy (Balbedie). The other lands in Easter Lochoreshire belonging to Sir James were Easter Capeldrae, Wester Raith, Polguild and Glennistoun.

Sir James played a prominent part in the affairs of the period but was deprived of his office in 1538 on the charge of corrupt administration. He was ordered to ward himself in Blackness Castle, but instead he fled to England and joined up with the Earl of Angus. For these acts he was found guilty of treason and his estates were forfeited shortly after his death in 1540.

Sir James married firstly, Alison Bruce, daughter of Sir David Bruce of Clackmannan and secondly Margaret Forrester of Garden. He had several children including James, his lawful heir, Robert already mentioned and two daughters. He had also two illegitimate sons, Robert, the progenitor of the Colvilles of Cleish, and James from whom was descended the Colvilles of Culross, and Alexander whose son was the first of the Colvilles of Blair.

Robert Colville of Cleish was one of those who sought reform within the Church. He was also known as the man who exposed a hoax staged by several fradulent clergy who had devised it in an effort to arrest the fast decaying credit of the Church and to restore its authority over the people by attempting to deceive them into believing that a miracle had been performed through the intervention of the Saints.

After it was made known throughout Edinburgh and the neighbouring towns that a token of the divine power was to be exhibited at the chapel of our Lady of Loretto at Musselburgh, the conspirators erected a high stage so that all those assembled could see. A man was then brought forward who for some time past had been seen walking about the neighbourhood with a guide and had the appearance of, and had been accepted by all, as being blind. As he stood on the stage it was clear that the white orbs of his sightless eyes could be seen, but after the incantations of the clergy these changed to those of one who had suddenly obtained his sight and his expression was one of complete surprise and in feigned gratitude he praised God, the Lady of Loretto and the Saints, also the priests and friars who had been the means of restoring his sight.

The onlookers, believing what they had seen to be genuine, applauded and showered gifts upon the man, but the laird of Cleish had his doubts and resolved to probe the matter further. He gave the man a gift and offered to employ him as his servant, an offer to which the clergy readily agreed. In Colville's lodgings in Edinburgh the man at length confessed to his part in the deception and revealed how it had been carried out.

Since a boy, he had acquired the ability of turning up his eyelids to show the white of his eyes. This propensity, accompanied by a hesitant walk displayed the characteristics of a blind person. The clergy, to whom he had become known, saw in him an excellent opportunity of restoring the power of the Church in the minds of the people. The man consented to their plan and was concealed in a vault in the nunnery of Sciennes near Edinburgh for a period of seven or eight years until all recollection of him by the public had gone. Although out of sight of everyone except the sisters of the nunnery, he had all these years been well cared for. He was for a short period before his appearance at the bogus miracle, paraded through Edinburgh, Dalkeith, Leith and Musselburgh, where he played his part so well that even his guide was deceived.

His confession to Colville was not enough; the people must be told the truth. Accordingly, the man made a public announcement the following morning at the cross in Edinburgh as to how he had along with the clergy deceived the public. Colville stood over the man with a drawn sword in case of reprisals, and as soon as he had finished speaking, both mounted horses which stood nearby and made for the Queensferry and eventually reached Cleish Castle.

Robert Colville and his wife Francisca Colquhoun received the barony of Cleish in

1537. He held the office of the Master of the Household to Lord James Stuart, afterwards, the Regent Moray. In 1560 he joined the forces of the Lords of the Congregation and was present at the attack upon the French troops in Leith where he died. His son Robert, who married Margaret Lindsay of Dowhill, succeeded his father in the barony and died in 1584.

Sir James Colville II

James Colville was a boy of eight years when his father died. Although the family had been stripped of their father's estates they had people in high places working on their behalf. It was thus in 1543 that James Colville, as heir to his father, had his estates restored to him through the influence of Cardinal Beaton. He was appointed Steward to Margaret, Queen of James III and was knighted sometime between 1547 and 1553. He died in 1580. Of his marriage to Janet, daughter of Sir Robert Douglas of Lochleven, he had two sons. James the elder, succeeded him in his estates.

In 1579, the year previous to Sir James Colville's death, following the murder of his kinsman, James Colville, bailie of Culross, by John and George Wardlaw and John Wardlaw their cousin, Sir James was made a gift of the fines imposed on the Wardlaws amounting to three hundred merks. Sir James's eldest son James conveyed by charter in 1586 the lands of Balgreggie to George Boswell, minister of Auchterderran and his wife Isabel Sibbald, reserving the rights of the occupant, Michael Balfour.

Sir James's second son was probably called Robert. In 1586 a Robert Colville who is described as the son of James Colville of Easter Wemyss gave to John Dick and Elizabeth Kinninmont, his wife, on the payment of one thousand merks, the life-rent, and to their son in heritage, the lands of Easter Cartmore. The receipt of sasine went direct to John Kinninmont in Colquhalie. Among the witnesses to the King's charter of confirmation of the following year signed at Beath, were George Boswell, rector of Auchterderran, James Colville of Culross and James Colville of Balbedie.

Sir James Colville III

James Colville was born about the year 1550. He entered military service at an early age and attained distinction in the French Wars under Henry of Navarre. He was granted in 1589 the lands of Culross, Valleyfield and Inzievar which were erected into the temporal barony of Culross and in 1609 he was created Lord Colville of Culross. James Colville married firstly Isabel, daughter of Patrick Lord Ruthven, and secondly Helen Shaw widow of Robert Mowbray. His son and heir James who had married Elizabeth, daughter of David Wemyss, predeceased his father in 1595. On the death of Lord Colville in 1629, he was succeeded by his grandson James Colville second Lord Colville of Culross, at whose death in 1654 the lands of Easter Wemyss were bought by the Earl of Wemyss and became once more part of the barony of Wemyss.

Alexander Colville I of Blair

Alexander Colville was the son of Sir James Colville I by his second wife, Margaret Forrester. In 1572 he was appointed one of the Senators of the College of Justice and a Privy Councillor. He gave up his rights over the property of the Abbey of Culross in 1587. These were afterwards conveyed by James IV to his nephew, Lord Colville. By his marriage to Nicholus Dundas, his eldest son and heir John Colville became titular Commendator of Culross. James Colville, a younger son, acquired the sunny half of the village and lands of Balbedie also half of the mains lands of Easter Wemyss in 1619. The sunny half of Balbedie had formerly belonged to John Boswell of Balmuto and had been purchased by a James Colville, probably his cousin, in 1591. This James Colville had held Balbedie under the Boswells during the previous twenty years.

It was largely through the efforts of the laird of Blair that the church of Beath was rebuilt. It was at Beath about the year 1540 that the Protestant Lords first met to discuss the state of the Church and the religious life of the people. The outcome of the movement was the Reformation. Alexander Colville has left an account of the situation at Beath church during this period. Fourteen years after the Reformation, when the spiritual needs of each congregation in Fife had been supplied, the people of Beath were still without a minister being "lyke wandering sheepe without a sheephard". The church stood neglected and was used as a sheepfold at night. Instead of the parishioners meeting to worship on a Sunday they danced to pipe music, played football, indulged in drinking and occasionally brawled and fell to wounding one another. All this, Mr Colville tells us, he saw "from his owne windowe". From this it is believed that the Colvilles were at this period in possession of Blair under the Wardlaws.

At length, in order to do something for the poor neglected folk, Mr Colville met several people at Kelty Sheills and sought their assistance in rebuilding the church. The response was instantaneous. One and all agreed to do his share in providing men and horses, and soon the building of a new church was in progress. Mr Colville provided the money and Mr John Hodge in Leuchat's Beath was appointed overseer of the work. The roof was to have been slated but as the slates were to be brought from Tipermoore some sixteen miles distant, it was agreed that for the first year "ye kirk should be sarked with deales".

The opening day was a great occasion. People came from all around and many "out of everie sitie". The kirk was so "thrang" that there was hardly any room to provide a temporary raised platform from which the minister could address the congregation. Alexander Colville died in 1597.

Alexander Colville II of Blair

Alexander Colville was the fourth son of Alexander Colville I. He married Agnes Wardlaw, daughter of Andrew Wardlaw of Torrie and Inchgall, and had in 1618 a confirmation charter under the Great Seal of the house and lands of Blaircowsnye with pasture for one hundred and sixty sheep on Benarty Hill, for an annual rent of £3. In

1633 he acquired the shady half of the lands of Balbedie which had formerly belonged to Robert Richardson, burgess of Burntisland. As a landholder in these parts he, along with his neighbour Michael Arnot, petitioned the Privy Council in 1620 on behalf of the parishioners of Ballingry and Portmoak to be allowed to extract toll money from the people using the "brig o' trees" over the river Leven at the gullets. In view of the dangerous condition of the bridge the Lords of Council agreed that Colville and Arnot be allowed to charge "tua pennyes of the footeman and four pennyes of the horseman" travelling that way during eight days before and after the four annual fairs during the following year.

Alexander Colville of Blair held the shady half of Balbedie for only ten years. With the consent of his wife and his son Alexander, he disposed of the lands to his brother James. By a confirmation charter which he received from the King in 1640 James Colville was now in possession of the whole of the lands of Balbedie.

Alexander Colville was appointed Lord Justice Depute sometime before 1643. In 1662 he, along with a jury of neighbouring landholders, presided over the well-known trial of the Fossoway witches. *

Alexander Colville III of Blair

Alexander Colville was the second son of the marriage of Alexander Colville and Agnes Wardlaw, and first appears in a charter of 1643 relating to the lands of Balbedie. The death of his mother was the final break in the chain of events which had connected the Wardlaw family with the barony of Inchgall for a period of over two hundred years. She had lived to see the gradual decline of her family's fortunes and the ultimate sale of the barony of Inchgall, the first step in the break-up of the old barony into small estates to be held by many proprietors.

Alexander Colville was in possession of Blair in 1669. He was a staunch presbyterian and, although a Justice of the Peace during the period of Episcopacy, he resolutely refused to sign the bond, as issued by the Privy Council, whereby those who signed undertook not to attend conventicles and to bring to justice all those who transgressed the law in religious matters. Mr Colville took an active part in the life of the parish and although he declined the office of eldership he nonetheless appears to have been an active member of Ballingry church. In this respect he followed his family's tradition as many of his forebears were prominent churchmen. The Blair estate remained in Mr Colville's family until the year 1796, when it was purchased by Mr John Syme, Writer to the Signet.

---

* Alexander Colville was also Auditor General of the Covenanters' Army. As Justice Depute he presided at the trial in 1640 of John Stewart Younger of Ladywell on the charge of slandering the King and his Council. Stewart was found guilty and beheaded by the "Maiden".

THE BEATONS OF CAPELDRAE

34

It has been said that part of Capeldrae lay within the parish of Ballingry. The writer has found no evidence of this. It is clear from charter evidence that Easter and Wester Capeldrae lay wholly in Auchterderran parish and that the various proprietors down through the years gave their teind sheaves to Auchterderran church as well as the teinds for the parsonage and vicarage there. The lairds of Capeldrae also had the right of a "room" (seat) in that church. It is noteworthy that Capeldrae does not appear in any of the Wardlaw or Malcolm charters. From this and the foregoing, it is clear that the lands of Capeldrae did not constitute part of the barony of Inchgall but were situated in Easter Lochoreshire.

Following the death of David de Lochore, when Lochoreshire came to be divided between two heiresses, Capeldrae was among the lands that went over to the Wemyss family. It was subsequently held by various families in succession before it came into the possession of the Beatons.

Each successive laird of Capeldrae had a seat in Auchterderran Church, but as these lands lay some distance from that church most of the folk who lived there attended the church at Ballingry. Not surprisingly, when Capeldrae emerged from a "ferm toun" to a thriving mining community it identified itself with the village life of Ballingry and Lochore rather than that of Auchterderran.

The progenitor of the Beatons of Capeldrae was Archibald Beaton, fourth son of John Beaton of Balfour and Marjory Boswell of Balmuto who were married in 1458. Archibald Beaton had five brothers and five sisters and was closely related to many persons well known in history. His eldest brother John, who succeeded his father in the estate of Balfour, married Isabella Monypenny of Pitmilly. Their numerous family included David Beaton, the Cardinal who was assassinated in 1546, Walter Beaton, parson of Ballingry and afterwards Archdeacon of Lothian, George Beaton, parson of Govan, James Beaton, father of James Beaton, Archbishop of Glasgow, Elizabeth, who married John Wardlaw of Torrie and Inchgall and Margaret who married John Graham of Claverhouse.

Archibald Beaton's second eldest brother David acquired the lands of Creich about the year 1502. He was brought up from his youth with James IV, and was appointed Lord High Treasurer and afterwards Lord High Chancellor and Captain of

Falkland Palace. He married a lady whose christian name is uncertain; a daughter of Duddingston of Sandford in Fife, by whom he had two sons and three daughters. His eldest daughter, Janet married Sir Robert Livingston of Easter Wemyss, and afterwards James Hamilton, first Earl of Arran. Elizabeth, David Beaton's youngest daughter was mother by James V of Jean, Countess of Argyll. David Beaton's eldest son John succeeded his father in the estate of Creich. He married Janet Hay, daughter of the provost of Dundee. Their eldest daughter Janet married as her third husband Sir Walter Scott of Buccleuch. She is best known through the writings of Sir Walter Scott of Abbotsford. In his *Lay of the Last Minstrel* Scott gives her a prominent place. She appears to have been possessed of a masculine spirit as she rode at the head of her clan to avenge the death of her husband. Sir Walter, speaking of her says "she possessed the hereditary ability of her family in such a degree that the superstition of the vulgar imputed them to supernatural knowledge". The belief that she was the possessor of witchcraft led many at the time to believe that she influenced Queen Mary to the murder of her husband Henry Darnley. Janet Beaton's sister, Grizel, married Sir Walter Scott junior, of Branxholm, Mary Beaton, a niece of Janet and Grizel who was spoken of as "a very fair beauty", was one of the Queen's "four Maries".

Archibald Beaton's third eldest brother, Robert, was in succession Abbot of Coupar Angus, Melrose and Glenluce, while Archibald's immediate younger brother, Andrew or Henry, was Prior of St. Andrews. James, his youngest brother was Archbishop of Glasgow and later Archbishop of St. Andrews. Archibald Beaton's sisters Janet, Margaret, Grizel, Isobel and Elizabeth all married gentlemen of note.

Archibald I of Capeldrae

We first hear of Archibald Beaton in the year 1504 when he was made a gift of the lands and goods belonging to the deceased — Littlejohn by reason of Littlejohn's son and heir being outwith the law. In 1506 he had a charter of half of the lands of Ballingall along with the mill there and also some lands in Perthshire. Two years afterwards he had a three years lease of a quarter of the lands of Falkland and Balbrekie at an annual rent of £4 plus a specified amount of barley and oats and twenty-four capons. It is not known for certain when Capeldrae came into the possession of the Beaton family although it appears to have taken place before 1513, as Sir Robert Livingston of Easter Wemyss with whom Archibald Beaton had entered into an agreement on Capeldrae, died at Flodden. It was in 1513 that these lands along with others in the parish of Auchterderran were annexed to the barony of Glassmount. In 1530 the superiority of Capeldrae was conferred upon Sir James Hamilton of Finnart, a natural son of the first Earl of Arran who was related to Archibald Beaton. Beaton had, by his wife, whose name is not known, a son and a daughter. He died shortly after the year 1530.

Archibald II of Capeldrae

In 1532 Margaret, daughter and heiress of Sir Robert Livingston and wife of Sir

James Hamilton raised an action against Archibald Beaton for the return of Capeldrae. The case came before the Lords of Session in July of that year and was deferred until November to allow a clerk of the court to "pas our and examin the auld failzeit personis allegit that best knowis this matter because thai air waik personis and in danger that thai deces in the meyntym". Nothing more is heard of the case, but the evidence of the "auld failzeit personis" must have been in Beaton's favour for the family continued to possess Capeldrae.

In addition to Capeldrae, Archibald Beaton possessed the small estate of Pitlochie in the parish of Kinglassie. He also held the lands and mill of Easter Hailes in the lordship of Musselburgh, and some lands in Renfrewshire. However, it is through his office of Chamberlain of the regality of Dunfermline that he is best known, and as Justicier and bailie his name appears regularly in the Dunfermline Register from 1531 to 1538. From the latter date till his death in 1547, he was Granitar and Chamberlain to his brother James, Archbishop of St. Andrews.

As a cousin of David Beaton, the laird of Capeldrae often accompanied him in his journeys out of Scotland. As in 1533 and again in 1536, when the Cardinal had to travel "to the partis bezond the sey, for certain grate materis concerning the commone wele of us, oure realme and leigis", and in 1537 when he had to go to England. In 1541 when the Cardinal had to "pas to the partis of France and utheris partis bezond the sey", quite a number of his relations travelled with him. In addition to Archibald Beaton there was on occasion Archibald's son-in-law George Forrester who had a lease of half of the lands of Crosshill. Quite often the Cardinal's sister Elizabeth and her husband John Wardlaw of Inchgall were among those who travelled with him.

In 1539 Archibald Beaton came into the possession of certain lands following the death of his uncle James Beaton, Archbishop of St. Andrews. These lands which appear to have been considerable, were situated in the shires of Edinburgh, Roxburgh and Stirling. Two years afterwards he was given the superiority of the lands of Capeldrae.

Things did not always go smoothly for Beaton. The year 1543 saw him at variance with the law. In March of that year an official of the court in Edinburgh was instructed to proceed to Capeldrae to charge Beaton to be in the town of Dalkeith within the period of six hours! and to remain there in ward at his own expense and not to travel a mile beyond the town until such times that he was freed by the court. He was cautioned "that he send na writingis to his toune (Capeldrae) to na maner of personis undir the pane of tressoune". These were strong measures especially when no formal charge seems to have been brought against him and one wonders what was behind it all. However, Archibald's kinsman, Sir Walter Scott of Branxholm, and James Douglas of Drumlanrig came forward and stood surety for his observing the court's ruling, and by the twentieth of the month he was allowed to return to Capeldrae on condition that he remain in ward within the sherrifdom of Fife.

Two years after this, we meet with Beaton again. In the year 1545 and again in 1546 he is made the recipient of certain goods which, prior to the process of law, had belonged to others. The records are interesting as they show how the law dealt with persons who ignored the summons to arms. The law required every man between sixteen and sixty years of age to equip himself with defensive and offensive armour in proportion to his status in life. The lower ranks of society were to be "sufficiently bowit and schaffit", in other words sufficiently equipped with a good bow and an ample supply of arrows, as also a sword a buckler and dagger and to be prepared to take the field when summoned, with provisions for fifteen to twenty days. It was usually the duty of the Justices of the Peace to compile lists of all able-bodied men within each parish. This was done with the help of the church Communion rolls.

In order that every man should become efficient in the handling of the bow, every parish was to have at least two "bow marks". The "butts" were usually set up in the churchyard and all male inhabitants were expected to practise every Sunday and to shoot at least six arrows. The duration was from Easter to all Hallow-mas. To ensure there were no counter attractions to the practice of archery and to the muster and inspection of arms which was to take place four times in the year, golf and football were "utterly cried down". Those who failed to appear at the bow butts were liable to a fine of two pennies, and to absent oneself from the wapenshaws could result in a fine ranging from 40/- d to £10 in the case of a landed gentleman and 10/-d to £2 in that of a bow man, depending on the number of absences. These fines were heavy according to the period but stronger measures were taken against those who failed to answer the general summons to arms.

This was the period before the emergence of the professional soldier when the Scottish laird went to war accompanied by his kinsmen and vassels who, unlike their English counterparts, were not paid. As a consequence, there was a general reluctance to do military duty when there was a possible way out. Perhaps the only incentive for the rank and file was the probability of gaining from the spoils of war in the form of booty. Cattle lifting and the like from across the border was considered military duty and plundering the "auld enemy" was looked upon as patriotic. There was also the possibility of receiving a share of the ransom money paid for the release of prisoners of note which at times could be considerable.

In 1545 the Privy Council dealt with John Melville of Touch, near Dunfermline and also John Clerk and William Haig. These men were stripped of their possessions including "all gudis movable and unmovable, cornis, steadingis, obligations, soumes of money, gold, silver, cunyeit and uncunyeit", all of which was gifted to the Laird of Capeldrae. The case against these men arose out of what the Privy Council called their "treassonable remaining and byding at hame fra our soverane lady's last oist and army deviset to pas with my lord governour to Lauder, the XI day of September last bipast, for the defence of this realme against our auld inymeis of England". A similar action was taken against David Merschale, Johnne Kilgour, Henry Criste and George Criste in Dysart for their "tressonable remaining and byding at hame". Here again Archibald Beaton is made a gift of the goods belonging to these persons.

As the wording in these and similar cases is almost identical, it suggests that the phrases were taken from the style book of the period without any reference to the nature of the goods belonging to the persons convicted, nonetheless it is fairly certain that the delinquents would lose most of the goods which they possessed. If the penalties imposed on these men were severe, even harsher measures were taken against three delinquents who lived within the barony of Inchgall.

In 1565 the case of John Dick of Lumphinnans, John Dick of Easter Cartmore and John Anderson of Balbeggie (near Inchgall Farm) came before the Privy Council. They were apprehended for "tressonabill remaining and byding at hame fra their majestries oist, raid and army convenit at Striveling the XXVIII day August bipast". The truth was that the three arrived at Stirling on the first day of September, four days late! By this date Archibald Beaton was dead and all their belongings were given to "Maister Johne Stewart". These included "all landis guidis movabill and unmovabill, dettis, stedings, actis, contracts oblyationis, sowmes of money, cornis, cattell, gold silver, jowellis and uthiris goods quhatsumevir". John Stewart was empowered to "intromit and tak up the saids eschete guidis and dettis at his awin handis quhairevir the samin may be apprehended and to occupy the said takkis and stedingis with his awin proper guidis or to set thane to tenentis as he sall think expedient frelie and quietlie".

Of course the annals of the period are not confined to recording matters relating to the lesser folk only. We are afforded a glimpse from time to time into the activities of the lairds and in time of national distress they figure more prominently. In this way it has been possible to gather fragments of information of a somewhat military nature. Going back to the year 1508 we find the Squire of Cleish superintending the casting of a gun and in recognition of his expert knowledge he received 14/-d. Four years afterwards he appears to have been in command of one of the King's ships patrolling the Forth. In 1513 when preparations were being made for an entry into England by the Scottish Army, an enterprise which ended in the disaster at Flodden, the laird of Lochleven provided a number of oxen which went to make up the team of sixteen animals which were required to haul each of the great guns. We note too that the men who drove the oxen from Lochleven to Edinburgh received 12/-d in "drinksilver". Again, in 1545 when the country was being ravished by the troops of Henry the VIII, John Wardlaw, brother of the minister of Ballingry and the nephew of Cardinal Beaton, on the instruction of the Cardinal, and on behalf of his father, manned the Castle of Inchgall and put it in a state of defence.

There was during this period and for many years previously, a dearth of timber for the building of ships and other commodities. It is not clear why the people of nearby Muckhart should have been singled out for a timely warning, but the King felt it expedient to write to the laird of Lochleven commanding him to warn his tenants of Muckhart that they must "help to draw tymir". The situation was no better in 1548 when the Castle of Broughty was held by the English and was being besieged by the Earl of Argyll. The lack of timber which hampered the enterprise was overcome by Robert Colville the Laird of Cleish, who supplied the besiegers with "tua dosoun of doubill dalis" which he then had at Dundee.

Four months prior to the siege of Broughty Castle, Archibald Beaton II of Capeldrae was with the Scottish Army. Some say he fell at the battle of Pinkie in September 1547, but this is not so. To be precise he was killed on the day previous to the battle.

The Scottish Army under the Earl of Arran had taken up its position behind the river Esk, awaiting the approach of the English Army under the Duke of Somerset. The English appeared in due course and, after a period of reconnaissance, they finally occupied the brow of Falside Hill facing the Scots. As had happened before, during the period before an impending battle, the Scots were restless and difficult to restrain from engaging the enemy. They could not refrain from skirmishing in front of the English lines and on Friday ninth September the day prior to the battle a body of Scottish horse, under Lord Hume, galloped tauntingly before the enemy's lines. A company of English cavalry took up the challenge followed by a thousand men-at-arms. The engagement which followed resulted in the capture of Hume's son and six other officers and two priests. Hume's cavalry were cut to pieces. He himself was hurt and was carried to Edinburgh while most of the Scottish foot-soldiers who took part in the action shared the same fate as the cavalry. The records of the century refer to the action as the battle of Falside and the name of Archibald Beaton "of Capildra" appears in a list of landowners who died that day. Three other Fife men of property Robert Douglas of Kirkness Beaton's kinsman, Henderson of Fordel and master Alex. Kynnymont all died at Pinkie the following day.

Archibald the II of Capeldrae married Janet Duddingston of Sandford by whom he had one son and four daughters. He also had a natural son named Archibald and it is of him that we will have something to say.

Archibald III of Capeldrae

We first hear of him in 1565 when he is witness to a Deed in which he is referred to as "of Capeldrae", and in the year following he is mentioned as being present at Queen Mary's court having newly returned from France bearing four thousand gold scudi, a present to the Queen from James Beaton the Scottish ambassador in Paris. In 1567 the Privy Council passed a precept of legitimation making him the lawful son of his deceased father, and by now he was one of the ushers of the Queen's chamber and was present at Kirk-o-Fields when Lord Darnley was murdered. He gave evidence at the inquiry into the murder and while a certain degree of suspicion rested on him as to the possibility of his being in the plot, he was subsequently cleared of all suspicion. Archibald Beaton, as the Queen's usher, had in his possession the keys of the chamber in which the Queen slept, which was directly under that used by Darnley. The Earl of Bothwell, on more than one occasion, tried unsuccessfully to obtain the keys but on each occasion Beaton remained faithful to the trust placed in him. Archibald Beaton remained in the Queen's service during her imprisonment and during her flight to England. In 1571 he, along with his kinsman Andrew Beaton and others, was expressly forbidden to remain in the Queen's household and he is last heard of as being in France where he probably ended his days. In 1578 he along with many others who had adhered to the Queen's cause (including the Earl of Bothwell) were declared traitors and the lieges were commanded not to help them in any way whatsoever, and as for those who had gone abroad, the masters of ships were forbidden to transport any of them or their servants back to this country on pain of death and the confiscation of their ships.

John Beaton of Capeldrae

John Beaton first appears in 1548, the year following his father's death, when he had a charter of the lands of Finglassie, a small estate in the parish of Kinglassie. He married Isabel Scott some time before 1555. He does not appear to have come into possession of Capeldrae right away, at least not to have enjoyed the fruits of the estate. In terms of a Deed signed at Holyrood House in January 1577, Michael Balfour of Monquhamie was made a gift of the proceeds from the lands of Capeldrae which had accrued since the death of Archibald Beaton. The gift was to remain until the entry of the lawful heir to the estate. In addition to Finglassie, John Beaton possessed the estate of Wester Cartmore and in 1568 he gave sasine to David Gaw and Elizabeth Forrett his wife for these lands at a yearly rent of £9 19/-d Scots.

This year, 1568, found John Beaton holding tightly to a dark secret, a secret perhaps only known to two persons in the neighbourhood, the other person being John Beaton's half cousin James Wardlaw, brother of the Laird of Inchgall. Another associate in the enterprise to which they had pledged their assistance, was James Hamilton of Roughbank, a son of Gavin Hamilton who figured in the stirring days of the period. Although each was to play a small part in the plot, they along with many other confederates, were hopeful of its success. This was to be the third attempt at achieving their objective and any delay would make their task all the more difficult. Moreover, Queen Mary had now recovered from her recent illness and was all the more able to play her part in her escape from Lochleven Castle.

35 *Lochleven Castle in 1770*

The first attempt, which was to have involved the use of a large boat which lay at the landing stage at Kinross and was used for transporting coal to the castle and capable of holding upwards of eighty-eight men who were to have stormed the castle and carried off the Queen, had not advanced much further than the discussion stage. It was

117

frustrated in its early stage by William Drysdale, the officer of the guard within the castle who, having become aware of what was afoot, gave orders to have the boat laid up on the shore and secured with chains so that the scheme never really got off the ground.

In the second attempt the plotters chose the age-old stratagem of impersonation. They planned that the Queen would momentarily assume the role of a washerwoman who made a weekly call at the castle to collect the Queen's laundry and who by now had become well-known to Sir William Douglas, the Queen's custodian, and his retainers as she came and went in a small boat rowed by two men. George Douglas, Sir William's younger brother was, from the beginning, foremost among those who schemed to effect the Queen's escape. He soon gained the confidence of Margaret Aitken, a Kinross woman who was the Queen's laundress (work for which she received two and a half chalders of Fife barley).

On having the proposed scheme explained to her, and the part she would play, Margaret Aitken agreed to participate, and on the 25th March, the day for her next visit to the castle, she set out no doubt with a little trepidation. On reaching the island, she went as usual to the Queen's chamber. There, by arrangement, the Queen changed into Margaret's outer dress and, putting on a hood and muffler and carrying a fardel of linen in her arms, she passed through the castle courtyard unsuspected by anyone and reached the boat. However, the hood and muffler seen at close quarters by the boatmen aroused their suspicion and when one of them teasingly tried to remove the hood saying "lets see what kind of dame this is", the Queen exposed her white and delicate hands. The boat by now was a short distance from the island and although she charged them on peril of their lives to row her to the shore, they refused and returned to the castle.

The upshot of this almost successful escape by the Queen resulted in her being removed from the Glassin tower situated on the barmkin wall to the main tower of the castle, and George Douglas was forthwith expelled from the castle island. This however, did not weaken his resolve to do all in his power to work for the Queen's liberation. His removal on the orders of the Regent Moray caused an estrangement between the two brothers. George Douglas continued to remain in the vicinity of Kinross and openly made his presence known to the occupants of the castle. He appears to have been in the habit of taking his horse into the loch and riding out into the shallow water as far as safety would allow. There he would wave a white cloth in the hope of attracting the Queen's attention to assure her that he was still working on her behalf. His behaviour greatly annoyed Sir William, so much so that on one occasion he ordered a cannon shot to be directed at his brother. By now the only person remaining in the castle whose sympathies lay with the Queen was Willie Douglas, a page of doubtful parentage but generally believed to be a natural child of his guardian, Sir William.

Meanwhile, George Douglas succeeded in securing the support of several of the nobles who still espoused the Queen's cause, the foremost of these being Lord Seton. There was also John Sempil, the husband of Mary Livingston one of the Queen's "four Maries", and John Beaton of Balfarge, brother of the Archbishop of Glasgow and nephew of the parson of Ballingry, and therefore a second cousin of John Beaton of Capeldrae.

Among those who knew of the efforts being made to effect the Queen's escape, was

36 *Mary, Queen of Scots*

Mary Fleming, her cousin. She somehow managed to have a ring conveyed to the Queen on which was depicted Aesop's fable of the Lion and the Mouse. Remembering how the mouse in the fable gnawed through the hempen ropes which bound the lion and set it free, the Queen saw in the ring a token of assurance that her friends were doing all in their power to enable her to regain her freedom.

The strict injunction of the Regent Moray forbidding George Douglas to enter the castle, appears to have been somewhat relaxed so that we find the Queen entrusting him with a letter to be delivered to the Regent Moray. Moray, for his part, had obviously abandoned his former suspicions and entrusted Douglas with his reply to the Queen, but he had no sooner done so than he began to have his doubts as to the wisdom of his action and immediately sent a messenger with all speed to instruct Sir William Douglas that on no account was he to allow his brother to enter the castle. Somehow, George Douglas became aware of this and he made every effort to outstrip the messenger. He arrived at Kinross before his competitor and straightway made for the loch. The letter bearing the Regent's seal was sufficient warranty for his commanding a boat to take him to the island and on entering the castle he immediately sought an audience with the Queen. With a rider hot on his heels, he made the most of the little time he had by throwing the letter on the table and immediately turning to the subject of her liberation. He acquainted her of the many friends she had on shore and of a scheme he had in mind, and stressed the need for her to make a friend of Willie Douglas, who had a better opportunity of serving her than most as he was in charge of the boats and was constantly coming and going between the castle and the shore.

Moray's messenger was seen about to leave the shore for the castle and this was the moment for George Douglas to depart. The Queen gave him a communication to be delivered to Lord Seton. As she was deprived of writing materials, she contrived to write a hurried message using soot from the chimney in place of ink and a napkin for paper. At the last moment she gave George Douglas a pearl earring which, if it could be returned to her, would serve as a signal that the scheme was finalised and she would know to be ready to play her part.

The Queen soon won over Willie Douglas with little presents of money and other kindnesses and it was not long before he was daily absorbed in working out little stratagems. He was a bright, intelligent youth, inclined to be over zealous, and at times his actions bordered on recklessness. It was one such indiscretion that induced Sir William Douglas to be suspicious of his actions and at length he too was expelled from the castle.

This turned out for the Queen's adherents not such a disaster as it first appeared. With Willie Douglas now living in Kinross, George Douglas and his fellow conspirators had ample opportunity of discussing their scheme with him. Now that he knew exactly the part he was to play in the plot, the difficulty was how Willie Douglas could be re-instated in his post. It was decided that this could best be achieved by approaching someone residing in the castle. So it turned out that George Douglas contrived to meet his sister by the merest chance (for so he made it appear) on one of her visits to Kinross. He appealed to her to intercede with her father to have Willie re-instated in his former post in attending to the boats at the castle. As the person appointed to take charge of the boats since Willie Douglas's expulsion was then suffering from a gunshot wound, Sir William needed little persuasion to accept his daughter's suggestion. With Willie back once more in the castle there was now no reason for any further delay in putting the scheme into operation.

In order to allay any suspicion of a pending plot, George Douglas had some days previously acquainted his mother, the Dowager Lady Douglas, and his brother, Sir William, of his intention of seeking his fortune in France. It so happened that the day following Willie Douglas's return to the castle, Lady Douglas rowed over to Kinross to say goodbye to her son before his supposed departure. With every detail of the enterprise complete, George Douglas seized this excellent opportunity of returning the earring to the Queen, the signal to her to be ready. On presenting a small packet wrapped in dirty paper containing the earring, he said to his mother that one of the boatman had found it on the shore and had offered to sell it to him, but as he recognised

37 *Queen Mary's escape from Loch Leven Castle*

it as belonging to the Queen, he had kept it until he had found an opportunity of restoring it to her. It was thus that Lady Douglas, who was the last person who would willingly have taken part in such a scheme, was the innocent bearer to the Queen of an object that was to set in motion a chain of events calculated to result in her escape from the castle within the short space of twenty-four hours.

No sooner had George Douglas succeeded in returning the earring than he proceeded to advise by special messenger all those who were loyal to the Queen to be ready to assemble with their armed retainers at a moment's notice. These included the laird of Inchgall and his kinsman Alexander Wardlaw, laird of Riccarton. A little earlier, John Beaton of Balfarge had crossed the Forth to make final arrangements with Lord Seton and Lord Hamilton for their crossing over to Fife with a sufficient number of horsemen to act as a bodyguard to the Queen. The hours that were to follow were the most crucial when it would be seen if the long weeks of preparation were to end in success or failure. Meanwhile, as part of the plot to ensure that the occupants of the castle would not observe any unusual activity on the shore near Kinross, Willie Douglas announced that he would treat the household to a special meal the following day to be followed by a little festivity, the cost of which was secretly provided by the Queen. This was ostensibly to celebrate his return to the castle, but the astute Willie obtained Sir William's permission to hold the meal in a small guest chamber, the only apartment within the castle where it was impossible to look out on the village of Kinross.

Willie Douglas had arranged the day well. The members of the household were entertained by their host. Willie succeeded so well that he had everyone laughing at his mimicry. Then he called upon the company to partake in one of the popular burlesque pastimes of the period and as "The Abbot of Unreason" Willie gave each of his guests a small branch and from the Queen he extracted a promise that she would follow him wherever he went for the rest of the day. In this way he was able, when out of earshot of the rest of the company, to impart vital information to the Queen concerning her escape which, if everything went as arranged, was only a matter of a few hours away.

It was the late afternoon before the frolics and jesting began to abate, but as supper was not until seven in the evening, Sir William and his lady must somehow be detained in the guest chamber as long as possible. With this in view the Queen remained there knowing that Lady Douglas, whose duty it was to be forever with the Queen, would remain in the guest chamber, and as it was a Sunday evening Sir William was in a more relaxed mood and remained there also.

At length, as the evening wore on the Queen returned to the tower accompanied by Lady Douglas. As the Queen lay resting on a couch, Lady Douglas got into conversation with the woman who kept the inn at Kinross. Overhearing the conversation, the Queen learned that a company of horsemen headed by Lord Seton had passed through the village that day, news indeed! and that George Douglas was still staying at the inn. These items of news, especially the first, must have told the Queen that the preparations on the shore were moving rapidly, and she would no doubt reflect that the success of the enterprise, upon which she was now about to partake, depended almost entirely on the dexterity and sagacity of Willie Douglas. A little before supper she replaced her ordinary dress with a red kertle belonging to one of her attendants and covering it with a long mantle, she went out into the garden where she met the Dowager Lady Douglas. As they walked and talked, the people who were out for their Sunday evening walk along the shore of the loch were seen quite plainly. It was then that Lady Douglas saw a small company of horsemen on the road coming from the direction of Benarty Hill.

Earlier in the day, James Wardlaw, acting as guide led forty of Lord Seton's horsemen to a secluded part of the hill overlooking the loch. They probably took the route through Ballingry so as to avoid being seen by the folk of Kinross. No doubt the efforts of James Wardlaw and John Beaton of Capeldrae, acting as guides would be welcome, as their local knowledge would be of considerable value. There is a tradition that, in addition to the horsemen situated on Benarty, there was a company of mounted men to the number of sixty posted at the West Lomonds overlooking the loch in the vicinity of Balgeddie. Here again, if tradition is founded on fact, in all probability they took the route by the east side of the loch as, coming from the south and using the west route, they would require to pass through the village of Kinross in full view of the inhabitants and run the grave risk of someone sending word to the keeper of the castle that something unusual was afoot. John Beaton of Capeldrae was probably the one who led this company over the treacherous ground which lay between Kirkness and the hamlet of Scotlandwell. This stretch was notorious for its swamps and marshes. At this period there was no timber bridge over the river and only those who knew the way were certain of negotiating its many hazards.

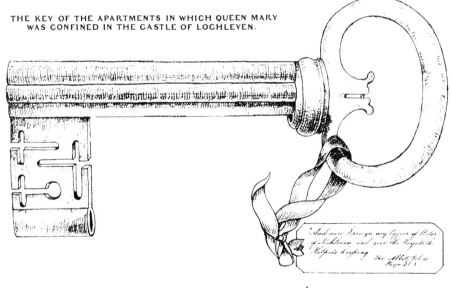

THE KEY OF THE APARTMENTS IN WHICH QUEEN MARY
WAS CONFINED IN THE CASTLE OF LOCHLEVEN.

38

THE GIFT OF SIR WALTER SCOTT TO LORD CHIEF COMMISSIONER ADAM
Printed by B Wilson Glasgow

The sight of horsemen as seen by Lady Douglas so aroused her suspicions that she was on the point of calling for a messenger to go and find out who they were and the reason for their being in the neighbourhood, when the Queen sensing that they could be none other than a detachment of Lord Seton's men, promptly engaged Lady Douglas in conversation until it was time for supper. As was his custom, Sir William waited on the Queen while she was having supper and it was not until this was over that he went to the room immediately below to have his evening meal with his wife and family. While still in the Queen's apartment, Sir William was casually looking out of the window overlooking the boats when he saw Willie Douglas engaged in some mysterious goings on — he was actually fouling the chains of all the boats except one. Sir William was furious and upbraided him from his position at the window and no doubt would have gone further had not the Queen, perceiving what was taking place, called out that she felt unwell and would Sir William bring her some wine. Meanwhile, George Douglas and John Beaton of Balfarge, who were staying at the village inn, had all but completed their preparations. On the pretence of having a slight headache John Beaton announced to the folk in the inn that he was going for a walk, and as pre-arranged George Douglas said casually that he would accompany him. The real reason for their exit was to go to the stables near the shore belonging to the Laird of Lochleven. On arriving there they broke open the door and saddled two of Sir William's horses and thereafter gave the prearranged signal by placing a light in a window in the old manse to let Willie Douglas know that they were ready and standing by.

The Queen having by now finished her supper, Sir William withdrew leaving in the room his youngest daughter and a niece to watch over the Queen. With supper being served in the common hall Willie Douglas was about to enter upon the most exacting part of the plot. It was his duty to serve at the table, in particular to attend to his master's needs and how he was to accomplish the difficult task of extracting the key of the castle gate from under Sir William's ever watchful eye, was surely uppermost in his mind as he went about his duties. Likewise the Queen, knowing that the meal was in progress downstairs, needs must be ready if and when she received the signal. Her difficulty was how to get away from the watchful eyes of the two girls. With her, as always, were her two female attendants, Jane Kennedy and Maria Courcelles. At length the Queen made it known that she wished to go to the room immediately above her own (usually occupied by her surgeon) in order to perform her daily devotions. Maria Courcelles helpfully remained in the room with the girls and succeeded in diverting their attention away from the Queen's movements. Jane Kennedy accompanied the Queen upstairs and each set about changing into the dress of country women. The Queen took off the mantle which had concealed the red kerkle she was wearing and by putting on a hood she completed her disguise. Jane Kennedy was somewhat similarly dressed and there was now nothing more to be done other than wait. Meanwhile, Willie Douglas, who was busy serving the table, was ever on the watch for an opportunity to seize the key as it lay on the table beside his master. As each course was finished, it became increasingly necessary for Willie to act, otherwise the meal would be over and the vital opportunity lost. Wine was called for, and as he entered the hall with the flaggon and goblets, he braced himself for the all-important manoeuvre. In handing the wine to Sir William, a napkin he was carrying slipped from his arm, as if by accident on to the table, covering the key. Willie casually as it were, lifted the napkin with the key enclosed in it and immediately left the hall. The surgeon who was sitting beside Sir William (so it is said) saw the manoeuvre expertly performed and engaged Sir William in lively conversation so that the incident passed almost unnoticed.

On his way to the courtyard, Willie Douglas gave the signal to the Queen's attendant at an upstairs window. Immediately the Queen and Jane Kennedy began to descend the spiral stair, passing on their way the room where Maria Courcelles was playing with the children. Further down they slipped past the doorway leading into the hall where the evening meal was all but finished, and out on to the outer stair of the tower which descended into the courtyard. Meanwhile, Willie Douglas had unlocked the courtyard gate and the three conspirators passed out, not without being noticed. One or two of the domestics looked on in bewilderment, while a washerwoman who understood more readily what was taking place, recognised the Queen, but Willie Douglas called her name and told her to hold her tongue. After locking the gate from the outside Willie threw the key into the mouth of a nearby cannon and conducted his charges to the one and only boat which was serviceable. The Queen concealed herself in the bottom of the boat, while Willie Douglas and Jane Kennedy took to the oars. When they had gone some distance from the castle the Queen stood up and gave the pre-arranged signal to those who were concealed on Benarty and to those who were waiting at Kinross and Balgeddie, by waving a white veil fringed with red. The spot where the Queen landed is not known for certain. As the surface of the loch was four and a half feet higher than at present, the margin of the loch must have been much nearer Kinross. Tradition has it that the boat landed in the vicinity of the Sandport.

On stepping ashore, the Queen was met by George Douglas and John Beaton along with ten horsemen. In a few moments the company was mounted, all except Jane Kennedy who was to follow as soon as an outfit could be obtained, and were off heading south for Queensferry. As they approached Benarty, they were joined by Lord Seton and the Laird of Riccarton and forty horsemen. Upon receiving the Queen's signal they had come out of their place of concealment on the hill and had headed westward to join the Queen's bodyguard. No doubt those in the castle of Inchgall who were in the secret, would cast many an anxious eye in the direction of Blaircrambeth that evening, looking for a company of horsemen pressing southward from the direction of Paran Well, a sight that would tell them that the plot so far had been successful and that the Queen was indeed free again.

The road at this period, if a beaten track could be named as such, as it skirted the west shoulder of Benarty Hill, lay to the east of its successor, the Great North Road, more or less equal to the distance that this road lies to the east of *its* successor, the modern dual carriageway. This trio of roads lies in what was known of old as the Pass of Benarty. The Queen's party took the high ground at an elevation probably a little less than that occupied by the targets of the modern rifle range. Like most of the medieval roads having no foundation, the pounding of animals hoofs and travellers feet soon turned them into sunken paths or hollow-ways. This characteristic is still discernible, but just, on the line of the old road as it approaches Paran Well. In William Adam's day it was more easily seen, and to mark its position where the road to Ballingry crosses it, he erected a monumental arch to mark its width where, if one looks towards the hill, there can still be seen a slight hollow in the adjoining field.

The Queen did not rest that evening until she had reached Niddrie Castle, the home of Lord Seton. Shortly afterwards Henry Wardlaw, Laird of Inchgall, and his son Andrew, joined the Queen at Hamilton and were present at the battle of Langside. In consequence of their actions they were, along with many others, found guilty of treason, but action was deferred on the authority of the Regent Moray.

The Queen's imprisonment lasted from 17th June, 1567, to 2nd May, 1568, during which time the amount of food consumed in the castle included 116 geese, 512 capons and 672 poultry. The records of the period give the total cost of maintaining the Queen as £1,389.1.0d.

Returning to John Beaton of Capeldrae, we meet with him again in 1577 when he paid to the Exchequer £300, a sum that had accrued in respect of the lands of Easter Capeldrae. In this year he is also referred to as "of Pitlochie", a small estate in the parish of Kinglassie that had been acquired by his father. By now John Beaton must have had some thoughts of parting with Capeldrae.

In 1579, the King at Stirling Castle confirmed a charter by John Beaton of Pitlochie who, with the consent of his son and heir apparent, John Beaton, had sold in 1577 the eastern half of Capeldrae and the meadow there to Andrew Arnot, minister of Scotlandwell and Isobelle Spence his wife, who up till then had, along with Archibald Dick, been his sub-tenants. From now on the Beatons ceased to be mentioned in connection with these lands. John Beaton is last heard of in 1585 when he possessed the mill of Duchal in Renfrewshire, and in this same year he appended his name to the confirmation charter of King James VI to the Burgh of Dunfermline. He had a sister called Margaret, who married George Forrister of Strathhenry who held half the lands of Crosshill under the Wardlaws. His son and heir, who agreed to the sale of Capeldrea, stood surety in 1575 to the amount of 2,000 merks for his kinsman Alexander Beaton, in order that he be allowed out of Blackness Castle where he had been held prisoner.

John Beaton, junior, married Barbara Trail after 1577. In this year he and his future wife were given sasine of the lands of Middle Baldridge and the Masonlands in Dunfermline by the monastery there. From now on he may have lived in the neighbourhood of Dunfermline.

Before leaving the Beatons, we would mention that Archibald Beaton the First of Capeldrae was the progenitor of the branch of the Beatons who settled in Skye. They became the hereditary physicians to the clans MacDonald and Macleod and for their services they were offered as much land as they desired. It was agreed that as long as their sept remained on the island, one Beaton of each generation would practise medicine. Farquhar Beaton, the sixth in descent from the Laird of Capeldrae, was a distinguished surgeon and for his services to the hundreds of men from Skye who fought at the battle of Worcester in 1651, their leader Sir Norman McLeod of Bernera, commended him for his outstanding gallantry in the action.

Almost one hundred years later, another Beaton of Skye and his newly wedded wife gave succour to Prince Charles and his guide. Beaton and his wife remained unaware as to the identity of their guests until, following the offer of a drink of milk which was accepted, the elder of the two men produced a gold cup so that his youthful companion might drink from it. The wayfarers in due course continued on their way across the moors, but before leaving the house, the elder man offered his host three gold pieces, and confirmed what they had by now guessed, that the youth was indeed Prince Charles Edward Stuart.

Following the death of the Rev. Andrew Arnot and his wife, Capeldrae passed to their son George who was in possession in 1630. In April of that year, Patrick Murray of

126

Williamston and John Sinclair of Balgreggie, both heritors in Auchterderran, complained to the presbytery that George Arnot of Capeldrae had taken possession of their rowme (seat) in Auchterderran kirk. George Arnot maintained that he had a right to the rowme in question. It appears that this was only the tip of the iceberg and that the whole question of the allocation of seats in the kirk required urgent investigation. Four months afterwards during which time the matter had been fully discussed an amicable solution was found and each of the thirteen heritors was assigned a seat in a new position in the kirk.

It may be that the Laird of Capeldrae was prone to act high-handedly, for in 1634 he lodged a complaint with the presbytery that Mr Chalmers the minister would not allow him to take Communion. The presbytery got over the difficulty, at least for the moment, by advising him to put his complaint in "wreat" (writing). We hear no more of George Arnot, and in 1636 it is one David Arnot who is in possession.

In 1662 Capeldrae was held by Andrew Arnot the son and heir of George Arnot. Andrew found himself in straightened circumstances and in 1665 Capeldrae was apprised in favour of James Arnot of Ferney, his kinsman, who received the sum of £1,042. In the following year James Arnot assigned his interest in the estate to William Arnot, Andrew Arnot still being the proprietor.

In all, the Arnot family held Capeldrae for a little over a century. In 1682 when the estate was sold to David Dewar of Muirton, Advocate, by reason of so many apprisings, the consent of Major William Arnot, David Arnot and Archibald Turner, an Edinburgh minister and others had to be obtained. With the resignation of David Boswell of Balmuto as superior of the lands, they were sold to David Dewar for the sum of £1,726.0.4d.

On 15th March, 1685, parliament ratified a charter of novadamus in favour of David Dewar of the lands of Muirton, Pitkinny, Capeldrae, and the shadow half of Balbedie. By the turn of the seventeenth century, a family by the name of Abercrombie had an interest in Capeldrae under the Dewars. By the middle of the nineteenth century the estate belonged to James Aytoun, Advocate, son of Major-General Roger Aytoun of Inchdairnie and Jean Sinclair, his wife who was descended from the Sinclairs of Balgreggie. James Aytoun could claim descent from John Aytoun of Over Pittadie in the parish of Kinghorn who appeared there in the fourteenth century. The estate had not long come into the possession of the new laird when he set about developing its mineral resources. Along with the Goodall family of Bowhill he established the Capeldrae Cannel Coal Company.

James Aytoun, who was unmarried, spent much of his time in the family town house at 39 Heriot Row, Edinburgh, along with his sisters. He was an admirer of the works of Robert Burns and published a booklet (now exceedingly scarce) which contained a translation into the French language of the poems, *Tam o' Shanter* and *The Twa Dogs*.

James Aytoun was succeeded in the lands of Capeldrae by his youngest brother Robert Aytoun, Advocate, who married in 1844, Helen Louisa Adelaide, daughter of George Reid Maughan, London. Robert Aytoun died in 1874.

39 *Commemorative Arch at Paran Well erected by Chief Commissioner William Adam*

THE LESLIE FAMILY

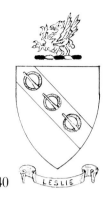

40

The family of Leslie derives its name from lands in the district of Garioch in Aberdeenshire where Malcolm son of Bartolf their ancestor received the lands of Lesslyn from William the Lyon in the late twelfth century. Sir Norman Leslie of Leslie acquired Fythkill in the thirteenth century and changed the name to Leslie and thus established the family's connection with Fife.

John Leslie, 6th Earl of Rothes, who came to own Inchgall was a half-brother to Agnes Leslie, wife of Andrew Wardlaw. In the Register of Royal Letters there is a note to be found addressed to King Charles I, dated 31st July 1632 which appears to have accompanied a deed of conveyance, which reads as follows:

May it pleas your Matie

These conteyne ane disposition by your Matie to Johne Erle of Rothes his heyres — male and assigneyis of the particular landis above written, all erected in one baronie called the baronie of Inchgall, patronage of the personage and viccarage of the kirk of Ballingrie vpon the resignation of Andro Wardlaw of Torrie and Mr. David Ayton with ane new gift of the whole lands and others forsiads, and ane union of the samyne in ane frie baronie, to be called the baronie of Inchgall and that ane sasine to be takin at the place of Inchgall sal be good and valide for the whole, to be holdin of your Matie and highnes successours in frie heretage and frie baronie for ever, for payment of the dewteis and performeing the services and conditions conteynit in the old infeftments payed to your Matie befor the Resignation — Oatlands, last day of July 1632.

The Earl had the following royal charter of the lands and barony of Inchgall signed at Whitehall on 3rd November 1632:

"The King with consent granted and of new gave to John, Earl of Rothes, Lord Leslie and of Ballinbreiche, and his heirs male, and of tailzie contained in his infeftment of the lands and the barony of Ballinbreiche and their assignees whosoever, the Maynes of Inchgall with the manor house, the lands of Flockhous and Bowhous of

129

Inchgall with the loch of Inchgall, the castle, the patronage of the Chappell and Chaplanrie of Inchgall, with the mill, the lands of Balbegie, Clune, Cairthmoir, Lumphynnanes Souther and Norther, Lochheid, Spittal, Ballingrie, Navitie and Quonthill, the hill called Bannerthy, with the patronage of the parsonage and vicarage of the parish kirk of Ballingrie, a quarter of the lands of Blaircrambethe and Kinnaird, half of Drumlochthornoche and Byn, the lands of Laddathe, Blaircusnie, with the village and lands of Corshil above Inchgall, the lands of Balfarg with the loch and mosses, with mills, fishings, coal heughs, lochs, moors, tennants etc. in the barony of Wester Lochoreschyre in the shire of Fife, which lands David Aytoun servitor of Andrew Aytoun of Logie, advocate (at whose instance they were apprised from Andrew Wardlaw of Torrie, son of the late Patrick Wardlaw of Torrie), also the said Andrew Wardlaw and his testamentary tutors resigned in favour of the said Earl, as assignee of the said Mr. David, these follow a ratification of prior charters, in addition the King incorporated all the above written into the free barony of Inchgall ordaining the tower and manorplace of Inchgall to be the principle messuage".

The Earl at first opposed King Charles' measures in Scotland and strongly supported the Covenant and was one of the commissioners deputed to settle the pacification of Berwick in 1639, and in the following year he was nominated by the Scottish Parliament to treat with the English. He latterly became reconciled to the King and endeavoured to modify the Scottish Parliament's measures towards the Monarch in view of the King's impending visit to Scotland. The Earl took ill in London and could not accompany the King and died there six weeks after the King's departure from London in 1641. John Leslie married Lady Anne Erskine and had one son and two daughters.

John Leslie, 7th Earl of Rothes

John Leslie was eleven years of age when he succeeded to the title in April 1642. He resided with his father-in-law the Earl of Crawford at Struthers until 1650 after which he took up residence at the family house at Leslie. When King Charles II arrived in Scotland in 1650 the young Earl came into close contact with him and in the following year he carried the Sword of State at the King's Coronation. He accompanied the royal army into England and was taken prisoner at the battle of Worcester in 1651 and was imprisoned in the Tower of London and in 1654 was taken to Newcastle. Through the intervention of the Countess of Dysart, he was set at liberty in 1655, but his estates were sequestrated in July of the following year. The lands of Leslie, Ballinbreich and Inchgall, with the exception of north and south Lumphinnans, were apprised by Robert Dempster of Pitliver in satisfaction of a debt amounting to 24,832 merks, 12 shillings and 4 pence.

The deed which was subject to the legal reversion was granted by Oliver Cromwell. Two years afterwards the Earl was again imprisoned, on this occasion in Edinburgh Castle on the orders of Cromwell. After remaining there for almost a year he was allowed to return home largely through the intervention of General Monk. Following the restoration of King Charles II, the Earl had a distinguished career. He was appointed High Chancellor of Scotland and was created Duke of Rothes. He died at Holyrood House in 1681 leaving two daughters.

THE MALCOLM FAMILY AND ITS TIMES

41

The person who followed the Earl of Rothes as Laird of Inchgall in 1656 was John Malcolm who had been Chamberlain for Fife since 1641. We hear of him as possessing the nearby lands of Balbedie belonging formerly to James Colville of Balbedie, when in 1645 he petitioned Parliament to grant him permission to alter the direction of the highway as it passed by his house.

The Malcolm family's interest in Balbedie arose out of the conditions of a loan which John Malcolm had given to James Colville in his time of need. The laird of Balbedie died shortly afterwards and the lands of Balbedie devolved on his son, Robert. As the loan had not been repaid within the specified period of seven years, the shady half of the lands of Balbedie was apprised in 1645 in favour of John Malcolm from Robert Colville for the sum of £12,093, the amount of the loan.

In a charter of confirmation which John Malcolm received the following year, the King granted him the sunny half of Balbedie along with half of the Maynes lands of East Wemyss, which lands had also belonged to James Colville. From this time onwards the Malcolm family were in possession of the whole of the barony of Balbedie.

It was also about this time that John Malcolm purchased from Sir George Erskine the lands of Innertiel, near Kirkcaldy, for £40,000 and in 1668 he had a charter under the Great Seal annexing the lands of Glengarnock in Ayrshire to the barony of Innertiel.

The Act of Parliament dealing with the road at Balbedie states that "the hieway gaitt and passage that leides by the south syde of the duelling house of Balbedie and by the barne and barne yaird thereof and by the houses of his tennentes and doores which by all men on horse and foot travelles and has travelled is verie hurtfull noysome and prejudiciall to John Malcome now of Balbedie and his tennentes and may be more commodiouslie hade ane other way by goeing northward at the eist end of the said house and yairdes". In consideration of the foregoing John Malcolm is given full power and liberty "to alter and change the sid gaite and passage from any farder going or comeing in tyme comeing which hes bene in use to be in tyme bygone and to caus the said gaitt be made and used in goeing north at the eist end of the syde house and yairds and thereafter west by the north side thereof which new way and passage the said John Malcome and his foirsaides shall be haldine to cause make and repair in ane sufficient and large gaitway and passage for horsemen and footmen and for cairtes slaides loades and otheres comeing goeing and travelling that way and for this effect gives power to cause stopt bigg up and condemnne the said way and passage by the south syde of the duelling house".

This of course was the highway leading to Leslie, whereabout two miles further north it came to the River Leven where no doubt the river would be crossed by means of a brig-o-trees. Whether Parliament's concession to John Malcolm had anything to do with his having to build a stone bridge over the river, no one can say, but this he was obliged to do. The inscription on the old Auchmuir bridge reads as follows:—

"Ken ye this brig, wi a' its largess,
Was built at Balbedie's proper charges;
Let no man o' Balbedie yet boast,
Quile this brig served him at Balbedie's cost."

In the following year (1646) John Malcolm had a Crown charter erecting the "sunny" half and the "shady" half of the lands of Balbedie into the barony of Balbedie with the Manor-place of the easten half to be the principle messuage. He was in 1651 one of the signatories to the "Submission of the gentlemen of Fife", wherein the subscribers stated their willingness to comply with the powers set forth by the English Parliament as relating to the affairs in Scotland, The Submission was drawn up and signed at Auchterderran on 6th October of that year.

In 1654 we find him journeying to Newcastle to see his friend the Earl of Rothes, who had been held a prisoner in the Tower of London following the battle of Worcester. Two years later, in 1656, John Malcolm was granted a charter under the Great Seal of the lands and barony of Inchegall, with the exception of North and South Lumphinnans, which lands were still in the possession of the Earl of Rothes. The charter dated Edinburgh 7th August is given under the name of the Protector Cromwell.

The charter reads as follows:— The Protector grants to John Malcolme of Balbedie his heirs and assynees whomsoever, the lands and barony of Inchegall, to wit, the Maynes of Inchegall with the Manor-place, etc., thereof alias Lochorshyre. The Flockhous and Bowhous of Inchegall, and the loch of Inchegall, with the tower and fortalice thereof, the lands of Milntoun of Inchegall, with the mill etc., thereof, the lands of Balbegie, the lands of Clunie, the lands of Carthiemore, the lands of Lochheid, the lands of Spittall, the lands of Ballinyris, the lands of Navitie, and Quothill, the hills called Bannartiehills, the quarter of the lands of Blaircramboth, the quarter of the lands of Kinneire, the half of the lands of Drumquodurnoch and the half of the lands of Byne, the lands of Layache, the lands of Blaircushney, and toun and lands of Corshill above Inchegall, and the lands of Balfarg and the loch and myre thereof, with the mill, woods, fishings etc., thereof, all in the barony of Inchegall called Lochorshyre and

133

sherrifdom of Fif:— excepting from the said disposition the lands of Souther and Nother Lumphennans, which were part of the said barony, notwithstanding which exception the tennants of the said excepted lands, pertaining to John, Earl of Rothes, Lord Leslie, shall be astricted in all time coming to the said mill of Inchegall:— which lands, barony, mill etc., pertaining to the said Earl and were resigned by him in favour of the said John Malcolme and his foresaids:— one sasine to be sufficient:— to be held of the Protector for the rights of services contained in the old infeftments.

John Malcolm of Lochore

Two years later in 1662, after the restoration of the Monarchy, John Malcolm received a new charter erecting the lands of Balbedie and Inchgall into one barony. In this charter, the right given in 1511 to erect the town of Crosshill into a free burgh of barony is renewed. He is given power to buy and sell all sorts of merchandise and to choose and elect magistrates and freemen and to have merchants and all kinds of tradesmen within the burgh. Friday of each week was to be a market day and there was to be a two-day free Fair held on 22nd and 23rd March and 27th and 28th June in each year when all kinds of goods made within the burgh were to be bought and sold. In 1669 he successfully petitioned the presbytery of Kirkcaldy to transfer his estate of Balbedie from the parish of Auchterderran to that of Ballingry, so that from henceforth the lands comprising the barony would all be within the one parish.

One can imagine that the erection of a village to the status of a burgh of barony would be looked upon as a great benefit to be welcomed by all the inhabitants. Apart from the fact that bailies and other officers could be elected to look after the welfare of the villagers, the Royal Charter conveyed to the inhabitants the right to set up local crafts and to sell their wares at the weekly market. While recognising the benefits which could have resulted from the implementation of the charter by the laird, it is to be said that of the 1511 charter very little record of the burgh life has survived. Indeed, it has to be said that it very soon decayed and disappeared altogether and had become in effect a "parchment burgh" only. This, to some extent, may have come about by the untimely death of the laird, be that as it may, there is evidence that burgh life was revived to some extent under John Malcolm.

It was about this time that the Malcolm family decided to style themselves "Malcolm of Lochore". It will be recalled that following the death of Sir David Lochore, the barony was divided into two parts, the parish of Auchterderran forming Easter Lochoreshire with Ballingry parish constituting Wester Lochoreshire, or Inchgall, as it was invariably called. While collectively the small estates situated for the most part in the parish of Ballingry constituted the barony of Inchgall, none was known by the name of Lochore. Certain evidence implies that the family residence was known initially as Inchgall House.

In order to give substance to the change the Malcolm family re-named the small estate of Ladath, Lochore estate, and Inchgall House situated as it was on this estate became known thereafter as Lochore House. It was in this way that the present-day Lochore estate come into being, there being at that period no village of that name. Of course the change did not take place over-night. For the past 300 years or so Inchgall had been the name by which the place was known. In more than one semi-official document reference is made to the *parish* of Inchgall — in error of course — but it is indicative of the universal use of the name by the local inhabitants. It is not improbable that, had the name of the barony been allowed to remain, the present-day village would have been known as Inchgall instead of Lochore.

In 1662, the year in which John Malcolm received the new charter combining Balbedie and Inchgall into one barony, he was appointed Sheriff Depute of Fife. For many years his name appears among the Commissioners appointed for the trial of witches and other offenders in many parishes throughout Fife. In 1663 he received a Crown charter of the lands of Blackford in Aberdeenshire and in the following year he was given many lands in the sheriffdom of Perth and Kinross. These grants were augmented in 1667 by a further grant of the lands of Binn, including the mill and mill lands and also the right to work the "peats and divotts" on Benarty. These lands, formerly part of the barony of Tullibole, were now to be incorporated in the barony of Inchgall.

The seventeenth century was a period in which political and religious struggles occupied the minds of most people. The average Scot, brought up in the staunch Presbyterian tradition, strongly resented the Crown supremacy over the church, and when matters came to a head many were prepared to show in no uncertain manner their opposition to the King's authority.

The century saw the unsuccessful attempt made by James VI to modify the Presbyterian form of worship by persuading the General Assembly to pass the Five Articles of Perth thus conforming more closely to Episcopacy. The attempts made by his Dunfermline-born son, Charles I to renew Jacobean Episcopacy, and the resultant persecution of the Covenanters and the religious struggles which brought about the execution of that Monarch, were followed by a somewhat quieter period under the rule of Oliver Cromwell. The restoration of the Monarchy under Charles II, who declared that Presbyterianism was no religion for a gentleman, saw the renewal of the savagery of the killing times. Fines, imprisonment, banishment and worse were the order of the day for those who were apprehended for being at conventicles. The Presbyterians in Fife had been so zealous in their attendance at conventicles that the King and his prelates came to speak of them as the "fanatics of Fife".

The death of Charles II and the rise of the Jacobites in support of his brother James VII brought about a change. James, a Roman Catholic, gave complete tolerance to all his subjects and persecution came to an end, but a return to Roman Catholicism was feared. It was not until towards the close of the century that peace returned under the reign of William of Orange. All these important events did not take place without affecting in some way the lives of the parishioners of Ballingry and as we will see, a number of people in Lochoreshire did take an active part in the events of the period.

The earliest notice of the opposition to the innovations in the worship of the church by the douce folk of Ballingry is to be found in 1620. Of the Five Articles decreed by the Assembly held at Perth in 1618, that of enjoining the kneeling position at Communion aroused hostility. At a Diocesan Synod held at St. Andrews, the Bishop asked the Rev. David Anderson of Ballingry if he had administered the Communion. The minister answered "No". On the Bishop demanding the reason, Mr Anderson replied, "My parishioners will not receive it efter that manner from me". "Is that the laird of Torrie that bade you say so" enquired the Bishop, "Tell him I bade him goe hang himself". While it does not appear that any reprisals were taken against the parishioners for their disobedience, nonetheless John Scrimgeour, minister of Kinghorn, who held land in Bowhill, was deprived of his living for opposing the Five Articles of Perth.

Things seemed to have gone along smoothly for a while after 1620. In 1634 the parishioners raised £6.11/- for the "captives of Kirkcaldy". This seems to imply an armed engagement of some sort, but its nature is not disclosed. Two years later the heritors and church elders think it is time there was a school in the parish and towards this end they agree to "stent" themselves to the amount of 100 merks (£5.11/-) to provide for the yearly salary of a schoolmaster. In 1641 Robert Bruce was admitted minister of the parish after he had taken the oath of allegiance to his Majesty, Charles I.

Ten years later, in the month of July, something occurred to break the even tenor of the village life. A few days after the battle of Inverkeithing, part of Cromwell's army passed through the village on its way to Perth, when Cromwell halted at Kirkness House and was the guest of Sir William Douglas. In September of the same year Cromwell gained his decisive victory over the Royalist forces at the battle of Worcester when the Laird of Inchgall was taken prisoner and George Bruce the minister's younger brother lost his life.

We have it on the authority of the Privy Council that field conventicles were first held in Fife and that they spread afterwards to other counties. They were first introduced by John Welsh who became famous as a field preacher. The fines imposed on those who were apprehended for attending these "disorderly meetings" were double the amount for house conventicles, but as field conventicles became more numerous the fines became much more severe. The first instance of the Privy Council having to deal with this kind of offence occurred after a conventicle held at Hill of Beath on Sunday 19th June 1670 on land belonging to Robert Moody, when it was estimated that upwards of a thousand persons attended. It was not a gathering of local people only, but a well-organised assembly with people coming from as far afield as St. Andrews, Kirkcaldy, Edinburgh and Stirling and from most of the parishes within these limits, including Ballingry, and as a sign of the unsettled condition of the times many came armed with swords and pistols.

Two services were held, conducted by the Rev. John Dickson of Rutherglen who had that year held a field conventicle at Glenvale near Kinnesswood, and the Rev. John Blackader, minister of Troqueer until he was ejected in 1662. The preacher at the forenoon service took as his text Corinthians XV-25 "for he must reign until he hath put all enemies under his feet". The speaker in the afternoon preached from Cor. IX-16 "for though I preach the gospel, I have nothing to glory of: for necessity is laid upon me; yea, woe is unto me, if I preach not the gospel". James Lamb of Dunfermline led the singing of the psalms.

It would have been surprising if such a gathering could be held without some kind of military intervention. As it was, a dragoon appeared during one of the services and tried to frighten the people by galloping among them, hoping that they would scatter. However, an armed member of the congregation at one point made a dash after the dragoon and succeeded in holding on to his horse's bridle. He asked him to remove peaceably and pulling out a pistol, he told him he would shoot him dead if he were not quiet. The dragoon was compelled to sit on horseback for the remainder of the service and at its conclusion he was allowed to go on his way.

As one can readily imagine, such conduct would not go unnoticed. By the end of the month the Privy Council was actively engaged in meting out reprisals upon those who were known to have been present at the conventicle. Adam Stoby of Luscar, William Adam of Culross, and Robert Welwood of Touch were summoned to appear before the Council under pain of rebellion. The first two ignored the summons. Robert Welwood admitted his offence and was fined 500 merks and was to be imprisoned until he paid the fine. He was also cautioned not to be present at any conventicle in the future under pain of a fine of 2,000 merks. Stoby and Adam were again summoned on 14th July along with Robert Moody of Hill of Beath, James and Alexander Hastie and James Lamb all from Dunfermline, and John Robertson from Navitie and many others living in St. Andrews, Stirling and Edinburgh. Stoby and Adam appeared personally and were fined 1,000 merks and 900 merks respectively, and Alexander Hastie was fined 300 merks. As no one would give the name of any other person who had been present at the conventicle, further punishment was administered. Stoby, Adam and Hastie were to be put in irons and imprisoned in the Tolbooth in Edinburgh while others were to be similarly treated and placed in the Canongate Tolbooth. In the case of Robert Moody and John Robertson, the Council showed some leniency. Both acknowledged having been present at the conventicle and declared themselves sorry and promised not to attend any in the future. They were accordingly dismissed without being fined. Those persons who failed to appear were forthwith denounced as rebels and their belongings forfeit.

Meanwhile the work of sifting out the names of guilty persons went on apace. Thomas Tenant of Moss-side was at Hill of Beath, but on being questioned he refused to comply with the injuction not to attend conventicles in the future. He was therefore fined 100 merks and imprisoned until the fine was paid. Margaret Martin and Bessie Young, servants of Lady Colville, on refusing to divulge the name of persons, were ordered to be put in prison. They remained there for a period of nine weeks until the magistrates of Edinburgh were ordered to set them at liberty. Among the lists of persons who were cited to appear before the Council are the following names of people who resided in and around Hill of Beath — Robert Kirk of Keirsbeath, David Dykes of

137

Netherbeath, Catherine Stewart, daughter of Lady Beath, Margaret Beveridge of Keirsbeath, John Collier of Dunfermline, Beatrice Cunningham of Kinnaird, John Reid of Cairney Bridge, Thomas Hutton of West Luscar, and "the good man of Craigtoun and his wife in Cleish Parish." James Dundas, son of the Laird of Dundas, refused to give information concerning people who were present at Hill of Beath. He was accordingly ordered to be imprisoned in the Tolbooth in Edinburgh until such time that he could be transported out of the Kingdom. The sentence would have been carried out had it not been for the intervention of James Dundas, his uncle. He petitioned the Council that his nephew be recalled and given the opportunity of answering the questions put to him. This was done and Dundas was set at liberty. An entry of 16th August shows others to have been made of sterner stuff. Under this date the Council considered the cases of Adam Stoby, William Adam and Alexander Hastie, also James Shish, David Mather, John Rankin and James Duncan. As they had all refused to disclose what they knew concerning the conventicle, they were one and all sentenced to be banished furth of the Kingdom. They were to be shipped to the plantations in America at the first opportunity, meanwhile they were to remain in the Tolbooth in Edinburgh. In the week that followed Robert Welwood of Touch had managed to pay his fine of 500 merks and was accordingly released from prison.

The period was one of mounting pressure imposed by Parliament upon Presbyterian ministers and their congregations. The Act of 1662 held that all ministers who had entered on their charges before 1649 must leave their churches and manses unless inducted in Episcopal order before November of that year. Almost four hundred ministers left their charges and took to preaching in private houses and afterwards in the open. This was the origin of the field conventicles. Many of the field preachers had sums of money placed on their heads and when apprehended they were imprisoned and afterwards banished. Penalties became increasingly severe following the Pentland Rising and at the height of the persecutions a person could have been shot for attending a conventicle.

Fines were imposed for non-attendance at church and for attending a church other than in the parish where one resided. The "outed" ministers were severely dealt with. Acts were passed forbidding them to come within sight of their parishes. To speak to or to give food or clothing or give shelter to an ejected preacher or anyone declared a rebel was to run the risk of being fined or thrown into prison. Conversely, it appears to have been an offence not to protect or shield a "King's" minister, or anyone engaged in carrying out the orders of the public authorities. An instance of this judicial madness occurred in 1682 when David Arnot, late of Capeldrae, was flung into the Edinburgh Tolbooth and fined £226, for not going to the assistance of the Rev. George Drummond who had been attacked by the parishioners in the church of Dron while he was reading an edict for the settlement of a minister presented to the church by Charles II, but whom the people did not want. The Privy Council ordered all those who had been in the church, young and old, to be questioned, and those who had not assisted the minister were to be either fined, imprisoned or scourged as an example to others. Arnot who was one of the heritors of the parish appealed against his sentence maintaining that he was not present in the church when the disturbance took place. Common sense prevailed and he was acquitted.

By 1674 many conventicles had been held in Fife. During the first half of that year more than a score are known to have taken place. Following one held in the Lomond Hills when the dragoons were met with armed resistance, Parliament gave orders for troops of horses and companies of foot soldiers to be stationed in such places as were best suited for searching out and seizing vagrant preachers. A reward of 2,000 merks was offered to anyone who would apprehend an "outed" minister and the fines imposed on anyone who was found guilty of being present at a field conventicle were to go to the informant. By mid-summer forty persons mostly heritors were cited to appear before the Privy Council for their part in these unlawful meetings. The fines ranged from £49 to £1,000 Scots.

Meanwhile, arrangements were being made for the quartering of troops in certain places throughout Fife. The Commissioners of Excise under John Malcolm were to fix the prices at which oats, hay and straw were to be sold to the dragoons for their horses. They were also to see to the provision of bedding, pots, pans and candles for the soldiers. By 1675 a garrison consisting of half a company of foot soldiers and twelve horsemen was stationed at Dowhill Castle, a little to the north of Kelty under the command of Captain Buchan. Other companies were placed at Culross, Falkland and Cupar where each was responsible for patrolling a given area of the county.

Notwithstanding the presence of these armed patrols, house and field conventicles continued to be held and by 1667 Auchterderran, Ballingry, Cleish, Kinnesswood, Balbedie, Kinninmont, Kirkness, and many places further afield were the venue of many an illegal gathering. Not surprisingly, the number of persons apprehended had by now increased considerably. The list is a long one and we will only mention these persons who lived within our neighbourhood.

John Collier of Lochgelly was denounced a rebel at the market cross in Dunfermline and among many others who were "put to the horn" and had their estates confiscated were David Barclay of Auchterderran, George Gray in the Bowhouse, George Barclay of Kinnaird, Patrick Hutton in the Blair, Alexander Barclay in East Blair, Lindsay elder and younger of Dowhill, George Birrel and George Miller in Kinnesswood and David Barclay, Robert Robertson, James Reid, Robert Meldrum and George Gibson in Ballingry.

In the following year (1678) John Collier of Wester Lochgelly, Peter Davidson of Findaty and John Paterson portioner of the Milton agreed to "keep the peace". As none of them could write, they authorised William Malcolm the notary who presented the bond, to subscribe it on their behalf. A similar bond was subscribed at Cupar by Michael Malcolm, second eldest son of John Malcolm. In the main, the heritors defied the law by peremptorily refusing to sign a bond which would bind them not to attend conventicles and to be answerable for their cotters and tenants, also to have no communication with or harbour "outed" ministers or vagrant preachers, and to apprehend any person who contravened the Act and bring them to justice or have them removed from their lands. Those heritors who refused to sign the bonds were David Arnot of Capeldrae, James Scrimgeour of Wester Cartmore, John Malcolm of Balbedie and Lochore, Lady

139

Kinninmond, the Earl of Rothes, James Betson of Cluny Craig, John Creig of Ballingry, Andrew Chalmers of Crosshill, Alexander Colville of Blair, John Mitchell of Ballingry and John Robertson of Navitie.

In the same year David Barclay of Colqually in Auchterderran parish, along with David Arnot of Balbedie, Alexander Findlay of Bucklyvie, and James Millar of Kirkcaldy, were sentenced to be transported to the plantations. Meanwhile they were to lie in prison until such times that a ship could be had to carry them to the West Indies. In December of that year orders were given to the magistrates of Edinburgh and the bailies of the Canongate to deliver these men along with Adam Stobie of Luscar to a company of guards. They were joined by a great number of prisoners, including many ministers, who had been taken at a conventicle in Cathcart earlier in the year. The whole company was escorted to Leith harbour where they were handed over to Edward Johnstone, captain of the *St. Michael of Scarboro*. Johnstone was to take his cargo to Ralph Williamson of London who was to transport the prisoners to the West Indies where they were to be sold as slaves. However, the ship arrived at Gravesend five days late and Williamson was not to be found. The captain's sympathies may have had a leaning towards the prisoners confined in the hold of his ship, some sixty-seven in all, as he does not appear to have exerted himself in trying to locate the whereabouts of Williamson. He therefore probably took advantage of the circumstances to assuage his conscience by setting all the prisoners ashore and allowing them to escape.

In May of this year another field conventicie was held at Glenvale near Balbegie when the Rev. John Dickson preached to a great number of people. The meeting was almost finished when Thomas Brydie, one of the sentinels posted on the West Law, sounded his horn, the signal that the dragoons had been sighted. The gathering scattered in many directions, some heading for Kinnesswood, others for Gospetry and Glenlomond; the less agile were soon left behind. The remainder of the story is best told in the words of a contemporary writer.

They had all got out of sight before the troopers cam' ower the head of the glen, but auld John Gibb, the farmer at Pittendreich. John was running past Powmill when he saw Laird Crawford among his stacks. He ran up to the Laird crying, "Oh Laird, Laird, you'll surely ne'er see an auld neebour harmed. Oh hide me, Laird". Crawford glowered at him and said "Sae the troopers are efter ye, Pittendreich? A sensible auld man like yoursel' micht hae mair wit than gang tae thae kind o' meetins'," but he grinned and said "jist you gang tae my hoose and creep intae the box-bed in the kitchen and pu' the door efter ye. The troopers will ne'er look for a Saint in Hell". When the troopers came along and asked the Laird if he had seen a man passing, "deed aye," he replied, "I saw him runnin' that way," and pointed in the direction of his house. The troopers then galloped off past the house in search of their man and "Pittendreich" escaped. Two of the number, Michael Glass and Robert Steedman were subsequently caught and imprisoned in the Tolbooth in Kinross.

Strict as these measures were, they were to be intensified in 1679 following the assassination of Archbishop Sharp on Magus Moor. On 3rd May, the day after the assassination, the Privy Council issued a proclamation. This was to be read in all churches on the following Sunday. It commanded the heritors in Fife and Kinross to bring their male tenants, cotters and man servants of sixteen years and over to certain specified towns throughout the shires. The ministers of each parish were also to be present with their Communion rolls. Those from Ballingry were to be at Kirkcaldy by ten o'clock on the morning of 20th May and to remain there until questioned by the Sheriff Depute and seen by certain witnesses. Anyone who failed to appear would be considered an accessory to the crime. In the meantime the dragoons were busy rounding up suspects, one such, while trying to escape, was shot in the back, when he was found to be the son of Aytoun of Inchdairnie in Kinglassie. He afterwards died of his wounds. His companion, Henry Shaw of Kirkcaldy, was apprehended and sent to prison where he remained till December when he was released on bail of 1,000 merks. John Henderson, an old man, a tenant of the Laird of Dowhill, was imprisoned in Edinburgh Tolbooth from June till December of that year for allegedly harbouring his two sons following their part in the assassination. He was released on bail of 2,000 merks.

42 *Inchdairnie House, Kinglassie (now demolished)*

John Malcolm had, by his wife, Margaret Arnot, daughter of Sir Michael Arnot, four sons, John, Michael, Alexander and James and a daughter Margaret. We have already mentioned Michael Malcolm, but it is from now on that his brothers appear in the annals of the parish. In 1680 John Malcolm along with three of his sons, John (now

141

Sir John of Innertiel), Michael of Nuthill and Alexander, Advocate since 1676, were appointed Commissioners of Excise and for the Militia in Fife and Kinross. In the same year Alexander Malcolm was appointed Sheriff Depute of Fife.

As the struggles between church and state continued, Parliament passed in 1681 what was known as the Test Act. Under this Act ministers were required to furnish lists of all who withdrew from public worship so that they could be brought before the magistraes. All those in office of public trust were to subscribe to the Act before January 1682, whereby they acknowledged the King as "supreme governor in all causes, ecclesiastical and civil:—that it was unlawful to take up arms against the King or to enter into Covenants, or to endeavour to change or alter the mode of Government either in Church or State".

As was the case in the previous bond, many heritors refused to subscribe to it. However, towards the end of the year a number of lawyers, including Alexander Malcolm, had taken the test although his father had not. As the Sheriff of Fife was among those who refused, he was deprived of his office and Alexander Malcolm was appointed to fill his place with full powers to administer the test to members of the court and to heritors, also to preside over the Commissioners of Excise and Supplies and to attend to the public affairs of the shire which, because of the foregoing, had somewhat fallen in arrears.

The closing date for subscribintg to the test having now passed, John Malcolm was the next person to be seized upon by the Privy Council. His reply to the Lords of the Council on the threat of dismissal was that it was expressly stated in Parliament that no Chamberlain need take the test, as Chamberlains were but factors and had no public trust. Nonetheless he was willing to take the test. The lords agreed that John Malcolm be allowed to do so, but as the date for subscribing had passed some two months earlier, it was uncertain if his subscribing now would be valid. They therefore agreed that the point raised by John Malcolm and the questions of the validity of his signing be debated, and in the meantime the appointment of John Bannerman as Chamberlain be left over until a decision had been reached. The decision of the Privy Council was probably in his favour as there is no evidence of his having relinquished his post. Later on in the year he headed a Commission for adjusting the valuation of lands in Fife. As the work of the Commission grew, new members were appointed and in 1684 we find his eldest son, Sir John, along with Micheal and Alexander Malcolm, appointed to the Commission. The last two were also made Justices of the Peace.

In 1684 the King appointed delegates from the Privy Council to visit specified shires with the object of "suppressing religious disaffection". Those chosen for Fife and Kinross-shire were the Earl of Balcarres, the Lord Livingstone and Colonel Graham of Claverhouse. A squadron of the King's guards was sent to Fife to be quartered where the Earl thought fit, and the Earl as Sheriff Principal was given authority to call out parties of the militia when required. In the absence of the Earl, authority was to be given to Alexander·Malcolm to convene certain land-owners who, when required, were commissioned to raise a hundred armed men under the command of James Lundin of Strathairlie. They were also empowered to call out heritors and liferenters between the ages of sixteen and sixty years sufficiently armed and with provisions for twenty days. The purpose of this force was to suppress rebels and disaffected persons, and in doing so ships and boats were to be examined, suspected houses were to be searched, suspects apprehended.

It was in this year (1684) that the case of Andrew Chalmers, portioner of Crosshill, Writer in Edinburgh, and his wife Isobel Pudziel, came before the magistrates. The Privy Council ordained in 1663 that no one should absent himself from attending church for a period of more than three consecutive Sundays. Failure to do so would result in a fine. To enforce the law, government officials were empowered to present themselves at the church door with lists of the people in the parish; names were checked and the absentees noted. On other occasions a company of soldiers would take over. The officer in charge would occupy the pulpit and would receive from the minister a list of the defaulting parishioners against whom proceedings were immediately taken. Probably the first of these procedures took place at Ballingry.

In February 1684 Chalmers and his wife were fined £600 Scots for their alleged attendance at conventicles and withdrawing themselves from worship in Ballingry Church. The decree was given in Chalmers' absence and was held as confessed. In July of the same year, Chalmers appeared before the Privy Council and appealed against the fine on the ground that he as a heritor had taken the Test when administered by the Earl of Balcarres, that he had always lived orderly and had never withdrawn from his parish church. He admitted that during the time of the Indulgence, his wife had, contrary to his own inclination, withdrawn herself from public worship, but had since frequently attended Ballingry Church and that his wife's "sometymes not frequenting was occasioned by her being a nurse".

In support of his case Chalmers produced a certificate from the heritors and elders of the parish, as the post of minister of Ballingry was vacant by the death of the minister. The Lords of Council having heard the case as presented by the petitioner, gave judgment as follows: "finding that he had taken the Test and given bond to the Earl of Bellcarras for the orderly behaviour of his wife, family, tenants and servants, hereby sist all exeution for the foresaid fine, until it appears what the petitioner's future obedience to the law and good behaveour shall be". Andrew Chalmers and his dependents probably complied henceforth with the requirements of the law as we hear no more about the case.

In 1685 we find John Malcolm holding the office of Procurator Fiscal to the Sheriff of Fife, a post obtained no doubt, through the influence of his son, Alexander. In February, 1687, Alexander Malcolm became a Senator of the College of Justice with the title of Lord Lochore, and in the following year he became a Lord of the Privy Council and Lord Justice Clerk. His younger brother James in this year succeeded his father as Chamberlain of Fife. He was also appointed quarter-master of the militia, and later on he held the post of clerk to the Committee of Trade.

The holding of illegal meetings continued. A forenoon and afternoon service was held in a barn at the Manor House of Cleish when William Mackie from Limekilns and Andrew Thomson from Inverkeithing officiated. The former held a further meeting two weeks afterwards at Scotlandwell, and on the same day William Spence from Edinburgh conducted a service in the house of James Ballantyne near Kinross. Coming nearer home, William Mackie was invited to and did preside over "ane Presbyterian house meiting" at Kirkness on 30th October, 1687. During this period an encounter took place near Pitlochie in Kinglassie Parish, between a company of dragoons and several people headed by one John Archer. A little further west on the ridge of high ground above Auchterderran there stood a Foley House or watch tower. The ruins (they are still discernable) were long pointed out as a place used by the Covenanters as a look-out post to warn of the approach of the dragoons.

On the whole the good people of Ballingry parish appear to have been fairly law-abiding: at least, if they did transgress the edicts of the day, they somehow managed to evade the rigours of the law, for the total sum of all the fines imposed on the inhabitants did not exceed £600. This was a very modest sum when compared with the total fines in the neighbouring parishes. Portmoak parish exceeded the lot with £32,700. Next came Kinglassie with £11,800, followed by Auchterderran with £5,040. The small parish of Auchtertool amounted to £4,500, and Orwel parish, £1,500.

The situation at the close of the short reign of James VII found many of the local lairds occupying opposing sides. John Malcolm and his son Sir John, along with many of the lairds in the neighbouring parishes, supported William of Orange. The more ardent ones in Auchterderran and Kinglassie accused their ministers of not praying for the King and Queen and sought to have them removed from their charges. On the other hand, Lord Lochore, along with his brother James, and John Scrimgeour of Bowhill maintained their loyalty to the House of Stuart, and as they were on the losing side, they paid dearly for it.

The Earl of Mar, as Lord President, was granted a warrant on 8th April, 1685 to arrest anyone who was suspected of plotting against the Government. Following the discovery of a letter written by the late King James VII then in Ireland, concerning a proposed landing in Scotland, Lord Lochore and the Earl of Balcarres and many other prominent people were immediately arrested and put in the Edinburgh Tolbooth. After a week in prison, most of those who had been arrested were allowed out on the payment of 10,000 merks as surety for their keeping the peace, but as the Earl and Lord Lochore were considered the prime movers among those who were opposed to the Government, they were to remain in prison. However, on the 29th April Lord Lochore appealed to the Scottish Estates for his release and was allowed out of prison on condition that he would remain within the town and would appear when called.

With so many Jacobite sympathisers abroad in the town it was not surprising that they should convene in secret to consider their next move. At length a plot was conceived whereby they hoped to gain control of all the governing bodies. It was intended to seize His Majesty's Commissioners, members of Parliament and members of the Privy Council. This was to take place in the early part of July, 1689. A number of those who were to take part in the plot were officers of the garrison in the castle, and several English and Irish Officers were also in the town ready to take part in the rising.

144

There is little doubt that the plot would have been put into effect had it not been that a day before the conspirators had agreed to act, the Lord President received a letter from an unknown writer revealing everything. The upshot was that forty-three persons were arrested, including the Duke of Gordon, the Earl of Hume and Lord Oxenford. Those from Fife, included Lord Lochore and his brother James who had recently returned from the north having been with Viscount Dundee as Commissioner-General of the Jacobite army; for his treasonable rising in arms he was now a declared rebel.

It was known from those who were apprehended that it was intended to set the town on fire in several places simultaneously and to open the Tolbooth and other prisons so that the Jacobite prisoners would escape. It was also intended to raise a force of 2-3,000 men and march north to join the insurrection under Graham of Claverhouse, now Viscount Dundee. The Earl of Crawford was now removed to the castle for greater security and Lord Lochore was again placed in the Tolbooth. Some leniency however was shown towards James Malcolm, but he was no sooner released from prison than he headed north again to join Claverhouse. He was present at the battle of Killiecrankie and saw Dundee lying dead from his wounds and was himself wounded. On his return home he was again apprehended and appeared before the Privy Council on the Charge of treasonable rising in arms. After a month in prison he was given his freedom after swearing his allegiance to the Crown and paying the sum of 500 merks as surety for his living peaceably. Lord Lochore also petitioned the Privy Council in August of this year and again in March and April 1690. He was finally released on bail of 20,000 merks. His brothers, Sir John Malcolm and Michael Malcolm stood surety for him. The conditions of his release were that he would do nothing to prejudice the Government; that he would not converse or correspond with any Jacobite and that he would not travel beyond a mile outside Edinburgh. Because of his Jacobite loyalties, Lord Lochore was no longer allowed to hold any office of public trust or responsibility. He was stripped of his judicial posts and ceased to be a public figure. He died at Cupar in 1691 at the age of forty-one and was buried in the Malcolm aisle in Ballingry Church beside his father who had pre-deceased him by seven months. Little is known of Lord Lochore's private life. We do know, however, from the writings of his friend the Rev. Doctor Munro, one time minister of Kinglassie and an ardent Jacobite, that Lord Lochore had in his possession a collection of interesting letters known to scholars as the "Buchanan Epistles". The letters, which were in Latin, were written by George Buchanan, the historian and tutor to James VI.

Colin, Earl of Balcarres, was released from prison at the same time as his close friend Lord Lochore. Almost immediately he left for France and eventually arrived at St. Germains where he stayed at the court of James VII. Meanwhile James Malcolm was brought before the Lord Advocate and closely questioned as to what he knew about the late battle at Killiecrankie. It was surely with some reluctance that he gave an account of many distinguished persons who had been present at the battle. James Malcolm soon followed the Earl to St. Germains. After a year at the Jacobite court they both returned home. Shortly afterwards James Malcolm acquired the estate of Grange, near Earlsferry.

The preparations which were afoot for the landing of the Old Pretender brought James Malcolm once again into the forefront of Jacobite stratagem. A somewhat feeble attempt was made in 1708. In March, several vessels left Dunkirk with the Pretender on board along with a large company of men and arms, and were due to anchor off Crail under darkness on a pre-arranged date. In the meantime the Earl of Errol had arranged with James Malcolm and an Aberdeen skipper to pilot the vessels the following day from Fifeness to a town further up the Forth, so that men and ammunition could be landed. Although the vessels' guns were fired as arranged and Malcolm boarded the foremost one and assured the company of the help that awaited them, there was no response from the shore. Instead, the English fleet had become aware of what was afoot and as soon as daylight broke they pursued the French ships of which all but one managed to escape. For his taking part in the rising, James Malcolm was attained and his estate forfeited, but his position was saved by his sister Margaret, who afterwards purchased the estate on its being resold. These deprivations did not dampen his loyalty to the Jacobite cause and when the 1715 insurrection was mooted he was soon actively preparing for it. In 1714 the Earl of Mar, his close friend, called him to London and offered him a ministerial post at £500 a year. This he refused as he could not take the oath of allegiance. Be that as it may, there appears to have been other things afoot, as he returned with what to him was interesting news. With George I on the throne, the Earl was now preparing for raising a rebellion in favour of James Stewart, the Old Pretender. As Commissioner-General of the army, James Malcolm was soon on his way to the Highlands confiding in his Jacobite friends with the purpose of raising troops.

In August 1715 he invited a large company of gentlemen to dinner when he announced that the Earl of Mar had left London some days earlier on board a collier, bound for Newcastle, in disguise under the name of Maule, accompanied by General Hamilton. From there they had arrived at Elie in a hired vessel the previous night and were now at the house of James Bethune of Balfour, from which place the Earl had sent for him. Mar's march was by way of Crail, then northward crossing the Tay to Dundee and on to Kinnoul and Perth. Meanwhile the insurgents with a force of 4,000 men occupied most of the coastal villages from Burntisland to St. Andrews. Malcolm persuaded not only his old friend the Earl of Balcarres to join him but also his son and successor, James, who, with the help of the Master of Sinclair, raised three troops of soldiers. The Pretender was proclaimed in most of the villages in the East Coast of Fife and an unsuccessful attempt to proclaim him was made at Kinross.

As the roads leading to the south were held by Royalists, the only way open to the insurgents to meet with their numbers in the south was by crossing the Forth. This undertaking was largely left to Malcolm to organise. With 2,500 men distributed in small companies in the fishing villages in the East Neuk, he was ready when wind and tide were suitable to ferry his force across the Firth in small boats. In the darkness of night the first detachment crossed successfully, the second was intercepted by the King's ships and forty men were taken prisoner. Other detachments were forced back to Fife and many, including the Earl of Strathmore, took refuge on the Isle of May. Despite the general confusion and the darkness, another detachment from Elie succeeded in crossing and making contact with the rebels in the south. Altogether, the exercise was deemed a failure and Malcolm came in for much criticism from the Earl of Mar.

We next hear of James Malcolm at Perth. From the garrison there he, along with Major Graham and Gordon of Glenbucket, was sent by the Earl of Mar to collect the tax from the town of Dunfermline. The detachment consisted of eighty cavalry and three hundred Highland foot soldiers. They were not to go direct but to take the longer route by way of Castle Campbell in order to taunt the Duke of Argyll's garrison who were stationed there. After despatching nine horsemen to the village of Saline and a similar number to Culross so that they could be warned if Argyll's men should follow, they entered Dunfermline. All the foot soldiers occupied the old Abbey and the horsemen were billeted throughout the town. Not suspecting trouble, and with the usual lack of discipline in the rebel forces, neither Malcolm or the other officers in command took adequate precautions to place sentries in sufficient numbers to ensure the safety of their men. Spies were soon at work and by 4 o'clock in the following morning, Colonel Cathcart with a company of dragoons and foot soldiers surprised the rebels, many of whom were wounded and killed and about twenty were taken prisoner and marched off to Stirling.

The second foray into Fife is more interesting as it touches on our own neighbourhood. Early on a Sunday morning in October 1714, a friend of the Master of Sinclair arrived at the South Inch in Perth to tell him that he had ridden all night from Burntisland, that the purpose of his coming was to advise him that a small ship had entered the harbour there loaded with arms and munition from Edinburgh Castle and destined for the Earl of Sutherland, the King's lieutenant in the north. He believed the arms amounted to 3,000 pieces. This interesting news was conveyed to the Earl of Mar who sent for the man in question and also for James Malcolm. After much discussion it was agreed that Sinclair and Colonel Balfour would leave for Burntisland that evening, taking with them eighty horses including fifty baggage horses. All the ports of the town were to be closed an hour before their departure to lessen the possibility of any information about their exploit reaching the Duke of Argyll, who was stationed at Stirling.

If the project was to proceed it was essential that they reach Burntisland by midnight as the ship was to sail on the full tide. At the given time the whole company rode out of the north port so as to conceal the direction of their journey. James Malcolm acted as guide and led them all the way, avoiding as far as possible, any villages. As a precaution they took with them anyone whom they met on the way. Meanwhile the Earl of Mar despatched five hundred foot soldiers under the command of John Stuart of Inveritie to occupy Kinross against the likelihood of Argyll sending his dragoons from Stirling to cut off their return to Perth.

When the company was three miles from Burnisland, they found Sinclair's friend waiting to tell them that the ship had gone out of the harbour but was still in the roads, so they continued their march in darkness. A halt was made about a mile from the town and twelve men who knew the town went on in front in order to seize the skipper in his house and to post sentries at the harbour to keep any boats from going out. When the company arrived they found all had gone well. Several small boats were seized and, with the help of several of the town's men whom they had pressed into action, they rowed out and brought the ship into harbour. Sinclair, standing up to his knees in water, received the arms but the number was disappointing, only three hundred and a bag of flints, two small barrels of ball and two or three barrels of powder and some boxes of cartridges. Another ship in the harbour yielded about twenty-five flint locks and a barrel of powder and from the town's guard they seized thirty firearms.

The booty was loaded on to the baggage horses and after the sentries had been called and those who had gone off through the town looking for drink had been rounded up, the company got under way between three and four o'clock in the morning. The return march was by Auchtertool where the Earl of Mar had sent John Farquharson of Inverie with five hundred of his men to be in residence in case Argyll's troops should come on the scene. When Sinclair arrived he could only see about forty of the Highlanders, the rest were all about the countryside plundering. Sinclair tried to take command but the Highlanders pretended not to understand his orders and some of the soldiers even pointed their pistols at him. At length one of his officers appeared, and in order to make some headway, Sinclair told him to tell his men that Argyll's soldiers were only a matter of three miles distant. Sinclair galloped off observing that this had had the desired effect, for the Highland soldiers appeared from nowhere and ran after the horse and even overtook the column. The stratagem however was short lived for before long they went off again in search of plunder. Sinclair complained to their commander in vain. The company passed through Ballingry on its way north. It does not appear that James Malcolm called on his brother at Lochore House. There is a tradition, however that as the column with the officers at its head approached Kirkness House, they encountered a wedding party travelling towards Ballingry. One of the officers gallantly offered to kiss the bride to be, but she appeared not to have favoured his advances, much to the merriment of the Highlanders and the displeasure of the officer. It is said that a halt was made at Kirkness and the grass at The Greens provided fodder for the horses. This, it is said was the last occasion that the grass at The Greens was cut.

After crossing the gullet bridge they travelled a good mile along what was anciently known as "the causay" till they reached Scotlandwell. At Kinnesswood pillaging broke out again. Sinclair's horse and Farquharson's Highlanders were joined by Stuart's five hundred foot soldiers who had been stationed at Kinross. It was again given out that the enemy was in the vicinity in an attempt to bring the Highlanders together, but the ruse was only a partial success as Farquharson's men continued to run about in groups of ten or a dozen and paid little heed to the orders of the command. Sinclair so abhorred the plundering tactics of the Highlanders that he suggested to Stuart that they should halt and search each man and return the spoil to the poor people who by this time had grown to a considerable number and were following the column and shouting their complaints. Stuart said that the Highlanders would not stand for that and if those in command were to reach Perth with whole skins they had better leave the foot soldiers to their own ways. On his advice the three companies dispersed and arrived at Perth separately. Sinclair with his column of baggage horses returned at 5 o'clock having marched over forty miles and having accomplished the mission in twenty-four hours.

Malcolm's failure to ferry the Jacobite force across the Forth was somewhat mitigated when the Earl of Mar had occasion to say that James Malcolm had done the King (the Pretender) more service than any man in Perth. We do not know if he was present at the Battle of Sheriffmuir; he probably was.

In conclusion, we would mention that Sir Walter Scott writing to Jane Jobson in 1825, refers to "two honest gentlemen hewn in stone", who were described to him as lying under the gallery of Ballingry Church, that is, in the Malcolm burial aisle. "Honest gentlemen" of course is an allusion to Jacobite sympathisers and seems to imply that Lord Lochore and his brother James were buried in the Malcolm family aisle*.

Sir John Malcolm, of Lochore

Sir John Malcolm, the eldest son of John Malcolm, was created a baronet of Nova Scotia in 1665, and on succeeding his father, he became the first baronet of Lochore and Innerteil. He became patron of the Church of Ballingry in 1701 and in this year he established a "New Fair" at the Milton. In common with Fairs held at Kinglassie and Kinross, dues were paid by ancient custom to the Burgh of Inverkeithing. These were collected by the Burgh officer who came attired in his official dress and mounted on a white horse. The Fair lasted long enough to be "a memory" among the old people living in the village at the end of the last century when it was known as the Weaver's Market. As chief heritor, Sir John figured largely in the life of the church and in the sub-division of the several Commonties in the parish. He was a Member of Parliament for Kinross-shire in 1722 and died in 1729 in his eighty-third year. By his wife Emilia, daughter of the third Lord Balfour of Burleigh, he had five sons: John, his heir; Robert, who succeeded his uncle James Malcolm in his estate of Grange, and who accompanied him in many of his Jacobite exploits; Michael, later of Balbedie; Charles; and James of Nuthill and Lathrisk.

Sir John Malcolm II, of Lochore

Sir John Malcolm succeeded to the barony of Inchgall in 1729 at which time he was following the business of a Writer in the town of Kirkcaldy. He had travelled much in his youth and his early adventures were the source of a fund of greatly exaggerated stories for which he became well known. He was, according to his friends, a little eccentric and was frequently subjected to ridicule. He was a member of the celebrated Anstruther

---

*The Malcolm burial aisle has now been made into the entrance vestibule to the church.

club known as "The Sovereign and Knights of the Beggars Benison". This club, according to tradition, had its origin in one of King James V's escapades when he travelled incognito in the Kingdom of Fife. It so happened that the King found himself faced with the difficulty of having to cross the Dreel burn near Anstruther which at the time was in spate. While the Guideman of Ballangeich was wondering what to do, an old tinker woman appeared and offered to carry him across. The King gladly accepted the offer and the woman kilted her skirt and carried him across on her back. This greatly amused the King and before long he was welcomed into the tinkers' camp and the remainder of the evening was spent merry-making in the local inn with the tinkers.

Many of the Fife lairds were members of this convivial club and Sir John who, it is said, was unduly inclined to boast, found ample scope for his story-telling. This propensity of Sir John's brought forth a ballad from a member of the club. The first three verses go as follows:—

> "Ken ye ought o' Sir John Malcolm?
> Igo and Ago:
> If he's a wise man I mistak' him,
> Iram, coram, dago.
> "To hear of his travels talk,
> Igo and Ago:
> To go to London's but a walk,
> Iram, coram, dago.
> "To see the leviathan skip,
> Igo and Ago:
> And wi' his tail ding owre a ship,
> Iram, coram, dago.

These lines were known to Burns who wrote a parody on them commencing, *Ken ye ought o' Captain Grose*. Sir John married Isabel, daughter of John Balfour of Fernie, the son of third Lord Balfour of Burleigh by whom he had three sons and five daughters. He died in 1753 aged seventy-two and was buried beside his father in the Malcolm aisle. He was succeeded in the barony by his second son Michael.

Sir Michael Malcolm of Lochore

Sir Michael probably spent some of his early days in the neighbourhood of Balgonie as the following lines assert:—

> "Balbedie has a second son
> They ca' him Michael Malcolm,
> He gans about Balgonie dykes,

150

Huntin and hawkin';
He's stown away the bonny lass
And kept the widow waukin' ''.

The Malcolm family did not escape the misfortunes which befell many a Scottish family during this period. We find that Sir Michael, when he came to the family honours, was following the trade of a joiner, first in Kinross and afterwards in London. The year before he succeeded to the barony he married Catherine Bathurst, daughter of Lord Chancellor Bathurst whom he first met in the following unusual circumstances. Mr Malcolm as he then was, being related to Lord Balmerino, the staunch old Jacobite and veteran of the battles of Falkirk and Culloden, was summoned to the Tower Hill, London in 1746 to be present at his Lordship's execution. Although a contemporary description presents Sir Michael as being in no way handsome, nonetheless, we are told that as soon as Miss Bathurst saw him standing on the scaffold, she fell in love with him on the spot.

The following year (1747) saw the return of dragoons to the neighbourhood. The veteran Major-General Humphrey Bland who was present at the battle of Culloden, was this year given the command of the King's forces in Scotland and was then stationed at Stirling from whence he despatched a troop of dragoons to Blairadam to be quartered there under the command of Sir William Erskine for the purpose of flushing out Jacobite sympathisers in West Fife. Blairadam had come under the notice of the Jacobite rebels two years earlier when they seized and took away a valuable horse belonging to Mr Adam. Blairadam by now was proving in all respects a suitable place from which to reconnoitre the surrounding countryside. Accordingly, in 1760 preparations were being made to have a further two companies of dragoons stationed there.

It was early in Sir Michael's lairdship that there occurred a case of alleged witchcraft in the parish. It concerned Mr Marr the schoolmaster at Ballingry who was also precentor in Ballingry church.

Although Sir Michael's early training and education had hardly prepared him for the duties which in later life he was called upon to undertake, he was nonetheless animated by a spirit of service in promoting the well-being of the community and his name appears largely in the annals of the parish. His activities were not confined to the parish only, as a story told of him shows.

One day while presiding over a Magistrate's Court at Kirkcaldy, he was hard-tested by a sharp-witted shoemaker whom he was sentencing to a fortnight's imprisonment for a trivial offence. "I want to know", said the shoemaker, "the meaning of these Latin words in the sentence". Sir Michael was so taken aback at being asked a question to which he did not know the answer, that he could only call "give that fellow two months more for contempt of court". Albeit his friend and neighbour, William Adam of Blairadam, spoke of him as "a character of great singularity and talent, and an excellent man".

Sir Michael in his old age is said to have composed the following couplet when a revolution in France looked imminent:

151

"Happy is the man who belongs to nae pairty,
Who sits in his ain hoose and looks out on Benarty".

Sir Michael died in 1795, the last of the Malcolm family to reside in Lochore House. Of his family of three sons and a daughter, none survived him and the barony devolved upon his cousin James Malcolm of Grange, who became fourth baronet, not of Lochore, as he decided to part with the estate, but of Balbedie and Grange. Even so, adverse circumstances appeared to have compelled some of the future baronets to occupy humble stations in life. Sir John the seventh baronet is said to have been a coach painter in Kinross and to have married a fisherwoman from Buckhaven, while Sir James the eighth baronet followed for many years the humble occupation of a ditcher. The family appears to have sold the estates of Balbedie and Grange in about the year 1901, as from that date they no longer appear in the title.

LOCHORE HOUSE

The precise date of Lochore House is not known, but on charter evidence, it appears to have been built between 1654 and 1661 at which time it was known as Inchgall House. It was probably built in 1658, as in that year John Malcolm of Lochore made a gift of a bell to the church at Ballingry, an act which seems to imply that he was by then the resident proprietor.

The house is thought by many to have been built to plans made by Sir William Bruce of Balcaskie and later of Kinross, who became Master of Works to the Crown under Charles II. Among his many works is Kinross House and the "new" part of the Palace of Holyrood.

John Malcolm and Sir William Bruce are known to have been close friends which makes the conjecture all the more probable. If so, it must have been one of his earliest works. Sir William started out on his architectural career in Fife by adding a wing to the Castle of Stravethy in 1653. There is a tradition that William Adam, the Kirkcaldy builder and architect and later proprietor of Blair Adam estate, and father of Robert and James Adam the famous architects, commenced his architectural career as an assistant to Sir William Bruce.

If a perspective drawing of Lochore House made in 1811 can be relied upon, it is evident that the servants' quarters and courtyard to the rear of the house had not yet been built. The house was flanked by two small buildings similar in design. Each stood a short distance from the house and were placed somewhat to the rear of it.

New marble fireplaces were added to the house at a period which can be determined, as the ornamental knobs on the lovely brass ashpans bore the head and inscription of George III. The original stone fireplaces, after removal, appear to have been built into the factor's house at the steading. It is fairly certain that these and other alterations took place during Captain Park's occupancy. It is known that the courtyard and servants' houses were in being by 1825 by which time the two small buildings already mentioned had been removed. These later alterations were probably carried out by Mr Jobson.

The house has undergone considerable alteration and mutilation in recent years following its being made into a Youth Club Centre, so much so that the courtyard and servants' quarters have been demolished and the house gutted so that only the shell remains. It has now become the headquarters of the Fife Spastics Association; but it may interest the reader to learn something of the place as it was formerly. The house is square on plan and faces east, and looks out on what must have been a pleasant rural setting, with Loch Ore and Inchgall Castle in the middle distance and an extensive view of the Ore valley. The front facade still presents, despite all its vicissitudes, a simple and dignified appearance.

The entrance is flanked by four doric columns, two on either side, supporting an entablature and above the door-way is a half-circle arch with a keystone. This arch and keystone treatment is repeated on a Venetian window in what was a first floor room immediately above. This window is not dissimilar to one to be seen at Balcaskie House where it occupies a similar position in relation to the main entrance. The length of the facade consisted of a room on either side of the entrance hall and the house was three rooms in depth. In height it comprised ground floor, first floor and a suite of attic bedrooms.

A spiral staircase leading from the hall, with pen-checked stone steps, gave access to the rooms above. Beneath part of the entrance hall and gained by means of a flight of stone steps, is what was originally a wine cellar. It has an arched roof consisting of hand-made clay bricks and the stone shelving is still in position. A withdrawing room situated on the first floor had a lovely white marble fireplace with a free-standing basket fire and ornamental brass ashpan. Displayed on the breast of the mantelpiece was a beautifully carved oval panel depicting a young lady feeding poultry. Also on the first floor facing south, was a small circular room referred to sometimes as the "study". The panelled door in this room, was curved to conform to the shape of the walls. The floors of the entrance hall and the kitchen premises were originally paved with flag-stones. These were replaced with timber floors in 1919, and while this work was being done a rather unusual apparatus was discovered.

Beneath one of the flag-stones on the kitchen floor were the remains of a whisky still. We were fortunate enough to have a first hand description of the apparatus at the time*. There was a boiler of a kind and a spiral copper pipe and some other vessel of copper, all concealed within a small chamber under the floor, but what displayed the keenest sense of ingenuity of the whole surprising affair, was a flue which led from the chamber to a near-by chimney, so that the smell from the whisky in-the-making was taken into the open air at a height which rendered it undetectable. The still was "discovered" again a few years ago and because the finders were unaware of its history, the fact received some publicity in the local press. There is no reason to believe other than that the still was installed when the house was built; we may therefore conclude that John Malcolm kept a good cellar.

The law respecting these things was not enforced in these days as it is now, and it would seem that quite a lot of illicit distilling was carried on in the district. We read of "Whisky Lizzie" of Craigside, perhaps now Craigend outside Auchterderran, who carried on illicit distillation at the turn of the eighteenth century. Another still is known to have been in operation in a secluded part of Benarty Hill. It is interesting to note that, about a hundred years ago, Lochore House was one of the few places in the parish where exciseable liquor was allowed to be sold.

Coming to more recent times; when workmen were putting in attic windows in the roof of the house about the year 1926, there were found lying on one of the heavy beams which support the leaded flat roof, a large quantity of hand made nails and a curiously fashioned spirit level of unknown date. It was also interesting to see written on the lead of the roof at various places, the names and addresses of workmen who had from time to time been engaged in carrying out repairs. Most had added the date, and quite a few went back over a hundred years. Also deposited in the roof space was a number of old news sheets, some dating from the time of Scott and one very old fragment referred to

* The writer's father was present at the time of the discovery.

154

43 *Lochore House in 1811*

the treaty of Ratisbon. No doubt the older ones had been brought by the Malcolms from their house at Balbedie.

Entrance to the courtyard was by means of a huge arched doorway. The doors swung on crook-and-band hinges of generous proportions and were kept in position by means of a large iron "sneck". A large wooden lock, whose dimensions were equal to the door on which it was bolted was reinforced with iron plates. By using both hands to turn an enormous key, the bolt of the lock slid into position and rendered the place secure. The courtyard was enclosed by two storey buildings on three sides; the back wall of the mansion formed the fourth. The ground floors on three sides consisted of domestic offices while immediately above were dwelling houses for the estate workers. At a height midway on the enclosing walls and sloping towards the centre of the paved courtyard was a continuous covered-in walkway the roof of which was supported on cast iron pillars.

One of the ground floor premises held a rather interesting domestic apparatus in the form of a clothes mangle. Although when last seen it had long since been abandoned, we recall its dimensions after the lapse of more than fifty years. The mangle consisted of a table-like form constructed in heavy timbers some seven feet long and two and a half feet broad, on the top of which were placed four wooden rollers about five inches in diameter, their length corresponding to the width of the table. On top of two of the rollers was placed a large wooden box about half the length of the table. The box, which was about one foot in depth, was full of water-rolled stones which must have weighed about two hundredweight. A rope was attached to each end of the box and each rope was wound round a windlass which was fixed at either end of the table. By turning the handle of one of the windlasses the box was pulled from one end of the table

155

to the other. It was thought at the time that the manner in which the mangle operated, was for the clothes to be wrapped round the rollers and placed on that part of the table not occupied by the box. As the box was pulled by the windlass it pressed down on each of the rollers in turn as it travelled along the length of the table. The rollers in turn would revolve under the weight of the box. No doubt the box would be pulled backward and forward over the rollers until the clothes were sufficiently mangled.

Before leaving Lochore House, we would remark on a fine sundial which was to be seen in the centre of the extensive garden, until recent years. Following the removal of the houses at the steading in 1962 the sundial was taken to the manse at Ballingry for safe-keeping, but it has since been lost. Its pedestal was of finely-grained freestone and stood on a circular stone base. In addition to the dial on top of the pedestal, which was of the "lectern" type, there were cut out on three sides of the pedestal, other dials of varying designs and ingenuity. Although the copper styles which had been set into the stone for the purpose of casting a shadow on the dials had nearly all eroded away, the finely cut lines and numerals on the stonework were distinctly visible. One wonders if this unusual recorder of centuries of sunny hours, had at one time graced the courtyard of Inchgall Castle.

Of the many adjuncts to the house, and a reminder of more leisurely days, was a small pheasantry which stood a little north of the courtyard. This no doubt would at one time be under the care of John McLeod whose work on the estate in his capacity as gamekeeper was noted by Sir Walter Scott. Another memento of days long since gone, when water for domestic use had to be carried in buckets and from a source which cannot in this case be described as being near at hand, is a hand-operated pump which at one time stood in the shade of a long avenue of ancient trees. The trees have all gone. The pump no longer responds with a gush of cool clear water to the pull of the lever. It creaks under the rust of centuries and its very where-abouts is almost forgotten.

The original approach to the house was from the east, that is to say, the one leading from the Kirkton of Ballingry. This may well have followed the line of an earlier track as the presence of Ladath House implies a road of some sort. The avenue leading westward likewise appears to have followed an earlier route as in this direction lay the Bowhouse of Kildownie, the Bowhouse of Inchgall, and at least one other dwelling. In old maps the route is given the name of "Loanhead". There is a local tradition that Scott gave the name "Cleikum Inn" to the lodge which stood near the entrance to the west avenue. It is true that in March 1825 Scott examined the west entrance to the estate and found that, as a very small portion of the neighbouring estate of Benarty intervened between Lochore estate and what was the logical approach to the public road, the makers of the avenue had perforce to make a right-angle turn and negotiate an awkward and steep incline in order to reach the road. Scott wrote to Jane Jobson in June of the same year pointing out the advantages to be gained if the line of the avenue were to be taken across the intervening ground which lay between it and the public road and suggested that the laird of Benarty estate be approached on the matter. Scott concluded by offering to meet the cost of the work himself. That the little project was carried through is evident, but contrary to what one would expect, Cleikum Inn was not built as a lodge. It was fortuitous that the new entrance stopped short of the house and it was

44 *Lochore House c.1925*

probably included in the negotiations with the laird of Benarty. It was of the simple "but-and-ben" construction and had its back to the public road. It is known to have stood on this site for some fifteen years before Scott saw it, but no doubt it received its name from Scott when it became attached to the Lochore estate.

45 *Cleikum Inn Lodge*

157

LADATH HOUSE

Pre-dating Lochore House by at least a century, was Ladath House. After the coming of the Malcolm family, the lands of Ladath became known as Lochore estate. The name Ladath is very old, and is mentioned in 1477, while "Ladath House and Steading" is referred to in 1545.

The house was L-shaped and appeared to have occupied the south-west side and part of the south-east side of the steading, and was built at a time when some provision obviously had to be made for the safety of its occupants. The approach was from the north-east where the ground is relatively level. On the south-west it was flanked by the Ladath burn, and here the wall was carried to a considerable height, and was five feet thick at its base. The house was two storeys in height, and where the configuration of the ground demanded, there was a basement which had a stone vaulted roof. On the north-west it was flanked by a range of buildings which formed part of the steading. To the north-east, where it was least secure, the walls were in parts three feet thick, and the windows small. These, in some cases, were rendered more secure by vertical iron bars set into the stonework.

The entrance to the house was by way of an arched doorway in the north-east wall of the courtyard. The two main apartments had plastered cornices. From the many fragments found, it was evident that the designs included "egg and dart" and bunches of grapes in semi-relief. The apartments also had mantelpieces made of freestone. One had a carved bolection moulding, which was probably the older, and the other, a design which has been recognised as belonging to a period around 1650.

In what was probably the kitchen premises were two built-in stone lavers or basins each with a channelled outlet for conveying the water to the outside of the house. The house had been roofed with stone slates.

The house and steading had undergone certain alterations from time to time and the Malcolm family appear to have enlarged the steading. From this time onwards, the steading was taken over as an adjunct to Lochore House, for the housing of the estate workers and partly for stabling and a coach house.

It is evident from the old writings that Ladath House was used by the family who lived in the castle and that it was at one time the Dowager House for the barony. Its garden became the garden for Lochore House.

About a hundred yards south of Ladath House, stood a rectangular dovecot with a lean-to roof and crow-stepped gable walls. Internally, the whole of the back wall was fitted with stone nests.

THE BEATSONS OF CLUNE CRAIG

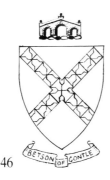

46

The Beatsons, whose name is derived from the son of Bat or Baty, were a border clan who lived in the Esk valley during the fifteenth and sixteenth centuries. One of the earliest accounts of the family concerns grants of land in the barony of Wester Ker given by King James II to John Batisoun, Nicholas Batisoun and Robert Beatysoune for their services at the battle of Arkenholme in 1455. A century later the family appears in Eskdale and Liddesdale; and in 1587 the Beatsons along with the Armstrongs were jointly involved in cattle-stealing (no doubt from across the border), when they carried off six hundred kye, six hundred sheep and thirty five prisoners.

By the end of the seventeenth century the name appears in Fife and Kinross-shire, mostly in connection with the transfer of land, and it is during this period that we find the name appearing locally in the person of James Beatson who occupied the Flockhouse of Inchgall in 1605. Thirteen years later, John Betsone of Eistertoun de Baith bought from Patrick Wardlaw the lands of Clune Craig and Contil (now Glencraig) in the barony of Inchgall. The charter was confirmed by King James VI in 1620. In 1636 his name appears as John Bedsone in a list of the heritors of the parish of Ballingry; and in 1648 he is referred to as John Beatson in Clune Creige. He was succeeded by "Jacobus Beatsone de Cluny Craig". James Beatson was in all likelihood his son. By now, the name appears in other parts of Lochoreshire and beyond, although the relationship between the various holders cannot be determined.

In 1624 David Beatson of Glennistoun bought from George Mertene de Cardoun the lands of Cardoun in the parish of Easter Kinghorn. These lands were annexed to Auchterderran parish in 1642. By the year 1630, Beatson was successfully working coal on the estate and by 1643 he was employing eight coal heughers. James Beatson of Glennistoun, mentioned in 1635, may have been his son.

Returning to the Beatsons of Clune Craig, we have seen that John Beatson was succeeded in his estate by James Beatson sometime after 1648. Now, there occurred in 1631 one of these incidents in the church which from time to time breaks the tranquillity of the village life and affords an excellent topic of conversation among the village busy-bodies.

159

The Rev. Mr Anderson of Ballingry complained to the presbytery about the conduct of Agnes Grig, the wife of James Beatson, in that she "troubled the Kirk"; and as the next meeting of the presbytery was to be held in Kirkcaldy, Agnes was summoned to appear there on the fifteenth of September. Her husband, appearing on her behalf, asked for an extension of the summons as they were busy with the harvest. It was agreed that the hearing be postponed for one month when his wife would require to appear before the presbytery at Dysart. Agnes, however, was in no way subdued. Two weeks afterwards the minister made a further complaint that Agnes Grig "had abused his daughter in the kirk of Ballingry with her speeches upon one Sabbath day and he offers to prove the samyn".

On the twentieth of October, Agnes and her husband set out for Dysart. Having in mind the awful condition of the roads in these days, they would no doubt go on horseback. Under the reconciling influence of the presbytery, the contending parties agreed "that the matter may be taine away peaceablie and friendlie" and submitted themselves to the judgement of Mr Chalmers, minister of Auchterderran, Mr Melville minister of Kinglassie and Mr Colville of East Blair.

In 1635 we meet with a James Bedsone in Ballingry but whether he and the preceding James Beatson were one and the same son of the laird of Clune Craig there is no way of knowing. On first October of this year (1635) he and James Andersone of Navitie declared themselves willing to accept the office of constables of the parish. The office of constable in these days did not carry the criminal connotation associated with the modern police officer but was more that of a public servant. We are on somewhat surer ground in 1641 when James Betsone of Conthill, as ruling elder for the presbytery, approved the expenditure of work done in repairing the manse of Auchterderran. Four years afterwards he appears again when he obtained a tack for sixteen years of the lands of Nother Kilrie and Pasker Milne from the Earl of Moray. He subsequently acquired the lands of Kilrie in 1668. When the question of having a school at Ballingry was under consideration, he readily agreed to contribute to the cost of the building and of providing an adequate salary for a schoolmaster.

James Beatson of Clune Craig and Contil was granted a Coat of Arms in 1671, and these appear on four silver Communion Cups which he gifted to the church at Ballingry. This public-spirited heritor also built the Clochrat Bridge at Clune Craig in 1671 to replace the ford there. He died on 13th July 1695 at the advanced age of ninety-four. By his wife, Marjorie Walker, he had Robert his heir, David of Vicars Grange, and William of Glassmount. Robert was also heir to the lands of Kilrie and his descendant Robert Beatson was in possession in the early part of the nineteenth century. William Beatson is commemorated in the following laudatory lines.

"Under this tombe here William Beatson lies
Was generous and honest in his ways
He virtuous was, and had an issue fair,
Powerful in riches and in knowledge rare"
Both Robert Beatson and his brother William bore Coats of Arms.

The Beatson family was to possess Clune Craig for many years to come but their descent is not clear. Among the persons bearing this name, other than those already

47 *Glencraig House (now demolished)*

mentioned, there is Thomas Beatson a church elder whose actions are recorded during the last quarter of the seventeenth century, James Beatson in Lumphinnans in 1704 and James Beatson of Clune, a church elder, in 1711. There are also those who are known from the inscriptions on the grave-stones in Ballingry churchyard, whereon the year of their deaths are given, namely Andrew Beatson, 1704, Bess Beatson, 1738, George Beatson, 1752 and M. Beatson, 1767.

Fortunately, the Rev. David Jamie has left an account of the way in which the Beatson lands came into the possession of the Henderson family, a branch of the Hendersons of Fordell. He also shows us that the name Glencraig is not older than the year 1830.

The last of the Beatsons who owned Contle and Clune was a bachelor as was David Henderson the owner of Inchgall (the lands adjoining Inchgall Mill). The old men were great friends and each made his will in favour of the other so that the possessions belonging to the one who died first would go to his friend.

Mr Beatson outlived Mr Henderson and thereby acquired Inchgall. He now possessed Contle, Clune, Templeland and Inchgall.

The old man, the last of his race, was known to Sir Walter Scott. Scott mentions him in a letter which he wrote to Jane Jobson in 1825. Mr Beatson died in 1829, but had neglected to make out a new will. As his will still stood in the late Mr Henderson's favour, Mr Henderson's next of kin moved in and claimed the four small estates. Collectively, they were to be known in future as Glencraig.

As to the identity of the last of the Beatsons, although Scott refers to Mr Beatson without giving his Christian name — and Mr Jamie likewise — he was in all probability the "John Beatson of Contle" whose name appears in a list of the principal heritors of Fife in the year 1803.

The person who succeeded to the lands of Glencraig was John Henderson, a cousin of the late David Henderson. John Henderson died in 1831 and was succeeded in the estate by his eldest son Robert. Following his demise in 1869, the estate passed to his younger brother William who held it for a short period before he sold it to James Constable in 1872. James Constable's son George sold the estate in 1894 to John Wilson of Airdrie, afterwards *Sir* John.

GREIG OF BALLINGRY

48

In 1623 John Greig of Balquhumrie bought the small estate of Ballingry from Patrick Wardlaw for £5,000 and established the family of Greig of Ballingry. The family resided in the Mansion House of Ballingry, not the ruined house that today is incorporated in the farm steading, but an earlier one that appears to have been a handsome dwelling, excellently situated with a number of cotters' houses in its neighbourhood. A few finely sculptured stones that were to be found lying in the farm yard long years ago showed that much taste and skill had gone into the mansion house that adorned the place in the seventeenth century.

John Greig had not been long in Ballingry when his daughter Agnes married James Betson of Contle and Clune. It has been said that John Greig and his brother Patrick were in no way remarkable, but it is to his credit that John Greig as a heritor and church elder was one of those who as early as 1635 advocated the need to establish a school in the parish. He was present when the ministers of the Presbytery met in Ballingry church in October of that year to promote the setting-up of a school and the setting aside of one hundred merks for the salary of a schoolmaster. In 1640 John Greig's brother Patrick had become a heritor and was also admitted to the eldership of the church.

In the matter of establishing a parish school, progress was exceedingly slow. In 1668 thirty-three years after it was first discussed, the Presbytery convened a meeting at Ballingry for the purpose of going ahead with the building of a school and the appointment of a schoolmaster, but only four heritors appeared including Patrick Greig and his relative James Betson. Nor did the Privy Council, agreeing to a supplication from the heritors in 1669 that the sum of three hundred merks be used for the building of a school, have the effect of speeding up matters. The three hundred merks represented a half year's stipend which had accrued from a vacancy in the ministry of the church. A further fifty-four years had to elapse before a school was established at Ballingry.

In 1676 we meet with John Greig again. The occasion is his refusal, along with most of the heritors of Ballingry, to sign the bond as issued by the Privy Council to abstain from attending conventicles and to bring to justice those who had transgressed the law in refusing to do so. John Greig applied for and was granted a Coat of Arms sometime between 1672-1677.

The estate of Ballingry passed out of the Greig family during the first quarter of the eighteenth century when it was acquired by a Mr Crawford who, as a heritor, was foremost in most of the affairs of the parish, maintaining always a very active interest in matters concerning the poor. His wife held the title of Lady Ballingry. Contrary to what may be supposed Lady Ballingry was neither the wife of a knight or a baronet, but as she was the wife of a laird, she had according to Scots law a right to the feudal title of "leddy". As her title arose out of lairdship, she was known as Lady Ballingry, not Lady Crawford.

CAPTAIN ALEXANDER PARK OF LOCHORE

49

It is not known for certain when Captain Park bought the Lochore estate from Sir Michael Malcolm, but he was in possession by the year 1788. He had a lot to do with the church life of the parish, first as chief heritor and later as a church elder, but it is through his industrial activities that he is best known. He was not long in the parish before he set on foot his project for draining the loch whereby he hoped to regain about one hundred and fifty acres of good pasture land. He also for a time worked limestone and ironstone deposits on the estate. A reminder of the latter was to be found in a small stone-built house, long since demolished, which stood a little to the south of the present railway bridge at Lochore, called Ironstone Cottage.

The new proprietor had his plans for the draining of the loch well advanced by 1791. The first thing he did was to purchase the Templelands through which he hoped to drive a cutting in order to drain the loch. For the payment of £700 he obtained the Templelands from Mr Watson the proprietor and straightway resold them to Mr Betson for the same amount reserving to himself the right to make the cutting. He afterwards built a "howff" to hold the workmen's tools. This stood on the south side of the river Ore near what is now the entrance to Park Street.

It may help the reader to understand how things appeared at this period if he can imagine an isosceles triangle with the main road as its base-line. To the north of the base-line, the river Ore formed one side of the triangle. At a distance of twenty yards or so south of the river on the base line, the mill lade formed the other side of the triangle. Both the river and the mill lade met at the apex of our imaginary triangle, some three hundred yards to the east. Now, what Captain Park did, was to drive a cutting approximately halfway along the base line and straight through the apex. Where his cutting crossed the road, he built a stone bridge and the road surface was raised considerably. The project had gone well by 1791 and continued for another year as it proved very hard work cutting down through the whin rock.

Following the actual draining of the loch in 1792, a deep and wide ditch was made for most of its length with small lateral ditches extending over the whole area. The project turned out to be only a partial success as there tended to be flooding during the winter months, so Captain Park decided in 1795 to deepen the cutting if possible. It appears that the "bottle-neck" was in the region of the stone bridge. The writer remembers being told some fifty years ago by an old residenter of ninety years, whose father undertook the work for the Captain, that it was the Captain's intention to lower the cutting by three feet, but after some success the work had to be abandoned as it was feared it would endanger the foundations of the bridge.

Probably because of the difficulties he encountered and the fact that the work had already cost him almost £1,000, Captain Park sold the estate in 1798. He took up residence in another part of Fife by which time he had attained the rank of Colonel. The person who bought the estate from him was John Syme W.S.

The amount of land reclaimed added considerably to the size of the Lochore estate. We have a plan of the estate at this period before us as we write, on which is shown the reclaimed land divided up into fields each named and showing acreages. In all one hundred and fifty-five acres were added bringing the total acreage of the estate to a little over five hundred and forty-nine acres. The Glencraig estate was enlarged to the extent of the reclaimed land which lay to the south of the main ditch. The fields yielded abundant crops of good meadow hay which was sold in lots at anything from £5 to £9 as the old receipts show.

As for the workmen's howff, being substantially built in stone it was turned into a dwelling house with an additional room, by which means it attained the dimensions of a "but and ben". It was long the home of old Jenny Dick a well known worthy who dwelt there towards the end of the last century. Jenny's favourite walk was to the east end of the Milton, where she would rest on the "parliament stone" before returning home. The house was used during the second world war as a Rescue Brigade Headquarters. It was eventually demolished in 1945.

JOHN SYME OF WESTER CARTMORE

50

By the end of the ten years or so during which Captain Park had been the proprietor of the Lochore estate, the character of the neighbourhood had changed dramatically. The loch, the dominant feature around which for centuries the whole history of the place had revolved, had gone. Inchgall Castle, although roofless for a century and a half was reasonably entire and retained many of its architectural features. It is therefore to Captain Park that we must attribute the positive robbing and destruction of the Castle. Up till 1792 it had been to some extent protected by the loch, but with the departure of the waters it became easily accessible and subject to increasing acts of destruction. As the laird by his actions had shown little regard for its antiquity, it is not surprising that in the years that followed, this time-honoured symbol of feudal days had been allowed to lapse into a sadly decaying ruin.

To a practical man like Captain Park the loch was a useless sheet of water. To him the revenue from the sale of meadow hay meant more than any pleasure that could be derived from having on the estate a picturesque tower set in the middle of a loch. The laird saw in the barmkin wall, the round towers and the subsidiary buildings a convenient quarry where good stone could be had for the building of the retaining walls of the main cutting for the draining of the loch. The greater part of the causeway was also removed probably for the same purpose or for the building of the bridge and the nearby workmen's howff.

Mr Syme of Wester Cartmore, Writer to the Signet, was no stranger to the district. He showed considerable interest in Captain Park's project and when it was mooted that the Captain was pulling out, he bought the estate from him believing that if he carried on where the Captain had left off he would profit from all the hard work which had hitherto gone into the project.

Cartmore, during the early eighteenth century, became an attractive proposition with its profitable coal deposits. This may have induced the Mr Syme of the period to purchase the estate from the Malcolm family. Like other properties situated in the barony of Lochore its history goes back many centuries. The earliest form of the name was Gartmore and may mean The Large Enclosure. When the barony came to be divided at the end of the fourteenth century, Cartmore was divided also. Easter Cartmore being in the parish of Auchterderran became part of Easter Lochoreshire, while Wester Cartmore, being in Ballingry parish, became part of the barony of Inchgall.

Easter Cartmore can claim a slightly earlier mention than its neighbour. The names of those who had an interest in this small estate whether owner or tenant, include Roger de Boswell in 1367, James Colville in 1530, John Dick in 1576 and James Dick in 1587, William Knox in 1658, David Knox in 1693 and John Knox son of David a Dunfermline merchant, in 1762.

Wester Cartmore is mentioned in 1393 under James de Vallance of Inchgall, David Gaw in 1568, Andrew Wardlaw in 1622, John, Earl of Rothes in 1632, John Malcolm in 1656, David Scrimgeour in 1670, James Scrimgeour in 1676. James Scrimgeour was followed by a Mr Syme probably the grandfather of John Syme, who was in possession of Wester Cartmore in 1680. A lintel stone in the old farmhouse bears two sets of initials separated by a lozenge. The first are J. S. probably for John Syme, the second are M. M. no doubt those of his wife.

51

In a legal document Mr Syme of East Blair states that he inherited Wester Cartmore from his father and it was here that he resided before he acquired other properties in our immediate neighbourhood. He was the eldest son of David Syme and was apprenticed in the legal profession to Samuel Mitchelson. He married in 1795 Barbara, daughter of James Spottiswood of Dunipace. Mr Syme had a younger brother who resided in the village of Aberdour where he is said to have written his well known treatise on *Political Economy*.

In the late 1790s John Syme in his capacity as a lawyer was employed by Sir John Henderson of Fordell in the management of the affairs of his estate, and it was in 1798 that he bought the Lochore estate from Captain Park and in 1799 he was in possession of the estate of East Blair with its long established coal mine. In 1803 he acquired the lands of Binn which marched with his own estate of East Blair. Mr Syme succeeded in doing all this by borrowing the greater part of the purchase price.

Although on the completion of his legal work in 1809 Mr Syme had received from Sir John Henderson a substantial sum, Sir John had been unable to implement his part of an agreement and a considerable balance had still to be paid to Mr Syme. By 1812 Mr

Syme had retired from the legal profession in order that he could give more attention to his mining projects and to improving the profitability of his estates. However, the debt he had incurred was proving an embarrassment to his affairs and the fact that his own funds were being withheld from him greatly aggravated the situation. He was at last compelled to take legal action against the laird of Fordell in order to recover his money, meanwhile his own creditors were pressing rather heavily on him.

Placed in this situation, Mr Syme decided to place the whole of his landed property in trust for his creditors and in so doing he appointed a Mr Selkrig as his trustee whose first act was to sell the estate of Binn which was valued at £18,000. As the circumstances were not favourable for selling, Mr Selkrig had to let it go for £16,000 in 1810 to William Adam of Blairadam. This was followed by the sale of the Lochore estate which went for £32,000 to William Jobson of Dundee in the early part of 1812. Here the sum obtained was considerably less than expected as an independent valuer had valued the estate at £51,371.6/6d, but as Mr Syme's creditors were pressing their demands, Mr Selkrig had no option but to sell.

By now Mr Syme had come within a relatively small amount of clearing off his loans entirely. Meanwhile Sir John Henderson who still owed Mr Syme money was having difficulties of his own, and while he could not repay Mr Syme, he pledged a ship belonging to him named *Margaret of Queensferry* worth £1,200 which was daily expected to arrive at North Queensferry with a cargo of timber from New Brunswick. Although Mr Syme held the ship as security for payment, it did not relieve him of his immediate anxieties. His creditors were suggesting that Mr Selkrig should realise more of the trust-estate, but he had no desire to sell any more of Mr Syme's land providing he could pay up the balance. Mr Syme was spurred into having further recourse to the law, and for a short period Sir John Henderson was incarcerated in the Tolbooth of Canongate, Edinburgh.

Matters appear to have been resolved amicably as Mr Syme continued to own his paternal inheritance of Wester Cartmore and to occupy the Mansion House of East Blair. Like his predecessor he took an active part in the life of the parish and was known for his acts of liberality and his gifts of free coal to the poor were long remembered.

Although he held Lochore estate for only fourteen years he appears to have done much to improve it. In addition to continuing the work commenced by his predecessor in cutting ditches and preparing the ground for cultivation, he had a plan made of the estate showing that by the year 1811 the estate had increased in size to six hundred and ninety-nine acres. The ground occupied by the former loch is shown on the plan divided into fields each with its individual name. In order to work the new ground Mr Syme built a farm steading on the site of the Castle of Lochore to be known later as Chapel farm.

In 1814 John Syme was appointed Deputy Lieutenant of the county and in 1817 he was made a Justice of the Peace. He died in 1821, his wife in 1835 and was succeeded by two sons. David, Advocate, Sheriff of Kinross-shire, who succeeded his father in Wester Cartmore, was still in possession in 1857. He sold East Blair to William Briggs sometime after 1831. He died in 1880. Mr Syme's second son James became the well-known Professor of Clinical Surgery in Edinburgh University and Surgeon to the Queen in Scotland.

52 *Sheriff David Syme, of Wester Cartmore*

JOBSON OF LOCHORE

53

The person who purchased the estate from Mr Syme in 1812 was Mr William Jobson,* a Forfarshire landowner who belonged to a well-known Dundee family which was prominent in the eighteenth and the nineteenth centuries. He was a successful merchant in the fish-curing trade and did much business in Dundee and London. He married Rachael, daughter of John Stuart of Stenton, a lady who claimed descent from Robert II, she being one of the Atholl Stuarts descended from the Wolf of Badenoch. Mrs Jobson was a sister of Lady Margaret Ferguson (formerly a Mrs Lyon) wife of Captain Sir Adam Ferguson, depute Keeper of the Scottish Regalia, and friend of Sir Walter Scott and Chief Commissioner William Adam of Blairadam. Sir Adam had frequented Blairadam since he was a youth and it is highly probable that it was through his good services that the Jobsons came into possession of Lochore. Sir Adam and Sir Walter Scott were schoolboy companions and it was in Sir Adam's father's house in Edinburgh that the youthful Scott met Robert Burns.

Although Mr Jobson was very capable in business, it appears that in the home it was his wife who was the dominant figure, and Jane, the only child of the marriage, was very much under the thumb of her mother. Mrs Jobson in appearance was short and rather stout and walked with a firm heavy step. By nature she was strong-willed, argumentative and domineering. She also seems to have lacked certain lady-like qualities which made her generally disagreeable in company, and taxed to the limit the patience of her closest friends. Her one concern in life, the more so after the death of her husband, was the future well-being of her little daughter Jane.

Mr Jobson, when free from the pressure of business, appears to have played his part in the public life of the community. He was appointed a Justice of the Peace in 1817 and continued to serve in that Office till 1821. He is also known to have had a more positive interest in the well-being of the neighbourhood, for when he died in 1823 it was disclosed that he had left the sum of £100 for the poor of the parish. On the death of her

---

* Mr Jobson did not occupy the estate until the following year. Meanwhile, he planted many trees on the estate and built the servants' quarters to rear of the Mansion House.

171

father, Jane who was twenty-two years of age, succeeded to the estate.* From now on till Jane's marriage in 1825, Mrs Jobson and Jane tended to live more in their town house at six Sandwich Place, Edinburgh and Isaac Bayley, a cousin of Jane, managed the estate on her behalf. He and his wife left their home in Edinburgh and lived for a short time in Lochore House. With the departure of Jane Jobson, Lochore House saw the last of its resident proprietors.

From this time onward her mother's sole concern was the future well-being of her daughter. Jane was thus enjoying the sheltered protection of her mother when for the first time she met Sir Walter Scott's elder son Walter. The meeting, according to a contemporary writer, the assistant minister of Ballingry, took place in 1824 at Blairadam. Earlier in the year the Fergusons had dined with Scott at his town house at thirty-nine Castle Street, Edinburgh, taking with them their niece, a small shy and rather dull girl, when Sir Adam suggested to Scott that young Walter should meet Jane, being careful to add that Jane would not be averse to selling her Fife estate which was worth between £45,000 and £50,000 as she did not admire the neighbourhood, and that her personal property amounted to £20,000. Sir Adam considered that Jane's income would be in the region of £1,500 to £2,000 a year. The suggestion was quickly taken up by Scott. The prospect of a marriage between young Walter and the niece of his life-long friend had its attractions. Scott, in writing to a friend during this period, alludes to Jane's financial position by remarking "there is gold in her garters". Of course it was clearly understood that the young folk would have to be mutually attracted to each other. With these thoughts in mind, Scott wrote to his son then stationed in Ireland.

In June 1824, Sir Adam and Lady Ferguson were staying at Blairadam as the guests of William Adam, and Mrs Jobson and Jane had presumably gone over from Lochore to see the Fergusons. The company was further increased by the arrival of Scott who had come for the annual outing of the Blairadam Club. Scott conversed freely with Jane and, although she was very shy, he found her totally devoid of any affectation, and thought her "little innocent pensive face looked very pretty". His opinion of Mrs Jobson whom he had now met for the first time was however not so favourable. In a letter to his son Walter, Scott speaks of her as having "a singularly unhappy manner" and in a more outspoken passage he described her as a "straight-laced Presbyterian dragon of a dame". Meanwhile, Cornet Scott had come home from Ireland and met Jane and the couple had become very friendly, but Mrs Jobson was far from happy.

A visit by Sir Walter Scott to Mrs Jobson's house was the occasion for a further outburst from Mrs Jobson. The Fergusons had been staying with her when Sir Walter called. When the subject of Jane and Walter Scott was mentioned and Mrs Jobson became aware of what was afoot, she upbraided Sir Adam for saying nothing to her about his match-making plans and protested that she had not been previously consulted, whereupon Scott, in order to take some of the heat out of the discussion, ventured to remind Mrs Jobson that it was customery to find out the mind of a young lady in such matters before approaching her parents; but this did little to appease her.

---

* Jane in the previous year had been presented along with her aunt, Lady Ferguson, to George IV by Lady Montagu Scott at a levee in Dalkeith House.

172

54 *Sir Walter Scott, second baronet, last laird of Lochore*

She believed that it was not so much her daughter as it was the Lochore estate that was the attraction. Mrs Jobson became so angry that she ordered Sir Adam and Lady Ferguson out of her house. Scott's own opinion was that the real reason for her extraordinary behaviour lay in her desire to centre her daughter's affection upon herself. Scott wrote "she is a bold high-spirited Highland woman wrapt up in her child or rather wrapping her up like a child and her exorbitant affection made her unreasonable and violent, and of having never seen such a hyena, and a perfect alligator on the banks of the Nile and all for nonsense of the first water". Jane was deeply distressed as a result of these squalls, but displayed a quiet delicate tact and an unexpectedly degree of firmness. She found much comfort in the knowledge that all her relations were delighted at the match.

55 Sir Adam and Lady Ferguson

On the occasion of the young couple's engagement, great festivities were held at Abbotsford, when Jane was spoken of as "the pretty heiress of Lochore". Lockhart, in describing the scene, says "It was the first regular ball given at Abbotsford and the last. Nay, I believe nobody has ever danced under that roof since then. I myself never again saw the whole range of apartments thrown open for the reception of company except once — on the day of Sir Walter Scott's funeral".

On Mrs Jobson being congratulated on the forthcoming marriage of her daughter, said "the young people were attached, otherwise her Jane might have looked higher, it was only a barony and of quite a late creation". Jane Jobson was married in her mother's house in Edinburgh in the evening of third February 1825. She and her husband were of the same age but of contrasting appearances. Walter Scott was a strapping soldier over six feet while Jane is described as being very small. The couple spent their honeymoon at Abbotsford. Under the conditions of the marriage contract, Sir Walter had already settled the estate of Abbotsford on the couple with his life rent, and power to raise a mortgage of £10,000 on the house, if required. Jane's marriage dowry amounted to £60,000.

Walter, unlike his father, hated books. He loved outdoor life, was a good horseman and a fine shot. He attended the High School in Edinburgh and at the age of eighteen he joined the eighteenth regiment of Hussars as a cornet. Meanwhile, Chief Commissioner Adam had been speaking in high places on Walter's behalf and the Duke of York had promised a commission at an early date, so it was at the time of his marriage he held the rank of lieutenant. His father had previously been planning to purchase a captaincy for him and Chief Commissioner Adam wrote to his son, Sir Frederick Adam, who had been newly made Governor of the Ioman Islands, to give Walter a post on his staff. Four months after his marriage Walter was gazetted Captain. This cost his father £3,500 plus £360 for his regimental outfit and £200 for two mounts. Scott's outlays about this period also included £500 in purchasing jewels for Jane. It has also to be said that Jane, following her marriage, was very generous to her mother. Among other things she provided her with the means of keeping a carriage if she so desired.

Nothing seems to have come out of Adam's letter to his son Sir Frederick, for later on in the year Captain Scott returned to his regiment in Ireland. The couple were visited by Sir Walter and later on by Mrs Jobson. Before the year was out Captain Scott was appointed aide-de-camp to Lord Wellesley, the future Duke of Wellington, and in August 1826 he and Jane returned from Ireland when Jane and her mother went for a short stay at Abbotsford. Jane though not very brilliant was quiet and understanding, her mother however gave no end of trouble with her vulgarity and bad manners. She was very difficult to please, so it was "one continued wrangle the day long". Scott's daughter Ann had hoped to join the men folks in an excursion to Lochore and Blairadam but Mrs Jobson had no desire to leave Abbotsford, so Ann complained at having to endure "the old torment" all on her own while the rest of the company were away. On this occasion Captain Scott and Jane spent a few days at Lochore House.

When we next hear of the couple they had gone south to Brighton to spend the winter of 1827 and Mrs Jobson had gone with them. As Mrs Jobson's Edinburgh house would be standing empty for some time, it was arranged to let Sir Walter have it for four months at a rent of £100. In February 1828 Captain Scott was raised to the rank of Major and was transferred from Canterbury to Hampton Court. Meanwhile, Mrs Jobson had taken a house in Brighton and in October 1829 Major Scott and Jane stayed with her for a short time. The Major, in a letter, says that Jane was fattening on shrimps, prawns and bottled porter and her mother was "in an awful state of inquietude, she positively shakes the room when she walks across it and her sitting down endangers the beams and rafters of the house". It is in this year that Major Scott as laird of Lochore in right of his wife, appears in the public records of the county. As, "Walter Scott of Lochore" he was appointed one of the Commissioners of Supply and held that office till 1837. In following the couple, we move on another two years. On 17th October 1831 Major Scott obtained leave of absence and arrived in London to accompany his father on a holiday abroad in an effort to restore his failing health. A week later the rest of the family arrived at Portsmouth to say goodbye to Sir Walter. It was not yet known if Jane would accompany her husband on the voyage. Ann Scott thought Jane mysterious until it was explained that Jane suffered dreadfully from seasickness and was ill even when crossing the Irish Sea. It was decided therefore that Jane would stay in Brighton with her mother. The last glimpse we have is that of Jane and Mrs Jobson standing on the pier at Portsmouth waving goodbye to the party on board the frigate *Barham*.

On the death of his father in 1832, Major Scott became Sir Walter Scott second baronet of Abbotsford and Jane became Lady Scott. It is surprising that Lady Scott held on to the Lochore estate for so long. Knowing how she and her husband felt about the neighbourhood, one would have expected that they would have disposed of the estate not long after their marriage. In the dark days following his father's crash, Major Scott wrote to his father offering him financial help. In a letter he writes "I think there is a good deal of Jane's money invested in the funds, she says to the amount of £14,000" and further on he writes "that land must be sold, why then Lochore will go first". In a further letter in which he discusses the proposed sale, he remarks "it is clear enough that I can do this without any great difficulty, as Lochore is a place which I never shall go to and shall dispose to the first good bidder; that will always give a good sum of ready money". Sir Walter of course refused all offers of help. "My own right hand shall pay my debt", he wrote. Lochore stayed with the Scotts and brought in about £1,200 a year in rents. Meanwhile, we find "Sir Walter Scott" in the lists of local Justices of the Peace for the years from 1835 to 1838. In 1839, by which time he had gained the rank of Lieutenant Colonel, he went with his regiment to India and after a period of seven years there he contracted fever and died in 1847 while returning to this country on board the *Wellesley*.

From this time onward Lady Scott lived most of her life in London. She sold the Lochore estate to the Capeldrae Cannel Coal Company in 1867 for £60,000. She died at her home in London on 19th March 1877 at the age of 76, and was buried in Dryburgh Abbey beside her husband and her illustrious father-in-law.

We end this short account of the Jobsons with a verse from a poem written by Sir Walter Scott in which he makes reference to his daughter-in-law. It will be seen that she is called "Jeannie" in the poem. This was her pet name and one by which she was known to the people of Ballingry. The poem is in manuscript and in the handwriting of Scott, and is a light-hearted invitation to Sir Adam Ferguson, Jeannie's uncle, then residing at

176

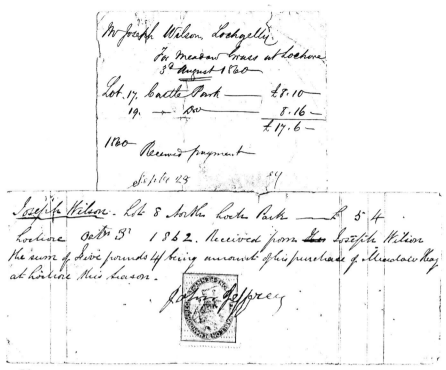

56 *Receipts for purchase of hay at Lochore Meadows during the time of Lady Scott*

Gattonside House on the other side of the river Tweed, to come to Abbotsford for dinner.

COME OWER THE TWEED, ADAM

Being an excellent new song to the old tune of
"Come Ower the Sea Charlie"

(The third verse goes thus)

> With wine we'll regale ye
> We'll draw punch and ale ye,
> And song, verse, and tale ye,
> Shall have at your call.
> Twill be worth a gold guinea
> To hear Mrs Jeannie
> Lilting blyth as a queenie
> In Abbotsford Hall.
>
> Then come ower the Tweed Adam,
> Dear Adam, Sir Adam,
> Come ower the Tweed Adam,
> And gladden us all.

177

Of the portraits of Jane Jobson, none so far have been traced, although enquiries have been made in all the likely places. In 1825 Sir Walter Scott commissioned William Douglas, a portrait painter, to paint a miniature of Jane for which he paid fifteen guineas. Three photographs are known to have existed (or perhaps still exist) showing Jane Jobson in later life. Those who have seen them say they show her as a gentle and kindly old lady. With this description we will have to be content.

THE CONSTABLE FAMILY

57

The family name of Constable, although frequently met with in England, is found in a much lesser degree in Scotland and few indeed who have this name are to be found in Fife; and yet perhaps the best known person to bear this name in more modern times was the Fife-born Archibald Constable, the well-known publisher of the early works of Sir Walter Scott.

Great antiquity is claimed for the surname. During the time of the Roman Empire *Comes Stabuli* denoted the "Count of the Stable" an office of considerable importance. In the continent at a much later period the person holding this office was in charge of cavalry, and during the Middle Ages his successor in office was in command of the King's forces in the field.

In Scotland the Constable was responsible for the security of the King's person and for maintaining the peace for a distance of twelve leagues from where the King was residing. *Constabularius* appears frequently in connection with castles in Scotland during the Wars of Independence when the person who held this office was responsible in the absence of the owner for the security of the castle under his charge. There were also Constables of towns and villages. It has been suggested that the surname in Scotland is derived from the holder of these latter offices.

During the reign of David I the office of Constable became hereditary in the great Anglo Norman family of Moreville. Hugh de Moreville is known to have become Constable of Scotland sometime before 1140. During the period of the Wars of Independence the title was conferred on the family of de la Haye by Robert the Bruce in the person of Sir Gilbert who became Constable of Scotland in 1314. William de lay Haye was Constable in 1330. By now the holders of the lesser offices were beginning to accept Constable as their surname.

The Constable family which is first heard of north of the Forth settled in Perthshire for many generations where it multiplied and acquired what was described in 1456 as "the Constable lands". Many of this name appear as burgesses of Dundee from the year 1563 to 1800. Descended from this stock was George Constable, son of John Constable "trader in Dundee", the life-long friend of Sir Walter Scott's parents. George

Constable, an Edinburgh lawyer, was a confirmed bachelor and an antiquary of considerable learning. He inspired young Scott with his recollections of the Forty-Five and other exciting reminiscences so much so that Scott in later years confessed that George Constable was the original of Jonethan Oldbuck the Antiquary of Monkbarns, in his novel, *The Antiquary*.

The first representative of the Constables of Benarty, James Constable, of Bonnytown in the parish of Rattray, was probably descended from others of the name who appear from 1329 onwards in the persons of "Symon the Constable" and John Constable who with others in 1360 rendered their accounts as collectors of the third contribution for the ransom of David II. Another John Constable, who was known as "Agricola" and "Fermorer" lived at Wester Randellstone in the parish of Errol. His son also called John was baptized in 1758.

James Constable

James Constable, the progenitor of the family, was the father of George Constable who married in 1659 Marjory, daughter of John Moncur, farmer at the Hillock of Rattray. There were three sons of the marriage, John, George and James.

John Constable

John Constable, the eldest son, was born in 1660. He married Margaret Chalmers whose progenitors were husbandmen at the Abbey of Coupar Angus. Of the marriage there were three sons, George, James and David.

George Constable

George Constable, the eldest son of John Constable, rented the lands of Blackhill of Rattray and afterwards rented the Mains of Bendochy. He married firstly Margaret, daughter of James Playfair, farmer in Couttie by whom he had four sons and three daughters. He married secondly Isabella Kinmond, widow of Alexander Alison, tenant in Melginch by whom he had two sons.

John Constable

John Constable, who was the eldest surviving son of George Constable, married in 1757 Margaret, daughter of William Johnston of Millhall who had issue two sons, William and George.

William Constable

William Constable, the elder son of John Constable was born in 1759. He studied for the ministry and was licensed by the Presbytery of Meigle in 1785. In 1801 he was presented by George III to the charge of St. Martin's in the Presbytery of Perth and in February of the following year he was ordained assistant and successor to David Bannerman M.A. William Constable married in 1814 Anne Briggs, daughter of Andrew Briggs and had by her seven daughters and two sons. His name appears in 1831 along with those of his kinsmen, Patrick Constable of the Mill of Errol and William Constable of Bendochy as a subscriber to James Knox's *Topography of the Basin of the Tay,* a scarce book wherein the early history of Lochore and Blair are entered into.

William Constable died in 1836 and his wife in 1861. Their family in order of seniority were Margaret, born in 1815, Anne, born in 1816, Janet, born in 1817, all of whom died in 1820. Georgina, born in 1818, died in 1898. Elizabeth Briggs, born in 1820, married her cousin James Constable of Glencraig. William Briggs Constable born in 1821, succeeded to the estate of Benarty and died in 1882. Margaret Anne, born in 1823, Andrew, born in 1825, died in 1916. His twin sister Anne (second of the name) died in 1915.

As recorded in an earlier chapter, the Blair estate remained in the Colville family until about the year 1796 after which it was sold to Mr John Syme an Edinburgh lawyer. Following Mr Syme's death in 1821 the Blair estate along with the estate of Wester Cartmore passed to his elder son, David.

David Syme, Advocate, was made a Justice of the Peace and a Commissioner of Supply for the County of Fife in 1830 and in 1838 he was appointed Sheriff Substitute for Kinross-shire, an office he held till his death in 1880. He was in possession of Blair in 1831. After this date he is designated as "of Cartmore". It was during David Syme's ownership that Cleikum Inn Lodge was transferred from the Blair estate to the Lochore estate. On being approached about a suggestion made by Sir Walter Scott, Mr Syme readily agreed to allow a right of access through a small portion of his estate in order that the west avenue leading from Lochore House could join up with the public road. On completion of the avenue, a small house which stood near the new entrance was gifted by Mr Syme to Lochore estate to serve as a lodge. The house was demolished in 1946.

William Briggs of Blair

The surname Briggs, a varient of Brigg, is derived from the Scots pronunciation of Bridge(s). The name in its various forms goes back to the fourteenth century. It is to be found frequently among the landowners in Fife during the eighteenth and nineteenth centuries when the holders of the name appear to have followed the naval and military professions. Among those who followed the latter profession was John Briggs who rose to the rank of General. As a young officer he went abroad and served in the Madras infantry and took part in the Malratta wars and accompanied Sir John Malcolm in his mission to Persia in 1810. Sir John, the Indian administrator and diplomat, belonged to a younger branch of the Malcolms of Lochore.

William Briggs, as far as the scanty records show, appears to have belonged to the second generation of a small shipping family domiciled in Alloa who did a brisk trade with ports in South America in the late 1700s. It is not known for certain when he acquired the estate of Blair. He probably came into possession in the year 1832 when most of the arable land on the estate was being worked by James Ramsay, tenant farmer. In 1838 he was appointed one of the Commissioners of Supply for the County. His name appears in the local records in 1846. In 1848 he subscribed to and was present at a presentation to Peter Craig on his retiral as schoolmaster in Cleish. We have little more than a hint that during his short period of ownership he desired to improve things about the estate. He is known to have removed the ruined walls of a small enclosure attached to the east wall of the church at Ballingry, probably the remains of the chancel of the pre-Reformation church. It had long been known as the Blair aisle and was the place of burial of the lairds of Blair. He erected iron railings to enclose the site, no doubt to establish afresh an ancient right. Mr Briggs is also known to have built the present Benarty House to replace the old house of the Colvilles. In addition, he had a town house in Perth known as Bertha Cottage. It was there that he died on 15th October, 1849.

William Briggs Constable: I of Benarty

Mr Constable was the eldest son of the Rev. William Constable and a nephew of William Briggs. He probably succeeded to the estate on the death of his uncle, but his name does not appear locally until 1858 in which year he was made a Justice of the Peace. Two years later in 1860 he was appointed one of the Commissioners of Supply for the County of Fife. He will be remembered as the proprietor who changed the name of the estate. This took place in 1866 when the old appellations were dropped and the estate received its new name of "Benarty". He married Marion Meikle Nelson, third and youngest daughter of George Nelson, farmer of Broomhouse, Haddingtonshire, by whom he had three sons, William of whom presently, Nelson and Andrew and a daughter Marion. He and his wife died at Perth in 1882. Nelson Briggs Constable was born in 1854 and died without issue in 1917 and was buried in the Dean Cemetery, Edinburgh. He married in 1901 his cousin Margaret Wyllie Constable who died in 1950. Andrew Henderson Briggs Constable was born in 1865. He received his early education at Kinross Public School and Dollar Academy and passed to Edinburgh University with a view to studying law where he took his M.A. and L.L.D. degrees and won the Vans Dunlop Scholarship in 1888. He was foremost in the various student activities; and as President of the Students' Representative Council he represented the University students at the Ceto-Centenary of the Bologna University.

He was called to the Bar in 1889 and such was his skill in the various branches of the law that he soon acquired a lucrative practice which on occasions took him to various parts of the country while acting as defending Counsel in criminal cases. Mr Constable studied Parliamentary procedure in which he was an acknowledged authority. In 1900 he stood as Unionist candidate for East Fife against Mr Asquith but was unsuccessful.

By 1910 he had contested a further three Parliamentary Seats but was unable to reach Westminster. As an Advocate of distinction he was appointed in 1917 to the office of Sheriff of Caithness, Orkney and Shetland. In 1920 he became Sheriff of Argyll, only to hold the office for a short period as he was afterwards elected to the Faculty of Advocates as Dean of the Faculty. Again, he did not hold this office for long, for he was soon elected one of the Crown Council to hold the office of Solicitor General. In 1922 he was appointed a judge of the Court of Session with the courtesy title of Lord Constable.

Lord Constable was obliged to retire prematurely owing to ill-health. During his few years of retirement he continued to take a keen interest in the welfare of the students of his University and was appointed a member of its Court. In recognition of his services the University conferred on him in 1928 (the year of his death) the Honarary degree of Doctor of Laws. He was buried in the Dean Cemetery, Edinburgh. Lord Constable married in 1895 Elizabeth, daughter of James Simpson of Mawcarse, by whom he had two sons.

Marion Nelson Briggs Constable, daughter of William Constable first of Benarty married in 1889 John Beveridge of Kinneston. She died in 1939. There were no offspring of the marriage.

William Briggs Constable: II of Benarty

Born in 1852 he succeeded to the estate of Benarty on the death of his father. In 1886 he was appointed a Commissioner of Supply and continued in that office till his death in 1898. He was buried in the Blair Isle of Ballingry church. Of his marriage in 1890 to Euphemia Harris, daughter of Robert Harris of the Green Hotel, Kinross, he had one son, William and two daughters, Marion and Georgina. His wife died in 1946.

Marion Meikle Nelson Briggs Constable was born in 1892. She married in 1916 Major Henry Watson Locke of Ormiston, Hawick, by whom she had one daughter, Enid Marion and three sons, James, William and Andrew. Mrs Locke died in 1960.

Georgina Johnston Harris Briggs Constable was born in 1898. She married in 1924 Gordon Mitchell Wright by whom she had two sons, John and Hedley. Mrs Wright died in 1983.

William Briggs Constable: III of Benarty

The late Lieutenant Colonel William Briggs Constable was born in 1896. As he was only two years of age when his father died the responsibility of managing the family estate rested solely on his mother until he reached an age when he could take over the responsibility himself. At the age of five years he entered Edinburgh Academy where he received his early education. In attaining the Upper School he was a member of the army class of boys intending to make the army their career. He excelled in sport and won many trophies particularly for running. He was also a member of the first Cricket XI and the first Rugby XV.

Shortly after the outbreak of the First World War he passed the entrance examination for the military college at Woolwich. After a short training course owing to war conditions, he was commissioned into the Royal Regiment of Artillery in February, 1915 and posted to Gallipoli. Following the end of that disastrous campaign he took part in the evacuation of the forces and was afterwards posted to Mesopotamia where he was engaged in desert warfare near Baghdad and was present at the relief of Kut under General Townsend. He was awarded the Military Cross during this campaign. After a short period in India he was again in Mesopotamia following the second Arab Rising. From there he was posted to Turkey as part of the Allied Control Commission under General Harrington. The years 1923 to 1929 were taken up with postings in Britain followed by a further three years in India, followed by two years in the South Irish Coast Defences. The year 1937 saw him in India once more.

On the outbreak of the Second World War the Laird of Benarty was recalled to form a regiment of reservists, and within a fortnight he was in France with his regiment. By now he was temporarily commanding a Field Artillery Regiment under General Montgomery in an advance on Brussels followed by the retreat to Dunkirk. After some days on the beaches he got across the Channel in an old Brighton Paddle Steamer, one of the hundreds of light craft called upon to get the troops out of France. After serving in various parts of Britain and in Orkney he was towards the end of the war posted to command a garrison in Sierra Leone in West Africa. On his return from overseas he retired from the army in 1948 with the rank of Lieutenant Colonel. In 1952 as a retired officer he was invited to accept a post at the Scottish Command. This he accepted and held the post for four years.

On his retirement from the army he devoted much of his time to the management of his estate particularly in carrying out his scheme of afforestation. Even so, he managed to find time to take part in national as well as local activities. He was Vice-Chairman of the Kinross Territorial Association and Secretary of the Help Society for Kinross and Clackmannan and afterwards for West Fife. He was latterly Honorary Vice-President of the West Fife branch of the Society and the first Chairman of the Fife Union of Boys Clubs.

In the political field he was a member of the committee for the West Fife Conservative Association and became Honorary Vice-President of the Central Fife Association. On the lighter side of his many activities he was for a time Chairman of the Kinross Curling Club and Honorary Secretary of the Scottish Skating Association and at all times an active member of the Kinross-shire Jolly Beggars Burns Society. He was also from its founding, an Honorary President of the Benarty Antiquarian Club.

Lieutenant Colonel Briggs Constable long had a desire to contribute materially to the on-going life of the church at Ballingry but the opportunity did not present itself until, during the work of enlarging the church building in 1966 the stonemasons found they had insufficient dressed stones to complete the work. Happily, it was not long before the Laird of Benarty was on the scene. As the ruined walls of the ancient house of the Colvilles were built of similar stones, he caused the walls to be carefully demolished and the stones transported to Ballingry. No doubt it was with justifiable pride and satisfaction that the laird viewed the work and saw how beautifully the weather-beaten stones from Benarty had added to the beauty and dignity of the old church. On the occasion of the re-opening of the church for worship, Lieutenant Colonel and Mrs Constable gifted a beautiful oak reading desk. Following his retirement the laird of Benarty was ordained an elder. In this office his desire for Christian service found expression in assisting the minister along with his fellow elders in promoting the spiritual care of the church in the various Christian activities throughout the parish. William Briggs Constable married in 1921 Edith Selkirk Allan Oswald, daughter of Doctor David Robert Oswald of Kinross by whom he had one son, William and one daughter, Edith Ann. Mrs Constable presently lives at Kingussie but takes an active interest in Benarty estate.

William Briggs Constable: IV of Benarty

The present laird of Benarty married in 1978, Barbara Jayne, daughter of F.C. Flury of Bletchley, Buckinghamshire by whom he has three sons, William Briggs, Adam Briggs and Peter Briggs. He has retired from his partnership in an oil-related business in the Orkneys and now attends to the management of his estate. Of all the old families who once held lands in Lochoreshire, the laird of Benarty is the last to reside on his estate.

THE CHURCH OF BALLINGRY

Time not only brings changes, but with time many hitherto unknown facts come to light. The Rev. David Jamie has dealt fully with the church's history from the Reformation onwards, but the earlier history of the church was denied him. The session records prior to 1669 were destroyed by people who should have known better but who obviously were unaware of their undisputed value, so we today are left with only a very vague idea of what they probably contained. How far back in the history of the church they would have taken us no one now can tell. However, from what has been disclosed since Mr Jamie's time it is possible to fill in, in very rough outline, the church's history prior to the Reformation. As Mr Jamie rightly says "The Culdees of Lochleven would not disdain to christianise Ballingry. They would never leave men almost within hail of their walls in the darkness of heathenism". To show that Ballingry did come within the enlightenment of the Christian faith through the evangelising power of the early Celtic church, we would refer to the name Crosshill with its ecclesiastical connotation. A cross stood there long before the formation of the burgh of Crosshill and the erection of a mercat cross. Probably belonging to this period was a sculptured stone to be seen some sixty years ago on the Commonty of the Milton Moss of Inchgall at a rather significant point where the loan divided, one path going towards the Milton, the other to Ballingry. The stone which is lost, has been described as displaying numerous figures in low relief.

No one can say for certain when the first church was built in our neighbourhood. In the present state of our knowledge we would put the chapel of Lochore as possibly the earliest place of worship. This chapel was part of the castle complex during its second phase and may have dated from before the mid twelfth century. It was at first a private chapel built by the baron of Lochore and endowed by a priest whose main duty probably was to say "soul-masses". With the removal of the feudal barons from Lochore Castle to Inchgall Castle the chapel became known as Inchgall chapel and although situated some distance from their island home it continued to be used and is mentioned in charters as late as the early seventeenth century.

Of the chapel of Bothedillach or Buthadlach belonging to the Abbey of Incholm and situated on the Clune hill very little is known. The lands of Bothedlak lay in the neighbouring parish of Beath.

In tracing the early history of the church at Ballingry it is necessary to go back in time to the Culdees of Lochleven. In the year 842 Brude V the last of the Pictish kings gave the island of Lochleven to St. Serf and the Culdees who were living there. This is the earliest record of the Culdees in Scotland. In about the year 942 Ronan, their "Monk and Abbot" made over the island to Fothad, Bishop of St. Andrews in return for the provision of food and clothing. Macbeth and his queen Gruoch as we have already seen gave the Culdees Kirkness and its boundaries, while Maldunus, bishop of St. Andrews gave them the church of Markinch, and Tuadal the church of Scoonie. Later on Queen Margaret made them a gift of the "Vill of Balcriste". In 1059 Fothad II Bishop of St. Andrews made them a gift of the church of "Hurkendorth" (Auchterderran), while Ethelred, son of Malcolm Canmore and Queen Margaret, gave them Auchmoor at the east end of the loch, thereafter King Edgar gave them "Petnemokane" near Kirkness.

By this time steps were being taken to reform the old traditions within the Celtic church, and in the reign of King David efforts were made to have the Culdees replaced by new religious Houses which were within the continental orders. In 1144 David founded an Augustinian priory at St. Andrews and in time the Culdees there were transformed into the Collegiate Church of St. Mary on the Rock. About the year 1150 St. Serfs isle was given to the Augustinian canons that they might establish a cononical order there and ultimately supplant the Culdees. To the Culdees, David gave the choice either of accepting the new order and becoming Canons or of being expelled from the island, but as time passed these provisions were somewhat relaxed. The Culdees, however, continued to retain their identity for almost another two centuries and are last heard of in St. Andrews in 1332 by which time they had been all but absorbed into the Augustinian Order.

Now, we have seen that in 1059 the Culdees of St. Serfs were given the church of Auchterderran by Bishop Fothad II. From this time onwards we may be fairly certain that the clergy would on many occasions pass through the lands of Ballingry in their journeyings to and from Auchterderran using probably the Common already referred to. This saddle-track stretched from Ballingry to Kirkcaldy and it is just possible that it was the clergy from St. Serf's Isle who first established this ancient right of way. It is not surprising therefore to find a chapel dependent on the church of Auchterderran established at Ballingry in the thirteenth century. There is a strong probability that this small preaching station was set up by the priory of Lochleven.

What follows is of interest as it is probably the earliest allusion to a chapel at Ballingry. It is to be found in a list of churches and chapels situated in the province of Fothrif in the year 1177, showing the stipends attached to the cures. The list contains "De Hurwharderich (Auchterderran) cum Capella XXX merks". The entry is preceded by the church of Portmoak and followed by that of Kinglassie which is known to have been a Culdee holding in the twelfth century. Another interesting fact relating to the chapel at Ballingry has come to light, thanks to the discovery of a fragment of a mid-sixteenth century manuscript copy of Bagimond's taxroll of Scottish church benefices for the year 1275 found in the binding of an old book in the Register House in Edinburgh. From this we know that the church at Auchterderran and the chapel at Ballingry were taxed for the financing of the crusades during this period. The Auchterderran-Ballingry relationship no doubt goes back to Celtic times. According to the ecclesiastical rules of the period, while Ballingry remained a dependent chapel the parishioners would require to travel to the baptismal church at Auchterderran to attend communion and to have their children baptized as the function of a subordinate chapel was for the preaching of the Word only. This again points to the use of the ancient right-of-way.

With the setting-up of the chapel at Ballingry, there would be a need to provide land for sustaining a priest appointed to officiate. The chapel of Lochore served the barony and for reasons which will appear shortly, it is unlikely that the baron of Lochore of the period provided the land. Whether the endowment took place early in the life of the chapel is not known. It is noteworthy that none of the early barons of Lochore ever appear to have held Ballingry. The earliest allusion to secular ownership is in the person of Ricardo de Ballingry in 1395, and even then Ballingry is stated as belonging to the church there.

The absence of any reference to Ballingry in the records of the Lochore family and the Vallance family suggests that these lands belonged solely to the church, firstly to the Culdees to whom they were returned after the verdict of 1128 and afterwards by the canons of St. Andrews who succeeded them. It is known that Navitie which was part of Ballingry belonged to the canons. The probability is that the Culdees endowed the chapel with their lands of Ballingry which lands we believe were included in Kirkness. It is not until 1477 that Ballingry appears in a list of lands which made up the barony of Inchgall.

58 *The Church of Ballingry in 1948*

The church had become parochial some time prior to 1424 when William de Masterton was its rector. It will be seen that the new status of the church coincides more or less with the coming of the Wardlaws as barons of Inchgall. The Mastertons took their name from a place in the neighbourhood of Dunfermline. In 1422 a William de Masterton conveyed the lands of Masterton to the monastery there, but it is not known if the benefactor to the monastery was also the rector of Ballingry, a post which at this period carried a salary of £20 a year. In 1424 the rector proposed to resign his charge in favour of his son John. So we learn that he supplicates that the Pope would commit power to the precentor of Dunkeld (probably Nicolus de Atholl) to receive his resignation and assign the church to his son. It is further said that, although John is the son of William and an unmarried woman, and the rule of chancery which forbids anyone to succeed to the benefices of his father, it is hoped that no prejudice will arise in these parts on account of this. We are not told if John Masterton succeeded his father as rector of Ballingry.

Thirty seven years afterwards in 1461 the little-known chapel of Ballingry emerges from obscurity to become a prebend of the Collegiate Church of St. Mary on the Rock at St. Andrews. We move another fourteen years further on to the year 1475 to find that one, John Tyrie, in witnessing a deed of this date adds that he is the rector of the parish church of Ballingry. From what is known of this man it is possible that he had held this post for the previous ten years. Several of John Tyrie's relations were churchmen, others were men of considerable standing in the town of Perth and stood high in the king's favour. John was the son of Alexander Tyrie, Provost of Perth, and his wife Janet Lauder. John became chancellor of the church of St. Andrews in 1460 when he is designated "Bachelor of Degrees" having received Crown presentation from King James II. In 1479 he was elected one of the "masters" to assist the venerable Robert Boswell, rector of Auchterderran, in his newly appointed post of rector of the University of St. Andrews.

We meet with several John Tyries, all related, during this period. There was a Sir John Tyrie, Provost of the collegiate church of Methven who, in 1488 received £5 from the king to buy a gown made of twill. In the following year we hear of another John Tyrie, writer in Perth, who received fourteen shillings for writing a letter for the king, and yet another John Tyrie who was vicar of Crammon in 1512. It was, however, Sir John Tyrie, of whom we have already spoken, who was the king's favourite. When the king came to Perth in 1490 it was Sir John's town house he lodged in and on that occasion the Lord High Treasurer paid Sir John £7 "to by a pwncion of wyne to lay in his hous in Sante Johniston again the kingis cuming thare". Two months later the king is again staying with Sir John and on this occasion a James Balfour is sent to Perth with £10 16/- to give to the king who is to play at cards with Sir John and the laird of Halkett.

A charter dated 27th February, 1512, shows that John Tyrie was still rector in Ballingry, but he must have left the church sometime between 14th August and 29th October of that year during which period he was paid £10. James Wardlaw, son of Sir Henry Wardlaw the laird of Inchgall who succeeded John Tyrie, received a like sum within the same period thus bringing the total to £20 being the annual salary attached to the rectory.

Little more is known of James Wardlaw beyond the fact that he was married and had a son called John and that he gained a Bachelor of Arts Degree at St. Andrews in 1476, and five years later he received the degree of Master of Arts. He probably did not hold the post of rector of Ballingry for very long. He is known to have been succeeded by his sister-in-law's brother, Walter Beaton, brother of the Archbishop of St. Andrews. Walter Beaton relinquished his post at Ballingry sometime before 1535. Four years later he appears as rector of Govan.

In 1535 and probably for some years previously, the rector of Ballingry was Alexander Wardlaw, the son of John Wardlaw laird of Inchgall, and Elizabeth Beaton his wife, and nephew of his two immediate predecessors. His name appears in 1536 and again in 1541 when he received £20 as rector. After a lapse of twenty years we meet with him again by which time the reformed church was taking shape, involving changes in church discipline and procedure. As Alexander Wardlaw retained his conservative views in religious matters, he held out against the ways of the Reformation and clashed with the church authorities. We will return to this shortly.

Following the Reformation we meet with the term rector less frequently, the name being replaced by "minister" or "parson". Although rectors were expected to reside in the parish and officiate, in many cases the spiritual needs of the parish were met by a substitute in the person of a residing vicar. While the rector enjoyed the larger share of the fruits of the church in the form of corn teinds, the lesser teinds went to the vicar. The Wardlaws were probably the only rectors who resided in the parish.

In the case of Ballingry, on the church becoming a prebend of St. Mary on the Rock, it would appear that part at least of the church's revenues was diverted from the parish and appropriated to the mother church and that, in addition to the rector, the cure was served by a pensionary vicar, both rector and vicar receiving a set emolument in place of a share of the church teinds. The first known pensionary vicar of Ballingry appears during the incumbency of Alexander Wardlaw in 1538 in the person of Sir Andrew Sym. In 1539 Sir Andrew received £20 2/- and £28 12/8d in 1541, during which period he had acted for Master Andrew Oliphant, Dean of Fothrif. In this year when witnessing a deed he is designated "Andrea Sym vicario penfionario de Ballingry". He probably held the office for the following eight years.

In 1549 a new vicar is appointed to the church. On 31st October of this year, in the presence of Henry Wardlaw the eldest son of the laird and brother of the minister, Andrew Oliphant, notary public "gave institution or possession to Sir James Stanis of an annual pension of the parish church of Ballingry and elected him to be vicar pensioner of the vicarage of the said church for the whole of his life in terms of a letter of pension by the Archbishop of St. Andrews under his round seal and the subscription of Mr Andrew Oliphant in form of an instrument made to Sir James thereupon". As James Stanis had like his predecessor taken the degree of Bachelor of Arts he was given the courtesy title of "Sir". On the same day the newly appointed vicar witnessed a deed wherein David Ramsay of Ballingry acknowledged having received from Henry Wardlaw in pure gold and silver the sum of one hundred merks Scots for the redemption of the lands of Navitie. Things seem to have gone on well enough for the next fourteen years or so, but the vicar's conduct began to be the subject of some concern in the parish and in time it came to the notice of John Wynram, the superintendent for Fife and Fothrif. On 12th January, 1564 Sir James and one Maig Symson were summoned to appear before the superintendent and the church court at St. Andrews. As neither of them responded to the summons, the court decided in their absence "accordying to the determinacion of the holl kyrk in thar generall essemble, haldyn at Edinburgh in December last" to issue letters of excommunication against Sir James and to summon Maig Symson again. The records are silent as to what action the vicar took after being deprived of his office. In all probability he repented of his wrongdoings and in other ways may have satisfied the superintendent's court as to his suitability for readmission to the ministry.

That he was reinstated in Ballingry is clear, but how long afterwards is not known. He was in office in 1573 when last heard of and was given the vicarage for life. He probably died in that year or shortly after.

To return to Alexander Wardlaw: he held the office of rector of the church for at least a quarter of a century prior to the Reformation and on the eve of the Reformation

59 *Tombstone of John Wynram of Kirkness, Superintendent of Fife*

he, as rector and James Stanis as vicar, were responsible for the spiritual life of the parish. One of the rules of the Reformed church was that no minister could dispense the sacraments without being permitted to do so by the superintendent. Now, although in other respects Mr Wardlaw appears to have been a sound man, he had a violent temper which, when not controlled, led him into trouble even with his own relations. However, many of his neighbours and relations did not treat him fairly and he had on more than one occasion to seek the aid of the law against those who sought to deprive him of his teind sheaves. He could not bring himself to acknowledge John Wynram as the newly appointed superintendent, so ignoring the rule, he continued to administer the sacraments as before. The superintendent therefore found him to be "inobedient" and had him replaced by Peter Watson a former canon of St. Andrews and now a qualified minister, but although Mr Watson had been sent "to support the rowm of ane minister in Ballingrye", Mr Wardlaw "stoppit hym to frequent thar manest and hostil hym and stoppit hym to come to solemnizat matrimony betwix two personnis", and in order to make it impossible for Mr Watson to perform the marriage, Mr Wardlaw shut off the chancel by erecting a row of "Jedwood staiffs", a kind of spear, which he kept in the

"Qweyr" of the kirk.*

Faced with this situation the superintendent had no alternative but to proceed to Ballingry in order to solemnise the marriage himself although he had little time to spare having come "fra otheris grat business". While he was there he "caused ane minister to be admitted to baptis ane bairn" to which Mr Wardlaw strongly objected and "injurit the superintendent and said he "hundit the hayl cuntre agains hym, and that he wes verray parciall". He "affyrmand hymself to be minister of that kyrk, lawfullie chosyn and providit tharto, and that he wald not be ane reader to John Knox nor ony other in Scotland". The superintendent took this occasion to admonish Mr Wardlaw and the parishioners for their neglect of the fabric of the church and called on them to have the church repaired. This was in accordance with an enactment of the General Provincial Council of the previous year which stated that ruined or decaying churches were to be rebuilt or repaired; the chancel by the rector and the nave by the parishioners. Mr Wardlaw however stood out against the injunction of the superintendent and said "the devill ane penne he wald spend upon the kyrk; gevand evyll exempill and occasion to the parrochinaris to leif undon thar deuete". The following day the heritors convened a meeting in the church when they desired Mr Wardlaw "to concur wyth thame according to the admonicion mayd be the superintendent" regarding the repairing of the church. Among those present were his brothers Henry the laird of Inchgall and Andrew Wardlaw, and his two uncles John Wardlaw and James Wardlaw. This, however, was the occasion for a further outburst from Mr Wardlaw when he declared "he wald do nathing in that behalve, nor obey ony admmonision or command of that fals, dissaitfull, gredy, and dissimblit smayk, for he wes ane of tham that maist oppressed, smored, and held down the Word of God and now he is cummin to it, and professis this same for grediness of gayr, lurkand and watchand quhill he maye se ane other tym. And farther ekit and sayd befoyr the sam personnis above wryttyn or I war not revenged of that fals smaik, I had lever renunce my part of the kyrk of God".

As the matter concerned Wynram himself, he handed over Mr Wardlaw to the jurisdiction of the kirk session of St. Andrews; so in due course he was summoned to appear before the minister and session "to ansuer to sic headis and articlis as salbe obeckit aganis hym for inobedence contenpsion and blasphemows spekyn aganis the superintendent of Fyiff".

Patrik Ramsaye appeared for Wynram while Mr Wardlaw conducted his own defence. During the hearing of the case several witnesses were called. The first of these was James Wardlaw who declared that "he wes present in the kyrk of Balingry upon the sext daye of Julii as he belevis, hard and saw Mr Alexander Wardlaw stop Peter Watson

---

* This is not the first occasion in which Jedwood staiffs are mentioned. This form of spear, along with other weapons, figured in a skirmish which took place at Lumphinnans some twelve years previously. One can well imagine that quite a number of spears would be required to seal off the chancel. The fact that they were kept within the church is of interest as it suggests that the church at this period was used as a repository for arms. The spears were probably placed there for safekeeping to be handed out among the menfolk who lived in the cluster of houses surrounding the church in times of danger. The storing of spears and other warlike weapons in religious Houses, if not a common practice in times of stress, at least is known to have taken place in Fife and elsewhere on occasions to the number of several hundred, but this probably arose out of unusual circumstances.

minister to preche, to minister baptisme or solemnizat mariage, and for the sam caws of set purpos, the parson had Jedwod Staiffis in the qweyr". He saw Mr Alexander, minister, "baptisme efter inhibicion gevyn to him by the superintendent". The second witness, Thomas Lodean, confirmed all that James Wardlaw had said. The third witness, Peter Watson, minister, spoke of "the manesing and bosting bayth in word and wryt, be Mr Alexander and also impediment was mayd to hym bayth wyth wordis and wapins vidz; Jedwood Staffis, provydit in the kirk be Mr Alexander for the nanis". Martyn Hearing and Andro Law, both of whom lived at Kirkness, added their testimony to what took place in the church and in due course the sixth witness was called in the person of "Jhone Jowsie, dwelland in Balingrie". On being questioned he answered that "he hard Mr Alexander Wardlaw inhibit fra ministracion be the superintendent; and hard be common voce and fam, that tharefter Mr Alexander baptised ane barn of Jhon Bruc in Capildra". The other charges "he confessis to be trew, as common voce and fam of the parrochyn of Ballingre recordis, bot he wes nocht present hym self tym tharof".

Alexander Wardlaw confessed to some of the charges, others he denied. His judges however found the charges sufficiently proven and Mr Wardlaw was summoned to appear "in the public assemble wythin the paroche kyrk of the citie of Sanctandrois and thar oppinlie confes his falt and offence don agains God and the superintendent, in blasphemyng, injuryng and contemptnyng of hym, and offending of hym injustlie; and tharof ask God mercy and the superintendent forgyfnes". Mr Wardlaw was likewise to appear "in the public assemble wythin the parrochie kyrk of Balingrie and in presenis of the minister that salbe appoynted to be thar that daye, publiclie confes the foyrsaidis offensis, at sic tym as the minister, thar present for that, sal reqir the sam to be don of hym; and thar ask God mercy, and the minister in name of the superintendent forgyfnes, and the hayll congregacion forgyfne of his sclander gevyn; pronunsing and desyring tham in tym cuming to obey all superiors, and to tak no occasion nor evyll exempill of hym, by the foyrsaid thingis be hym raschelie and injustle don. And thyr premissis to be don be the sayd Mr Alexander under the payn of excommunicacion and gyf he faleis excommunicacion to be executed and used aganis hym wyth al severite".

60 *Communion Tokens*

Mr Wardlaw seemed to have complied with the decision of the kirk session, but it is some years before we meet with him again, meanwhile Mr Watson continued to administer at Ballingry till 1567. Probably Mr Wardlaw was translated to Kinross for it is on record that an Alexander Wardlaw was reader there in 1563. In 1569 he reappears as exhorter at Ballingry with "the thryd of the parsonage as his stipend". At this period the combined stipends of parsonage and vicarage amounted to £33, 6 8d. Three years later in 1572, Mr Wardlaw regained his full status as minister of the parish, and in 1574 he had the assistance of a reader whom he paid out of his own salary of £36 per annum.

His troubles, however, did not cease with his becoming "persoun, minister of Ballingarie". In November, 1574 "Maister Alexander" raised an action in the Privy Council against his brother Henry who had succeeded his father as laird of Inchgall. On Sunday, the last day of October 1574, Henry Wardlaw had "contrair to all gude nychtbour heid, causit brek the said Maister Alexander's fauld upon his Kirklandis of Ballingrie and chaisit his and his cottaris cattell furth thairof, extending to fiftie heid of nolt (black cattle) or tharbie, and causit put thame in ane hous", for the purpose that they should injure each other, the intention being that Henry Wardlaw would impound the cattle for any damage they had done to his property. The minister's actions appear very fair under what must have been very trying circumstances. He sent four "newtrall" men in the persons of Johnne Steidnan, Robert Alexander, David Redy and David Haxtoun all of them tenants in Kirkness, to examine the ground at Ballingry, and to see "the skayth done be his cattell". They were also to offer Henry Wardlaw "sufficient amendiment quhidder they (the cattle) had done skayth or nane." To this effect Henry could retain "ane, twa, thre or four of the cattell, the best he plesit according to the dampnage and skayth", but Henry "ulluterie refusit". The minister travelled to Edinburgh to appear personally. Henry Wardlaw being "ofttymes callit and not comperand" was denounced rebel and put to the horn and ordered to restore the cattle to his brother.

Alexander Wardlaw was married, but his wife's name is not known. He had two sons and two daughters: John, probably the eldest of whom little is known; George, who was sheriff clerk of Forfar, who figures in the Register of the Privy Council for the year 1607 when he quarrelled with his cousin's husband Sir David Wood; Catherine, who married John Dick of Lumphinnan in 1571; and Margaret who was the wife of James Miller, son of Robert Miller burgess of Kirkcaldy. Alexander Wardlaw died before 20th January, 1581.

The story of Ballingry church from the time of Alexander Wardlaw to the close of the nineteenth century is given in interesting detail by the Rev. David Jamie and requires no retelling. Many stories however, relating to Ballingry church were quite current about the middle of the nineteenth century. These ranged from mischievous boys throwing divots at one another during worship to the presence of dogs and poultry in the church during the service.

It was still the custom for lairds and shepherds to bring their canine friends with them to church. One can easily imagine the commotion when two or more dogs began quarrelling during the sermon. This was the occasion for the minister to appeal to the beadle to restore order and an excellent opportunity for John, the beadle, to exhibit his unrivalled ability to eject the offenders and his witty reply to the minister.

Sleeping in church was an offence greatly looked down on by the minister who, when he caught anyone "nodding", would call out "some are no listening", and if they do not sit up "I'll name them oot". Church discipline which had been so rigorous in days gone by had by now been greatly relaxed although still retained to some degree at Ballingry. It is on record that Mr Greig on many occasions rebuked folk from the pulpit, so it was, that a member of the congregation who happened to "gang a kenin rang" ran the risk of being "namet oot".

Of the stories told about Ballingry, those relating to Ballingry burials excel all others. These, while portraying the Scottish manner and customs of former days, contained, as the reader can imagine, a source of quaint humour and the shrewdness of the Scottish character which so often expresses itself when the tale touches the macabre.

Of the old church at Ballingry, evidence is very scanty. Some interesting facts have emerged, however, as the result of desultory reading in various sources.

When the Culdee missionaries from St. Serf's priory came to this part of Fife they would probably erect a cross at a chosen place from which they would then and thereafter preach the Word. As time went on, in order to provide for the spiritual needs of the people, a small church would be built at the place of assembly to replace the earlier cross. A small religious community would thus become estabished whose modest place of worship, consisting probably of wattle-and-daub walls and a thatched roof, appeared at Ballingry. In all likelihood the present church marks its site. This is in keeping with the religious thought of past ages. Once a church had been established on consecrated ground, the ground was considered sacred and each succeeding church down through the ages was thought to take to itself some of the veneration and sanctity of the place.

The earliest church at Ballingry, of which there is any record, was a long and narrow building with its long axis running east and west, consisting of a chancel, choir and nave and a transeptral aisle to the north. It was a low building, stone built with probably a thatched roof and of course it had no "lofts".

The earliest reference to the church is during the Reformation period. It was then in much need of repair. Andrew Wardlaw, the laird of Inchgall and David Ramsay, who held the lands of Ballingry under the Wardlaws, were willing to do their part in repairing the nave, but the minister who was responsible for keeping the chancel in good repair was most unwilling to do so.

In about the year 1658 the walls of the church were raised so that lofts could be formed at the east and west ends of the church although the transeptral aisle appears to have remained as before and probably had now become ruinous as it stood open to the sky. The ruined walls which once enclosed the Blair aisle were probably the remains of the chancel. The belfry from the earlier church was incorporated in the new church and in 1658 John Malcolm the new laird made a gift of a new bell. The bell bore the latin inscription "Felices quos haec Balingria cimbala Cristi ad pia sacra vocant", which being translated means, "Blessed are they whom these Ballingry chimes call to the sacred worship of Christ".* The church had now a slated roof.

---

* This bell did service for almost 300 years. In 1966 a new bell was cast from a mould taken from the old one.

Three years afterwards the laird had the idea of using the transeptral aisle as a family burial place. He accordingly had a wall built to shut it off from the church leaving only a small communicating door. He also had the outer walls raised to the same height as the walls of the church and had a roof put on it. While this work was going on it would no doubt occur to him that there was a need for a window and that he must somehow find a suitable one. His obvious choice was the chapel of Inchgall. The Chapel had been long in disuse and was fast becoming ruinous. Forty years after this period it was little more than "a rickle o' stanes".

61 *The Malcolm Window*

The window which was to be built into the north wall of the burial aisle, either through years of neglect or more probably on its removal from its original site, sustained injury. The keystone was damaged and had to be replaced by another which was made from a different kind of stone from the rest of the window, and on that occasion the words "death where is thy sting" were carved upon it no doubt at the direction of the laird. Likewise, a mullion and tracery of inferior workmanship and design took the place of the old, with the result that the tracery when viewed in relation to the jambs of the window is seen to be out of balance.

It is most unusual to find dates appearing on windows of this period and as the numerals 1661 occupy the panels below the mouldings on the pilasters on either side of the window, it suggests that these were added when the window was rebuilt. The window remained unglazed until 1966 when the burial aisle became part of the church once more. The aisle was probably first used for burial after the death of John Malcolm in 1691. During this period, when the laird came to church with his family and servants, they occupied one of the side lofts, probably the west one.

In 1678 the church again comes under notice when it is observed that it is very ruinous and that the slates are altogether off the south side of the roof of the nave. The heritors are urged to have the necessary repair work carried out.

With the departure of the Malcolms from Lochore House, the family burial aisle was no longer used. Accordingly, sometime before 1825, the communicating door between the church and the aisle was built up and the upper portion of the dividing wall demolished so that a loft could be constructed partly in the roof space. We gather from the writings of Sir Walter Scott that this loft was used by the occupants of Lochore House. By the year 1831 there was a need to have the church enlarged in order to accommodate the increasing number of worshippers. The church was accordingly made longer and broader and had as before two side lofts which were reached by means of two doors set in its south wall, all much the same as it was before, only the south wall was now increased in length and of course built in a new position further south than formerly. The church had now a seating capacity of three hundred and twenty. Things remained so until 1876 when a door with a pointed arch was inserted in the west wall of the church and the west door in the south wall permanently closed.

Coming to our times, the church which was considered small and cramped by present-day standards, was remodelled and opened for worship in 1966. It incorporated much of the old fabric in its new design. The church was extended southward so that it is now orientated north and south instead of east and west as formerly. It is entered through the Malcolm burial aisle whose walls contain memorial panels commemorating the ancestors of the Malcolm family, and which now functions as an entrance porch. Two memorial windows gifted by Mr David Grieg in 1951 in memory of his great uncle the Reverend James Greig, occupy a fitting place in the new part of the church.

The work carried out during the years 1965 and 1966 afforded a valuable opportunity of observing any evidence which pointed to the antiquity of the place. The excavations in the graveyard and the removal of the kirkyard wall to the south revealed that the graveyard had been considerably levelled up at one time. The line of the original surface showed that the ground had fallen away quite sharply and that the ancient church had stood on a natural mound or knoll. Considering the level of the road at the north side of the church in its relation to the graveyard, it is not improbable that here too the ground had to some extent been levelled up at some remote period. Beyond the limits of the graveyard in what was the manse garden old stone foundations were exposed.

By a chance discovery a stone of unusual interest afforded strong presumptive evidence of an early Christian settlement. While workmen were cutting through the east wall of the old church in order to insert a window, they found built into the wall the upper portion of a cross-slab. The head and arms of the cross which were cut in relief and slightly wedge-shaped were chipped in parts and showed signs of weathering. The slab was lost not long after its discovery, but not until it had been carefully examined. Expert advice was sought and one authority assigned it to the period from the tenth to the twelfth century.

Another relic of a very different nature belonging to the body-snatching period, was discovered while work was in progress on the extension to the church. Following the removal of the tombstone and the dis-interment of the remains of the Hendersons of Glencraig to make way for new foundations, it was discovered that one of the coffins had been enclosed in iron bars. Although the workmen appear not to have recognised the true nature of the relic, there need hardly be any doubt that what they had found were the remains of an iron mortsafe. It had been placed over the coffin in order to protect the body from the resurrectionists.

Among other relics of special interest that were allowed to disappear during the extension to the church was the ancient "lectern" sundial which had been deposited in the manse grounds for safe-keeping until a suitable place could be found for it in the churchyard, also the two stone cannon balls which for centuries had surmounted the pillars of the entrance gate to the church. The cannon balls were believed to have been placed there during the Malcolm period and in all likelihood had come from Inchgall Castle.

FEUDS, FELONY AND FANTASY

Although law and order were becoming increasingly observed in the early seventeenth century following the Union of the Crowns, there were those who still took the law into their own hands, and while the cases about to be cited may seem tame compared with the stories of clan fighting in the Highlands, they nonetheless show that even in the more governable parts of central Scotland, some lairds held the law in contempt and carried things through with a high hand, and even the lesser folk on many occasions settled their quarrels by force of arms. The following incidents are taken from the records of the period covering a little over a century and culminating in the siege of Lumphinnans. The inhabitants of Lochoreshire were of course not in any way less law-abiding than their neighbours and the unlawful use of arms was more or less still commonplace in other parts of Fife. We are still in the period when men considered themselves not properly dressed unless they wore a sword or carried a firearm discreetly on their person.

In 1539 Alexander Ramsay of Kynmont had all his goods seized for having set upon a person by the name of Barclay. His belongings were given to Adam Lindsay of Dowhill. Ten years afterwards a more serious incident occurred at the "toun" of Lumphinnans where Alexander Dick and eleven others lay in waiting on Robert Stewart at his house of Lumphinnans where they attacked him with an axe and several spears. Stewart had a miraculous escape although he sustained a broken shoulder. His assailants were outlawed. In 1550, James Davie in Inchgall was outlawed and had all his goods seized and disposed of for having taken part in the slaughter of David Balfour in Urquhile.

In this same year grave news came out of Kinglassie. In the month of September George Winchester of Kinglassie, whose family were tenants of these lands under the Archbishops of St. Andrews and were therefore the leading proprietors in the parish, was stripped of a "tenement and fair house" belonging to him in St. Andrews, and had also his lands and goods taken from him. Having been convicted of heresy by the church, all his possessions became crown property and were gifted by Queen Mary to one Arthur Cairns. Winchester's "crime" was that he had in his possession a bible written in English and was known to have read it.

In 1577 an Act was passed making the wearing of culverins, dags, pistols or any other firearms without a licence punishable with the loss of the right hand, but this attempt to suppress crime seems to have had little effect, at any rate locally, for two years afterwards the Ballingry minister's two sons John and George Wardlaw were convicted of the mutilation of James Colville, bailie of Culross and fined three hundred merks.

The year 1583 saw something which must have caused quite a stir among the inhabitants of the turf and thatched hovels that went under the name of Easter Lochgelie. We have seen that the Wemyss family had a half share in the mill of Lochore as early as 1296. A little over a century later this family had certain rights over Loch Gelly, and in 1427 Sir John Wemyss gave John Melville of Raith permission to construct a lade through his lands of Powguild in order to bring water from the loch to a new mill which the laird of Raith was constructing at Pitconmart, to be known later as Shaw's Mill.

While the Wemyss family and the Melville family as neighbouring proprietors were always on good terms, this cannot be said of the other neighbouring proprietor, Boswell of Balmuto. This rather turbulent family in the person of John Boswell, challenged in 1583, the Wemyss family's right to the fishings in Loch Gelly. It was thus that a feud developed between David Wemyss and the Laird of Balmuto. Rumours of the trouble reached the Privy Council in the early part of that year and in April both contestants were summoned to appear before the King and council when it was agreed that both parties would withdraw their forces and not resort to violence and that the question of the fishing rights would be dealt with by a panel of people representing both parties. However, after a lapse of only three weeks, John Wemyss, the laird's eldest son, "bodin (forced) in feir of weir (war) of the speciall causing and hounding out of David Wemyss", gathered together his friends and servants to the number of one hundred and twenty persons and planted themselves on the south side of the loch. There they built a fort and dug a ditch on all sides so that the water from the loch formed a moat around their stronghold. They then manned the fort and furnished it with ammunition and warlike weapons and to assert their laird's right, they put a boat on the loch and defied the laird of Balmuto to remove it. This, we are told was done "to the greit inquietatioun of the cuntrie".

The King, when he heard of what had been done, gave orders to each party to "skail thair forces" and to appear before him on 8th June under pain of rebellion, meanwhile there was to be no fishing on the loch. The King in the end settled the feud between the two lairds but three years elapsed before it finally came to an end.

The year 1577 saw many cases of people in the neighbourhood being summoned before the courts for acting outwith the law. John Beaton, son of the Archdeacon of Lothian and late minister of Ballingry, was one of many local persons by the name of Beaton who, along with many others to the number of thirty appeared at Falkland fully armed. The purpose of their convening there was to prevent a court being held. Word of their coming had reached Falkland beforehand and a number of mounted men successfully prevented them from achieving their objective. The offenders were summoned to appear before the Privy Council, when some were warded in Edinburgh Castle and others who had ignored the summons were denounced rebels.

During mid-summer the peace and quiet of the rural life of Auchterderran was broken by a quarrel that had arisen among several of its inhabitants. Michael Balfour in Balgreggie, Alexander Clerkson in Bowhill and Patrick Crawford at the Kirk of Auchterderran were at variance with Henry Maul the laird of Balgreggie. The quarrel, whatever its nature, was extended to the minister's widow Isobel Sibbald, David Boswell her son, and John Law in Pitcairn. Each had to find surety in a sum specified by the court ranging from one hundred merks to one thousand pounds, as a guarantee of his or her keeping the peace. David Sibbald of Letham stood cautioner for Isobel Sibbald, while two Edinburgh burgesses stood cautioners for the others, for their future good behaviour.

Towards the end of the year we find Henry Orrock of that ilk and Henry Dick of Gartmore standing as sureties in the sum of five hundred merks that Henry Dick of Lumphinnans will not injure Patrick Halkett of that ilk.

In January, 1607 John Dick of Colquhallie and John Gaw were brought before the Privy Council by Sir George Bruce of Carnock, who was the foremost mining engineer of his day. Sir George, whose coal works were at Culross, used water power to drive a machine which he constructed to lift water from his mine on the principle of the Egyptian water wheel system. By means of a large wheel to which a long iron endless chain with thirty-six buckets were attached at regular intervals, he was able by lowering the chain down the mine shaft and by setting the wheel in motion, to raise eighteen buckets of water from the mine at any given time.

Now, Dick and Gaw held a grudge against Sir George and resolved to visit his coal mine with the intention of causing harm. They tried first of all to alter the course of the water supply to the water wheel but found this beyond their resources. They returned at a later date along with eight others armed with lances and blocked up the water supply to the mine at its source at the water dam in the moor above the village. They then returned the following day and broke down the dam. The onrush of water caused considerable damage and the amount of water lost would, according to Sir George, have been sufficient to have worked his machine for the following four months. Sir George, in his complaint to the Privy Council said that he had now to use horses and men where in the past this had been done by water power. Out of the reverence he had for the King and Council he had "forbeir all violent revenge" upon Dick and Gaw and was content to seek remedy at law. Both defenders were found guilty and committed to prison in Edinburgh Castle. They were released a month later on the payment of one thousand pounds by John Dick of Cartmore.

Still in the year 1607, we find Patrick Halkett of North Lumphinnans, brother of the laird of Pitfirran, at loggerheads with James Masterton in Beith who he attacked in the Kirk of Dunfermline during divine service. Halkett picked out Masterton sitting beside the bailies and straightway went up to him and hit him on the face with his "fauldit neve". Not content with this, he waited until the minister was leading the congregation in prayer and seeing Masterton in a posture of devotion he stuck a dirk into his back and would have finished him off had not the bailies and others intervened. Halkett was summoned before the court to face a serious charge.

Later on he again appeared before the court on a charge of wearing hagbuts and pistols and of molesting the laird of Inchgall and Robert Ladaich his servant, and for damaging the laird's dykes, also for pursuing David Kynnymonth of Glennistoun with a drawn sword and killing his horse. He was found guilty, and sent to Edinburgh Castle, but was released by the end of the year when his brother, Sir Robert Halkett, stood surety for his good behaviour.

Ministers of the gospel were not exempt from being set upon and sustaining injuries. In 1607 David Wemyss, son of the laird of Pitkinny, was put to the horn for wounding John Chalmers, minister of Auchterderran and was released only after having found caution in the sum of one thousand pounds. By the middle of the year 1608 rumours began to circulate that two contending parties were planning to settle a dispute by armed combat. By the month of July it was clear that there was some foundation for the general apprehension that something unusual was afoot. The parties in dispute were George Martin who lived in Cardoun Tower at Cardenden and Lord Sinclair. There were to be four persons on either side, George Martin and his three sons challenged Patrick, Lord Sinclair, his two sons and David Seton of Parbroth. By now, as the place of combat, time and the kind of weapons to be used had been agreed upon, there is every likelihood that the contest would have gone ahead had not some neighbouring lairds intervened in order to avoid unnecessary bloodshed. The affair came to the notice of the Privy Council who acted quickly and within a week the contending parties were summoned to answer for their conduct. Lord Sinclair and his company obeyed the summons and were straightway put in prison, but the laird of Cardoun and his sons having ignored the summons, the Captain of the Guard was ordered to proceed to Fife and apprehend the rebels. The case came before the Privy Council on 4th August.

Alarming as the attack on the Rev. John Chalmers of Auchterderran must have been, an even more dastardly assault was made on the minister of Ballingry in 1609. Its severity stunned the folks in the neighbourhood and shocked the clergy of the Presbytery. James Forrester, a falconer, and a nephew of Sir Robert Forrester of Strathenry, appears under circumstances which are at once dreadful and alarming. Concerning a matter, the nature of which is not disclosed, Forrester called at the manse of Ballingry in the afternoon of the 20th of October, 1609, "upone sett purpois, provisioun, foirthocht fellonie". He asked to see the Rev. David Anderson who at that moment was in his study. Forrester appears to have declined to enter the manse but desired the minister to "come out to his yeard to speak to him". Mr Anderson, having complied with his request, he began to threaten and "maist inhumanelie tuke him by the hair of his beard, and with all his force rugget the same of purpois to have drawin furth the haill of his beard". He then drew his sword and attacked the minister and in the struggle that followed Forrester struck off the minister's right arm.

The case came before the Privy Council in the following month. All the ministers in the presbytery appeared on behalf of Mr Anderson, but the defendant did not appear and was accordingly denounced a rebel. Meanwhile James Forrester had hastened to Sir Robert Forrester's house in an attempt to evade the consequences of his actions, by which time there was a warrant out for his arrest. He was now being sought on an additional charge along with his brother and cousin and Robert Douglas, servant of George Douglas of Kirkness, for unlawfully carrying hagbuts and pistols.

It is not known how long Forrester evaded arrest, as it was not until the 19th of September, 1610 that he appeared before the Privy Council. He confessed to the crime and humbly craved the King's pardon and that of the minister. The verdict was given by Andrew Cockburn, chancellor to the Privy Council that, as Forrester had confessed to the mutilation of Mr Anderson, he was to be committed to the tolbooth of Edinburgh and to remain there as a convicted person until advised by the Privy Council as to "his doom". It was not until the 13th of June of the following year that James Forrester knew what his future would be. He complained to the Lords of Council that he had now been detained in the tolbooth for more than a year, but since his conviction, Mr Anderson had been willing to receive from him some reasonable satisfaction for the injury he had

62 *Cardoun Tower, Cardenden*

received, but as he was still in prison he could not himself make that satisfaction, nevertheless some of his best friends had given him bonds for the payment of two hundred and fifty merks to the minister, which sum was not fifty merks less than that which the minister himself craved. But now "upoun mony frivole pretenses" the minister refused to accept the sum offered and would not consent to him being set at liberty, "bot will laif him to die miserablie in the waird throu famyne".

After hearing both parties the Lords agreed to release Forrester, as the minister had now agreed to having received satisfaction for the injury done to him but it was felt that Forrester should be made an example of, and remembering the "cruell and barbarous persute of which he was guilty and finding it a crime meriting severe punishment to the terrour of uthris to commit the lyke againis ministeris and prechairis of the evangill in tyme coming", ordained that he be banished from the Kingdom and not to return without the King's permission under pain of loss of his right hand. Some years afterwards, Forrester petitioned the Privy Council to be allowed to return home but whether this was granted or not is not known.

In February of this year we are made aware of a feud which existed between the families of Douglas and Colville, when measures were taken to prevent Sir George Douglas of Kirkness from avenging the death of Lord Torthorwald on Lord Ochiltree.

In the following month the laird of Inchgall and Torrie was carrying things with a high hand in his domain of Torryburn. Having donned some pieces of gaudy armour and carrying a sword and other weapons he went with three of his servants to the house of David Russell and Maisie Fotheringhame his wife. There he commanded his men to break to pieces a "pleugh" which belonged to Russell. The laird returned the following day with more of his servants when they broke down a stable door with fore hammers and took away a horse belonging to Russell. The laird himself attacked Russell's wife with a cudgel to the effusion of blood and left her for dead.

In this same month John Chalmers minister of Auchterderran sought the protection of the law from the "boists minasses, shoiris" (threats) of Sir George Boswell of Balgonie who avowed he would have his life.

In November of this year we are told that John Stewart, son of Lord Doune and brother of Lord St. Colm, had evaded the law for four months after wounding John Gibb of Over Lassodie. In order to find out his whereabouts the Privy Council ordered that certain of his known friends should be questioned. These included five persons living in the vicinty of Kelty, three in Aberdour and David Redie, servant of John Bugyall, flesher in Crosshill. Stewart was brought before the court within two weeks when he was found guilty of fatally wounding John Gibb with a dagger whereby he died within two days. The case is given in great detail and describes how, following a quarrel between Stewart's horse-boy and his own servant of which John Gibb was entirely innocent, Stewart sat drinking in a house in Keltyhaugh and openly expressed his "deidlie feid haitrent and malice" towards John Gibb. The others in the company obtained a promise from Stewart that he would not molest Gibb, but that he would that night go to the brig of Gairny. However, no sooner had Stewart left his friend's house than he turned his horse about and rode towards Lassodie. It was now late at night and on reaching Gibb's house, Stewart called him by name. Gibb recognised his friend's voice and although he was in bed he instantly got up and, wearing only his "night sark" he opened the door. It is clear that by now Stewart was acting under the influence of drink. Without giving any reason for his untimely visit or any mention of his supposed grievance, he struck his dagger into Gibb's breast, "neir the heart". In November, 1609 Stewart was sentenced "to be tane to the place of his executioine and thair his heid to be strucken from his body".

By the close of this year a complaint had been sent to the Privy Council against the younger sons of Douglas of Kirkness and the Forresters of Strathenry who held part of Crosshill, that they continued to strut about the neighbourhood armed with hagbuts and pistols to the fear of the inhabitants.

The next ten years or so passed off peacefully in Lochoreshire, at least no serious incidents are recorded. In 1620, Robert Law raised an action against Andrew Martin, son of the laird of Cardon, for the brutal assault upon his son George who was the servant of the laird of Dogton. The charge against Martin was that, while George Law was going about his peaceful occupation, he came up to him on horseback and harangued him, then he drew his sword and "gaif him ane grite straik in his fute and hes lamed him thairof". When Law fell to the ground, Martin "come rynning upoun him and with guardis of the swerd gaif him ane deadlie straik upoun the head and hurte and woundit him in sindrie uther pairts of his body", leaving him for dead. Martin did not answer the charge and the Lords of Council ordered him to be denounced rebel.

In the year following we have a typical example of the overbearing haughty and disgraceful attitude of a laird towards his servant. Because James Boswell failed "to do them courtesy", Sir John Boswell of Balmuto and Sir George Boswell, his brother, attacked him in a most brutal manner. They first tried to trample him under their horses feet, then Sir John dismounted and gripped James Boswell by his beard and dragged him for several yards "continewalie utterring mony injurious, reprotchfull and disgraceful speitshes against him". As if this were not enough, Sir George struck James Boswell on the back, head and face with a stick and Sir John having released his hold of Boswell's beard, struck him likewise. The Lords of Council acquitted Sir George Boswell of his part of the charge, but found Sir John Boswell guilty and committed him to Edinburgh Castle.

After a lapse of eight years we meet with Sir John Boswell again. On this occasion he was accompanied by his wife, Janet Scott, who appears to have possessed some of her husband's aggressive nature. It so happened that David Beaton of Garden raised an action against Sir John, charging him with some irregularities. The papers were sent by Thomas Allan, messenger, who delivered them to Sir John personally at the Kirk of Auchterderran. The messenger was taking his leave when he was called back by Lady Boswell. After a word with her husband, she dismounted from her horse and disgracefully upbraided Allan, "calling him dastard, villain, common thief, how durst thow persoom to charge the laird of Balmowto". She seized Allan and struck and buffetted him with her feet and fists and threatened to put a sword through him. It was only through the intervention of some of the kirk folk that her Ladyship was prevented from doing further harm to the poor messenger. It is not known if Thomas Allan received any redress for the injuries he received. All too often the authorities condoned the lawless actions of the "landed people" but, as we shall see later on, the law caught up with Lady Boswell in a later incident.

An equally turbulent family were the Halketts of Lumphinnans, a branch of the Halketts of Pitfirrane, a family who were related to the Lochore and Vallance families. They held the lands of Lumphinnans from the late fourteenth century and one named Philip is referred to in history as Lord of Lumphinnans.

Patrick Halkett, who we have already met within these pages, held the lands of Lumphinnans under the Wardlaws, but for twelve or fourteen years prior to 1630 he and his near relations and dependents had defied all attempts by the Wardlaws and others to have them removed and had "maisterfullie and violentile keeped and possest" the lands of North and South Lumphinnans "in contempt of law and justice". In March, 1630 the case came before the Privy Council when the offenders were denounced rebels and put to the horn. The order to flit and remove themselves, their tenants, servants, goods and gear "furth and fra" Lumphinnans had no effect whatsoever. They continued their "violent possession with ane sattlad purpose and resolution to maintane thair possessioun be way of deid" (death).

In 1632 the Earl of Rothes bought the barony of Inchgall and forthwith took steps to have the Halketts removed and to have David Aitoun put in possession of

Lumphinnans. The sheriff was empowered to eject the Halketts and to arrest anyone who resisted. James Smith the sheriff depute was entrusted to put the law into effect. Meanwhile, Patrick Halkett and Isobel Boswell his wife, and their two sons John and Andrew, also John Meldrum and David Dewar their tenants, having heard of what was afoot, busied themselves to meet what was to them an invasion of their premises. They laid in a store of food also "powlder, leade, muskats, hackquebuts, pistolls, garnets and other warrelike provisiouns". They then built a small fortification on the west side of the house and set up their guns. Fearing that their numbers were insufficient to meet the sheriff's forces, they enlisted a number of soldiers recently returned from service in the Continent. Having completed their stronghold they awaited the appearance of the besiegers determining to fight it out to the last.

63 *Balmuto Tower*

The sheriff depute had with him a number of his servants, also James Anderson, a notary, John Chalmers, minister of Auchterderran, and Andrew Fairful, minister of Leslie. Seeing all the warlike preparations, the sheriff depute "being loathe to enter in blood", decided that the two ministers and the notary should go forward and ask the occupants of the house in the name of his Majesty, to surrender the house to him. The request was met with "ane plane and direct refuisall of obedience, protesting with manie fearfull and execreble oathes that they would never rander the hous bot would stand to their defence to the ultermost and should have the lyffes of some of the best of the componpanie before they randered, uttering their blasphemous words they cared not altho the devill tooke thame, for they behoved once to dee".

As the sheriff depute did not possess a warrant of fire and sword, he and his company could only withdraw and report back to the sheriff. The Privy Council retaliated by instituting "ane most regorous and sharpe course for punishing the actors and preventing the forder grouth of such disobedience".

The sheriff was given wide powers. Having received a commission of fire and sword, he and his deputes commanded all and sundry of his Majesty's lieges and

206

subjects in arms within the sheriffdom of Fife, to meet when and where the sheriff should decide. They were to "use all kinds of force and warlike engines to pursue and assiege the house of Lumphinnans, to cast down the fortifications and search out and seize the rebels". It was made clear in the commission that should the sheriff and any of those under his command incur slaughter, mutilation or fire-raising, it would not be considered a crime.

These strong measures appear to have paid off. There is no clear account of what took place on the second approach to the house, whether the Halketts gave a good account of themselves or peacefully gave themselves up. What is known is that a little over two months after the first attempt at their arrest, the sheriff brought them before the Privy Council where they were charged with having held the King's authority in contempt and possessing forbidden weapons. John and Andrew Halkett were committed to prison within the tolbooth of Edinburgh and Patrick Halkett was incarcerated in the tolbooth of Drysart. A court held in Edinburgh on the 13th of June, 1632 decreed that John and Andrew Halkett were to be banished from the Kingdom for the remainder of their lives. Meanwhile they were to remain in jail until a ship was found to take them out of the country.

After eighteen months in jail Patrick Halkett applied unsuccessfully to be released. He was, however, allowed eight shillings daily and his jailor two shillings, which sums were to be paid by the Earl of Rothes. By April, 1634 he had been removed to the tolbooth in Edinburgh when the Provost and Magistrates allowed him his freedom on condition that he would remain within the burgh of Edinburgh and town of Leith. His freedom lasted for a period of seven months, till his death in prison in November of that year. Andrew died in exile sometime before 1635. Thus came to an end one of the worst cases of insubordination and defiance of the law to come before the courts.

Under the date 1634, we are made aware of a foul deed done in Lochgelly in the previous year. Robert Lambert in Kinghorn had been in prison in the tolbooth in Edinburgh for over a year on a charge of having taken part in the slaughter of Thomas Dow in Lochgelly. As Lambert was a poor man and had no money save what he could obtain by crying out from the "yronhouse", the lords agreed to his remission and instructed the bailies of Edinburgh to release him.

We hinted earlier on that we would meet with Lady Boswell again. In 1643 the Earl of Moray took up the case of his tenant, James Betson, in Pascar Mill and his son David. The Earl in his disposition stated that Lady Boswell and her husband Sir John conceived a grudge against James Betson anent "ane water draught" beside the mill and were determined to do him harm. To this end, Lady Boswell, along with two of her servants and a servant of Captain Pitscottie, armed themselves with swords, staffs and other weapons and went to the smiddy of Moses Hill where David Betson was working. They put violent hands on Betson and carried him to Balmuto House where they kept him prisoner. Following this, Robert Hay at the direction of Lady Boswell, went to Pascar Mill and pursued James Betson for his life, at the same time warning him that should he come again, on the instructions of his lady, he (Robert Hay) would be better prepared. Answering the charge, Lady Boswell admitted that she had held David

Betson prisoner at Balmuto but only in order to teach him good manners! The Lords found the charge proven and Lady Boswell was warded in the tolbooth in Edinburgh. The other conspirators were put to the horn and their goods forfeited.

We have now reached the mid-seventeenth century. Of the working classes belonging to this period; weavers, colliers, sauters, crofters, packmen and others, perhaps the most harassed by the authorities were the gypsies. Their distinct mode of living tended to ostracize them from society. They were favourably dealt with during the reign of James V and in the time of Queen Mary, but they were unjustly persecuted during the reign of her son James VI. Because of their wayward way of living, and not conforming strictly to the law, they were all too often subjected to penalties which were harsh and unjust. Many ended their days on the gallows and slave ships. While there are allusions to the presence of gypsies in Fife in the preceding century, we have not found any case involving gypsies in Lochoreshire. It is possible therefore that the Lochgelly colony of gypsies had not yet been established at this period. It is not until one hundred years or more had passed before they make their appearance locally.

These itinerant families are called Egyptians in the old records and can be traced in Scotland from 1492 onward. They appeared on many occasions before the King in what may be called "command performances". The last on record was in 1530 when they danced before his Majesty in Holyrood House and received 40/- for their efforts. Whence they came is still not clear. They were certainly of eastern extraction and had at one time a peculiar dialect of their own which seemed to point to a north Indian origin. The Scottish gypsies styled themselves "Lords and Erles of Litell Egypt" and thereby strengthening the opinion of many that they originated in Egypt. Their swarthy olive complexion, jet black hair and eyebrows and keen penetrating eyes were distinctive characteristics of their race. Yetholm was their headquarters in Scotland and the last of the gypsy "kings", Charles faa Blythe, died there in 1902. There is a tradition that one of the gypsy headquarters was at the little village of Pattismuir, south of Dunfermline, where there was a gypsy "palace" inhabited by a gypsy "King".

The gypsies who established themselves at Lochgelly probably did so in about the middle of the eighteenth century. Their first known leader was Charlie Graham, who in 1798 led his band of ruffians, consisting of men, women and children to the number of fifty, in a desperate attack upon the stalls and stall-holders at the Hairst Fair held in Dunfermline. It had been their custom for many years to visit all the fairs and markets in the neighbourhood and to steal what they could as the opportunities arose. In this year the gang went on the rampage. They knocked over the sweetie and clothes stalls in the High Street and caused a great disturbance. Charlie Graham was arrested and "run into the black-hole" (the jail), but the rest of the gang managed to get him out. Knowing that the magistrates would now issue orders for his arrest, he immediately made his getaway in the direction of Perth followed at some distance by a company of Militia. At Kinnoull Hill he hid among the thickets and whins and probably would have eluded arrest had it not been for the devotion of his dog. Anticipating what might happen, he tried to quieten the animal and placed his hand over its mouth, but the noise of the approaching soldiers was too much, the dog sprang out from his hiding place and Charlie was arrested. He was shortly afterwards tried and executed.

Fifty years or so passed before we hear of the Lochgelly gypsies again. We are told they were on very friendly terms with a tribe in Linlithgow and many a fearless escapade they had together. Their mutual respect may have arisen from the fact that in the early part of the eighteenth century, both tribes were led by women. Ann McDonald was gypsy chieftain in Linlithgow while Lizzie Brown led the Lochgelly tribe in all their desperate fights. This amazon is reputed to have presided over her tribe with considerable authority and to have assiduously trained the young boys herself in the art and skill of thieving.

Their common enemy was a tribe from the north amounting to over two hundred persons under the leadership of Andrew Gordon. This gang frequently visited the Queensferry, Dunfermline and Stirling fairs and markets, where they stole merchandise from the stalls and acquired many other things by means of stealth. They are known to have had many affrays with the Linlithgow gypsies. It is said that of all the joint exploits of the Linlithgow and the Lochgelly gypsies against their common enemy, one which took place at Raploch near Stirling was by far the bloodiest.

The Lochgelly tribe were not one whit behind the others in all their cunning and art of deception and thieving. Like Burns "Nannie", it could be said that Lizzie Brown "kept the countryside in fear", not only in Fife but in the Mearns where many a desperate fight took place. Will Faa, who was of the family who claimed hereditary kinship among the gypsy fraternity, was a notable swordsman as well as an accomplished smuggler. He stayed for some time in the gypsy camp at Lochgelly during his visit to Fife. It was said that many a hen-roost bore evidence of his presence while he remained in the neighbourhood. His "accomplishments" must have served him well for he died at the ripe old age of ninety-six in 1847.

The breakup of the gypsy settlement followed the loss to the village of the Muir ("moor"), part of which had been used as a gypsy encampment and always looked upon by the villagers as common ground. The fraternity scattered, and took to camping on various right-of-ways and waste ground. It was a common sight as late as the first quarter of the present century to see gypsies camping on the "Old Loan", east of Crosshill although by this time they had shed much of their aggressive tendencies and had acquired more of the habits of tinkers and hawkers than the old customs of the real gypsies.

The memory of their low-set tent made from curved withies covered with oil-cloth turned black with grime and held down at ground level with stones, a camp-fire placed in a small circle of stones a short distance from the entrance with a boiling-pot hanging from a tripod made from three straight sticks, several fragments of clothing drying on a nearby hedge, a child or two running about, brown as berries and half naked, the figure of a woman with large earrings sitting at the entrance of the tent smoking a clay pipe, a small piebald pony with panniers slung across its back, grazing nearby, a shallow ramshackle cart holding a clothes basket or two in the making and a barrel intended to be cut down to make a washing tub, heather besoms, heather pot-cleaners, pans, kettles, horn spoons, and many other pieces of handiwork all destined to be hawked from door to door, an emaciated dog or two tethered to the cart wheel, is still clear to the writer and many people living in the neighbourhood who, as children, passed by with much fear and trembling as they saw these "gain-aboot buddies" settle down for a night or two before the urge to move on caught up with them again.

Many of these cases show a strong disregard for the law. Too often the persons involved were the local lairds who meted out rough justice and scorned the consequences. Unlike the "landit men", the crofter was usually content with his lot and resorted to force only when subjected to unjust treatment.

The disciplinary control of the church over the parishioners in the post Reformation period was very strong. The period was one of strict Sunday observance. It was also the age of superstitious beliefs. At its height the enforcement of Sunday observance had almost become a fetish, while the efforts to wean the ordinary person away from the belief in a personal devil in the shape of "Auld Hornie" was no less difficult than having to pursue the delinquents of sabbath-breaking. People still held fast to the beliefs which had come down to them from earlier generations; legends and tales of the supernatural which doubtless date back to pagan times.

Of equal concern to the Kirk Sessions in Lochoreshire and beyond was the belief still held by many in witchcraft, fairies, elfs, brownies and the like. The period was one of intense activity real and imaginary. We read of the well-known coven of witches at Crook of Devon at whose trial Alexander Colville of Blair presided, and the strange goings-on in the manse at Kinross, the work of a mischievous poltergeist which kept the minister and his family in constant fear.

Of the unusual disturbance which took place in Ballingry church, the presence of fairies in Kinglassie, the spectre piper of Lochgelly fair and the white horse of Bowguild, we will hear of later. We have only to recall that Bessie Lochore was convicted and executed for witchcraft and to recall such names as The Deils' Stane, Satan's Castle, The Witches Brig, The Witches Brae, all to be found in Lochoreshire not to mention the Ballingry legend to realise how widespread was the belief in the supernatural not so very long ago.

The "sins" and petty offences which lay outwith the notice of the civil courts were quickly seized upon by the ever vigilant kirk sessions before which the offenders were summonded, to be gravely admonished if the charges were proven. The sin of sabbath-breaking was a recurring offence frowned on by those who were entrusted to supervise the morals of the parish. It was therefore news indeed when it came to the ears of the Ballingry Kirk Session that David Paton, who was a servant of James Betson in Lumphinnans "did drive right open on the sabbath day in time of divine service, through the parish of Kinross". Twice the delinquint was summoned to appear before the session but to no avail. With the weight of the Presbytery behind them, the Session at last secured Paton, who for the enormity of sabbath-breaking and the added offence of ignoring the summons, was most firmly dealt with and "sharply rebuked".

Among the many misdemeanours which troubled the Kirk Sessions from time to time was that of drinking taking place in certain houses on a Sunday, also "the ganging o' the mills", presumably the waulk mills situated at the Milton. If the Ballingry Session had their troubles in seeking out and admonishing the sabbath-breakers in their midst, their brethren in Auchterderran did not find the task any easier, indeed, in one instance they had to deal with what to them must have been a most painful situation. It became known that Mr Harvey their minister had been seen "stooking his corn upon a Sunday". In an age when the first day of the week was observed by maintaining a solemn demeanour throughout every action of the day, when apart from going to church there was little else that could be done, when work of every kind was proscribed and a kind of sanctimonious gravity settled on everyone, it is to be expected that the conduct of the minister when it became known, would shock the prejudices of the crofters and others who made up the hamlet of Auchterderran. Such a grave offence committed by their much-respected minister must needs be dealt with by a higher ecclesiastical court and Mr Harvey appeared before the Presbytery where he explained that he had stooked the corn when he thought it was in danger of being blown down by the wind. Notwithstanding his explanation his brethren deposed him for profaning the Lord's Day. Wiser councils prevailed, however, for in the month that followed the Synod of Fife removed the suspension. But the damage had been done, when an admonition in all charitableness would have sufficed. It was now too late and Mr Harvey who had been a very capable man, and a faithful minister demitted his charge and returned to his native Ireland.

It is claimed that names such as Navitie and Lochty are relics of a vanished race who dwelt in the neighbourhood. Navitie was originally part of Kirkness and was possessed by the Culdees. At some unknown date it became ecclesiastical property, probably attached to the preaching station at Ballingry. The root name Naompaite was coined long before Christianity came to these parts. It is well known that the early missionaries set up their churches near the site of the holy places of an earlier faith. This seems to have taken place at Ballingry.

The little stream which separates Navitie from Ballingry is of equal antiquity. Its origin is in Gruoch's Well and is one of many streams bearing a name which is pre-Christian and which was regarded by people of the remote period as the home of the water spirit, the origin of the cult of the Black Goddess. It is little wonder then with these ever-present relics of ancient faiths and beliefs, that some traces should have lingered in the minds of the inhabitants until comparatively recent times.

When it is remembered that a Ballingry clergyman believed that he himself had come under the spell of witchcraft, it is easy to understand what effect these beliefs must have had on the minds of the less enlightened folk. A hankering after a supernatural origin for many things was no less evident at Ballingry than elsewhere. Even the natural features of the local landscape has been assigned to the devil's handiwork.

In order to account for the prevalence of whinstone boulders in the parish, we are to conclude that in some far-off time "the deil had business on his hands". The legend a century ago was to the effect that while the devil was flying over Ballingry with his apron full of stones in an effort to fill up Loch Leven, his apron strings broke and its contents were scattered all over the parish. To show that oral tradition and folklore can change when passed from one generation to another, if we go back to the old chroniclers for their version, we learn that the devil was travelling in the opposite direction; that he had come from the north and was journeying south, and furthermore, he was not airborne at all. We are assured that the devil was striding across the country carrying the stones in his apron in order to build a bridge over the river Forth and as with mighty strides he

211

thundered through Ballingry when almost within sight of the water, the stones fell out of his apron and are to be seen lying scattered all over the place to this very day.

Lochgelly too has its legend. A piper who attended a fair there in an age long since forgotten, set out to return home to Kirkcaldy, but he had not reckoned on the uncanny power of the little folk. The hour was late, the night was dark. With pipes playing he entered the Belcrag cave and was seen no more. When conditions are favourable his pipes, it is claimed, can be heard by those who have the rare facility of hearing sounds no longer heard by lesser mortals.

No less credulous is the account of the white horse which at times frequents the stables at Powguild Farm. Who its owner was, and what strange impulse compels it to return to the land of mortals, no one can tell. Even today there are those who can recall happenings which lie beyond the sphere of ordinary experience.

If Lochoreshire was not the most prolific region for cases of witchcraft when the zeal of the kirk was at its height in eradicating it, it certainly had its share of the witchcraft trials. It is known that the lairds of Lochore and Blair were in attendance at many, and that some folk in the neighbourhood were summoned to give evidence at witch trials which took place beyond the limits of the shire. By far the most outstanding case of alleged witchcraft took place at Ballingry about the middle of the eighteenth century.

The relationship between the Rev. Robert Balfour, the parish minister, and the schoolmaster, could not be said to have been cordial. When Mr Balfour found that the church attendances were beginning to fall away, and that he had much difficulty in delivering his accustomed enlivened discourses from the pulpit, he began to look around for the cause of his failing popularity. It was not long before he became convinced that the schoolmaster was the cause of the trouble and that he had in fact cast a spell over him. Convinced that he had become the victim of witchcraft, matters came to a head one Sunday when Mr Balfour stopped abruptly in his sermon and announced to the congregation that he would not continue with the service until the schoolmaster had left the precentor's desk and removed himself from the church. The schoolmaster was about to take his leave while protesting his innocence, when Sir Michael Malcolm, amid the disturbance which followed, during which there were many raised voices and much pushing and pulling, rose from his seat in the gallery and proceeded towards the body of the church. He defended the schoolmaster and refused to allow him to leave. As a result of this unusual affair, a number of parishioners, it is said, left the church at Ballingry and established a Secession church at Lochgelly.

A no less astonishing case came out of Auchterderran in 1707. In that year, Thomas Russell, schoolmaster and clerk to the Presbytery, acknowledged having committed the "horrid sin" of writing the Lord's Prayer backwards. For this most "flagrant scandal" he was deprived of his office for a short period. In his defence the schoolmaster said that he had been asked by Mr Scrymgeor of Wester Bowhill to write the Lord's Prayer in this manner, as he was troubled with sinful thoughts. It was not until afterwards that the schoolmaster had learned that the writing of the Lord's Prayer backwards was made use of as a charm against witchcraft. It was only after he had appeared before the Presbytery and the congregation and had been severely rebuked for having committed "a sin of a very heinous nature" that the schoolmaster was restored to his former post.

It is not known whether the thoughts that troubled the laird of Wester Bowhill arose from the evil practices of "the strange woman who haunted the parish and who was suspected of witchcraft", but on the advice of the Presbytery, the minister was advised to put her out of the parish or have her brought to justice.

It was not the fear of witchcraft alone that troubled the minds of the people. There occurred in a house in the neighbourhood of Inchdairney, so foul a deed that it shook the tranquility of the village life of Kinglassie. The dastardly deed so shocked the douce folk that the owner of the house was prevailed upon to pull it down. However, after a little, he concluded he had been too hasty and made preparations to have the house rebuilt but, try as he would, all his efforts came to naught. At each attempt to rebuild the walls, he found the next morning that his work had been levelled to the ground. It never occurred to him and the good folk of Kinglassie that all this was the work of vandals. They looked for the cause elsewhere and soon became convinced that what they saw was the work of the supernatural. The old chroniclers tell us in all seriousness that the builder had not consulted the fairies and that the little folks' sense of justice had been so outraged that they were determined to use their supernatural powers to see that the house ever after should remain a ruin.

64 *The Crosshill Stone (now removed). The bowl-like cavity measured 6¼ inches in diameter narrowing to 5½ inches across the lip and 2¾ inches in depth*

Of all the accounts of the paranormal none perhaps awakens so much interest as a ghost story although seldom does one receive it at first hand. While no stories of the supernatural are known to linger around Gruoch's well or the monolith, with its neatly cut bowl-like cavity that stood on the lands of Wester Crosshill, or indeed the ruins of Inchgall Castle, one is drawn to the conclusion that the ghost of the courtier of a bygone age that is seen in the village of Crosshill from time to time, may somehow have a connection with the castle. We read from time to time of charters and legal deeds being

213

signed by statesmen, merchants, churchmen and others at Inchgall. This not only implies the presence of men of note, but also of armed retainers who travelled with them. There can be little doubt that the time-worn hall of Inchgall Castle saw many a gathering of soldiers, courtiers and servants and to provide accommodation for such a motley company must have caused quite a stir in the little village of Crosshill. No doubt many an incident would take place among these daring and hot-blooded men when tempers rose and swords were drawn and dark deeds done of which history has left no record whatsoever. It is said that deeds of violence can have an uncanny way of influencing the human mind that happens to be on the same "wave-length" at the right time and place, so that the beholder slips back as it were into a bygone age and experiences something which took place a long time ago. The present writer offers no explanation for the inexplicible occurrence which befell him and his companion, but simply relates his experience.

He encountered this denizen of a bygone age some sixty years ago on the lands of Easter Crosshill, in what was then Ballingry golf course. It was in the cool of the evening following a bright summer's day. The sun had set and soon the daylight would be giving way to dusk. The writer and his companion were approaching a

small hill when there appeared from the far side the figure of a man. The apparition, for that is what it turned out to be, was that of a well-built man of a little above average height, wearing a most unusual dress. His head and shoulders appeared first and as he ascended the hill more of this figure came into view until his whole person was silhouetted against the evening sky. He wore a large flowing cloak which reached down below his knees and had on his head a large broad-rimmed hat. He no sooner appeared than the writer's awareness was considerably increased by his running towards him as if he was fleeing from someone. When but a short distance away he stumbled and fell. The writer and his companion rushed forward but before reaching the spot where the figure appeared to fall, he had vanished. The whole incident was over in a much shorter time than it has taken to tell. The other person's face was drenched of all colour and the writer's own no doubt was no better as it was now realised that both had witnessed something "uncanny". A glance at the golf clubs brought both back to a world of reality and left both wondering what rational explanation could be found for such an unusual occurrence. The apparition had the appearance of that of a courtier of the seventeenth century.

To supplement our description, we would refer to the well-known poster that appeared many years ago advertising Sandeman's Port. Our older readers will recall the familiar picture of a tall figure wearing a long black cloak and a broad rimmed hat, and holding aloft a wine glass. This approximates very closely to the silhouetted figure … we would hasten to add, however, that the analogy ends with the figure, and that our experience had not the remotest connection with Port Wine! The apparition has been seen again on at least two occasions in other parts of the village, and the description given by those who have encountered it, are remarkably alike.

EARLY MINING IN LOCHORESHIRE

Although the earliest known reference to coal in the parish of Ballingry does not go back beyond 1560 there is every likelihood that it was being worked there at a much earlier date. The presence of coal in other parts of Lochoreshire is recorded at a slightly earlier period and something will be said about this later on. Going further afield it is evident that as early as the thirteenth century the monks of Fife were the mining experts of their day.

In 1291 the monks of Dunfermline obtained a charter from William de Obervill granting them permission to dig for coal in the lands of Pittencrieff for their own use only, and as the supply gave out in one pit they were empowered to open another. Many years ago, while workmen were preparing the foundations for the new bridge over the glen, they came across old coal workings believed to have been those made by the monks of the monastery.

The cloistered brethren soon realised that the possession of a coal heugh was a valuable asset and it wasn't long before they were extending their coal-getting activities to lands other than those belonging to themselves. Perhaps the work of winning the coal was done by bondmen belonging to the monastery. Most feudal landlords and barons of the period possessed heritable rights over their tenants (we have seen that Constantine of Lochore had a bondman). If the lower class of peasantry were not serfs, they could not have been far removed from a state of bondage. They were not allowed to move from one place of work to another, but were bound to remain on their master's land and when occasions arose they were sold along with it, or were gifted from one person to another. The monastery in about the year 1142 received as a gift from David I three bondmen — Ragewin, Gillepatric and Ulchell and there is evidence that they received other gifts of bondmen and their families from the same Monarch. In 1174 their labour force was increased by a gift from William-the-Lyon of Gillandrean MacSuthen and his children.

As time went on the number of bondmen belonging to the monastery greatly increased, and in common with other religious houses and great landholders, a register was kept which was of the nature of a stud-book. In it was recorded the members of each servile family, and the names of their sons and daughters and who they married. Each and all were slaves for life unless, as sometimes happened, they secured their freedom when a fine was paid to the lord of the estate. The marriage of a daughter of a bondman was the occasion of the payment of a fee to the master to compensate him for the loss of the woman's services. There is on record a case of serfdom as late as 1751 when the coal master of Kelty colliery was under an obligation to return a collier (he had probably been given on loan) to his rightful owner.

It is evident from the Dunfermline register that not all of the bondmen lived within the neighbourhood of the monastery, but some appear to have worked in other parts of Fife and also in far away Tweeddale. One of the monks' early activities must have touched the western limits of Lochoreshire for they appear to have had the mineral rights in part of the parish of Beath. In 1572, by which time they must have become expert mining engineers, the Commendater of Dunfermline granted to George Douglas of Lochleven in feu charter, the right to work coal in the Kelty coal heugh for an annual rent of £6 18 8d plus an augmentation of 6/8d Scots. The charter states that the coal heugh had belonged to the monastery "many years bygone beyond the memory of man". Why this should be, having in mind that the lands of Beath belonged to the Abbey of Inchcolm, is not at all clear. One reason perhaps was that the monks of Inchcolm knew very little about coal-mining and had come to an arrangement with their brethren at Dunfermline, acknowledging their superior knowledge in this undertaking.

As a plentiful supply of fuel was required to feed the enormous fires in Lochleven Castle, it is readily understood that George Douglas* would have a lively interest in the coal heugh at Kelty. It is known that a coal boat was kept on the loch for the purpose of transporting coal from the shore to the castle. This boat was much larger than an ordinary one and in contemporary records it is referred to as the "great boat".

Not only did the monks have an interest in the coal at Kelty, but we meet with them also a little beyond the eastern limits of Lochoreshire in Strathore near Thornton. In 1555 they gave to the tenant on their lands of Stentoun permission to work the coal at his own expense. Instead, however, of increasing the rent they stipulated that every ninth load of coal should go to the monastery.

Next in antiquity to the Dunfermline charter is the reference to coal pits in the lands of Rires situated of old in the parish of Kilconquhar. The pits were a going concern in 1293. They were held of the King of Scotland by Duncan, son of Duncan the late Earl of Fife who, during this period was a minor and a ward of Edward I of England. Edward appointed Walter de Cambhou in 1293 guardian of the lands of Rires during Duncan's minority. He managed the estate and the coal pits which were then held by Edward of England on behalf of Duncan. The pits, which were probably very small concerns, had a yearly value of 4/5½d. Going still further east we find an interesting situation at the priory of St. Andrews, for there, prior to 1420 one Thomas Puriok, canon of St. Andrews, obtained the consent of his superiors for himself and some of his brethren to work seams of coal on certain land belonging to the priory. An agreement was reached with the prior and convent about the revenue from the sale of the coal and all appear to have been happy in their profit-sharing enterprise. A little later in 1460 there was a colliery at Largo and another at Markinch which were the property of the Crown, and from which the exchequer derived thirty-two chalders of coal annually instead of £37 in money. It was coal from a heugh in Markinch that fed the many fires in the Palace of Falkland. It is known also that coal was being worked in the neighbouring parish of Wemyss as early as 1475. In a Deed of this date, in which coal is mentioned, John Tyrie the minister in Ballingry is a witness. Coming a little nearer home we find coal referred to in 1587 in a Deed dealing with the lands of Balmuto.

Tools used by the old miners have been found from time to time in abandoned workings. One such coal heugh at Blairburn in the parish of Wemyss, known to have been abandoned in the 1600s, was pumped dry in about the year 1901 when several ancient mining tools were found. These included shovels made entirely of wood, picks,

---

* The Douglases were the hereditary castellans of Loch Leven Castle which remained State property till about 1588.

mells of iron and pinches made of wood and shod with iron points. The pick handles were said to have been of great thickness. Of articles found within our neighbourhood we have to record the discovery in 1856 of a wooden shovel found in old coal workings situated to the east of Lochgelly, and within our own recollection the finding of a length of wooden water pipe in an old mine working on the Blairadam estate. The pipe had been made from an Elm tree trunk of about ten feet in length through which a hole about five inches in diameter was made. The pipe when found was partly filled with an ochreous substance showing that the water that had passed through it had contained a certain amount of iron. The narrow end of the tree trunk was shaped like a cone while the large end was hollowed out in a manner the reverse of the narrow end. It was clear that there had been a series of pipes laid down column-wise, the small end of each pipe fitting in to the larger end of the preceding one. No doubt the "cone" joints had been bedded in clay to render them water-tight.

Some forty years ago, three workmen in Benarty mine were afforded a glimpse into conditions which prevailed during the period of serfdom. On breaking through into very old workings, the men discovered a passageway which, because of its obvious antiquity, was named thereafter the "Monks' Road". The passageway, which was cut through the solid coal, was about five feet in height and about four feet in width at its base. In shape, it has been described as not unlike a keyhole.

Further examination revealed alcoves which were cut into one side of the passageway at somewhat regular intervals. The alcoves, which were made to form a kind of seat, were thought to have been used as resting-places by the women coal-bearers as they carried their heavy loads of coal to the surface. Beside one alcove were found the remains of a coal creel complete with head bands.

An equally interesting relic of former days was a primitive coal-pick made from the limb of a tree. A small branch on either side of the limb had been cut to the required length and shod with iron, tapering to a point. The discoverers were given only a brief view of the "finds". As soon as fresh air entered the workings, both relics fell to dust.

In the light of so much evidence of early mining to the east and west of Lochoreshire, it seemed almost a certainty that a little research would reveal that the early mining engineers had been active in that region also.

We have shown in an earlier chapter, that Lochoreshire included three parishes and portions of others. Commencing with Kinglassie it will be remembered that Constantine of Lochore renounced his claim to it in 1234 in favour of the Abbey of Dunfermline. Probably as an outcome of this, there appears in the register of the Abbey, a list of the descendants of one of its bondmen by the name of John Scoloc. They all, with a possible exception of two, died at Kinglassie and were buried there, the last being killed during the reign of John Balliol. They probably all worked at Kinglassie. Coal was being worked there in 1643 and for many years before this date by John Hamilton, the land proprietor. By 1668 the coal works were being managed by one James Riddell, a Leith merchant who employed Henry Mason as his oversman, along with eight coal heughers and Alexander Henderson as his coal grieve and John Harvie as carter. In addition to coal both Hamilton and Riddell had salt works at Kinglassie. The proprietors of Kinglassie had as early as 1579 the right under charter to have access

217

66 A wooden shovel found in 1856 in old coal workings to the east of Lochgelly

to the sea "for the karying and bringing of wraik and wair to the lands of Kinglassie".

The earliest reference found so far to the presence of coal in Auchterderran parish is in 1532 when it was being worked at Dundonald where it appears to have gone on more or less continuously until modern times.

At the end of the eighteenth century there were three pits there, although by the early nineteenth century this number had been reduced to one. The industry revived in 1836 under the management of R. W. Ramsay when seven colliers were employed producing a weekly output of one hundred and thirty-three loads (one load equalled one cwt.) which were sold at 8d the load. Fifty years afterwards the number of pits increased to two when sixty miners were employed at 4/-d a day. The daily output from both pits amounted to eighty tons. The workers were housed rent-free but paid 1/6d fortnightly for their quota of coal. It is not known how far back coal workings took place at Auchterderran, but by the time a century had elapsed after it is first recorded the reference to coal was common-place and appears regularly among the appurtenants of the barony.

To the east of the parish lie the lands of Cluny, one of the early coalfields of the neighbourhood. The colliery during the mid-eighteenth century was one of three collieries belonging to the Earl of Rothes whose family had been mining coal for centuries on their estate. In 1713 the Earl of the day, being short of labour, wrote to the town council of Dunfermline asking for the loan of two colliers. That august body reckoned they could spare the services of two workmen from their burgh mines so it was that David Murgain and George Brown were loaned to the Earl on condition that he would return the men to the council when requested.

It is evident from the foregoing that colliers were loaned by one master to another as circumstances required, just as if they were so many pieces of merchandise. A little previous to this period, there is evidence of six colliers and eleven coal bearers (probably women) being given on loan by a coal master in Fife to Christoper Seaton to work in his mine at Tranent so long as they were not required in Fife. In the mid-eighteenth century there is the instance of another Fife coal master who, being short of workers, instructed his manager to seek out those who belonged to him who had deserted their work and suggested also that he get some of the colliers who had lately been employed at a mine which had closed; as they were now in different parts of the country and "nobodies property".

Although still in a state of serfdom, some poor creatures had the courage to speak out against injustices and to withhold their labour, but as the law was on the side of the master and as they were thirled to his service, they usually had in the end to submit to the conditions laid down by him. The following is an example of the terms to which those who rebelled had to agree.

Are you content to sign on stamped paper that your satisfied to serve the E. of Rothes and his family as their bound Coalier and that not only yourself but yours.

Are you content to work his Crop Coal on the lands of Coallden just now going at 1/3 hacking money of each load Great and 1/3 each load small and to work all the seams of his Coalls at the said rate or as his Lordship shall think fitt and to do every other thing with respect to the working of the Coall and offsett any Down of Sinks or to do every other thing in his Coall work that is on use for Sink as you are to Due in and Concerning such Coallworks in all capacities.

Are you content to take what meall you shall want for your family from his Lordship and pay him twenty shillings above the price for each boll of his own meall or Use Country meall of a merk of each boll above what he shall pay for North Country meall if he shall be obliged to buy to serve you and the rest of his Coalliers.

Are you content to allow a load of Coalls each week free to his Lordships use and he is to give you a free house over a year and to maintain and keep the same to you.

In 1752 a number of colliers at Cluny struck work over a grievance. In order to put down the disturbance, a company of soldiers were despatched to the scene and six of the colliers' leaders were arrested. Three soldiers and a corporal marched three to Cupar where they were imprisoned; five soldiers and a corporal took the other three to a prison at Kirkcaldy. They were released only after each had signed a document agreeing to the conditions laid down by the Earl of Rothes. To prevent further trouble at Cluny the Earl issued the following notice "That the coulliers or their wives who shall be mutinous or abusive to their neighbours in interrupting them at their work shall be imprisoned until they acknowledge their fault".

Travelling eastward, the barony of Cardon in the mid-seventeenth century belonged to the family of Edmiston, first by William Edmiston and then by his son, during which period it was leased to several people in succession. In 1633 it was leased to David Beatson who, by 1643, was employing eight coal heughers working at his "great coale" which he sold at 3/6d a load. By 1657 the coal heugh at Cardon was in the hands of

67 *An impression of the monks' road and primitive coal pick obtained from an eye-witness.*

219

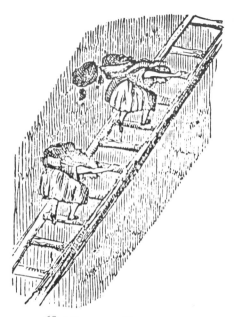

68 *Women coal bearers*

"William Rowane of Gaslee and Henrie Davidsone in Blacklaw" and four years afterwards "Andrew Kennedie, portioner of Lynktoun of Abbotshall", was in possession. By this time some advancement had obviously been made in the production of coal. In the year 1661 "engines" are mentioned. This probably refers to a horse wind-lass. Andrew Kennedie's sojourn in Cardon, however, was short-lived, and Messrs. "Archibald Angous, William Geed, Gilbert Hallyburton, John Wemyss and John Angous, ship masters and burgesses of Burntisland took over. By this time "coal machinery" is mentioned. It is known that during this period most of the coal shipped from Burntisland came from the Fordell colliery and was brought to the harbour in panniers on horseback. These men from Burntisland were of considerable standing: two were bailies of the town and Commissioners to the Scottish Parliament. They therefore took over the barony, not in their own name only but in the name of the other magistrates of the burgh. Their interest in the barony is readily understood and no doubt it would not be long before coal from Auchterderran was being taken aboard at Burntisland for shipment to the low countries. Travelling westward from Cardon, which was of old in the parish of Kinghorn but has been part of Auchterderran since 1642, we note that coal is mentioned in 1638 as being worked at Bowhill and likewise in 1636 on the lands of Little Balgonie. Further west we record the presence of coal on lands which at one time were in the parish of Ballingry, and barony of Inchgall. The first of these are the lands of Spittal where coal is mentioned in 1636. These lands were annexed to Auchterderran parish in 1891. The second of these lands are those of Lochhead near Lochgelly, which came to the Vallance family through the marriage of Agnes de Cranbeth and James de Vallance. In 1625 Patrick Wardlaw gave Arthur Forbes (probably a relative of his wife Margaret Forbes) power to work coal and limestone there. The coal spoken of as "all good burning colles" was subsequently

220

69 *Contemporary drawings of 1786 showing*
underground workers at Gilmerton Colliery, Midlothian

worked by the Earl of Wemyss and, in consequence of his holding these lands, he had the right to possess a seat in Ballingry church. The lands of Lochhead were annexed to the parish of Auchtertool in 1649.

Continuing westward we come to the lands of Lochgelly where no doubt coal had been worked from an early period. There is factual evidence to show that many pits there were worked out and abandoned by the mid-eighteenth century. By the beginning of the nineteenth century there was only one colliery working. This stood on the east side of the road leading to Glencraig and quite near to the railway station. It belonged to the Earl of Minto and was worked on a limited scale, employing only seven

221

colliers and six oncost workers. The output continued to improve and in 1816 a manager was appointed to supervise the works. Meanwhile, a second pit was sunk and in 1822 the Earl leased the pits to Messrs. Chisholm and Brown who in the following year sunk a third pit. This undertaking had all the latest machinery installed, including a condensing steam winding engine. After a period of about four years Messrs. Chisholm and Brown went bankrupt and the coal at the pit-head was sold to pay their creditors. The works reverted to the Earl of Minto and were leased on this occasion to Nicol Thomson who held them until 1831, when John Henderson obtained a lease of the coal field for ten years. The industry made great progress under Henderson's management, employing thirty-nine men and twelve women with a weekly output of one thousand three hundred loads (a load equalled one cwt.) which were sold at 8d a load. Three hundred loads were delivered by cart to Kirkcaldy each week. In 1841 John Henderson went into partnership with Messrs. Granger and Millar, Mining Engineers, Edinburgh, and obtained a thirty-one years lease of the coal and ironstone in the lands of Lochgelly and Cartmore. In 1846 Millar withdrew from the management and Messrs. Kinnaird and Russell joined the Company.

The new management, known as John Henderson and Company, set about building two blast furnaces to smelt the ironstone which was now being worked. These were in operation by 1847 and in 1851 the name was changed to The Lochgelly Iron Company.

Much progress was made and a further two furnaces were built in 1856. By the last quarter of the nineteenth century the Company possessed three coal-pits and four ironstone pits. In depth they ranged from twelve fathoms to one hundred fathoms and had a combined output of four hundred and sixty-five tons per day. The Company had, at this period, one hundred and twenty-four two apartment and eighty-nine one apartment houses for which their workers paid a fortnightly rent of 2/6d and 1/3d respectively.

Continuing westward we come to the lands of Easter Cartmore where again there is evidence of coal having been worked although perhaps at a little later date. In the mid-seventeenth century William Knox had a charter of these lands from David Boswell and David, Earl of Wemyss, as joint proprietors. In 1762 John Knox, a Dunfermline merchant was in possession. In this year Mr Knox had a plan made of the estate* and it is from this plan that we obtain an insight into the location of some of the old coal heughs around the village of Lochgelly. Given prominence on the plan is a coal pit under the heading "Present working 1762". The pit was situated in what is now the western half of Lochgelly golf course and if what is shown on the plan in any way reflects its output, it must have supplied a wide area. Roads leading from the pit read, "coall road to Bingrie", "coall road to Kirkcaldie", "coall road to Lochgelly, Aberdour and Burntisland" and "coall road to Beath". This was probably the pit known at a later date as the "Gig pit": if so it had ceased working before the middle of the following century. A hundred yards further north there is shown the site of eight pits marked "old coall pitts", and from there to the Beagle burn (written Bigell) is shown a "coall levell". This

---

* The plan which was produced by Robert Scotland, land surveyor is ornamented in a rather curious manner with drawings of Mermaids and stylistic representations of fish, birds and animals.

probably was a water course for draining water from the pits. Another feature of mining days is a row of collier houses situated at Launcherhead (written Laneshire Head), while to the south-east of Launcherhead, on the east side of the main road leading to Ballingry, is shown a group of ten "old coall pitts" under the heading "Lochgelly". Further north, probably to the east of the present railway station there are shown another four "old coall pitts" and a "coall levell" leading to the Beagle burn. Wester Cartmore at this period belonged to John Syme who is known to have been an early pioneer in coal mining.

70 *Raising water from mine by chain of buckets*

The adjoining estate of Lumphinnans, the westermost part of the barony of Inchgall, was in the year 1762 put up for sale. It is clear from the notice of sale that there were no coal pits on the estate, although it was stated that coal was believed to be had. It was not until 1826 that coal was being worked there. After a period of thirteen years the work force amounted to twenty-three workmen with a weekly output of five hundred loads. In addition to coal the output of ironstone was considerable and in 1853 two blast furnaces were built to smelt pig iron. In the 1870s there were two coal pits working, one of one hundred and ten fathoms and the other of seventy-five fathoms, producing a daily output of one hundred and fifty tons. The blast furnaces at this period produced twenty tons of pig iron daily.

The Company had by now built forty-four two apartment and thirty-six single apartment houses to accommodate their workers, and the Earl of Zetland, who owned the estate, built a school in 1864 for the education of the workers' children.

Before going on to give an account of early mining in the Lochore district, the following sketch of mechanical contrivances used in early mining in Lochoreshire and in Strathore may interest the reader.

223

The name "Gin pit" occurs fairly often in old mining phraseology and it was the "Gin" or "Gin horse", as it is sometimes called, that replaced the use of stairs in the mine shaft whereby coal was brought to the surface by women coal-bearers. It was in the year 1808 that the Gin was introduced into coal mining in Lochoreshire. In this contrivance which was a sort of horse windlass, the horse was harnessed to a large horizontal wooden drum which revolved on a wooden frame at a height which allowed the animal to walk underneath it. The horse was harnessed to the underside of the drum and as the animal was driven round in a circle it pulled the drum overhead with it. This apparatus stood a short distance from the mine shaft and by means of a rope which passed round the horizontal drum and over two wheels set vertically over the mine shaft, one end of the rope descended to the bottom of the mine where it was attached to a large wicker-work basket or similar constructed cage, the other end being fixed to a similar cage which hung at ground level, the horse was able to pull the loaded cage up the shaft while the other cage descended. On the full cage reaching the surface, the horse was turned about to pull the drum in the opposite direction thereby bringing the other cage to the surface.

A somewhat similar contrivance was in use for drawing water from the mines.

By means of gear wheels the power from the horse was transferred to a horizontal shaft which in turn operated an endless chain to which were attached a series of buckets set at regular intervals. The chain went down into the "pump sink" and as it revolved over the horizontal shaft, full buckets came up on one side while empty buckets descended on the other.

It is not until 1731 that "engines" are mentioned and it is clear that the motive power was other than horse-power. The greatest recurring difficulty in early mining was the seepage of water into the workings, especially where a level could not be run in from a nearby burn so that the water from the mine could drain into the stream. The chain and bucket system was not very efficient and in time it was replaced by the suction pump. Before this, it was not an uncommon occurrence for men to be moved from one mine to another until the water problem had been dealt with.

In 1736 a report was submitted by the architect William Adam of Blairadam and three others, containing detailed information on levelling that had been carried out at Easter Strathore for the siting of a water engine for the purpose of pumping water from the mine. From the nature of the observations made by William Adam, it is clear that he had a good knowledge of coal mining. As he himself was engaged in sinking a new mine on his own estate of Blairadam, this is not to be wondered at. Among the Earl of Rothes' many papers, there is a working drawing of a water engine. Although it does not bear Mr Adam's signature (the paper is torn and defaced where this may have appeared) it is almost certain to have been prepared by him.

The engine was to be powered by water from the river Ore which was to operate a water wheel twenty-one feet in diameter and two feet six inches wide. The shaft of the wheel was to have a crank on either side each with a two feet six inch radius. These were to operate two vertical timber levers which in turn were attached to two beams, each twenty-five feet long and one foot six inches square. The beams are shown centrally pivoted on top of a stone-built pillar thirteen feet six inches high, eight feet six inches wide and twenty-eight feet six inches long. As the cranks revolved they imparted a see-

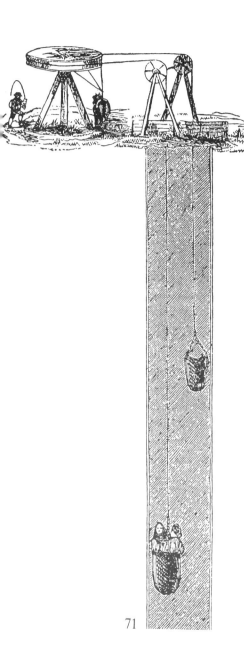

saw motion to the beams which in turn raised and lowered iron chains attached to pump rods seven and a half inches in diameter. The engine, when erected at a cost of £229. 19. 4d was capable of drawing water from a depth of one hundred and forty-four feet.

Contemporary with the water engine was a contrivance, the lower part of which consisted of timber levers and pump rods somewhat similar to the water engine but was worked by wind power and in appearance was not dissimilar to a windmill. The tower was some forty feet high and the wind sails were about fifty feet across. By means of gear wheels, the power from the sails was transmitted to a vertical shaft which occupied a central position in the tower and extended to ground level where other gear wheels provided an up-and-down motion to two timber levers which extended out through the tower where they lifted and lowered chains attached to pump rods. The windpump which was working in 1740 was capable of lifting water from a depth of eighty feet.

These contrivances postulate the presence of someone capable of keeping them in working order and in 1741 we meet for the first time with the "Colliery Engineer" in the person of one Stephen Row.

By the 1840's most of the pumping engines driven by wind and water had been replaced by steam-driven pumps. The earliest of these contrivances were most imperfect and by no means effective by later standards. With steam

225

escaping all over, the coal consumption was excessive and the engine was considered profitable only from the fact that it was fired on cheap fuel.

Improvement followed improvement, and by the mid-nineteenth century steam was being used much more as a motive power. It was in 1823 that the first of the steam winding engines replaced the gin-horse or windlass in Lochoreshire.

By the second half of the nineteenth century steam was being used to work a contrivance for operating bucket pumps in a mine at the Milton of Inchgall. This was done by erecting a fifteen horsepower steam engine at the mine mouth. The engine operated a bell crank which in turn raised and lowered two ropes alternately, which corresponded in movement to the rise and fall of the bell crank levers. One rope descended twenty fathoms to the bottom of the mine where one of the pumps was situated. The other worked a similar pump placed at the bottom of a dook which was driven at a steep gradient not far from the mine bottom.

72 *Engine erected in 1736 to pump water from mine*

We come now to the Glencraig and Lochore districts and if in tracing the progress of coal-mining there, we have allowed ourselves to go into the story a little more fully than has been done elsewhere, perhaps the reader will forgive us for so doing. The earliest reference to coal being worked in the barony of Inchgall is in 1560. Although coal-mining had obviously been going on for some time before this date, to attempt an earlier origin would be largely a matter of conjecture. No doubt the primary object in working the coal during its earliest period was to provide the laird with fuel for Inchgall Castle and probably for Ladath House. By 1560 coal-mining was already a going concern at Blaircushnie*, where there was a coal heugh under the management of William Skyrling, a tackman who had a lease of the coal heugh from the laird. From the known circumstances, it would appear that William Skyrling's lease was due to expire in 1560. In this year Henry Wardlaw the laird, made over the coal and coal heugh to his cousin John Wardlaw, a Leith merchant who held the lands of North Lumphinnans and who had been in possession there since 1532. One of the first things John Wardlaw did was to give notice to the tackman to remove himself and his servants from the coal heugh. This, William Skyrling refused to do, and on the matter going to court he was ordered to vacate the coal heugh. But still he refused, and on doing so he was pronounced a rebel and "put to the horn". By 1565 William Skyrling was dead and as his belongings by law fell to John Wardlaw, he made a gift of these to his son, James Wardlaw chaplain of Collihill, so that, in the words of the Deed dated 1565, James Wardlaw received "the gift of the escheat of all gudis, movable and unmovable, dettis, takkis, contractis, actionis, obligationis, sowumes of money, jewellis, gold, silver, cunyeit and uncunyeit and uthiris gudis quhatsumevir qucilkis pertenit to unquhile William Skyrling". Two years afterwards, when things had returned to normal, John Wardlaw not only possessed the coal heugh but he had sasine of the lands of Blaircushnie the lands of Ladath and a quarter of the lands attached to Inchgall Mill. For the next fifty years or so the only evidence of mining in the barony of Inchgall is to be found at Blaircushnie. However, from 1614 onwards coal is mentioned in the Inchgall charters and appears along with limestone, peats and divots as one of the appendages to the barony. It is in 1628 that coal appears in connection with the lands of Crosshill and as this implies exploratory "howkings" of some sort, it is doubtful if it remained so, it is more than likely that the Crosshill coal was being worked by this date. Meanwhile coal continued to be produced at Blaircushnie. In 1645 we read of one William Wannan, a collier in Blair, who confessed to the murder of Patrick Reris. There is no record of the prices paid for coal in Inchgall at this period, but they probably did not differ greatly from the prices at the neighbouring coal pit at Kelty where in 1680, small coal could be had for 1½d — 2d a load. Great coal was a little dearer at 3½d a load. By comparison, these prices were cheap, as peat was to be had at 4d a load! The coal heugh at Blair (by now the older name was seldom used) was still to the fore at the beginning of the following century, and in 1715 women continued to be employed there as coal bearers to bring the coal to the surface.

A short description of women coal bearers taken from an account by an eye witness may not be out of place here. Coal bearers were, as was necessary for their calling, generally robust and muscular and well fitted for hard work. In preparation for their work they put on a "Sod", a sort of hap which was well padded in order to minimise the pressure of the loaded creel on their backs. They next wore a "head brat" which was made of very strong material and protected their necks and shoulders from loose dross.

---

* Blaircushnie was the earliest name for Benarty Estate. It was also known as Blair and sometimes as East Blair to distinguish it from West Blair which was another name for Blairadam.

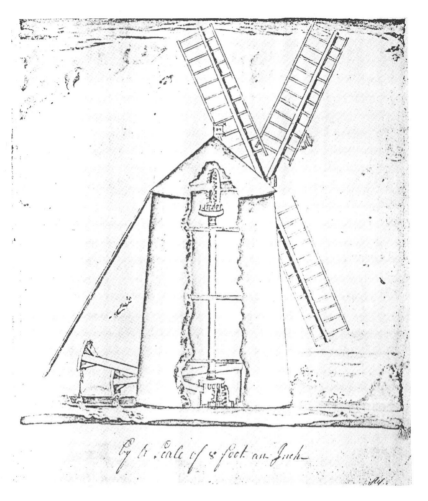

73 *Wind-driven pump erected in 1736*

They afterwards put on the coal-creel. This was made of wicker and has been described as resembling a cockle-shell. The creel was somewhat flat in order to lie on the womens' back and was turned up all round so as to contain the coal, and at the front there were attached two "tugs" (bands) which passed across the coal-bearer's forehead and helped to keep the creel in position. The average coal-bearer carried from the coal face to the surface, either up a gradient in the case of a mine or up winding stairs in the case of a pit, a creel containing one to two cwts of coal. As an aid to negotiating the long dark passages the coal-bearer held a "link" (light) in her hand.

Astonishing as this may seem, it has been known for the really strong and muscular bearers in a trial of strength to carry as much as three cwts of coal at one time.

The story of mining at Inchgall during this period is scanty. That there were ironstone mines on the Lochore estate in the last decade of the eighteenth century is known, and in all probability coal was being worked there also. It is certain that during the first quarter of the nineteenth century coal was being worked on the estate and in the near vicinity of Lochore House. Mr Syme, who acquired the estate in 1798 probably had a hand in this, and coal was still being produced during Mr Jobson's ownership. It was in the years following 1835 however, that coal mining really began to establish itself as the stable industry in the village. The family of Goodal of Bowhill, who held a lease of the Cluny colliery from the Raith estate and who had successfully worked the coal there, went into partnership with the Aytoun family who owned the Capeldrae estate, to form the Capeldrae Cannel (candle) Coal Company (sometimes known as the Capeldrae Gas Coal Company) with Thomas Goodal as its manager. Pits were sunk to the gas coal a little south of Kirkness House and near Capeldrae farm. These pits were known as Manorlees and Flockhouse. There was also a pit at Westfield called "The Squirrel". Shortly afterwards miners' houses were erected at Westfield and Flockhouse. The venture proved a success from the beginning, one of the chief consumers of the coal was the Kinross and Milnathort Gas Company to whom it was sold at about 14/-d a ton. By 1866, in addition to James Aytoun advocate, and Thomas Goodal, the management included Messrs. Crombie and Anderson of Lochgelly who already had an interest in the Balgreggie Colliery. In 1867 the Company was negotiating with Lady Scott to obtain a lease of the minerals in part of the Lochore estate, and in the same year Messrs. Nimmo and Sons, Coal Masters, were doing likewise for the remaining part. A memorandum addressed to John Jeffrey, the estate overseer, outlines the conditions of the leases. These, along with coloured plans of the estate lie before us, as we write.* It is generally believed that the Capeldrae Cannel Coal Company bought the Lochore estate from Lady Scott in 1867. No doubt mining operations would commence in that year under the mineral lease but whether the Company bought the estate before the year was out is not clear. In any event the mineral leases must have been of short duration especially that of Messrs. Nimmo and Sons. Lady Scott sold the estate for £60,000.

74 *Woman dragging truck on rails in Fife, 1841*

* See appendix No. 1

The Company now called the Lochore and Capeldrae Cannel Coal Company had sometime previous to 1867 built rows of houses for their workers on the west side of the main road on ground belonging to Hynds farm on the Lochore estate. It could be said that with the building of these houses, the mining village of Lochore came into being. They were long known as Caravan Row from the fact that the roofs of the houses were segmental in shape. They were supported on Belfast trusses, covered with timber sarking and tar-felting. The southernmost houses, which went under the appellation of Dandy Row and Candle-makers Row, stood on the site of a former lochan and almost identical with the site of the present village bowling green. By 1879 more houses had been built. They stretched midway to the crossroads at the north end of the village and a further two rows stood on the south side of Ballingry road, where the present library stands. The houses had ash-pits and shared dry privys to the rear. Water was had from iron stand wells at the side of the road. There were no wash-houses or coal cellars. The washing of clothes was done in the open; the floors in the bed recesses, instead of wood, were paved with square fire clay tiles. This was where the household coal was stored. Drainage was by open channel in front of the houses. There were eight blocks of houses in all amounting to ninety-three houses of which sixty-three consisted of single apartments. There were by now one hundred and seventy-eight persons residing in the village. Before this, most of the houses were situated at Crosshill and Milton. The shift of population, small as it was, marked the change in the industrial life of the village, from the one-time cottage-weaving industry at Crosshill, with the lint-pits and waulk-mills at the Milton, to coalmining as the staple industry.

By 1871 the Company had sunk two pits and one mine. Number one pit which stood a little north from where the Mary Colliery was sunk in 1902, reached the depth of twenty-five fathoms. A few nearby houses that served the colliery were known afterwards as St. Ronan's Place. Number two pit stood a short distance to the north of the present Country Park Centre and reached the depth of forty-seven fathoms. Both pits worked two seams of parrot coal, one two feet six inches thick and another fourteen inches thick of very superior quality. The mine produced ironstone from a seam five feet thick: one hundred miners and seventeen surface workers were employed and the daily output was forty tons of coal and fourteen tons of ironstone. Wages ranged from 5/-d to 6/6d per day.

By 1879 a further two surface mines (inguanees) had been sunk and of the three mines mentioned, one stood on the south side of the road leading to Chapel farm not far from where the Mary Colliery number two shaft was sunk. Directly opposite this mine, on the north side of the Chapel Road and halfway up Bowhouse bank, was another mine, the remains of which are still to be seen. The third mine was situated at Miller's Neuk on rough ground south of Lochore House.

Crude oil was also manufactured at Lochore. This followed after a similar plant had been set up at Lochgelly in 1865 where six men and two boys were employed.

Before the introduction of the railway, much of the coal and ironstone mined at Lochore was transported by horse tramway to Kelty.

Most of the mines of this period were quite small undertakings. In many cases the number of men producing coal did not exceed half a dozen. In a good week the profit to

75 *James Aytoun of Capeldrae*

the owner was in the region of £3, but if underground difficulties arose, this could be as low as a few shillings.

The Company continued to expand and in 1885 it had taken over the mines at Easter and Wester Crosshill and the Milton.

The Crosshill mines were opened in 1865 and employed fifteen miners who worked a seam of parrot coal and produced eighteen tons of coal daily. The Milton mine commenced in 1869 and employed twenty miners. They worked a seam of parrot coal two feet six inches thick. It was of excellent quality and was used for producing gas. The Company had by now shipping ports at Burntisland, Alloa, Leith, Glasgow and Greenock and Alexander Burns who was the Company's manager resided in Lochore House. Five years later in June 1890 the Company sold out to the Fife Coal Company, along with the much smaller Rosewell Gas Coal Company.

By 1890 other mining activities were going on in the barony south of the river Ore. The estate of Glencraig had been attracting the attention of mining men for some time. The area north of Glencraig House, which was ultimately occupied by the Glencraig Colliery and all its ramifications, is shown on old maps peppered with disused ironstone mines which were "old" by the mid-nineteenth century. The estate during the first half of that century was owned by the Henderson family. John Henderson's second son William, sold the estate to James Constable. George Constable, his son from whom John Wilson of Airdrie bought it in 1894, tried out its mineral resources by putting down several bores. In the following year the Wilson and Clyde Coal Company commenced sinking two shafts and established the Glencraig Colliery. The only houses at Glencraig, apart from the mansion house, was the stone-built Contle Row. These houses constituted the "village of Contill" referred to in 1701. The name goes back to 1546 at least, when the lands of that name were part of the estate called Cluniecraig. Things moved rapidly after 1895. North and South Glencraig came into being when houses were built for the colliery workers. The urgent need of water to supply so many houses was overcome in a somewhat novel way by tapping a source of water down the pit shaft and pumping it into a large tank placed high upon the pithead gear. From there pipes led the water, not to standwells on the street as had been done at Lochore, but into every house. In 1895 this was considered quite an innovation. A further development in the mining resources took place about 1901 when the Company bought Easter and Wester Crosshill.

76 Glencraig Colliery c.1900

By now the Fife Coal Company was formulating plans to work the deep seams of coal in the Lochore and Capeldrae estates and on first March 1902 work was commenced on sinking the Mary Colliery. A party consisting of directors and their wives travelled by special train from Kelty station using the mineral line, and the engine was gaily decorated for the occasion with green and red flags. Mrs Carlaw, the wife of the Company's manager, cut the first turf after which the party had lunch in a timber building erected for the occasion. The colliery shaft was to measure twenty-eight feet by eleven feet and was to go down to a depth of three hundred fathoms. The estimated cost of the colliery was £100,000. Early in the project a row of houses was built near at hand to accommodate the families of the men engaged in sinking the shaft. These houses were afterwards known as Peveril Place.

Along with the sinking of the pit came the building of the workers' houses. These were built on land belonging to Hynds farm which was of old on Ladath estate, now known as Lochore estate. The old farm buildings with their red pantile roofs stood for a long number of years in the centre of the village, and what was the farmhouse was converted into small flats and was thereafter known as Dumbiedykes. What may have been a corn loft in the farm steading was converted into a small hall. It was by then a very old building and as one wall had a decided bulge outwards it was supported by raking shores made of timber. These and an outside wooden stair, which reached the only door placed in the gable wall, gave the building an old-world appearance. Many a happy social gathering was held in Hynds Hall in the early days of the village. The houses in Caravan Row were in some cases renovated and received conventional slated roofs and were afterwards renamed Lochleven Road. After a year or two a workers' Institute was established which housed the Lochore and Benarty Working Mens' Library.

Mary No. 2 pit shaft was sunk about the year 1921 and the pithead frame which was constructed in concrete was one of the first of its kind in the country. Today when all traces of mining have gone, this pithead frame still stands and is likely to withstand the ravishes of time for countless generations to come.

On the pits closing down in 1966 the evidence of coal mining in the barony of Inchgall had extended for a period of a little over four hundred years, but there is every likelihood that coal was being worked in the barony long before the year 1560.

SOME NOTABLES IN LOCHORESHIRE'S PAST

The following persons have for the most part not appeared in our account of the old families of Lochoreshire. They have, however, by reason of their actions and personalities added a tincture to the colourful annals of bygone days. Many, of course, lived at a period long after Lochoreshire ceased to exist (the territorial designation went out with the Malcolms), but as they lived within the region once known by that name, they come within the limits of our purview.

Squire Meldrum of Cleish and Binns

The first of those whose actions we attempt to delineate was well-known in the sixteenth century. William, or Squire Meldrum was the son of Archibald Meldrum of Cleish and Binns and is said to have been born in Cleish Castle in 1492, and to have spent his boyhood days there and much of his early youth. After an adventurous life abroad he returned to reside at the Binns, a house that had been part of his father's patrimony.

The Bymnis, Bynnie, Byne and Byn, as it was variously called, situated a little west from the estate of Benarty was for generations held by the Wardlaws of Inchgall and latterly by the Malcolms. The lands of Binns were originally part of the barony of Crambeth and were annexed to Lochoreshire following the marriage of Sir James de Vallance and Agnes de Crambeth, and were probably Agnes' marriage dowry.

The Meldrums originally hailed from Aberdeenshire having taken their name from the barony of Old Meldrum. A branch of the family settled in Fife in the thirteenth century when Alexander de Melgedrum witnessed a Fife Deed in 1278. David de Melkedrum of Fife is also mentioned in 1292. The name appears locally in the person of Willelmus de Meldrom who was one of those who perambulated the boundaries of Kirkness and Lochore in 1395. Archibald Meldrum, who was probably the father of Squire Meldrum, was present at the perambulation of the west boundary of Fife in 1457 and again in 1466. Archibald Meldrum from the year 1501 till his death in about the year 1509 was a Royal Pensioner, and was known at court as the Squire of Cleish. The payments made to him were irregular, but appear to have been intended as by-monthly and although they were equally inconsistent, they may be said to have amounted to 14/-d. Along with each payment, which very often was made in "Franch Crounis", the Royal Clerk is careful to enter that it is made "be the Kingis command". From time to time he had a special mission assigned to him as in 1502 when he was given 28/-d to make a purchase in preparation for a journey to Denmark. In 1503 the Royal Treasury is depleted to the amount of £10 14/-d in order to purchase "VII elne of rede chamlot" for the making of the livery for the Squire. In October of the following year he was to accompany the King on a visit to Brechin, and to prepare for the journey a horse was bought at Inverkeithing for the sum of £5 6 8d, and a pair of black hose made for him at a cost of 12/-d. When it is remembered that the value of the Scottish shilling was equal to one English penny, the Squire's hose cost one shilling or in present day value five new pence. Perhaps the last of the special assignments given to the Squire of Cleish was the casting of "ane gwn", a task which brought him in 1508 the sum of 14/-d.

Following the death of Archibald Meldrum there is, as one would expect, no mention in the Royal accounts of the Squire of Cleish. However, after a lapse of two years the entries appear again, and they no doubt now refer to William Meldrum the new Squire. In order to make good the lapse in payments, the Squire of Cleish in 1511 received as his penion "XV lycht franch crouns" amounting in value to £10 10/-d and as a Court Servant he also received "VI elnis of rowans tanhy" to make his tulle livery at a cost of £6 9/-d. In 1512 the Squire of Cleish, at the age of twenty joined the navy and on the 24th day of July of that year "quhan he sald past in the schippis", he received the sum of £20.

For the story of the adventures of William, we have to rely on the metrical account given by his friend Sir David Lindsay of the Mount in his poem *The History and Testament of Squire Meldrum* written in 1550. The poem has most of the ingredients of a medieval romance in which the hero finds adventure in foreign parts, appearance at court, rescuing ladies in distress, love-making and personal combat, nonetheless, we are assured that it is the true life-story of the Squire.

Squire Meldrum joined the Scottish Navy during the period when it was being enlarged and several new vessels had been built including the *Great Michael*. It was also at a time when the relationship between the Scottish and English monarchs was anything but cordial. In 1513, the year of his entering, the first of his expeditions was surprisingly not under the command of Sir Andrew Wood of Largo, the King's captain, but under the Earl of Arran. Instead of obeying the King's orders to proceed to France, the Earl conducted his fleet to Ireland where he stormed Carrickfergus and it is here that we first hear of the Squire's exploits. He rescued a lady of that town who had been robbed of her clothes by two sailors. On refusing to return these to the woman they attacked the Squire with swords. He cleft one on the head who fell dead, the other was much stronger and after much parrying the Squire drew his dagger and struck him right to the collar bone. The lady in gratitude offered herself as his wife adding that she received a yearly sum of £1,000. At this the trumpets blew for all to return on board the ships but the lady continued to implore the Squire to take her with him. She gave him a ruby ring and wished to return with him to Scotland, but the Squire replied that he was bound for France and in any case she was too young to sail the seas. Undaunted by his reply she offered to go on board the ship dressed as a man, but the Squire made haste to reach his ship, promising that if perchance he came again in more peaceful times he would marry her and so he weighed anchor and sailed away. The navy put in at Brittany where the Squire was feted by the ladies.

He is said to have been liberal with his money, won the prize at every game he took part in and was virtuous and wise. He was likewise courteous in company and was liked by the seamen, the knights and the Admiral himself who, because of his courage and devotion to duty, gave him command of five hundred men. From there, the navy sailed to France to assist the French King in defending his country against the assaults of the English Navy, an enterprise which resulted in daily skirmishes in the neighbourhood of Calais and Picardy. It was not long before our laird of Binns was taking part in the enterprise. To this end he marched at the head of one hundred spearmen and a company of foot both "bold and stout" and was warmly greeted by the King of France who gave him a command in his army.

It so happened that for some time past an Englishman by the name of Talbart had constantly thrown out a challenge to any man in the French army to fight him with spear or lance, but so far no one had come forward. On hearing that a company of Scots had joined the French, Talbart repeated his challenge to include the Scots. The news greatly aroused the Squire and when he sought out the English champion, he, Talbart, half boastingly complained that he could find no one who would dare fight him. "It is a great shame" said Meldrum "that you should return home without doing battle. I myself will meet you in the field tomorrow on horse armed with spear and shield".

The challenge coming from the youth surprised Talbart and feeling rather insulted that from out of all the knights in the French and Scottish army no one should accept his challenge except an unknown Squire, he addressed Meldrum in humiliating terms telling him that he was too young and he had not the strength, he therefore counselled Meldrum, calling him "child" to let the matter drop, but the Squire was not to be put off so easily. For honour's sake Talbart had to accept the challenge, although to meet the young Scot he reckoned it would be a walk-over, and hardly justified the need for much preparation.

In their encounter both combatants had their lances broken and the contest was halted until others were provided. The tourney lance was of considerable length and made of wood with a blunted head, the object being to unhorse your opponent by aiming at his shield, a feat which required no little degree of horsemanship and considerable strength.

The contest had all the colour and pageantry of a medieval tournament. Both contestants rode on to the field clad in full armour and heralds sounded a flourish on their clarions to announce to the assembled host their arrival. The young Squire displayed on his shield a heraldic device depicting a silver otter — his family crest.

French Counts as well as English and Scottish knights and many others of lesser rank took up their positions amid a forest of penants and other war-like accoutrements, each hoping that the outcome would turn out the way he wished.

As both contestants had fallen to the ground following the shock of their encounter, the Squire took a little wine while Talbart secured another horse and as both were now furnished with a new lance, they rode off in opposite directions and turning round adjusted their helmets and awaited a blast from the heralds' trumpets to announce the second onslaught. Digging their spurs into their mounts, on they came at full speed and as the thud of spears on wooden shields was heard, it was seen that Talbart had broken his spear for the second time, but this was not all. The Squire had driven his challenger to the ground and was holding him there with his lance.

Talbart, having surrendered by the rule of tourney, ransomed himself with his horse and armour, while Squire Meldrum was led by the English Captain to his pavilion and Talbart had his wounds attended to afterwards. In the true spirit of chivalry, challenger and defender shook hands and went their way.

After journeying to France where he and his men took part in several exploits against the English, the Squire received honours at the French court and afterwards left Dieppe for Scotland in a well-furnished ship with a company of one hundred and sixty men. On his return voyage he encountered an English man-of-war when a fierce fight followed with guns firing from both ships followed by hand to hand fighting, when halberts, spears and hagbuts wrought havoc on both sides. The Scots at last overpowered their enemy with the loss of fifteen men and took possession of their ship and the crew of two hundred seamen. The captain and his senior officers were lodge in Blackness Castle.

The Squire's fame had gone before him and he was welcomed home on every hand. He did not return to his home at Benarty as one might suppose, but journeyed by way of Strathearn where he lodged in a castle, the home of Mrs Haldane, "the lady of Gleneagles"; the young widow of John Haldane of Gleneagles who had died at Flodden. He continued to stay at the castle and fell in love with its owner and she with him, but their betrothal was frowned on by the church as they were blood-related to a degree prohibited in matrimony, so that a special dispensation was sought from Rome.

We next learn of our Squire going off to the west country to wage war on the MacFarlanes who had forcibly taken possession of his lady love's property and lands of Boturich. After travelling night and day, he and his men arrived at Loch Lomond armed with halberts, hagbuts bows and spears and approached Boturich castle where they were met by the tenants and servants who rallied to support them in laying siege to the place, but before long they were exposed to a hail of arrows from those who were manning the battlements. The Squire in return ordered his men to shoot and soon there were casualities on both sides. An assault was necessary, and presently the Squire ordered his smith to "lay the ledderis to the hous". The Squire led the way in scaling the castle walls and his men followed like "busie beis dois to thair hyfe". The fighting was fierce and many were slain, but soon the Squire overpowered MacFarlane who gave up his arms and the fighting ceased.

William Meldrum on his return to Strathearn was greeted with much merrymaking and minstrelsy and to complete the joyous occasion his lady love presented him with a fair daughter, but events were to take a turn which none could have foreseen.

Time went by and still no papal dispensation was forthcoming. One, Luke Stirling, his rival knew this and being jealous of the Squire, decided to get him out of the way before he could obtain a licence to marry, and thereby have the lady to himself in marriage. He enlisted the help of his nephew, laird of Keir, who, along with sixty armed men stalked the Squire and his lady from Leith to Edinburgh. The conspirators set upon the Squire and eight of his retainers behind Holyrood Chapel and a fierce struggle took place in which the Squire, wielding his two-handed sword killed Keir's principal servant and struck Keir so that he was in danger of his life had not one of his company come to his aid. In all, twenty-six ruffians were either slain or wounded. Up till now the fighting had been man against man, but as the contest was going against the conspirators, Keir decided to employ other tactics. He ordered three of his men to come up behind Meldrum while he engaged him from the front. The Squire fell to the ground under the attack from behind, but even on his knees he continued to wield his sword about him until through exhaustion and loss of blood, he swooned. His attackers closed in and

237

giving him a final blow they left him for dead, but the laird from Lochoreshire was made of sterner stuff than they had imagined, and after being placed in good lodgings by his fair lady, (her father being the Provost of Edinburgh), he received the best of medical skill and in time he recovered.

Still no dispensation was forthcoming and as the years rolled by the lady of Gleneagles grew tired of waiting and at length she married another with whom there was no impediment to marriage.

History is silent as to where William Meldrum lived during this period but in all likelihood he resided at the Binns. He was appointed sheriff-depute of Fife under the hereditary sheriff, Patrick Lord Lindsay and held office from 1524-1530. It is to be remembered that the parish of Cleish was situated in Fife at this period.

In his latter years, the laird of Binns turned surgeon and practised medicine. He is said to have carried out his skills among the poor of his neighbourhood without recompense or reward. His final days were spent at Struthers Castle, the home of the Lord Lindsay of the Byris, where he died in about the year 1550.

John Sage M.A., Schoolmaster

John Sage was the son of Captain Sage in the parish of Creich who, under Lord Duffus defended Dundee when it was stormed by General Monk in 1651. His first post after leaving St. Andrews University was that of Schoolmaster at Ballingry. This was in the year 1670, and as the "commodious" school with its thick stone walls twenty-three feet long by thirteen feet broad and red pan-tile roof, lying hard-by the church, had not yet been built, it is not clear where the children received their rudimentary schooling, probably in the minister's barn.

From Ballingry, Mr Sage accepted a similiar post in Tippermuir, near Perth and afterwards became the tutor to the sons of Mr Drummond of Cultmalundie. On his pupils' education being completed, Mr Sage was without work and without future prospects. Through the good offices of Dr Rose, Archbishop of Glasgow he entered the Ministry and was appointed to one of the Glasgow churches where he remained as minister and clerk to the diocese till the Revolution in 1688. Mr Sage was by conviction an Episcopalian and a Royalist and was compelled to leave his charge in Glasgow. In Edinburgh, where he now resided he managed to scrape a living by writing articles all dealing with the controversies of the period.

At length he was compelled to leave Edinburgh and in his extremity he returned to nearby Kinross where he received the protection and friendship of Sir William Bruce, the architect and sheriff of the shire. He was given the post of tutor to his children and remained there until 1696.

When Sir William Bruce was imprisoned in Edinburgh Castle for his opposition to the new government, Mr Sage contrived to visit him but was suspected of disloyalty and had to flee for his life to the wilds of the northern hills. On assuming the name of Jackson he remained there for some time, wandering from place to place, destitute and without money, until the Countess of Callander, hearing of his condition, gave him shelter and appointed him domestic chaplain to her family and tutor to her sons. On the completion of the children's education, he accepted an invitation from Sir John Stewart of Grantully to become his chaplain and companion. He remained with Sir John until the continuance of the Episcopal order depended on new consecrations. He was prevailed upon to accept the office of Bishop and was consecrated to that office with its attendant personal danger, by the three deprived Archbishops of Glasgow, Edinburgh and Dunblane in 1705.

77 *Bishop John Sage*

The privations of his youth had weakened his constitution and not many years afterwards he journeyed south in the hope of improving his health. In Bath and London he was befriended by many distinguished people. He returned to Edinburgh in 1710 and although worn out by failing health, he set about preparing what was to be his last work, *An Introduction to Drummond's History of the Five James's*. He died in 1711 the year of its publication. Bishop Sage was the author of many works and he left behind several manuscripts on various subjects. These were published in London in 1714.

The Reverend Thomas Hardie D.D.

The Rev. Thomas Hardie was the son of the Rev. Henry Hardie, minister of Culross Abbey and was presented to the parish by Sir Michael Malcolm in 1773. He was not long in Ballingry when he acquired the small estate of Navitie and his name appears in many Deeds in connection with that estate, and as a landed proprietor he also had a claim on part of the Benarty Commonty.

After a ministry of ten years he was translated to the high church in Edinburgh, one of the four churches into which St. Giles had been divided. As the senior minister of the city he was present at the execution of the notorious deacon William Brodie in 1788 and had to endure the hated spectacle longer than was usually necessary, as the "bolt" on the apparatus failed to work on the first and second occasion. In contrast to the tense atmosphere created by such an unusual occurrence, Brodie, between each attempt, came down from the scaffold and conversed coolly with his friends. Mr Hardie was an attractive and eloquent preacher and was the author of several works chiefly of a religious nature.

78 *Rev. Thomas Hardie*

He was appointed Regius Professor of Divinity and Ecclesiastical History in the University of Edinburgh in 1788, and in that year was made a Doctor of Divinity. He rose to the high office of Moderator of the Church of Scotland in 1793 and was made one of his Majesty's Chaplains in Ordinary and a Dean of the Chapel Royal in the same year. Following his death in 1798 the estate of Navitie passed into the possession of Lieutenant Colonel Lindsay of the East India Company's service. It was he who built the present Navitie House.

Mr Hardie's sister married the Rev. Robert Liston, minister of Aberdour from whom was descended Robert Liston, the celebrated surgeon and fellow worker with Professor Syme in Edinburgh.

The Rev. William Blair M.A.

The Rev. William Blair was born at Clunie, in the parish of Kinglassie in 1830 and received his early education at the parish school in Auchterderran. From there he attended Mr Wilson's school in Pathhead and at the age of sixteen years he entered the University of St. Andrews where he took his M.A. degree. For some years afterwards he acted as a private tutor. In 1853 Mr Blair published *The Chronicles of Aberbrothock*, and four years later there appeared his *Rambling Recollections*, wherein he describes in detail many places in Scotland of historical interest, but what he relates about his native countryside and of Auchterderran and Crosshill, all within ancient Lochoreshire, should be of special interest to the reader.

David Page, F.R.S.E, F.G.S, L.L.D.

David Page, the son of a local stonemason and builder, was born at Lochgelly in 1814 and received his early education at Auchterderran Parish School. At the age of fourteen he entered the University of St. Andrews and afterwards attended Edinburgh University with a view to entering the ministry, but his inclinations leaned towards writing and for a short time he acted as editor of a Fife newspaper. While still in his twenties he became scientific editor to Messrs. W. and R. Chambers the well-known Edinburgh publishers. He studied the natural sciences along with geology and physical geography and in 1853 he was elected a fellow of the Geographical Society of Edinburgh, and in this same year he became a proprietor of the *Fifeshire Journal*, a business concern which he managed for four years. His many scientific pursuits and popular courses of lectures on geology and kindred subjects called for recognition, and in 1863 and 1865 he was elected president of the Geographical Society and two years afterwards the University of St. Andrews conferred on him the honorary degree of Doctor of Laws.

By the year 1866 Doctor Page had published upwards of ten text books of geology and in 1871 as an accomplished scholar in his sphere, he was appointed Professor of Geology in Durham University College of Physical Science at Newcastle-upon-Tyne. After holding this office for eight years he died at Newcastle on 9th March, 1879.

Professor James Syme

Professor James Syme was the second eldest son of John Syme of Cartmore, Lochore and Blair, Writer to the Signet. He was born in Benarty House, the old house of the Colvilles on 7th November, 1799 and received his early education at home. He became a pupil of the high school, Edinburgh and as a boy he showed an aptitude for anatomical pursuits. Among his early experiments in chemistry was the perfecting of a method of waterproofing cloth which was afterwards patented by Charles Mackintosh in 1823 and gave rise to the "Mackintosh Coat".

79 *Professor James Syme*
From a photograph in the collection of the Wellcome Historical Medical Museum

In 1815 James Syme entered Edinburgh University and became a pupil of Dr John Barclay the well-known anatomist. Three years afterwards he came under the notice of Robert Liston the eminent Edinburgh surgeon and in 1823 he succeeded Liston as lecturer on anatomy. After travelling abroad he started a private surgical hospital in Minto House where he commenced his lectures on clinical instruction by which he was in future to be recognised as the foremost authority. Ten years later, he was appointed Professor of clinical surgery in Edinburgh University and in 1838 was appointed surgeon to the Queen in Scotland. After a brief period as Professor in clinical surgery in the University College, London he returned to his old post in Edinburgh. Among the young surgeons who were attracted to Syme by reason of his extraordinary skills was

Joseph Lister who had come to Edinburgh from London in 1853. His admiration of Syme was unlimited and his close association with his master was to continue for sixteen years until Syme's death. Professor Syme's fame as a teacher as well as a surgeon continued to rise until he was recognised as the foremost living authority on surgery. In 1869 he resigned his post of surgeon to the Infirmary after an illness and was succeeded by his son-in-law Joseph Lister.

Professor Syme during his career contributed many papers to the science and art of surgery. These, along with his remarkable career received recognition from many Universities who bestowed on him honorary degrees. He died in 1870. Professor Syme was twice married. By his first marriage he had two daughters and by his second marriage a son.

80 *Sir Joseph Lister, BART, AET. C. 58*

Joseph Lister married Agnes Syme, Professor Syme's elder daughter, in 1856. The couple spent their honeymoon abroad when many famous schools were visited. On their return they spent a short period with Mrs Lister's uncle David Syme the proprietor of Cartmore who resided at Kinross. Lister's fame as a surgeon was international. He received the highest honours at home and in many countries. His name appeared in the honours list of 1883 when he was made a baronet and in 1897 he was raised to the Peerage.

81 *Agnes Lister about the time of her marriage*
From a photograph in the collection of the Wellcome Historical Medical Museum

Lady Lister died in 1893 but Miss Lucy Syme the younger daughter of Professor Syme was alive in 1927, the centenary year of Lord Lister's birth when she was over ninety years of age. Although unable to attend, Miss Syme was very interested in all that she had read concerning the forthcoming centenary celebrations.

Rev. Charles Rogers, L.L.D., F.S.A. Scot.

The Rev. Charles Rogers was the son of the Rev. James Roger* minister of Dunino. From the parish school where he received his early education, he passed to St.

* The Rev. Charles Rogers added an "S" to the family name.

Andrews University, where he soon showed signs of his leaning towards a literary career. He was still in his teens when he picked up and bought at a sale a manuscript volume of the poems by Sir Robert Aytoun a cadet of the Aytouns of Inchdairnie. This he published along with a life of the author, a venture which had the effect of bringing him to the notice of many persons of distinction. He followed this in 1849 with his *History of St. Andrews*. On leaving the University, he was licensed by the Presbytery of St. Andrews as a probationer of the Church of Scotland and in the capacity of assistant minister, he came to Ballingry in 1850. The Rev. James Greig being in his eighty-fourth year, there is little doubt that what Mr Rogers relates in his *Autobiography* and other works concerning the Malcolm family, Sir Walter Scott and Mr Jobson of Lochore, came from the lips of Mr Greig. It was Mr Rogers' ambition to succeed Mr Greig as parish minister. It was therefore a bitter disappointment to him, following the death of Mr Greig, to find that Lady Scott, as chief heritor had made other arrangements.

While residing in the parish, he lodged at Chapel farm. During his short stay he succeeded in re-opening the school at Ballingry. The schoolmaster of the period for some reason failed to attract children, and although he opened the school daily, no pupils turned up. It was thus that the case of the Ballingry school was raised in the House of Commons and was given as a reason that the education of children should no longer be left in the hands of the church. Mr Rogers gained the schoolmaster's confidence, assuring him that any change in the running of the school would not affect his salary in any way. Accepting this assurance Mr Laurence signed a document consenting to the appointment of an assistant, and on Mr Rogers being successful in obtaining a small salary from the heritors for the new assistant, the school was re-opened under more efficient management.

For the greater part of the preceding forty years during which period Mr Laurence had been at loggerheads with the Presbytery and the heritors, the school had been virtually closed. The education of the children was undertaken by a few parishioners who built and maintained a school at Flockhouse. In its latter days, this school building was used as a meeting place by the United Free Church. Before leaving the parish, Mr Rogers succeeded in establishing a local library. This was replaced by a Coats library in the village in 1908.

On leaving Ballingry, Mr Rogers spent some years at Bridge of Allan. In 1855 Doctor Rogers as he was now, was appointed Chaplain to the garrison in Stirling Castle. In his book *A Week in Bridge of Allan* he suggested that a monument to Sir William Wallace should be built on the Abbey Craig near Stirling. The propriety of erecting a monument was readily approved by many notable persons, and Doctor Rogers became the leading promoter of the project by addressing meetings throughout Scotland and the south, and by corresponding with many influential Scots abroad. His labours brought in a considerable amount of money to the project. The monument was completed in 1869 and in recognition of the vast amount of work which Doctor Rogers had put into the cause, a marble bust of him was afterwards placed in the entrance hall to the tower.

Doctor Rogers' most ambitious work was the *Modern Scottish Minstrel*. To gather material for his work he visited the places associated with writers whom he wished to

82

include in his book. In Alloway he visited Mrs Begg, Burns' sister and in Dumfries, he met Burns' eldest son Robert and the poet's two younger sons Colonels William and James Burns, from whom he received many interesting details of their father. He also met Baroness Nairne, the author of *Land o' the Leal*. In Galashiels Doctor Rogers met many people who had known Sir Walter Scott intimately. With Sir Adam Ferguson, Jane Jobson's uncle, he became slightly acquainted. The old knight—he was bordering ninety—spoke of the olden times and when Doctor Rogers suggested reminiscences of his meetings with Scott and the Ettrick Shepherd he burst into tears. On completing his tour of Ettrick Forest and Teviotdale, having meanwhile gathered much original material respecting James Hogg, John Leyden, Henry Scott Riddell, James Telfer and many other minor poets, he returned to explore central Scotland for Scottish bardic literature. The work was completed in six volumes, the first appeared in 1855.

Among his public undertakings were the founding of the *Scottish Literary Institute*, the *Caledonian Institute* and the *Grampian Book Club*. To the latter he contributed many original works. He was also Historiographer to the *Royal Historical Society*. His writings which were many, were the fruits of an intimate and scholarly study of Scotland's past, while in his *Scottish Life*, he gives an interesting account of the literati of his day, many of whom he had known and corresponded with. He latterly resided in London in a house gifted by many of his former associates. There he continued his literary career with unabaited zeal. His *Autobiography* appeared in 1876 in which he gives an account of many of his literary undertakings and wherein he speaks of his sojurn in Ballingry.

W. J. N. Liddell, M.A., B.A. of Navitie: Advocate

Mr Liddell succeeded to the estates of Navitie and Findaty on the death of his father in 1879 and in this year he gave up his practice on being called to the bar. He was one of the honorary sheriff-substitutes of the County of Kinross and on many occasions he acted as interim sheriff at Dunfermline, Kinross and Alloa. He also acted in that capacity at Portree in Skye during the trouble there arising out of the crofters' agitation.

Mr Liddell, although a kindly entertaining host at home, is said to have been of a somewhat litigious disposition and frequently had on his hands "a guid gangin law plea". He was well informed in the study of place names, and in 1896 he published a book entitled the *Place Names of Fife and Kinross*. He was of the opinion that the place names of Fife were of Goidelic origin and could be looked upon for the purpose of interpretation as belonging to ancient Ireland. The book has been superseded by more recent publications on the same subject. The "shirra", as he was known locally, died in 1907 and was succeeded in his estates by his son.

The Rev. David Jamie M.A., B.D.

The Rev. David Jamie received his early education in the burgh school of Cannongate, Edinburgh and commenced his working life as an apprentice house painter. From there he entered the employment of Messrs. Cowan and Co. stationers in that city, during which time he attended the Cowgate Port evening school and passed from there to Doctor Bell's school in Niddry Street where he came under the notice of John Hope, Writer to the Signet, the Temperance reformer who, from now on took a special interest in the boy who was showing so much promise. During this period Mr

Hope wrote of young David Jamie as "decidedly the top boy for his age of all the hundreds of boys I have to do with at present". Shortly afterwards, David Jamie entered the British League and became an assistant superintendent at the childrens' abstinence meetings.

83 *Rev. David Jamie*

In 1867 he gave up his employment in order to further his education and enrolled as a pupil in the Royal High School where in 1872 he carried off the MacGregor Gold Medal awarded to the dux of the school. Three years later he took his M.A. degree at Edinburgh University and in that same year he accompanied Mr Hope in a tour of Germany. In the years 1876 and 1877 Mr Jamie, through the generosity of his benefactor, attended the University of Marburg, during which time Mr Hope was kept informed of his progress by regular letters sent to Edinburgh. He was also encouraged to learn French, Mr Hope providing for him a French Tutor.

In 1879 when Mr Jamie took his B.D. degree Mr Hope proposed that he should study the French, German and Italian languages by travelling in these countries. He therefore offered to pay Mr Jamie's expenses for the duration of a year and a half so that he could undertake the course which he had planned for him. For reasons which are not disclosed, this generous offer was not accepted. Meanwhile Mr Jamie with the approval of Mr Hope accepted an offer of assistant minister in St. Paul's Church in Glasgow. A year or so afterwards he was offered a similar post under Doctor MacDonald of the High Church, Inverness and in 1882 he was ordained Minister of Ballingry, the induction dinner was held in Kirkness House, the last occasion in which an assembly of people took place within its historic walls.

In 1890 a Deed was drawn up creating the Hope Trust consisting of five Trustees of which Mr Jamie was one. Four years after Mr Hope's death in 1893, Mr Jamie wrote the life story of his benefactor and a full account of his many undertakings, under the title *John Hope, Philanthropist and Reformer.*

When Mr Jamie died in 1910, he had served the parish for twenty-eight years during which time he had seen Ballingry change from a quiet rural parish to an ever-expanding mining community with the creation of the villages of Glencraig and Lochore. In addition to his pastoral work, Mr Jamie helped the young people of the neighbourhood by holding classes in the manse on specialised subjects. In one of these he taught shorthand and at the end of each session he issued certificates to those who had completed the course.

Mr Jamie had a leaning towards the study of antiquities. He was especially proficient in deciphering old writings. He was also an active member of the short-lived Ballingry Antiquarian Club, whose members during the years 1890 and 1891 carried out exploratory diggings on the Clune Hill and successfully excavated the Bronze Age burial cairn at Harelaw, but above all he will be remembered as the author of *Old Church Life in Ballingry*, a book for which almost a century has been the sole repository of the annals of the parish.

The Rev. Archibald Houston M.A., B.D., D.D

The Rev. Archibald Houston hailed from Ayrshire. He received his early education at Symington village school and afterwards at Troon Academy. From there he entered Glasgow University where he obtained his M.A. degree. After filling the posts of assistant minister, first at Hyndland, Glasgow and later at Hillhead in the same city he came to Auchterderran in 1885 to be assistant to the Rev. Mr Grant, minister of the parish. Following the death of Mr Grant in 1889, Mr Houston was appointed minister. This was during the period when there was a great increase in the population of the parish.

In addition to his ministerial duties, Mr Houston devoted a large amount of his time in parochial and county educational affairs. Later in life he received the degree of Doctor of Divinity from the University of St. Andrews. He was the author of *Auchterderran Fife, a Parish History* which appeared in 1924. In this work Mr Houston did for Easter Lochoreshire what Mr Jamie had previously done for Wester Lochoreshire.

The Brothers Gray

Thomas and Andrew Gray were born at Lochgelly in the mid-nineteenth century. On leaving the village school, they were both apprenticed in the building trade, but continued their studies with a view to obtaining a higher education. Both attended Glasgow University and passed out with honours.

Thomas, who was the younger, accepted an appointment with the government of Japan as teacher of electrical engineering in the Imperial College in the capital. He became an authority on the study of earthquakes and along with two associates, David Milne and J. A. Ewing (both teachers in Tokio) he produced a seismograph for reading the movement of the ground during an earthquake. This instrument was latterly improved upon by others. The co-ordinated study of the three teachers produced various types of seismographs and under their direction seismology became an exact science and in due course the Seismological Society of Japan was founded. This society continued its work until Milne its chief organiser returned to England in 1895. Thomas Gray, PhD. on his return to Scotland was appointed supervisor of the work of laying the Trans-Atlantic cable system. He died in America in 1908 while occupying the post of Professor in the Rose Polytechnic Faculty.

Andrew Gray, on leaving the University, experimented in physics and became assistant and private secretary to Lord Kelvin. He wrote many books of a scientific nature and was appointed Professor of Physics at the University College, Bangor in North Wales. In 1896 he received the honorary degree of Doctor of Laws from the University of Glasgow. He was also made a Fellow of the Royal Society and was one of the experts attached to the Ministry of Munitions during the first world war.

Among the lesser known are James Brown L.L.D., born at Colton of Pitcairn in the parish of Auchterderran, who rose to the position of Professor of Natural Philosophy in Glasgow University, and the Rev. David Greig, fellow student of Michael Bruce the poet and James Campbell of Harran Hill, who was inducted to the Secession Church at Lochgelly in 1773 and laboured there for fifty years. One of his young adherents was John Dick who became well known as a theological writer and afterwards Professor of Theology to the Secession Church and who received the honorary degree of Doctor of Divinity from Glasgow University.

Another person of a bygone age worthy of notice is Mr Skirving of Strathrudie Farm in the parish of Auchterderran. He and three others who were known as "the friends of the people" were towards the end of the eighteenth century banished from the country because of their outspoken liberal politics.

Mr John Jeffrey, overseer of Lochore estate during the time of Lady Scott was the joint editor with Mr Charles Howie of a book entitled *Trees and Shrubs of Fife and Kinross*. Mr Jeffrey obviously knew a lot about Lochore estate and gives detailed information about Silver Fir, Willow, Common Ash and Common Beech trees all planted on the estate in the year 1812.

RURAL DAYS AND RURAL WAYS

The position of the average possessor of land in the barony of Inchgall was as elsewhere, one of dependence on the lord of the manor under whom he held his land and to whom he not only owed a money rent but an actual service such as a certain number of days spent in working for the laird during harvest, carting fuel in the form of peat, heath and brushwood, and sheep-shearing — depending on his degree of bondage. He was also bound by his feudal ties to have his corn ground at the laird's mill for which he paid heavily, a condition that still prevailed at Inchgall in 1656 and be he husbandman, cotter of feudal tenant, he was bound by ancient custom to assist in bringing home new mill-stones for the Mill of Lochore and latterly for Inchgall Mill, an undertaking which required considerable strength and skill. Apart from a coal mine at Blaircushnie which belonged to the laird and a few rural handicrafts estalished in the village of Crosshill, the chief occupation of the people in the barony in the seventeenth century was sheep and cattle rearing and crofting. The colliers were in a state of serfdom, the crofters were still labouring under poor if not servile conditions. The records from this period onward tell an interesting story of rural life.

The roads at this period were scarcely more than dirt tracks. They had no metalled surface and were devoid of any camber to shed off water, nor had they drainage ditches. They twisted this way and that in order to avoid peat bogs and pot holes, their course being marked only by an occasional ragged hedge or turf dyke. Carts were few and of small capacity being capable at most of carrying a five cwt load. Transport of goods in general was still by means of pack horses using pannier baskets.

The rivers Fitty and Ore were crossed by shallow fords or by timber bridges consisting of tree trunks trimmed and laid side by side and stretching from bank to bank, the whole being levelled up with small stones and gravel. The Lochty burn was still crossed by a ford. Further north, the river Leven, as it issued from the loch was crossed by a timber bridge, this too was probably a "brig-o'-trees". This bridge was repaired in 1621 and again in 1642 when the parishioners of Ballingry contributed towards the cost of the work. A toll amounting to four pennies for every horse and horse load and two pennies for every person on foot was levied from everyone passing that way. By 1682 the bridge was again badly in need of repair when servants and horses drawn from the neighbouring parishes were commandeered in order that the repair work be done as speedily as possible.

This road was the highway between Perth and Edinburgh by way of the Great Common through Crosshill to Pettycur near Kinghorn where the ferryboat crossed over to Leith. During the period of the timber bridges we read of the "maine deepe ditches and sinkin myres" on the road leading from Scotlandwell to Ballingry and of the many people who lost their lives while travelling that way. Almost everyone travelled on foot, the more prosperous rode on horseback although by this time horses could be hired at two pennies the mile on the outward journey and half this amount for the return journey.

These old right-of-ways, used mostly by cattle-drovers and gypsies, usually

252

covered a width of ground on either side of the track where animals could feed on the grass as they travelled. With so many animals travelling on these tracks, the soft earth became churned up, especially in wet weather, so that they became "hollow-ways". This is especially noticeable on a portion of the "Old Loan" where the track turns southward in the direction of Harelaw cairn. Before the passing of the Turnpike Act in 1751, parish roads were badly made and poorly maintained. In general, there was a lack of practical knowledge of roadmaking. By the mid-seventeenth century, the supervision of roads came under the charge of Justices of the Peace, and an Act of 1669 gave them power to demand from anyone residing within the parish six days labour on the roads each year. By statute the width a road was to be not less than twenty feet, but it was often much less. No doubt in most cases it would comply with a later injunction that it should be of "a competent breadth of twell foots", wide enough to allow two carts to pass.

Some idea of the prevailing conditions of the roads can be had from the fact that when a house was being built in the neighbourhood, the deals for flooring had to be brought from Kirkcaldy harbour. The only possible way of transporting the timber was by horse transport, a few boards being slung on either side of the animal. It must have been a painfully slow means of transport. We have already remarked on the condition of the road north of Ballingry. Fortunately the roads going south appear to have been better maintained.

In a report submitted to the Privy Council in 1629 on "the sighting of the hieway betwix Dunfermline and Falkland....for his Majesty's sure and sauffe journeying that way", it is said that the road as far as Maistertons brae is in good condition, but from there eastward to the old Bridge of Or there were parts which required to be "helped" (repaired) in order to make it passable for horses and carts. The report continues, "the road through Kinglassie is also in poor condition".

This refers to the visit of Charles I. It appears that the route through the lands of Easter Cartmore was one of the ways used by Royalty when travelling between Dunfermline and Falkland. There was no road through Lochgelly at this period. After travelling eastward by way of the Drum road from Beath, the traveller entered the lands of Easter Cartmore some distance to the west of the village of Lochgelly. At a point approximately halfway between the village and the Clockrat Bridge, the traveller turned eastward by taking the "Kirk and Kiln" road which crossed the river Ore at the "Bridge of Orr" and thence to Auchterderran, Kinglassie and beyond. The Bridge of Orr (probably a brig-o'-trees) was an acknowledged vital link in the early road system and was replaced by the Bowbridge (Brigghills) which was extensively repaired with timbers in 1698.

With the aid of an old estate map we are made aware of the various roads that existed between Ballingry and the village of Lochgelly in the mid-eighteenth century. Immediately south of the river Fitty in what is now South Glencraig there was at this period a large track of rough ground called the Common Moor on which the proprietors of Easter Cartmore, Lochgelly and Colquhally pastured their cattle. In it a road from "Lassodie to Auchterderran", made straight for the Clockrat Bridge (built in 1671). Continuing southward, about halfway across the Moor, a road branched off to the southwest in the direction of Lumphinnans marked "Road leading to Cupar by Leslie". The road to Lochgelly had by now left the Moor and was well within the lands of Easter Cartmore. Here it was traversed by a road leading from the direction of Cartmore Farm and proceeding eastward in the direction of Brigghills, marked "Kirk and Kiln Road". Proceeding southward at a point near the present Lochgelly railway station, it was joined by a road from the west marked "Road leading from Kinross by Kelty to Burntisland, Kinghorn and Kirkcaldy". A little beyond this point the road divides, one going in a south-westerly direction considerably to the west of "Lane Shire Head" probably to link up with the "Drum" road, the old back road to what is now Cowdenbeath, the other kept to a south-easterly direction and passed Lochgelly to the east of the village. It is marked "Road leading from Kirkcaldy, Kinghorn and Burntisland to Kelty and Kinross". In addition to the roads mentioned here, there were quite a few situated to the west of Lochgelly known as the coal roads.

The lands of Lochgelly are first mentioned in 1354 when they were held by Agnes de Crambeth. No doubt there would exist from an early period a cluster of turf-thatched hovels situated near the loch which went by that name, possibly at Lochhead which appears in 1432 as part of the lands of Lochgelly. The village was until the early nineteenth century approached only from the west, the one and only street terminated at "The Market Place" situated at the east end of the village. It was not until 1774 that the village had outgrown itself. In this year a plan was prepared showing a development and headed *The New Town of Lochgelly*. The plan shows how the rising ground to the south had been surveyed and streets laid out in grid fashion, but as yet the streets were un-named. Upwards of sixty feus had been built upon but a far greater number were standing vacant.

The town at this period did not extend westward beyond where today the Miners' Welfare Institute is situated, and the Main Street (although un-named) from this point eastward to the Market Place could only boast of one feu occupied on its north side and five feus built upon its south side. Knock Hill consisted of three buildings which formed a square with one side open to the south. The feu which was a fairly large one belonged to John Knox of Easter Cartmore in 1762 and contained ground to the west of the Square called Brewstead and a well called Brewstead Well. Bank Street, Station Road and Auchterderran Road were non-existent at this period. Heather and broom covered the steep descent to the north. During the first half of the nineteenth century when the village was extended northward, all to the west of Bank Street and Station Road was built on ground belonging to Easter Cartmore Estate.

The general appearance of the countryside during the seventeenth century was rather dull and bleak with large tracks of ground ill-drained, with heather, moss and whin prevailing. The whitewashed stone-built farmsteadings with their red pantile roofs had still to come. To emphasise the bare aspect of the neighbourhood we would mention that the neighbouring estate of Blaircrambeth, when bought by John Adam some seventy years later, could boast of only one solitary tree. There was but one cultivated enclosure on the estate, the remainder in general was either heath or covered with rank grass.

The houses of the ordinary folk of the period were built entirely of local materials.

Each cotter, probably with the help of his neighbour, built his own house. Land-gathered stones provided material for the walls, which in most cases did not exceed five feet in height, although very thick. The windows were correspondingly small. The floors consisted of hard-beaten earth or clay occasionally rendered more permanent with the addition of forge ashes. The houses had no ceilings and the roofs were thatched either with turf or reeds. The fire usually occupied a position in the centre of the floor and the smoke from the peat or wood fire hung about the rafters until it escaped through an opening in the thatched roof.

Many of the houses were very poorly built and have been described as miserable hovels. During a rainstorm in October 1655 quite a few of the roofs of these houses fell down upon the occupants.

The crofter's house of the period was slightly better and was built more or less to a common pattern, it consisting of an oblong building containing the dwelling house and a byre-cum-stable all under one roof. Separating the two compartments was a passage called the "through-gang" which was secured at the front with a door called the fore-door. If this passage had an additional door to the rear of the house, it was called the "yard door". Midway on either side of the "through gang" was a door, one giving access to the byre, the other to the dwelling house. In most cases animals and people entered the building through the fore-door, the animals turning into the byre by the "heck door" and the people into the house by the "trans-door". It was usual to have the byre at a slightly lower level than the other part of the building, particularly if the building was on a sloping site so that the effluent from the animals did not foul the living quarters.

As in the smaller houses, the walls were built of stone bedded in clay mortar. The roof couples were roughly-trimmed tree branches, with cross beams called "ribs" or "pans". The whole was covered with brushwood on which were placed divots or sods held in place with oat straw. Doors were seldom more than five feet in height and the windows were very small, and usually partly glazed, the lower portions having boards which could be opened when required. Internal partition walls consisted of stakes driven into the earthen floor, interlaced with a sort of wicker work and plastered over with clay mortar mixed with oat straw. The fire usually occupied the centre of the floor of the apartment or was placed in the gable wall. The fuel consisted of peats, dried turf, roots of trees and brushwood. All the daily activities of the household took place within this apartment. The sleeping quarters took the form of "box" beds with doors which are closed during the day. The contents of this apartment called the "in-seat", usually consisted of a rough heavy table of common wood, several stools, a meal chest, a sowen-tub, a spinning wheel and a household press, also the usual cooking and dairy utensils. Articles not in daily use were usually stored in the roof-space, called the "cranny". On larger crofts, there was occasionally an additional apartment leading off the in-seat, called the "spense". In this apartment the more valuable of the household articles were kept and it was here that the crofter and his wife received their guests. It could be considered the early equivalent of the parlour.

We spoke earlier of the absence of a chimney in the cotter's house. As time went on provision was made to enable the smoke from the fire to escape more easily from the dwelling. This gave rise to some novel ideas. One such idea was to be seen in the home of

James Brown, the miller of Inchgall Mill, who lived at Balbegie (the present-day cotter's house belonging to Inchgall farm). It could perhaps be described as an architectural curiosity—known locally as a "clay lum". The contrivance which occupied the centre of the apartment directly above the fire, was suspended from the roof of the house and was made of wicker work and consisted of a smoke vent, the lower part of which was considerably enlarged to form a bell-mouthed canopy to receive the smoke. The vent narrowed as it rose towards the roof and finally emerged through the thatch. The whole thing was plastered with wet clay, both inside and out, which by reason of the heat from the fire became "baked" and therefore very hard and presumably fireproof. It was said to be worth a whole day's journey to see.

The person next in importance to the laird in those days was the minister of the parish. The person who filled this office during the mid-nineteenth century was the Rev. Robert Bruce, second eldest son of Sir William Bruce of Earlshall in Fife. He had a yearly stipend of five hundred merks and one chalder of victuals and attended to the spiritual welfare of the two hundred and sixty souls that made up the total population of the parish.

The dress of the parish minister consisted of a short jacket buttoned up rather close at the neck with a belt at the waist, he wore knee breeches, long stockings and buckled shoes. His headdress was a close-fitting skull cap. The colour of his dress was by Act of Parliament ordained to be a "priest-grey".

With few exceptions, the manses in the neighbourhood were all built in the same style. They were two storeys high, so that when compared with the low-built houses of the ordinary folks, the manse of the period must have had an imposing appearance. On the ground floor one entered into a hall at the head of which stood the family table surrounded with stools and an occasional chair. A cupboard or two stood against the walls, for this was the dining room and the parlour of the house. In the wall behind the table was a door which gave access to the "workhouse" where food was prepared. On either side of the hall there was a door. One led to a room which served as a study. Against each side wall was placed an open ladder-like stair by which two upstairs chambers were reached directly from the hall. The open-plan staircase so much in fashion today, is really not a new idea after all. The hall and the workhouse were the only apartments which had a fireplace. In the case of Ballingry, water was had from a draw-well—situated a little to the east of the house—the remains of which were uncovered in 1965 while workmen were digging the foundations for the extension to the church.

The outhouses connected with the manse were a barn, stable, byre and henhouse and if Ballingry was no different from the neighbouring manses, there would also be a brewhouse. The roofs of all these buildings including the manse were of course covered with "thak and devots".

The chief occupation of the people in the barony of Inchgall in 1662 was agriculture and stock-rearing. Evidence of cattle and sheep rearing is to be found in such names as "Bowhouse" and "Flockhouse". Both are mentioned in 1605. The Bowhouse was situated on Harran Hill a little west of Lochore House called then Inchgall House, while the Flockhouse stood on the north side of the road leading to Capeldrae Farm on the site of the present Police Station. This house is not to be confused with Flockhouse School

84 *A farmsteading in West Fife about the year 1690*

(now demolished) which stood a little further north and was of fairly recent origin. The fields were unfenced and the stones which went to build the dry-stone dykes in the following century for the most part lay scattered over the ground except where here and there small plots of ground had been cleared for cultivation. By this time the run-rig system of cultivation using the heavy wooden plough had given way to the one-horse plough. There were in the barony in the year 1633 "twelve one-horse plows". Interesting evidence of early cultivation and the remains of a turf-wall rectangular enclosure belonging to this period are to be found a little to the north of Hunt Ha' Wood in what may have been part of the Common of Boglochty.

The old Scottish plough was a very heavy and cumbersome implement. Built on generous lines it was almost entirely the work of the crofter, the only part made of iron was the coulter. In some cases this too was made of wood, and shod with iron. Chains were non-existent in ploughing. Crudely-made ropes and strips of leather had to suffice. The plough was usually the common property of four or more crofters who, for economy, combined for the purpose of ploughing.

Unlike its modern counterpart, the wooden plough did not turn a "share", but produced a triangular rut in the soil rather than a furrow. This on occasion was so feeble that the ground had to be gone over a second time. The weight of the plough was such that it required a team of eight oxen to drag it, sometimes more. A "twal ousen plew" was not uncommon. Each crofter provided two oxen and along with his neighbours made up a minimum number of three men to drive the plough. One man in front led the team by means of a rope tied round the horns of the foremost animals. In other accounts he is described as walking backwards in front of the oxen while looking for stones which

257

would impede the progress of the plough. A second man, called a gaudman, carried a long pole with which he urged any animal that tended to linger. By gauding and frequent verbal ejaculations he kept the team of oxen on the move. A third man held the plough and manoeuvred it over the rough ground, while a fourth man followed behind breaking up the clods with a wooden mallet and generally preparing the ground for the wooden harrow that was to follow.

Striking evidence of the use of the early plough is to be seen on Harran Hill down from the ruins of the Bowhouse. Taking advantage of the dry ground up from the loch, the plough team worked the ground in a slanting direction down the face of the hill. This is seen today in the curious formation of ridges which occupy the greater portion of the hill and which terminate in oblique curves formed by the team of oxen swinging round to a halt at the bottom of the hill. It has been suggested, not surpringly, that the ridges are the result of old coal workings. There can, however, be no doubt as to their antiquity. A visitor to the parish in 1726 was careful to note the peculiar formation of the ridges but was unaware of their origin.

These remains of early cultivation are to be found elsewhere and are generally believed to cover a period extending from the Middle Ages to the 1600s. They have been described as "terraces", "rigs" and "ridges" according to the physical characteristics of each individual site. In view of their near proximity to the Castle of Lochore, it is difficult not to connect them in some way with the agricultural pursuits of the occupants of the castle. This possibility is strengthened by the remains of a broad path or unmetalled road which descends from the hill in the direction of the castle and which clearly is associated with the ridges. Similar evidence of bygone cultivation is to be seen at Markinch and Inverkeithing. At both these places, especially at Inverkeithing, the ridges lack the bold and impressive formation of those at Harran Hill.

85 *Cultivation ridges on Harran Hill as seen from the site of the Castle of Lochore*

We have already seen that most of the land not under cultivation was covered with heather and whin. When land had to be cleared the horse-drawn slype was almost the only vehicle used. As there were no divisions between grazing land and land under crop, flocks had to be herded to prevent animals from straying on to cultivated land and other people's property. James Beatson, who is mentioned in 1605 as living in the Flockhouse is described as a herd.

The records of the period afford a glimpse into the various pursuits and activities which went into the making of the rural life of the neighbourhood. We have seen that the Rev. Alexander Wardlaw kept a number of cattle and it appears his successors kept a number of animals as part of their livelihood till as late as 1780. What is known of the rights that the various proprietors had in the common ground shows that perhaps sheep-rearing was the predominant activity. There were quite a number of Commonties in the barony of Inchgall, each providing "foggage, fail and divots" but used mainly for the grazing of animals.

The furthest north, and perhaps the largest in extent, was the Commonty of the hill of Benarty. It is known to have exceeded one hundred and eighty-five acres and is alluded to in 1566. In 1623 Henry Mitchell and Michael Chalmers had a right to pasture two hundred sheep on the Common. Likewise the laird of Inchgall grazed sixteen head of cattle and one hundred sheep there. In 1620 Alexander Colville, laird of Blaircushnie had the right to graze one hundred and sixty sheep. The Commonty was divided in 1780 when a plan was made but since lost. Mr Hardy, minister of Ballingry as laird of Navitie, received sixty-six acres in lieu of his right of servitude; others who received portions were John McKenzie of Dolphington and Sir Michael Malcolm.

A little further west was the small Commonty of Nivingston in which the church of Ballingry had the right of one half of the servitude. This gave the Session the right to graze "two cows and their followers, one broad sow and a boar and their followers, one broad goose and a ganner and their followers". The Commonty was divided about the year 1795.

Not far from Nivingston was the Commonty of Kinneard in which the church of Ballingry also had an interest on behalf of the poor of the parish. In 1735 it is stated that the right of pasture on the Commonty went beyond "the memory of man". It was divided about the year 1800. Situated to the east of Benarty Hill was the Commonty of Boglochtie, also known as the Commonty of Strathruddie. It lay on the fringe of the barony of Inchgall although still in Lochoreshire. The Commonty consisted of one hundred and fifty acres of the ill-drained land near which the present Lurgie gas plant now stands. The proprietors of Pitkinnie and Muirton had grazing rights upon it. The Commonty was divided in 1759.

Hard-by the village of Crosshill lay the Commonty of the Milton Moss of Inchgall which probably included what is known today as the "Old Loan". In 1767 John Chalmers, Writer in Edinburgh, the occupier of Crosshill, raised a summons of division and in the following year the Commonty was divided among the proprietors of Crosshill and David Moncrieff of Boghill and James Malcolm of Balbegie.

On the south side of the River Fitty was the Commonty of North Lumphinnans. In a notice dated 1762 advertising the sale of the lands of Lumphinnans extending to seven hundred and nine acres, reference is made to a Commonty consisting of sixty-two acres which was then under submission to be divided. It was used for grazing by the proprietors of Cartmore, Colquhally and Lochgelly, and occupied the ground which today is known as South Glencraig.

These Commonties prior to being divided were not held by any one person under Charter, but were in effect the poor man's grazing ground. Collectively, they must have constituted a sizeable portion of the lands within the barony. While lands held under Crown Charter by the baron continued to be leased out to tenants as before, it is to be said that with the departure of the Wardlaw family, if indeed not some years before its final demise, the break-up of the barony of Inchgall had begun. The process was greatly accelerated under the Malcolms so that from the eighteenth century onwards there appears the names of more and more bonnet lairds and tackmen, until the portion of the barony which remained in the hands of the landholder-in-chief was acquired by a mining concern in the late nineteenth century.

But let us return to life as it was in the seventeenth century. By now the lands of Lumphinnans, Clunie-craig (Glencraig) and Capeldrae had been sold and quite a number of small portions of the estate were already leased at annual rents ranging from £3 to £6. As these rents were paid in pounds Scots and therefore worth one twelfth of the English pound, and six pound rent was equivalent to fifty pence of today's money.

The enclosed fields which lay scattered around the crofts were small, and bore the "furrow and rig" pattern. They were known as "infields" which received the meagre supply of dung from the croft. The patches of ground situated some distance from the crofter's house and only subject to occasional tillage were known as the "outfields". These were usually worked until successive crops exhausted the fertility of the soil when they were allowed to lie fallow until nature had to some extent restored the balance. near the house was the "kailyard", while close at hand was the perpetual "dunghill".

Crops usually consisted of corn, oats, barley, beans and peas, while flax was grown for home-spinning, although one can well imagine that much of this commodity would be grown locally to keep the waulk mills going at the Milton. The presence of so much whin, still to be seen in Easter Crosshill, reminds one of a practice of the period, of reducing the young green shoots of this plant to a pulp by means of a flail and giving it to cattle and horses as food.

Of the rural industries we would mention coal-mining. The coalheughs of Inchgall and Blaircushnie were going concerns as early as 1560 and from this time onwards coal is frequently mentioned. The methods used must have been very primitive. The names of those who worked in a neighbouring coalheugh in the year 1668 reveal that the task of bringing the coal to the surface was performed by women. In the year 1645 the Presbytery of Kirkcaldy had to deal with a collier in Blair, a Ballingry man, who confessed to the murder of Patrick Reirs.

Another rural activity was the working of limestone on the estate. This dates from 1622 when James Mitchell in Ladath was given power to work limestone in Navitie and Ballingry. The limestone in Ballingry was worked at a later date by Captain Park. The stone was reduced to a powder by burning after which it was used on the fields as manure.

Of the many places where folk were wont to gather in olden times none could replace the kirk and the weekly market. It was the custom for churchgoers to stand in groups in the kirkyard and recount the news of the past week, and to discuss their everyday business there until the minister appeared to commence the service. At the market "where drouthie neibors, neibors meet" the atmosphere was more convivial. This was the occasion for friends and acquaintances from further afield to exchange news since their last meeting and to chat over more personal matters over a pint-stoup of ale.

The Kirk Session records show the efforts made by the church to improve the moral tone of the parish, but despite his efforts the minister in 1640 reported to the

Presbytery his regret that there was "a profanity of the Sabbath be the ganging of the myles". Not only was work being done, but John Paterson, a church elder, did openly sell drink on the Sabbath and also entertained his friends on the Sabbath afternoon. For his misdeeds he was gravely admonished and told to abstain from breaking the Sabbath. A little before this time we obtain a glimpse, just a glimpse, of the social life of the "toun". Some persons had strayed so far from the path of rectitude as to go "Gyseing" (dressing up). Those responsible for this most unseemly behaviour were summoned to appear before the Presbytery.

To call at a neighbour's house for a friendly chat has been a custom enjoyed by most people down through the ages. During this period when womenfolk set out to spend an evening in another's house, they took with them their "rock", that is, their distaffs or spinning wheels so that they might "draw a thread" as they chatted away. This custom gave rise to the saying when a meeting was in the offing, "I am coming over with my rock".

We mention here The Herds' Annual Games, held on the summit of Benarty on what was originally the Benarty Common. The games appear to have been abandoned early in the nineteenth century, but may have had their origin at a much earlier date. Herding as an occuption began to go out of use about the middle of the eighteenth century with the increase in the amount of land being enclosed with dry-stone dykes. Herds from all over Fife and the neighbouring counties took part in the various contests, including golf which at this period was played with leather balls filled with feathers. Football was also played with sides numbering fifty persons and upwards, with little attention being paid to rules. There was also a game called "the wads", involving "hostages", about which nothing more is known.

BONNIE B'INGRY

On approaching Ballingry from the south, as seen from the heights of Lochgelly, one cannot but be aware of the one thousand feet high backcloth of Benarty setting out before it the waters of Loch Ore, the ruined castle of Inchgall, and the ancient Kirkton of Ballingry.

It is difficult now for anyone to picture the neighbourhood before it became overlaid with the incrustations of an industrial age. Albeit most of this has now gone with the creation of the Lochore Meadows Country Park, an ambitious venture carried out by the Fife Regional Council. The epithet "Bonnie B'ingry", so often on the lips of bygone generations, no doubt truthfully portrayed the quiet beauty of the place. Even Scott, in a moment of delight, alluded to what must have been an equally common saying when he spoke of Ballingry as "the earthly paradise, so called".

We refer to the period prior to the beginning of the nineteenth century when, according to Mr Greig the minister, there were not above seventy reeking lums in the parish. When it is remembered that Lumphinnans, Balbedie and part of the village of Lochgelly were in the parish, the minister's remark, couched in the homely doric, emphasises the sparseness of the population. The dwellings of this period were in the main, stone-built, low-roofed, red-tiled, or thatched and turfed single-ends which, seen in surroundings of natural beauty beside a sprinkling of sheep and grazing cattle, gave to the place an air of peacefulness and repose. It is in surroundings such as these that many people of note came to Ballingry, drawn by its past history and objects of bygone days.

Sir Walter Scott knew the hamlet fairly well and left his imprint with his reference to Loch Ore and Ballingry church in his novel *The Abbot:* but long before Scott's day people had been coming to the place. It could be said that Ballingry came into a little prominence among antiquaries and writers in the early part of the eighteenth century following the publication by Sir Robert Sibbald of his *History of Fife,* a work that is said to have first appeared in 1682 but of which a more correct copy appeared in 1710.

It was claimed by Sir Robert that there were to be seen the remains of a Roman camp situated on the north shore of Loch Ore. Ballingry, therefore, did not escape from the "Roman epidemic" that broke out among antiquaries about this time, and quite a few places in Fife were identified with the conjectured movements of the Roman army of the first century all of which have since proved negative. During the two and a half centuries that have gone, not a little ingenuity and much ink has been spilled on the subject of the Loch Ore site. It was not until 1951 that the spade finally settled the matter and revealed its origin.

Sir Robert was followed by Alexander Gordon, a land surveyor and celebrated antiquary who had newly completed his survey for the proposed Forth and Clyde Canal. He visited Ballingry during the first quarter of the eighteenth century and carried out his survey. Although he found the site so denuded that he could not make a complete plan, he nonetheless noted the various ditches and other features and published his description of the so-called camp in his *Itinerarium Septentrionale* published in 1727. The next person to visit Ballingry was William Maitland who, like

Gordon, measured the over-all length and breadth of the "camp", noted the turret beside the Loch and the remains of the ancient chapel of Inchgall. His *History and Antiquities of Scotland* appeared in 1757.

Ballingry by now was becoming well known among antiquaries and in 1760 Richard Pococke, Bishop of Meath, passed through Ballingry in his tour through Scotland. Writing to his sister from Dysart he says, "after visiting Lochleven, I turned south to Kirkness and two miles to Lough Or, where I saw what is called a Roman camp on the north side of the lake". The bishop also describes the remains of the castle on the island of Inchgall.

It was about this time that the professional soldier came on the scene. No doubt from his training, he would consider himself better equipped to work out Roman military strategy. General Robert Melville, an uncle of William Adam of Blairadam, had just completed a walking tour of Scotland in search of Roman camp sites when he arrived at Ballingry, and by his account he appears to have spent some time in the parish. Of course, the Loch Ore site was his first objective. After dealing with it, his enquiries throughout the neighbourhood revealed that a silver coin of the Emperor Pertinax had been found in a field immediately south of Harelaw about the year 1704. If General Melville was not the discoverer, he was at least the first to record the presence of a rectilineal enclosure wherein the coin was said to have been found. This enclosure was contained within a rampart and ditch and appears to have had a cobbled entrance on its west side. From surface evidence it appears to be medieval and is probably coeval with the second phase of Lochore Castle. The old name Balbegie, was probably first applied to it and denotes the home of the lesser man.

Meanwhile, Melville had been communicating his discoveries to his friend General William Roy, the father of the Ordnance Survey who, along with Colonel Watson had been engaged in the 1750s in making a survey of Fife. Melville's discovery of Roman marching camps in Strathmore and elsewhere had given a new impulse to General Roy's study of Roman antiquities. It is therefore not surprising to find Roy postulating on the position of the Loch Ore site in relation to the movements of the Roman army in the first century. The importance of Roy's work was soon recognised and was published posthumously in 1793 under the title *The Military Antiquities of the Romans in Britain*.

We move on to 1770. In this year John Clerk of Eldin, while residing at Blairadam, spent several days in the neighbourhood. He was the eldest son of Sir John Clerk, Baron of the Exchequer and the author of *Naval Tactics* and the inventor of the strategem known in naval warfare as "breaking the line". Clerk was an ardent antiquary and, along with his brother Matthew, he accompanied General Melville on his walking tour of the highlands. He possessed the gift of sketching in no small degree and executed a number of local sketches, including Blairadam and the Castles of Dowhill, Lochleven and Inchgall. He also made a sketch of Loch Ore as seen from the heights of Blairadam, in which are to be seen the Castle of Inchgall, and the hamlet of Crosshill. Accompanied by his nephew William Adam, then a youth, he spent several days measuring the Loch Ore site and produced a plan of the ditches and other features. It was his intention to have his plan inserted in *Roy's Military Antiquities*. Unfortunately, it does not appear there, nor is its whereabouts known. The plan is not to be found among the Blairadam papers.

Eleven years had passed before anyone of note came to the parish. Lieutenant General Henry Hutton, who for many years had been collecting material for a work entitled *Monasticon Scotiae* spent some time in Ballingry in the year 1781 and made a sketch of Loch Ore and the castle of Inchgall. General Hutton's work still remains in manuscript.

During this period, the noted traveller and historian, Adam de Cardonnel, was likewise visiting the ruined religious houses and castles of Scotland while preparing his guide to the *Picturesque Antiquities of Scotland*. In the second edition of this work which came out in 1793 a sketch and brief description of Inchgall Castle are to be found.

There was yet another fellow antiquary engaged at this period on a smiliar mission. Captain Francis Grose, a friend of Cardonnel, had long been travelling the country gathering material, antiquarian and legendary, for his *Antiquities of Scotland*. Grose enlisted the help of Robert Burns in collecting legendary lore in Kyle. In sending his contribution, Burns entrusted the package to Cardonnel for safe delivery to the Captain. In the package, Burns enclosed his well known poem "Ken ye ought o' Captain Grose", in imitation of the old ballad of *Sir John Malcolm*. The 1797 edition of *Antiquities of Scotland* also contains a sketch of Inchgall Castle.

The last of the old school of antiquaries to visit Ballingry was Lieutenant Colonel Miller. He explored the ground in the vicinity of the former loch in 1829 and from his detailed account of Harelaw Cairn, and what he calls traces of fortifications in what a century later was to become known as Lochore public park, where he says a stone coffin, some urns and many bones had been found, it is evident that he had spent some time in the neighbourhood. He informs his reader that, while standing on the Harran Hill looking towards Chapel farm, he could distinctly see the line of the three ditches of the camp in a corn field from the corn there being of a darker hue.

Colonel Miller, like most of the antiquaries before him, believed that the ninth Roman Legion had been attacked by the native tribes at Loch Ore where, according to the Colonel, tradition has it that there was a great battle.

Many writers since Miller's day have written about the "Roman Camp". Only recently the age-old story has been retold. The Roman Legion is again attacked and Benarty is once more resounding to the clash of arms! Tradition dies hard, but as has been shown earlier on, this ghost camp which has haunted the antiquarian fraternity for the greater part of three centuries, has at last been laid low. Laid low in more than one sense, for not only has it been shown not to be Roman, but it now lies beneath six feet of industrial waste.

AMONG THE MINOR POETS AND RHYMERS

To the north of Benarty Hill on the island of St. Serfs in Lochleven, Andrew Wyntoun, the Prior of the Monastery in the fifteenth century wrote his *Cronykil of Scotland* in verse, and further north, beyond the loch, in the little village of Kinnesswood, Michael Bruce, "The gentle poet of Lochleven" in the mid-eighteenth century was writing his poems in praise of his native Bishopshire.

No one would deny the contrast in scenery that exists on either side of the hill, still, it would be strange indeed if no one at any time in the long history of Lochoreshire did not feel the urge to compose a lilt in praise of his countryside or of the folks who lived there.

Probably the earliest reference in verse to the neighbourhood is to be found in the poem by William Drummond of Hawthornden in his *Forth Feasting*, written about 1620 where a trifling reference is made to the river Ore. Nor can we say more about the lines which appeared in the following century, as the author of the satirical verses on Sir John Malcolm of Lochore is not known.

James Campbell, a local youth who is believed to have composed several pieces of merit, but whose compositions are now lost, lived at Harran Hill a little west of Lochore House.* His poems, most of which were composed in the Scottish idiom, remained in manuscript. He was a close friend and devotee of Michael Bruce and was composing verse about the year 1767. Being a fellow student of Bruce at Edinburgh University, his aim was to become a minister of the Secession Church. His humble home at Harran Hill is known to have contained a small but well-selected library. About a month after Bruce's death, he wrote to his friend David Pearson of Wester Balgedie asking him to call on Bruce's parents and purchase from Mr Bruce his son's copy of *Cornelius Nepos*.

In a letter to a friend in 1769, Campbell refers to the death of Michael Bruce ("Amyntas" to his close friends) and concludes,
"But we may now with tears our care deplore
And mourn our loss, *Amyntas* is no more",
One of Campbell's poems is known to have survived as late as the middle of the present century, but all efforts to establish its whereabouts have failed.

It is not surprising that Benarty Hill which is so prominent a feature in the neighbourhood should arrest the attention of the poet. In a poem by an unknown author which appeared in 1796 we have the following lines:—
My lovely Delia...blooming as Aurora
In all her splendour rising in the east;
Than honey sweeter which the little bee,
Industrious, gathers on Benarty Hill;
And more ingenious than the blushing rose,
Whose op'ning bud breathes incense to the morn.

Again, Benarty is celebrated in the lovely Jacobean poem entitled *The Chieftain's Lullaby*.

---

* The ruined foundations of houses are still to be seen in Harran wood.

"Hush thee babe! the stag is bellowing
On Benarty dim and lone;
Hark! Oh hush! the hounds are yelling,
Who at morn will cheer them on?"

James Kennedy who in 1810 wrote his robust and expressive poem called *Glenochil* with its historical insight into happenings long ago, sang of the neighbourhood. Of Benarty he wrote:—

Green Ochil's child of steepy height,
That oft, in Leven's surgy curls,
Benarty, frowning on the sight,
The riven rock, rudely rattling, hurls.

Romantic hill! thy Alpine caves
Have rung with manly shouts afar;
Thy whistling heath sighs o'er their graves,
Who sternly braved the brunts of war.

Dark, on thy summit, nod no more,
In fatal form, great Gedor's towers;
Nor waft thy echoes, wide the roar
Terrific, of conflicting powers.

Relying on the generally accepted belief of his day that a Roman Camp existed at Lochore, he describes the scene in seven verses. Benarty resounds to the clash of arms and the ninth Roman Legion is all but annihilated.

Fortless, and rude, and robed in grey,
Towers o'er the lea renown'd Lochore,
Where, darkly pour'd in fiercest fray
Flow'd British mixt with Roman gore.

That clang of war — ah! fancy rears
Battlia of immortal men —
High gleam around their deathful spheres,
And chiefs awake to win their names again.

And so on. He concludes the scene thus:—

I hear the shouts — the clash of arms —
Each dying groan — each dismal yell —
'Tis past — and, o'er ambition's harms,
Maternal tears the Tiber's crystal swell.

He sings of Blair in these words:—

Then sweetly swell the turfty hills,
With blooming lawns and arbours fair,
Whose foliaged boughs arch rippling rills,
And silvanize the slopes of Blair.

Primeval Blair! whose mountain groves
Give beauty to its gay domain;

Where, 'mid a scene of rural loves
Truth, patriotism and honour reign.
To the ancient Paran Well he devotes four verses, the last two being:—
Where in a fresh, salubrious clime,
The spas of Paran sheerly well,
And, fringed with hairbells, heath and thyme,
Steal, pure and purling, down the dell.

At last, his tiresome travail done,
He quaffs, unpall'd, the healthsome spring,
Delighted, circles with the sun,
Invoking Bel the ninefold magic ring.

Coming to more modern times, there was Elizabeth Clephane the hymn writer who was born in Kirkness House in 1830. Although Elizabeth could not have been more than nine years of age when she left the neighbourhood she would no doubt know the village well and would worship in Ballingry Church where along with her parents and younger sister, she would occupy the Kirkness pew which was situated under the east gallery of the old church. Elizabeth in later life composed the well known hymn "There were Ninety and Nine" and the lesser known one "Beneath the Cross of Jesus".

We have two poems from *Hame Ower Lilts* by David Tasker in 1900. The first is a simple natural song, a true Scottish love lyric. It falls far short of the level of Burns but it is an honest and devout tribute by a youth to the girl he loves and his sincerity is felt in every line.

JANET SHAND

Whaur windin' Lochty wimples doon
To mingle wi' the Leven clear,
And drumlie Ore a drowsy tune
Hums to its castle ruins drear
There blooms as fair a flooer, I trew,
As e'er by lover's een was scann'd,
Eclipsed by nane, and matched by few,
Is dear kind-hearted Janet Shand.

Her velvet cheeks wear vermeil tints,
Dark broon her silken hair and een,
Wine-red her dewy lips, while glint
Twin raws o' ivory teeth atween.
But a' her ootward charms combined
My hert could never hae trepann'd,
If inward beauty o' th' mind,
Had graced nae gentle Janet Shand.

Lang pairted though we havena' been
I feel as lanesome, dull and wae,
As if her face I hadna' seen
For mony a lang and weary day.

267

To her by day my fancy turns,
By nicht I dream that hand in hand
'Mang flooery braes, by crystal burns,
I gaily roam wi' Janet Shand.

Speed on! ye langsome 'oors, and bring
That joyfu' day, when to my hert
I'll fauld her 'neath love's downy wing,
Nae mair on earth till death to pairt.
If wantin' her, though routh o' gear
Were mine, wi' flunkies at command,
I'd gladly yield them a' to share
Cauld puirtith's cup wi' Janet Shand.

Janet Shand lived at Spailinn, Lochcraig.

The second, *Bonnie Benarty* contains in its faltering lines some resemblance of descriptive writing.

BONNIE BENARTY

There's a far awa' hill in the kingdom o' Fife,
And in fancy I see it ilk day o' my life;
And at nicht, in my dreams, aft I wander fu' fain
'Mang its bracken and broom and red heather again.
There are hills in the land mair majestic and hie,
Though nane but itsel' I've a hankerin' to see,
Far, far wad I gang, and ne'er weary atweel,
The green sunny slopes o' Benarty to speil.
And what gars me lang frae my heart to be there,
It's no but there's scenes that I ken o' as fair.

Though whiles frae its tap, looking doon on Loch Leven,
I hae thocht it nae less than a glimpse into Eden.
But ayont, and ower a', 'tis a dream o' lang syne
That hallows the spot wi' a charm maist divine,
A fond recollection o' blythe days of yore,
When I wooed 'mang its woodlands the maid o' Lochore.

Oh can I forget in the gloamin' sae still
Hoo I sped ower the fields to the farm on the hill,
And lingered impatient aside the auld birk,
Till she stole to my side like the dawn through the mirk?
O' what wi' the bliss o' young love can compare!
In my journey through life I've ha'en joys less or mair,
But neither afore nor sin syne hae I kent
Sic rapturous 'oors as thegither we spent.

'Though nigh thretty milestanes I've passed on life's road
Sin' last there we pairtet, ilk pathway we trod

268

And ilk nook whaur we sat in my memory are green
As gin we had only traversed them yestreen;
And a licht that is shed not by sun nor by moon
Illumines the landscape and haloes it roon';
And it never shall fade while I treasure each thought,
And cherish the memories that cling round the spot.

Another descriptive poem came from the pen of David Hunter of Lochore in 1948. He was no mean musician and the music he set to the words are only one of his many musical compositions. The first verse of his poem is as follows:—

LOCHORE CASTLE*

As the sun sinks beyond the crest of the Ochils
And bathes all around with its radiant glow
The peak of Benarty is shrouded in darkness
A shadow is cast o'er the valley below
On the edge of the shadow the golden lit waters
Reflect on the Clune and the Castle once more
Majestic and regal she stands on the crest
Of the Isle of Inchgall in Bonnie Loch Ore.

Passing from Ballingry to Lochgelly we come within the childhood scenes of Lochgelly's poet, Alexander Brown. In this poem he sings of the village well. The first and last verses are as follows:—

86 *The Auld Stane Well*

* In reality, Inchgall Castle.

THE 'AULD STANE WELL

When summer blinks on flowery braes,
And whins in bloom are gay;
Where labour rests at golden eve,
And rosy children play;
How sweet to hear when evening's glow
Is fading in the dell,
The lisping murmur of the spring
That fills the village well.

Long be the Braes with gowans bright,
The whins with blossoms gay;
Long village sons thy memory keep,
Though far from thee they stray;
And long by thee may peaceful age,
With kindling glances tell
Of boyhood's days and boyhood's ways
Around the village well.

Equally well known was Peter Leslie, the soldier poet. Born in 1837, he commenced work at the age of ten in one of the local coal pits. He had a studious turn of mind and was unsuited for his occuption of driving a pony. He therefore joined the army and while serving abroad, he regularly contributed articles to the *Fife News*. These formed the basis of his book *The Autobiography of a Private Soldier*.

Peter Leslie died in 1905 and was buried in Auchterderran churchyard. He wrote under the pseudonym John Pinder. Most of his verses relate to local people and places. Among the better known are *Mary the Pride of Lochgelly, The Lass o' Pitkinnie, The Flower of Balgedie, Clune's Green Braes, The Kirk o' Auchterderran, Auld Laucherhead, Farewell to Lochgelly*, and *The Banks o' Clune*.

The opening verse of the last is as follows:—

I've mused upon Benarty's Hill
When nature's sweets were singing
And toddled oft by Inchga' Mill
When bonnie flowers were springing;
An' I hae roved thro Colin's crags
Her glens and lovely rills
An' mony a pleasant day I've spent
Upon the Torry hills.

Another rhymer of note was John Henderson a native of Lochgelly and a contemporary of Peter Leslie. His published poem *The Birnie Braes* extends to fifteen verses. The first goes as follows:—

Let ithers sing o' foreign lands
And a' their scenery praise;
Tae me there's not a spot on earth
Like oor ain Birnie Braes

'Twas close by them my mither lived
When first I saw the licht,
And there I lisped my little prayer
Beside her knee at nicht.

A well known writer of verse whose compositions are still read by those in Lochoreshire and beyond was Dr David Rorie, medical practitioner in the parish of Auchterderran, in the early part of the present century. As his vocation brought him in close contact with the parishioners he had ample opportunity of observing their manners and customs. These he portrayed in his many humorous poems written chiefly in the Scottish dialect. His books of collected songs and poems include the now well known song *A Lum Hat Wantin the Croon,* while some of his poems such as *The Auld Doctor* and *A Druggist's Shop,* touch on the duties and elements of his profession. Others, while displaying originality in humourous expression, contain an element of religious sentiment, such as the following:—

THE DEIL'S A BUSY BISHOP

Man, I was sayin' las' nicht to Jock—
    A canny billy, that!—
There's heaps o' queer things happen noo
    To gar ye won'er at;
O' godly thocts an' kindly deeds
    The lord gie us increase,
For the Deil's a busy bishop
    In his ain diocese.

While a' the warld's sotterin'
    Like tatties in a pot,
An' man's chief en' is naethin'
    But to cut his brither's throat,
O' godly thochts an' kindly deeds
    The Lord gie us increase,
For the Deil's a busy bishop
    In his ain diocese.

Gin ye canna lo'e your neebor,
    Try an' lat the crater be,
An' dinna yoke to whustlin'
    When ye hear he's gaun to dee;
O' godly thochts an' kindly deeds
    The Lord gie us increase,
For the Deil's a busy bishop
    In his ain diocese.

271

SCOTT'S VISITS TO LOCHORE

It is a local belief, fostered from time to time by contributions to the press, that Sir Walter Scott was a frequent guest at Lochore House. Some writers have gone so far as to apportion to him the round study, where they have him in their imagination ensconsed at his desk busily engaged in writing part of his novel, *The Abbot*. A little research, however, shows that Sir Walter was not so frequent a visitor as is generally believed. It has to be said that his connection with Lochore was not the outcome of his son's marriage with the heiress to the estate. Scott must have known of the place many years before. There was a tradition still current in the village of Auchtertool towards the end of the last century which was to the effect that Sir Walter as a boy, accompanied by an elder, witnessed the burial of one of the Skeins of Hallyards, an old laird who had taken part in the Jacobite rebellion of 1715.

The interment in the old church of Auchtertool was carried out in a most unusual manner. The weird undertaking took place during the hours of darkness. The account tells how the body of the deceased who had died in exile at St. Germains in France, was first taken to Hallyards and afterwards borne shoulder-high by old retainers of the family, accompanied by torchbearers and preceded by a piper playing a lament. The solemn procession went by way of the Lady Walk and afterwards straight across the fields towards the church. There, by the light of flickering torches which produced a phantom-like atmosphere, the interment ceremony followed the ritual of the Roman Church, and the family vault received the remains of the old cavalier.

The unusual nature of the burial ceremony would no doubt appeal to Scott's imagination and doubtless inspired him to include some of the details in his description of the burial of the Countess of Glenallan which appeared in his novel *The Antiquary* in 1816.

As a boy of fifteen years in 1786, he travelled north on a pony on his way from Edinburgh to Invermay by way of Queensferry. As the road led through the elevated grounds of Blairadam, he would have a good view of the Ore valley and a distant view of Loch Ore and its castle as the loch had not as yet been drained.

The sight that met the youthful Scott would be very similar to that sketched in 1770 by William Adam's uncle, John Clerk of Eldin. As the objects in the middle distance in the sketch lay within the environs of "Bonnie B'ingry", we are justified in believing that the neighbourhood at that time possessed features of natural beauty. Scott at a later period in his life spoke of the beautiful woods and valley of Lochore. From the elevated view-point at Blairadam, the whole valley of the Ore could be seen. William Adam, referring to the wider prospect, calls it the "Vale of Fife". The foreground sloping towards the loch was traversed by the road from the Queen's Ferry as it skirted the west shoulder of Benarty Hill, while the waters of the Ore descending from the high ground above Blairadam rushed on towards the loch. Loch Ore lay two miles distant, with the Harran Hill to the north and on its southern shore the elevated ground of the Clune, while at its furthest end, the solid mass of the castle and the island of Inchgall were reflected in its waters. Beyond lay the hamlet of Crosshill, while topping the middle horizon could be seen the tree-girt cairn of Harelaw. Away beyond, as far as the eye could discern, were the undulating lands of Fife framed in by the waters of the Forth, and out beyond where sea and sky met in distant haze, lay the Isle of May.

Scott may have known that Janet Beaton, who married his namesake, Sir Walter Scott of Buccleuch, to whom he gives so prominent a place in his poem *The Lay of the Last Minstrel* was a granddaughter of Archibald Beaton, the laird of Capeldrae. Nor was this the only connection with Lochore to which Scott could have justly laid claim, for had not another of his forebears, Sir Walter Scott of Branxholm married a grand niece of the same laird, and when adversity struck the House of Capeldrae in 1543, did not the laird of Branxholm come to its aid and stand surety for the head of the House so that he could return to Capeldrae and to his own folk.

There is another interesting fact which presupposes Scott's awareness of Lochore, a fact which we believe had until 1952 gone unnoticed.* It has already been said that the remains of the Motte-and-Bailey castle on the north side of the loch was considered by the old antiquaries, including Scott, to be the remains of a small Roman camp or outpost. It was not until 1727 that it was described in any detail by Alexander Gordon in his book entitled *Itinerarium Septentrionale*. Scott had a copy of his book at Abbotsford, and as all readers of his novel *The Antiquary* know, it was Sandy Gordon's *Itinerarium Septentrionale* that Jonathan Oldbuck took with him on his journey from Edinburgh to Fairport. Scott's description of the Roman camp in that novel is largely taken from Gordon's description of the so-called Roman camp at Lochore. As to Scott's more intimate connection with the neighbourhood, it is to be said that he was receiving letters from the Clephanes of Kirkness before 1815. In this year he was made an honorary member of the Musomanik Society of Anstruther. From 1817 onward he was paying visits to William Adam at Blairadam, and by 1821 as his fame as a novelist increased, he began to receive honours from public bodies. In this year he was made a freeman of the Burgh of Dunfermline. During this period from 1813 onward, the Jobson family were staying at Lochore and it is more than likely that at some time or other he would hear of the family from his friend Sir Adam Ferguson. It is unlikely that the Fergusons would take their niece to Scott's house for dinner without his having previously heard of the girl and her family.

William Adam, writing on the formation of the Blairadam Antiquarian Club says, "in the summer of 1817 I asked Sir Walter (then Mr Scott) and his two earliest and most intimate friends, Sir Adam Ferguson and Mr William Clerk, to accompany me to Blairadam, where we contrived to pass some very agreeable days strolling in all directions through the garden, the grounds and the woods". It was on this occasion that William Adam remarked to Scott how singularly the place was environed with castles of great antiquity, and he proceeded to enumerate them, from Castle Campbell in the west to Falkland Palace in the east, including his own little Castle of Dowhill and the ruined Castle of Lochore (Inchgall). "The enumeration, (he says), which I made generated an idea which was effectively carried into execution". It was agreed to add some other friends to the party and to make the visit to Blairadam an annual event. The meetings were to take place at midsummer and so arranged that the party dined at

* It was the subject of a paper read to the Benarty Antiquarian Club in 1952.

273

Blairadam on the Friday. Saturday and Monday were free for Club activities in "gratifying antiquarian curiosity in all directions". Sunday was a day of rest when usually the Club members attended the parish church at Cleish. The Club consisted of nine members. In addition to the four already mentioned there was Chief Baron Sir Samuel Shepherd, Thomas Thomson Advocate and Deputy-Register and Keeper of Records, his brother the Reverend John Thomson, minister of Duddingston and landscape painter, Captain (afterwards Admiral) Charles Adam, son of William Adam and Mr Anstruther Thomson of Charleton, brother-in-law of William Adam.

The ladies of the respective families were included in the house parties and when they chose to accompany the Club members on their outings, their chief role was to attend to the catering. The number was increased on several occasions by visitors. Lord and Lady Abercrombie came once, as did Lord Sydney Osborne. On another occasion Count Flahault turned up and Mr Cheape of Wellfield joined the party more than once. Several of Mr Adam's near neighbours in Kinross-shire also joined the Club members at Blairadam for dinner.

The first Club outing was in 1818 and took the form of a visit to Castle Campbell near Dollar. Scott was the first to descend "fearlessly down the yawning gulf into the dungeon" and was soon followed by other venturous members of the party who kept up a running commentary of what they saw, to the enlightenment of those who preferred to stay on top. It was agreed by all that the visit was worth all "the labour and the hazards". The return journey was by way of the Cauldron Linn and the Rumbling Bridge. At the Rumbling Brig Inn, the menfolk were met by the ladies where, after a light meal and much merriment, the company returned home to Blairadam.

The next three annual meetings of the Club were taken up by visits to Dunfermline Abbey and the ruins of the Monastery and the Palace, also Cleish Castle and other places of antiquarian interest. It was in 1821 that the heritors of the Abbey church of Dunfermline promised Scott the pulpit which had been taken out of the "Old Kirk". This was sent to Abbotsford the following year.

The year 1822 was outstanding in the Club's excursions. It was at Scott's suggestion that the party agreed to visit the high tower at Abernethy, Macduff's cross, Mugdrum cross and Lindores Loch in the course of the day's outing, and in order to do so it was decided to commence the journey at an earlier hour than usual. It must have presented a fine sight on that mid-summer morning to see the party aboard their horse-drawn carriages proceeding along the Great North Road en-route to Abernethy. Admiral Adam, Sir Walter Scott, Mr William Clerk, Sir Adam Ferguson and Mr Thomas Thomson in the landau drawn by four horses, followed by Chief Commissioner Adam and Chief Baron Shepherd in his chaise and pair. But even in the less mechanical age in which they lived, accidents did happen. As the carriages were approaching Dam-head (now the village of Glenfarg), Baron Shepherd's chaise broke an axle-tree at a point on the road where, fortunately, there was a blacksmith near at hand. As the morning was still early and the devout man and his family were at morning prayers, temporal necessities had to give way to spiritual devotions, so at length when the village artisan did appear he received instructions to have the carriage repaired.

The Admiral on board the landau, on seeing what had happened, weighed anchor

87 *Sir Walter Scott*

for a moment, then like all good mariners, hauled to and picked up the survivors, so with all seven on board the landau proceeded down Glenfarg. After breakfasting at Mr Murray of Ayton's beautiful place at the foot of the glen, the company re-embarked for Abernethy. They had no sooner reached the ancient tower than Scott dived into the vault and brought out a human skull which he proceeded to roll up in a pocket handkerchief in order to take it home to Abbotsford. Mugdrum cross was inspected on the way to Macduff's cross.

At the village of Newburgh enquiries began as to the whereabouts of the celebrated cross. Sir Walter thought little of Sir Adam Ferguson's attempt to obtain the required information from a local youth — "a foolish boy", as Sir Walter said. Instead *he* would enquire of a very old and infirmed man who was seen approaching the party, so assuming a knowledgeable air, and addressing Sir Adam, he said, "permit *me* to know how to get at the springs of antiquarian knowledge; I will suck the brains of this ancient inhabitant of the place", and in order to ensure that he would succeed where Sir Adam had failed, Sir Walter proceeded to search for a sixpence in his waistcoat pocket. Having secured the coin between his forefinger and thumb of his right hand, he demanded of the patriarch if he could tell him anything about Macduff's cross. "I can tell ye a' aboot it" was the encouraging reply. No sooner had he received the sixpence than the old man jumped to his feet like a sixteen year old, he twirled his stick above his head and displayed his delight in the form of a circular dance which he performed to his own vocal accompaniment. He turned out to be an itinerant idiot who knew nothing of the place. One can imagine it would be sometime before Sir Walter regained his usual composure. His mortified expression was the reason for the broadest of grins on the face of his old friend Sir Adam. As the transactions of this "most joyous and kindly Club" are silent on anything relating to Macduff's cross, we are left wondering if its members succeeded in finding its whereabouts.

The landau with its occupants passed Lindores Loch and at Inchyre the party saw the house of Mr Ramsay of the Edinburgh Courant. At the Trafalgar Inn upon the Cupar road, the landau hauled-to and the company disembarked to find that the owner had been imbibing too freely and was incapable of attending to his guests. Attendants there were none, so everyone had to do his part in preparing a meal. From the landau came a large basket containing everything requisite for a full meal, the work, care and forethought of Miss Adam. Scott laid the tablecloth and placed the wine on the table. The Chief Baron cleaned the glasses and acted as waiter. Sir Adam and Mr Thomson unwrapped the fowls and tongue. Mr Clerk and Admiral Adam produced the cold pies and bread, while the Chief Commissioner attended to the horses and their drivers. The landlord, on coming into the room somewhat recovered his senses on seeing such an unexpected sight. Much was eaten and many times the glasses were filled, for the company had not eaten since breakfast. Miss Adam was not forgotten. Scott called for a bumper to her health and a thousand thanks to her excellent catering. With the arrival of the landau at the door it was not long before it was filled both inside and on top. It was about ten o'clock at night when the party drove up the avenue to Blairadam House.

The Club meetings no doubt continued annually at the summer equinox although it was not until 1826 that we again hear of their activities, or to be more precise, their inactivity, for the oppressive heat in June of that year made any undue exertion out of

276

the question. Scott wrote "if we attempt any active proceedings we dissolve ourselves into a dew. We have lounged away the morning creeping about the place, sitting a great deal and working as little as might be on account of the heat". He also says "the Lord Chief Commissioner's family misfortunes and my own make our holiday this year of a more quiet description than usual". The Club's activities seem to have been much curtailed and amounted to driving about in the Droskie and walking in the evening.

It was probably some time prior to 1826 that the Club members on a Sunday afternoon climbed to the top of Benarty Hill. As the company lay on the grass enjoying the extensive view from their elevated viewpoint, Sir Walter remarked "what an extraordinary thing it is, that here to the north so little appears to have been done, where there are so many proprietors to work upon it; and to the south, here is a district of country entirely made by the efforts of one family, in three generations, and one of them amongst us in the full enjoyment of what has been done by his two predecessors and himself. Blairadam, as I have always heard, had a wild uncomely and inhospitable appearance before its improvements were begun. It would be most curious to record in writing its original state, and trace its gradual process to its present condition". Chief Commissioner Adam, referring to this many years afterwards remarks "this observation, which was assented to and enforced by the rest of the company, its originating with such a man, and confirmed by other friends highly flattered me and made a deep impression upon me". The outcome was a little book privately printed *Blairdam, 1733 to 1834,* in which the improvements on the estate are described in detail and all aspects of estate management discussed.*

The etymology of the estate is worthy of comment and shows the change from Crambeth to Blairadam, although down through the centuries, especially in the earlier periods there was inevitable overlapping. Throughout the thirteenth and fourteenth centuries it was known as Crambeth. In 1231 reference is made to a Robert de Crambeth whose son Gilbert owned the lands of Cleish. Bishop Matthew de Crambeth appears in 1288 and Master Hervy de Crambeth in 1296, when Crambeth Castle, known later as Dowhill Castle, was the seat of the family. Agnes de Crambeth is mentioned in 1354 and the estate was still known by this name as late as 1390. Blair de Crambeth is mentioned in 1493 and this form of the name continued till the middle of the seventeenth century when the "de" was dropped, but the prefix was retained when it is written Blaircrambeth and was still known by this name in the first quarter of the eighteenth century. Towards the end of that century it began to be known, at least locally, as "The Blair", although officially the name was Blaircrambeth. In about the year 1800 Chief Commissioner Adam dropped the suffix Crambeth and replaced it by his family name, since when it has appeared as Blairadam.

The summer of 1827 saw the Club's excursion bound for the east of Fife, its ultimate goal being St. Andrews. The usual trio Sir Walter, Sir Adam and Mr Clerk arrived at Blairadam, to be joined by Miss Adam and the company set off for the home of Mr Anstruther Thomson at Charleton, Miss Adam's uncle. There they were joined by Mr Thomas Thomson, Chief Baron Shepherd, Chief Commissioner Adam and Sir

---

* The writer has in his possession a leather-bound copy of this book beautifully ornamented in gold scroll-work, containing an autographed letter by Chief Commissioner Adam in which he refers to Sir Walter Scott.

Henry Raeburn. Mr Thomson his wife and daughters received their guests most kindly and everyone was in good spirit. The following morning the company set off for St. Andrews. They walked among the ruins of the Cathedral and climbed St. Rule's tower with the exception of Scott who, owing to his rhematism omitted the latter part but instead sat on a gravestone and recollected how thirty four years before, he had carved the name of his first love in Runic letters on the turf beside the castle gate and asked himself why it should still agitate his heart. The return of the company from the tower brought him back to reality. Leaving St. Andrews, Scott expressed a strong desire to visit Magusmoor and the spot where Archbishop Sharp was assassinated. During the weekend stay at Charleton the Houses of Balcaskie and Elie were visited also the church of St. Monan's, which at the time of the visit was being extensively repaired. On this occasion the Club did not return to Blairadam. Instead, it was agreed on leaving Charleton on the Monday for Pettycur Ferry on the return journey to Edinburgh, to visit one or two places on the way. A souterrain not far from Elie House was inspected, also Macduff's Castle (so called) and the caves on the Wemyss coast and finally Wemyss Castle. The company boarded the ferry in the early afternoon and so ended the excursions for another year.

The following year saw the usual gathering at Blairadam on the Friday evening. Saturday was taken up by a second visit to Castle Campbell, and a drive over the hill and round by the Kerry Craigs on the Blairadam estate took up most of the Sunday afternoon. On Monday, the Club passed through Lochore and Ballingry and on to Kirkness and took a boat to St. Serfs island in Lochleven. From there they rowed to the Castle island and talked much about the Castle and the Queen's escape with Scott joining in the discussions and conjectures with a demure face. On leaving the loch the Club went to see Burleigh Castle on the outskirts of Milnathort, from which Scott was successful in obtaining some old pieces of woodwork which eventually turned up at Abbotsford.

It was probably following the Club's visit to Lochleven Castle that Sir Walter presented William Adam with "a curious and magnificent key of great size" which had been given to him by one who believed it to have been the key of the apartments wherein Queen Mary was confined. The key according to tradition was found by a boy while walking along the edge of the loch.

The objective for the 1829 Club outing was Falkland Palace. Two carriages and a gig with the Club members to the number of six with Lord Sydney Osborne as a visitor, passed through Lochore, Balbedie, Strathenry and on to Leslie and Christ's Kirk on the Green. At Falkland they were met by Mr Howden the factor who showed them through the Palace. The company dined at Wellfield the home of Mr and Mrs Cheape where they were joined by some of the ladies from Blairadam. The sheriff substitute of Kinross dined at Blairadam on the Sunday and brought with him a gold signet which had been found at Kinross in April of that year. It is since thought to have belonged to Joanne of Beaufort wife of James I. An early dinner on the Monday allowed the company to return to Edinburgh and to their several homes.

The contingent from south of the Forth in the summer of 1830 was much smaller than usual. Scott accompanied by his daughter Anne and Sir Adam Ferguson alone

88 *Chief Commissioner William Adam*

made the journey. One wonders if the two knights, as they travelled to Blairadam on the Friday evening of the thirteenth anniversary of the Club, had any foreboding as to its future. Some portend of things to come seems to have been in the air as their numbers had sadly diminished. Chief Baron Shepherd had returned to England, William Clerk had a severe cold, Thomas Thomson was detained and on the Saturday morning, William Adam felt unwell and decided to remain at home. With an early start, the company set off for Culross which was to be the last of the Club's excursions. They breakfasted at the home of Sir Adam Rolland at Luscar, and arrived at Culross in weather conditions described by Scott as most impropitious, very cold and rainy. The Club was met by Sir Robert Preston then in his ninety-second year and shown over Culross House and Abbey and entertained to a sumptuous dinner. The following day being Sunday, it was decided to go to church at Ballingry but when they reached the church it was found — probably owing to the indisposition of old Mr Greig — there was to be no service that day. In order to pass the time the company looked over Lochore estate and thereafter returned to Blairadam. Monday was taken up by strolling about Blairadam and Scott wrote a long letter to his son Walter no doubt acquainting him of the conditions of Lochore. With his return to Sandwich Place, Edinburgh at eleven o'clock that night, Scott had come to the end of another of his annual visits to "The Kingdom", had participated in the last of the Club's meetings and had made his last visit to Lochore.

We have seen that Scott's visits so far had been as a member of the Blairadam Antiquarian Club, but it is known that he came to Lochore at least on two occasions outwith the period of the annual meetings at Blairadam. Since his first visit to Blairadam in 1816, he had become familiar with the neighbourhood and the idea of writing a novel associated with the surrounding district had arisen in his mind. The outcome was the publication of *The Abbott* in 1820. In the scene of that novel where Henry Seyton slays Jasper Dryfesdale in the howff of old Keltie, Sir Walter makes Seyton say to George Douglas "Tie a stone round his neck, and when the sun is down, have him to the loch of Ore, heave him in and let him alone for finding out the bottom". Sir Walter might not have given so graphic details of how to dispose of the body had he known that the waters of the loch were but four feet deep! He may have had his doubts, however, for he puts in the mouth of Douglas the reply "it shall not be so" instead the body of Dryfesdale is to be taken to "the chapel at Scotland's wall or to the church of Ballingry".

In March 1825, a little over a month after his son's marriage, he paid what he describes as a "twenty-four hours visit to Lochore" in the company of Mr Bayley, Jane's cousin and Mr Laidlaw, his estate Steward at Abbotsford. From what is disclosed of his visit, it is clear that he and the rest of the company had arrived in the afternoon or evening of the first day and had spent the whole of the next day in going over the estate, and had left possibly during the forenoon of the third day. This is the only occasion on which it is known that Scott resided at Lochore House. His arrival was welcomed by everyone except Jane's large yard dog, for although Scott made every effort at intimacy, the dog remained unfriendly. Scott made full use of all the hours available to him during his visit. He climbed Benarty, scrambled through the old crags, walked over the pasture lands and examined drainage ditches. He met John McLeod the gardener-gamekeeper who, having just returned from a shoot, showed Scott the result of his morning's work which included "ten wildcats, four polecats, five weasels, three whittrets besides sundry magpies". Little escaped his notice. He remarked "there is no need for railroads here you may send the cook-maid with the coal scuttle to dig out the coals she wants for the day". Scott visited Inchgall Castle and, as if by way of contradicting a remark made possibly by Jane Jobson on a previous occasion, he adds "it is not a stupid place". He almost lost himself in the morasses of the ill-drained loch and likened himself to the ninth Roman Legion which he believed nearly came to grief in the nearby Roman camp, so called. He was pleased with all he saw and was delighted with the efficient way in which Mr Bayley was managing the estate. He reckoned that the grasslands could be let at between £3 and £4 an acre and that the estate was worth between £40,000 and £45,000. Scott met James Greig the minister of Ballingry and a Mr Birrell who he described as a cheery little old gentleman, both of whom had been invited for dinner. Mr Birrell was John Birrell a land surveyor of the family of parchment makers who lived in Portmoak and who had surveyed and produced plans of several of the local estates. He was a friend and devotee of Michael Bruce the poet, and is *Varro* in Bruce's *Ode to a Man of Letters*. The conversation at the table would no doubt touch on the management of the estate in all its various aspects and while we would expect Mr Birrell to be quite knowledgeable on such a subject, Mr Greig being a son of a farmer, would no doubt add his contribution to the discussions. It is fairly certain that Scott received from the minister a description of the two stone effigies that lay under the centre gallery in what was known as the Malcolm aisle in the church. Scott, writing to Jane describing his visit to Lochore, says he had intended to go to the church to see what he calls "two honest gentlemen hewn in stone — some of the old knights of Lochore", but hail showers prevented his going. If Scott's use of the epithet "honest gentlemen" was intentional as alluding to their Jacobite sympathies, there can be little doubt that the effigies were those of Alexander Malcolm (Lord Lochore) and his brother James, both of whom were ardent Jacobites.

On the morning of their departure it was decided to take back to Abbotsford Jane's pony and chaise to be under the care of the coachman there in case Lochore House should be let to strangers. Scott was glad to inform Jane afterwards that her pony was being well cared for and that Lady Scott had been out driving in her pony and chaise.

The only other occasion on which Scott visited Lochore other than with the Blairadam Antiquarian Club was when he and his son Walter came over from Blairadam in August 1826. Despite a stormy day they went over the property and discussed the need for an alteration to be made to the west approach road to the house, a project which Scott had been turning over in his mind since March of the previous year.

Of Scott's visits to Lochore, very little oral tradition remains. He is said to have visited Lochgelly in order to gather information for an article which was to appear in Blackwood's magazine on the Lochgelly gypsies.

Of the following anecdotal fragment the present writer is the second removed from the original informant, a Lochore man who as a youth remembered seeing Scott during one of his perambulations of the estate. On seeing that Sir Walter was having difficulty in climbing over a dry-stone dyke (he was lame from infancy), he gave him a helping

KIRKNESS

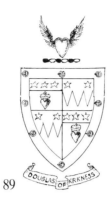

89

Kirkness, as we have seen, had from an early period become a place of local importance, as a Culdee possession. It emerged during the period when medieval man truly believed in the spiritual authority of the church, an authority which touched his life at every point. As Kirkness contained the Prior's Ward or residence belonging to the Priory on St. Serfs isle in Lochleven, it must have gained recognition long before the lands surrounding Loch Ore were erected into a Knight's fee. Long after the Reformation when it had become a temporal lordship shorn of its former status, it was annexed to Ballingry for ecclesiastical purposes.

Although Kirkness lay outwith Lochoreshire, it calls for inclusion in our study of local history if only on account of its interesting past and its early association with Lochoreshire. Kirkness lay within the lordship of Bishopshire and belonged to the regality of St. Andrews. Bishopshire, as the name implies, was probably created by the powerful bishops after the church had seized these lands, along with those later identified as comprising the parish of Portmoak, from the Culdees in the mid-twelfth century. As to the extent of Kirkness, we shall require to be content with a brief description of its boundaries at this period as extending "from a public road which leads from Inverkeithing to the Irishmen's Stone".

Some incidents in the history of Kirkness have already been recorded, the most outstanding being the dispute between the Culdees and the laird of Lochore. It will be recalled that this took place about the year 1128 and in all likelihood concerned the boundary between the two estates from the ford of Navitie westward. By the year 1395 when the question of the boundary between Kirkness and Lochoreshire was again raised, it was the stretch from the ford of Navitie eastward that was in dispute. The contending parties were John de Boswell and Robert de Livingston lords of Easter Lochoreshire on the one side and the successors of the Culdees who, by reason of a provision laid down by David I were now absorbed into the Augustinian order of canons regular. The clergy were represented by Andrew Wyntoun, the Prior of St. Serfs.

283

So it was that on 6th July, 1395 there assembled at the "ville de Balbechy" in the west corner of Kirkness a great company of distinguished people. From Navitie eastward the Lochty burn formed the southern boundary of Kirkness with the church lands of Ballingry. Further east the burn entered Bog Lochty with Kirkness to the north and Easter Lochoreshire to the south.

In order to settle the matter a company of nobles, churchmen and many others assembled on a rock overlooking Bog Lochty known at that time as the Bog of Polnabar. The company included Robert, Earl of Fife and Menteith, Walter, Bishop of St. Andrews, Alexander, Bishop of Caithness, Michael de Ramsay, Sheriff of Fife and Andrew Wyntoun the Prior. The local landowners included Henry de Arnot, Andrew de Gatemilk, John de Glen, John de Boswell, Robert de Livingston and Richard de Ballingry. Specially summoned witnesses were present, and as a few of their names appear later on in connection with other matters we know that they must have been local men. After much inspection and discussion the jurymen gathered round the Earl by the side of the marsh and their spokesman, Aye Jonson delivered their verdict which was unanimous, "As the course of the burn ceased to be distinguished after it entered the marsh, a straight line from that point through the bog to a point further east where the estates of Kirkness and Kinnimond meet, should be the boundary between the lands of Kirkness and Lochore". At the request of Andrew de Wyntoun and John de Boswell, an official report was drawn up on the spot by Thomas de Karnys, a notary public, in the presence of the two bishops. *

The family of Douglas was for many generations associated with Kirkness. Even before the Reformation, by which time Kirkness had become a temporal lordship under the Earl of Morton, the church gave Kirkness in feuferm to William Douglas, son of Robert Douglas of Lochleven. The Deed was drawn up by Cardinal Beaton at St. Andrews in 1544 and was witnessed by Archibald Beaton of Capeldrae.

There is a tradition that Cardinal Beaton used Kirkness House as one of his summer residences and made frequent visits there. This was probably the case as Kirkness lay adjacent to Capeldrae the home of the Beatons, and of course his sister Elizabeth Beaton was Lady of Inchgall. It is known from the St. Andrews Deed that the Prior of the Monastery on St. Serfs Isle had a "Ward" or house at Kirkness. Mention is also made of the "Cruives" or "Gulatis" at the mouth of Lochleven. These also belonged to the church and no doubt originated with the monks of St. Serfs. They were wicker boxes constructed in such a way as to trap eels. This form of eel-fishing continued at the river Leven until 1860.

When Sir William Douglas died in 1556, Elizabeth Brown (Lady Kirkness) his widow, her two sons and her daughter were granted the lands of Kirkness along with the use of the Prior's boat upon the loch.

Kirkness, following the Reformation came under the jurisdiction of John Wynram, Superintendent of Fife and Strathearn. Wynram had been an Augustinian Canon and Prior of the Priory in Lochleven. He had taken part in many trials and burning of heretics and preached at the trial of George Wishart. On the eve of the Reformation he embraced the Protestant religion and was appointed Superintendent

* See Appendix No. I

284

of Fife in 1561. In 1560 he is styled as "of Kirkness". In 1562 he, with the consent of James Stewart perpetual Commondator of the Priory of St. Andrews gave to Margaret Stewart, widow of John Aytoun of Kinaldie in consideration of a large sum of money which she had given for the erection of a manse and a large garden at Kirkness, the life rent of the manse and the manor house of Kirkness with its garden also five cotter's houses with small gardens attached which were occupied by David Smith, David Law, William Hogg, John Cleinan and John Hering. Margaret also received sufficient stone and turf and other things necessary for the upkeep of the houses and for the maintenance of the Prior's Ward. In addition she was to have the life rent of the Isle of St. Serfs in Lochleven along with the fishings in the loch and the right to fish with baskets (cruives) at the mouth of the loch. For all this Margaret Stewart was to pay an annual rent of 6/8d for the manse and St. Serfs Isle, and five merks for the right to fish, making a total of £5, 13 4d.

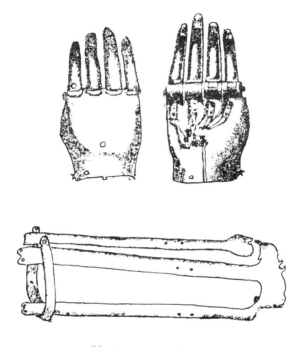

90 *The Carslogie Hand*

It is of particular interest to find it stated in the charter that the manse was to be used in future as the place where the barony courts of Kirkness were to be held. It seems that Wynram had more than a passing interest in Margaret Stewart for two years after the date of this charter he married the lady. Nineteen years afterwards, Kirkness was in the possession of the Aytouns of Kinaldie. There can be little doubt that it was through Wynram's influence that this came about. After his wife's death in 1573 Wynram had a dispute with the Aytouns over the right to retain several of his wife's gold trinkets and the succession to the rent of the manse of Kirkness.

285

The reason for his actions is not given, but in 1562 Wynram had several persons living at Kirkness "put to the horn" and their belongings confiscated. The Deed gives the names of the miscreants as Martine Heryne, Andrew Gregg, Robert Wilsoun, Robert Alexander, David Hakstoun, David Reid, Thome Wilsoun, James Burt and Andro Steidman all of Kirkness, and Johne Heyrne in the Greine (Green). All their belongings were to be given to George Wynram who was probably a relative of the Superintendent. In 1591 Kirkness with the Manor House of the Priors was still in possession of the Aytouns.

However, the Douglas family were acquiring more and more land in Bishopshire and at the turn of the century Sir George Douglas was in possession of Kirkness. In 1607 we read that George Oliphant of Buchiltoun sought the protection of the law from the laird of Kirkness who, along with others, had molested him. This laird was inclined to carry things through with a high hand and several Edinburgh merchants had to appeal to the courts in order to receive their due reward for services rendered.

The old church of Portmoak, situated at the edge of Lochleven, was now becoming ruinous and in winter it was not always accessible owing to the flooding of the loch. It was thus in 1645 that the laird of Kirkness was approached about a possible site for a church at Scotlandwell. Sixteen years were to pass before the new church was built: meanwhile Sir George Douglas died and his son Sir William became the laird of Kirkness. The new laird, however, had his own ideas about attending the church. While he was willing to give ground and contribute to the cost of building a new church, he much preferred to attend the church at Ballingry and in 1650 he appealed to the Presbytery to have Kirkness disjoined from the parish of Portmoak and annexed to Ballingry Parish. Things of this nature did not move any faster then than those of today. Two months afterwards, a deputation consisting of four elders visited the bounds of Kirkness in relation to Scotlandwell and Ballingry, and their unanimous decision was that "it was far more commodious for the laird of Kirkness and his servants to repair for heiring of the Word to the Kirk of Ballingry than to the Kirk of Portmoak". They pointed out that Kirkness lay one and half miles from Scotlandwell while it was only half a mile from Ballingry and that "the way being good and passabil at any time to the Kirk of Ballingry, and an evill way to the other, and many times impossible to travel upon it".

The Presbytery, however, was unwilling to rush into a decision right away. The matter came up on several occasions and at last the Presbytery unanimously approved the recommendations of the elders and recommended to the Lords, Commissioners of Parliament for the plantation of Kirks, to disjoin the "towne and lands belonging to Sir William Douglas of Kirkness in the paroshe of Portmoak and annex them to the paroshe of Ballingrie".

It was along this "evill way" to Scotlandwell that Cromwell led half of his army on his march to Perth in July of the following year after he had stayed overnight at Kirkness.

As we hear no more about the proposal to annex Kirkness to the Parish of Ballingry, we may conclude that the Commissioners accepted the Presbytery's recommendation, and that the change took place. Circumstances change with the years and in 1687 when religious feelings were running high and Mr Malcolm of Ballingry was the Episcopal minister, it is not surprising to find Lady Kirkness despatching one of her servants to intimate to her friends that a Presbyterian conventicle was to be held at Kirkness the following day on Sunday the 21st October.

Brigadier-General Sir William Douglas died in London in 1747 and was buried in the chapel at Kew. He left two sons, Robert, who was probably the elder, was in 1689 appointed one of the Commissioners to raise £228,000 Scots for the raising of troops for the security of the Protestant religion; and William, who joined the third Foot Guards was latterly Colonel of the regiment of the 32nd Foot. He died in the Netherlands in 1747.

Kirkness passed out of the Douglas family during the last quarter of the eighteenth century when George Clephane of Carslogie married, as his second wife, Anne, Jean Douglas of Kirkness, Sir William's widow. Shortly afterwards, the Celphane family's Seat was transferred from Carslogie to Kirkness. The eldest son of the marriage was Major General William Douglas Clephane, who married Marianne, daughter of Mr Maclean of Torloisk, Isle of Mull, and thereafter assumed the additional surname of Maclean. The Clephanes are said to have been well above average height and to have been a strong and courageous race. They were held much in awe by the local people and woe betide anyone who got in the way of their horses.

General Maclean Clephane was member of Parliament for Kinross-shire and was appointed Lieutenant-Governor of Granada. He died in 1804. His eldest daughter Margaret, who was born at Kirkness in 1793 married Spencer Joshua Alwyne, Earl Compton and second Marquis of Northampton in 1815. She died at Castle Ashby in 1830. Margaret Maclean Clephane was eleven years old when her father died, and Sir Walter Scott who knew her mother well, was appointed at their choice to be her guardian. Sir Walter arranged Margaret's marriage with Earl Compton and received letters from the future Marchioness written at Kirkness and posted at the Inn at Kelty Bridge.

91 *The Carslogie Horn*

287

In one of her letters dated Kirkness, 11th October, 1814, written shortly after the publication of *Waverley,* Miss Maclean Clephane wrote to Sir Walter clearly stating her opinion as to the authorship of the novel. She wrote — "In this place I feel a sort of pleasure not unallied to pain, from the many recollections that every venerable tree, and every sunny bank, and every honeysuckle bower, occasions; and I have found something here that speaks to me in the voice of a valued friend — *Waverley.* The question that rises, it is perhaps improper to give utterance to. If so, let it pass as an exclamation. Is it possible that Mr Erskine can have written it? The poetry I think, would prove a different descent in any court in Christendom. The turn of the phrases in many places is so peculiarly yours, that I fancy I hear your voice repeating them; and there wants but verse to make all Waverley an enchanting poem — varying to be sure from grave to gay, but with so deepening an interest as to leave an impression on the mind that few — very few poems — could awaken. But, why did not the author allow me to be his Gaelic Dragoman? Oh! Mr..., whoever you are, you might have safely trusted — M.M.C."

Scott was given the task of drawing up the marriage settlement, a task which he found not without its difficulties. He was anxious to ensure that Miss Clephane as Lady Compton, would be amply provided for from her own resources should she become a widow. Of course she was the heiress of her mother's property, "Torloisk" in Mull, but there were also her two younger sisters whose future had also to be provided for. The initial difficulty was overcome by her grandmother, Mrs Douglas Clephane of Kirkness and Manorlees. This old lady whom Scott had met some years previously and had thought rather odd, came forward with the generous offer of settling the estate of Kirkness on the bride-to-be. Through this marriage Kirkness became the property of the Marquis of Northampton.

Andrew Clephane, an uncle of the marchioness, was appointed Sheriff of Fife in 1820. He married a daughter of the House of Douglas and lived at Kirkness and after a distinguished legal career he died there in 1838. He had a son, a Lieutenant-Colonel of the 79th Highlanders, and two daughters. The elder daughter, Elizabeth, was born at Kirkness in 1830. After their father's death, the sisters left Kirkness and lived at Ormiston and latterly at Melrose. The two sisters were ardent church workers and were untiring in their work among the poor of Melrose. Elizabeth, although in poor health all her life, because of her cheery disposition earned for herself the sobriquet of "The Sunbeam". Elizabeth, as we have seen, was a successful hymn writer. She died in 1869.

Two heirlooms belonging to the Clephane family lay in Kirkness House for almost a hundred years. They were what became known in history as the Carslogie Hand and the Carslogie Horn. The former, according to tradition, was made on the order of Robert the Bruce for Alan Clephane, his follower, when he lost his left hand in battle. The steel hand was fitted with springs to enable him to hold his horse's reins when riding. Sir Walter Scott mentions this in his *Fair Maid of Perth.* The Carslogie Horn has been described as having ornamentation on it of Carlovingian work of the nineth century, consisting of carvings depicting chariot races and combats of men and animals. The two relics are now in the possession of the present Marquis of Northampton.

Surprisingly, the mansion of Kirkness retained traces of its former grandeur long after the departure of the Clephanes. As late as 1880, the fine library appears to have been more or less intact and contained many valuable manuscripts and rare books, the most notable of these was a small and extremely fragile volume containing the sermons of Bishop Hooper of Worcester who was burned at the stake on 5th February, 1555.

Kirkness at the turn of the present century was occupied by a Mrs Ballingall and in 1900 the estate was sold to Sir John Wilson of Airdrie. Two years afterwards when Mrs Ballingall was leaving Kirkness, she made arrangements to have the remaining treasures in the house gifted to the museum at Kinross.

From this time onward the house was allowed to fall into decay, its final demise came in 1920 when it was unroofed and in the following year workmen were busy removing the finely sculptured stones bearing the Coats of Arms of the families who had once resided there. The last of the gatherings to be held in the large upstairs drawing-room with its beautiful half-circle window looking out on Lochleven, as we well remember it, was an Induction dinner to the Rev. David Jamie when he came to Ballinry Parish in 1882.

It is a far cry from the days of Malcolm Canmore, when Mohan returned to his house at Kirkness and in desperation burned it down. How many houses have stood on this site no one can tell. The ruined mansion contains stones which appear to have come from earlier monastic buildings. Kirkness in its hey-day had a thriving village in its neighbourhood and a chapel. The remains of these can still be traced a little to the north of the ruined house. The old records tell of a Brewer and a Tailor in the village and gave the names of many of the cottars who lived there. The long tree-lined avenue set out in such a way as to give a distant view of St. Serfs Isle has gone, and The Greens which provided fodder for the horses of the followers of Prince Charles Edward Stuart is no more. With such a long and interesting past and as yet unspoiled by modern developments, Kirkness should prove an interesting place for the archaeologist to explore. Meanwhile, in the silence of decay, the old place holds fast to its secrets.

CROSSHILL: BURGH OF BARONY

Rural life in the barony of Inchgall was centred in the village of Crosshill, a cluster of houses in close proximity to Inchgall Castle which contained among other things the Mains lands of the barony, which lands were set apart for the laird's personal use and provided produce for the laird's table. One would suppose that the village had its origin as an appendage to the castle. Here lived the feudal vassals who were at all times subject to the laird's authority. Perhaps the village owed its beginning this way but its name suggests a much earlier origin. It testifies to the presence of a Christian symbol, probably a free-standing cross.

The lands of Crosshill lay astride one of the earliest routes in Fife, known of old as the Great Common, which stretched from Pettycur on the Forth through the lands of Dunnikeir and headed northward as Johnnie Marshall's Loan. It crossed the river Ore at Redford steps and, passing by the farm of Strathore, it headed westward through the land of Inchdairnie Muir, Mak-im-Rich and Strathruddie. From there it continued westward by way of Peatdykes, Coupmore, Shyrim Brae and Harelaw, descending towards Crosshill where it was known as the Common of the Milton Moss of Inchgall, to be known later as Torrie's Loan. It emerged from the lands of Wester Crosshill continuing westward towards the lands of East Blair passing on its way Ladath House. The west avenue to Lochore House when constructed in 1811 followed more or less the line of the old Common, passing on its way the lands of Rigwoodie. This part of the Common was known in olden times as Loanhead. From there it appears to have continued along the south side of Benarty, its line and direction marked by the modern road till it passed the lands of Binn and eventually joined up at Paran Well with the equally ancient route leading from Inverkeithing to Perth.

Not only are we to suppose that a wayside cross would of itself appeal to the emotions of the devout traveller in medieval times, but Crosshill, situated as it was on the Great Common, would also attract many a wayfarer as a convenient place in which to halt and be refreshed before continuing westward or journeying northward by way of the Gullet Bridge. As its inhabitants were the feudal tenants of the lord of the manor, working on his estate or employed in Inchgall Castle, the clachan drew to itself an ever-increasing number of clay-built hovels, the nucleus of the future burgh.

Some time in the early part of the sixteenth century Sir Henry Wardlaw carried out extensive alterations on Inchgall Castle and, probably in recognition of his efforts and his good services to the Crown, he was granted permission by James IV to erect his "toun of Corsehill" into a free burgh of Barony with power to erect a mercat cross and to hold a daily market and a special weekly market as well as a fair twice in the year. With the possible exception of "Serjandcroft" mentioned in 1546 which seems to imply the presence of a serjeant, there is as yet no evidence of a burgh having functioned under the Wardlaws. The serjeant was a person appointed by a burgh council to act as an official of the burgh court.

Crosshill, the village of the hand-loom, lost much of its character following the death of the last of the Wardlaws with the gradual decay of the island home and the final unroofing of the castle, but in 1617 the village was still enjoying its privileged position in the barony. In this year events outside the parish quickened the even tempo of the village life. The news from John Hunter provided an interesting topic of conversation.

The villagers would all be astir very early in the morning of 18th May, 1617. King James the sixth was visiting Scotland after a lapse of fourteen years and was residing at Holyrood House. One might ask how this had anything to do with the folk in Ballingry. The answer lies in the fact that it was the King's intention to visit St. Andrews and Dundee. He had a very large retinue and the amount of luggage that travelled with him was enormous.

Those whose business it was to arrange everything planned to cross the Forth from Leith to Burntisland and thence to St. Andrews. The transport difficulties were overcome by placing the responsibility of providing carts, carriages and horses on the parish constables. The number of vehicles and animals to be provided was to be assessed according to the number of ploughs in each parish.

John Hunter, the miller at Inchgall Mill in his capacity as constable* of Ballingry Parish, was instructed to find out the total number of ploughs in the parish. Having satisfied himself on this score, the miller sent his report to Edinburgh when he was advised in return that the parish was "stented to fifteen plewis". The miller was accordingly responsible for mustering fifteen carts, horse and drivers. Each contingent was to be at Burntisland harbour at six o'clock in the morning of 19th May to load the carts as the luggage was taken from the boats. Each loaded cart had a trace-horse but even so, considering the awful condition of the roads, it must have been a strenuous journey for both men and animals. The slow-moving column consisted of no less than eighty carts with their drivers and two hundred and forty horses, which number included the horses that pulled the carriages belonging to the nobility.

A similar occurrence took place on 5th July, 1633 when John Bugyall in Crosshill and Robert Meldrum in Inchgall Mill were parish constables. Ballingry parish on this occasion had to furnish twelve carts and twenty-four horses and drivers who, along with contingents from neighbouring parishes, had to be at Dunfermline Palace at 6 o'clock in the morning in order to convey the King's luggage to Falkland Palace. Five days later the contingents were to be at Falkland before three a.m. to uplift the Royal luggage and convey it to Burntisland harbour as the king (Charles I) was returning to Edinburgh. It is likely that as on a known previous occasion the king passed through the lands of Easter Cartmore on his way from Dunfermline to Falkland.

It may be asked what do we know of the town of Crosshill and the neighbouring lands during this period. Like most old land divisions, the lands of Crosshill were contained within natural boundaries and lay equally on either side of the highway going north. This gave rise to the terms Easter Crosshill and Wester Crosshill. Wester Crosshill had as its southern boundary part of the north shore of the loch facing Inchgall Castle, where there are still to be seen the remains of what appear to be very old dwellings probably the houses of the retainers of the castle. Travelling westward, these lands terminated at the Rosewell burn at a point between Crosshill and the lands of

---

* The office of parish constable carried an entirely different connotation from that of the police constable of today.

Ladath. The burn from the loch to its source took a circuitous route. Although today it is a mere ditch, it was until fairly recently easily identified by a mineral railway which followed the greater part of its course. At a point a little east of what is now Montrose Crescent, the march between the two estates went in a north-easterly direction, following as before the course of the burn to a point where the latter flowed out of a small lochan in close proximity to the highway. The site of the lochan is now the village bowling green.

92 *Sculptured stone from "Castlerags", Milton*

This northerly portion of Crosshill is shown in some old maps as Kirkland, on others Kirkhill. It is clear that the village Institute which stands on the site of the croft of Tushielaw lies surprisingly outwith the Lochore estate. Beyond the lochan was a very small stream, the overflow from one or two natural springs situated on the high ground in Ladath estate. Another source of water was the Rose Well. The overflow from these springs came from the direction of the crossroads at the north end of the village. It should be said that the term "Lochore estate" is of fairly modern usage. The old charters always referred to this part of the barony as Ladath. Mid-way up from the loch in Wester Crosshill and close to the highway stands a little knoll (now built upon); as the old charters always described Crosshill as being *above* Inchgall, it is more than likely that this is the "hill" alluded to in the name.

The southern-most point of Easter Crosshill where it adjoins the highway is at Crosshill cottage. It is here that the boundary takes a south-eastern course to march with the lands of Milton of Inchgall. To the east the lands of Crosshill are bounded by Torrie's Loan where, eventually veering north-west, they terminated at the crossroads at the north end of the village. This was the meeting place of four estates.

292

Looking northward, and commencing with the lands situated to the north-west and proceeding clockwise, they were known of old as the Kirklands of Ballingry, the lands of Flockhouse, the lands of Crosshill and the lands of Ladath. At a much later date when certain portions of land had been sold to others, these same lands appear as Craigie-Malcolm, Rosewell, Tushielaw and Lochore.

The present Crosshill cottage is well over one hundred years old and may be the last of a long line of dwellings to be built on this site. Built into the north wall of the garden of the house are three interesting stones. They appear to have been triangular pediments of dormer windows: one of the stones has carved upon it at its apex a mullet with two crescents underneath, while below are the initials I.P. and G.G. Further down are carved a hammer, tongs and a horse shoe and at the base of the triangle is the date 1652. The other two stones are also triangular: one bears the date 1659 and the other the initials I.K. and the date 1729. These stones were salvaged from a house in the Milton known as Castlerags. An old house near Crosshill cottage, recently demolished, bore the date 1625.

From 1511 onwards mention is made of the "Villum de Corsehill" and there is no reason to think otherwise than that the villa of Crosshill and its successors stood upon the site of Crosshill Cottage.

Situated a short distance on the rising ground to the north of Crosshill Cottage stood a row of stone-built houses on either side of the road. These houses with their red pantile roofs probably dated from the early eighteenth century and were known from their location as Easter Crosshill and Wester Crosshill respectively, all of which were demolished in the mid 1930s. These houses could be considered modern when compared with the "burgh" period. They were witness to the continuity of village life and perhaps marked the site of the one time "toun of Crosshill", as a ferm toun of the period could consist of as little as six or eight cottars' houses.

Returning to the various vocations that made up the life in the village of Crosshill, some idea of the character of the weekly market can be had from the writings of the period. The privilege of holding fairs and markets was repeated in favour of John Malcolm by Charles II in 1662. Under the patronage of the Malcolms a market was held every Friday and two free fairs annually on the 22nd of March and the 27th of June, each to last two days.

We can be fairly certain that the market was held in Wester Crosshill, probably up from the loch and opposite the Milton. The one and only street would no doubt be encroached upon as forebooths or stalls were erected in preparation for the day's business. We may rightly suppose that the local and the neighbouring tradespeople made up the generality of these public gatherings, each one in his day possessing a portable stall or booth and by his traditional skills and produce contributing to the well-being and progress of the community. The village traders, at most, must remain shadowy figures but we may with tolerable certainty include the following inhabitants among the stallholders of their day.

Such stable commodities as butter, cheese, milk and eggs were probably to be had at the stall belonging to Henry Dick of the Milton and Sarah Beveredge his wife, both of whom figured prominently in the 1600s. John Bugyall, who was living in Crosshill in

293

93 *A weaver at work at his hand loom (19th century)*

1609 and whose family was still to the fore in 1678, was the village butcher. He, with the help of his servant David Redie, would have joints of beef and mutton on display as well as poultry. Well-known attenders at the market would be Robert Meldrum the miller at Inchgall Mill and his wife Janet Thomson who were residing at nearby Balbegie in 1618.

One can readily imagine Meldrum chatting to the crofters and cottars enquiring as to how their crops were doing, especially their corn crops, knowing that sooner or later they all must come to his mill to have the corn ground into meal. James Mitchell, who was living at Ladath Steading in the 1600s and who worked the limestone deposits in Ballingry and Navitie with William Inglis as his overseer, would have samples of his produce on display in the form of lime fertiliser. Alexander Smith, another stallholder, was a nailor to trade and was going strong in 1641. He had hand-made nails of varying sizes on sale at an average cost of 8/-d Scots (8d) the hundred. The itinerant cobbler usually had a stall. He could make a pair of "shoon" out of a raw cowhide for £1.10/-d Scots and when necessary, could turn his hand to repairing horse harness. The stall occupied by John Paterson of Crosshill would no doubt be well patronised. His stall was always amply supplied with good light ale straight from Markie Beath a brewer at Kirkness, and from the Milton brewery, an institution first alluded to in 1546.

William Davidson and Patrick Murray were village carpenters and are known to have been plying their trade in Lochoreshire in the 1640s. Their stall would no doubt include among many other things, wooden rakes and harrows, flails, slypes, three-leg stools and an occasional peat barrow. Allied to the workers in wood was the village cooper whose stock-in-trade included tubs, luggies, lippie measures, coggies, potato mashers and perhaps an occasional display of wooden platters and horn spoons. Foremost among the indispensable artisans of the village was the "smithie" who is known to have held lands in the Milton as early as 1546. Blacksmithing, like most rural crafts was usually kept in the family, the son being apprenticed to his father down through the generations. It would be he who would make the "jougs" that hung on the wall of Ballingry Church, to which reference is made in 1642 when it was placed round the neck of Alexander Dick when punished by the kirk session for his misbehaviour. When not engaged in his usual task of shoeing farm horses and making "cues" for droving cattle, the smith usually found time to make such things as girdles, swees and pot-chains, oil cruisies, peat-cutters or the odd plough coulter for use on the wooden plough of the period, all for display at the village market.

In addition to the Mill of Lochore and Inchgall Mill there was one situated at the Milton referred to in 1663. Much earlier than this was the waulk mill at the Milton which was going strong in 1547. This mill was used in connection with the manufacture of linen. To "waulk" cloth was to thicken it. Other evidence of weaving is to be found in "litsters" residing at the Milton. These people were engaged in the dyeing of cloth. The weaver's stall would display coarse linen yarn and webs of material dyed and woven ready for use, also coarse woollen plaiding. Long hose woven in thick durable fabric were in use at this period and were sold at 1/-d Scots (1d) the pair.

In a make-shift enclosure hard-by the stalls were the farm animals. Here there were usually to be seen a score or so of sheep belonging probably to Henry Mitchell and Michael Chalmers or John Greig straight from the grazing on Benarty Common; also a number of black beef cattle belonging to James Mitchell of Ladath, all of which came under the critical eyes of the crofters, cottars and cowherds. Nearby a young horse or two tethered on a patch of rough grass stood patiently waiting to be led away by a new master. One can imagine that the tackman or coalgrieve from Blaircushnie coalheugh would be a frequent attender at the market looking for likely buyers among the limestone burners and brewers. Another probable attender would be the person who had the fishing rights on Loch Ore. In 1614 the fishings are referred to and it appears that salmon were to be found in the river Ore. The rental of the fishings on Lochleven at this period was £23 per annum, but in the year that Loch Ore was drained it had risen to £123. Fish from Lochleven were hawked through Kinross in creels and trout were kippered in the house chimneys like red herrings. Trout was sold at 4d the pound, perch, pike and eels at 2d the pound. Similar activities on a lesser scale may have prevailed at Crosshill. Probably alongside the fishmonger was the salt cadger from the salt works at Kinglassie which at this period belonged to James Riddell a Leith merchant. The "sautter" no doubt would be much to the fore as his commodity was among the foremost necessities of life.

Among those who frequented the toun on market days — ploughmen, threshers,

94 *The Jougs*

drystone-dykers and drovers — were the travelling packman and cadger or carrier. Bringing the latest news from the neighbouring touns, they were not infrequently sought out by the village gossips. The packman on paying a penny for custom was allowed to set up his stall and show off the contents of his pack. The cadger with his pack-horse sauntered from one stall to another chatting to the stallholders and in general making himself known and seen by all in the hope that someone would engage him to carry home newly bought merchandise to a neighbouring croft or biggin.

After forty years or so the market had lost much of its importance and presumably went into decline. It was replaced in 1701 by a "New Fair" established at the Milton of Inchgall by Sir John Malcolm. Similar to a New Fair set up at Kinglassie in 1703, the stallholders at the Milton were, by ancient custom, obliged to pay dues to the burgh of Inverkeithing. The Fair was known locally as the Weaver's Market. It continued according to tradition well into the nineteenth century. Most of the weaving done latterly was for Kirkcaldy merchants who supplied the weft. A weekly supply was sent by cart to Lochgelly.

With the increasing use of machinery in the 1800s, coupled with cheap rate piecework and standardisation, the hand loom weaving came to an end. No longer was heard the "Shiedeldy — Shadeldy" of the loom in the village. The weaver families by now had gone over to coal mining. The old customs of the hand loom weavers were soon to be forgotten in the changed ways of village life and within another generation all memories of hand loom weaving had gone forever.

296

Long before the closing of the Fair at the Milton there had been signs that Crosshill and the Milton were gradually losing their importance. Although a site for the parish school at the Milton was contemplated, it was Ballingry that won the day. The school was built there in 1722. It was about this time that the Shank of Navitie was becoming a self-contained little community. There had of course been an Inn there from very early times and rivalled the Spail Inn as a welcome place for travellers. Janet Bruce of the Shank, who was probably its proprietor, was selling ale and brandy in 1760, and James Westwood at the Shank was supplying ale and tallow candles there in 1765. By the following century the number of inhabitants at the Shank had increased many times and included John Brand, shoemaker, Robert Low, blacksmith and William Suttie, grocer and carter.

The Kirkton of Ballingry had by this time developed also, and included George Robertson, tailor and George Williamson who sold ale there. Other tradesmen in the neighbourhood included George Dick, tailor at Kirkness and James Anderson who sold ale in the village of Kirkness. There was also John Elder, joiner, who figures in the church records, and the tailor who plied his trade at Tushielaw.

Coming to more modern times we record the presence of a grocer at Glencraig in the person of Robert Wishart. As this was at a time long before the mining village came into being we may suppose that Mr Wishart had his small business in the Contle Row.

As with the rural markets and the hand loom weaving, coal mining has had its day, and life in the village has come full circle. Green fields brighten the Ore valley where King Coal once held sway and Inchgall Castle looks down once more on a quiet countryside.

THE MAKING OF A VILLAGE

With the sinking of the colliery at Glencraig in 1895 and the Mary Colliery at Lochore in 1902, there was a marked increase in the population of the neighbourhood. Previous to this period the small mines at Capeldrae, Lochore, Crosshill and Milton had employed a relatively small number of people. By the year 1903 the Benarty Colliery which had hitherto been the largest employer of local labour, was employing one hundred and twenty persons below ground and eighteen above ground. The Glencraig Colliery by now was fast developing its resources and was employing five hundred and sixty-four persons underground and one hundred and twelve above, while at the Mary Colliery one hundred and four persons were working underground and sixty-seven persons above.

As these collieries developed their underground workings the number of people coming to the district greatly increased. New houses were built at Glencraig and preparations were afoot for the building of the village of Lochore. It was during this early stage in the development of the village that a serious outbreak of fever occurred.

Up to this period the people in the neighbourhood had obtained water from draw-

95 *Old view of Kirkton of Ballingry*

298

wells and natural springs. As a good supply of water is essential in the everyday life of a community, when every drop had to be carried, it is not surprising that the wells of old were never far removed from places of habitation.

Starting at the extreme wester limits of Lochoreshire and travelling eastward, there was the Paran Well near the Binns, known as the site of the attempted ambush of Mary, Queen of Scots and her husband Darnley, Cardies Well near Benarty House which, like the other two wells of this name in Fife, may be associated with Gilolamo Cardano of Milan, the celebrated physician, Gruoch's Well near Ballingry farm of which we have already spoken, the Manse Well on the site of the present Ballingry church hall, Ladath Well near Lochore House, the Butter Well near the Flockhouse, Rose Well at the crossroads in the village of Lochore, Tushielaw Well north-west of the former railway bridge at Lochore although really in Wester Crosshill, the Milton Well near the river Ore, and Shirum Well a little to the north of Inchgall farm. Other wells with historical associations in Lochoreshire were the Stane Well in Lochgelly, the Holy Well in Auchtertool, the Priest's Well in Auchterderran and St. Glassin's Well in Kinglassie. No doubt there would be more wells of which there is no record.

96 *Old View of Contle*

The miners' houses which had been recently erected at Glencraig had a piped water supply from a tank at the colliery, but there was no such thing at Lochore, and for many years previous to 1903 there had been cases of fever in the village. When the Mary Colliery was sunk the Coal Company provided a water tank at the colliery from which workmen filled their flasks and the people living at the Mary Row (known later as

299

Peveral Place) carried water from the tank for their daily use. The water came from the Ladath burn which passed close by the steading near Lochore House where there was a nearby open ash-pit. Not surprisingly, the water became contaminated and there were twenty-one cases of typhoid fever at Mary Row during the month of July. A little later there were eight more cases in the village of Lochore. After the initial outbreak, a supply of water was obtained from a spring situated a little to the west of the Ladath burn, but this too became polluted through the deliberate acts of persons who broke down nearby water troughs and allowed contaminated water to enter the stream. Before the month was out, fifteen persons had died and over one hundred and fifty cases had been admitted to Thornton Hospital. Almost every family in the village had suffered. Two trained nurses were sent to reside in the village to attend to the sick, their wages being paid by the Coal Company. Pure water was brought to the village daily in carts and in order to ease the anxiety of many of the people, the Coal Company made advances of money. The distress in the village had now gained such proportions that the matter was raised in the House of Commons. A relief fund was started to assist those

97 *Flockhouse School (now demolished)*

who had suffered most, and plans were discussed for a temporary water supply to be piped to the village. During the months that followed many schemes were proposed but none seemed satisfactory, meanwhile water continued to be brought to the village in carts. At length in December 1903, the burgh Council of Lochgelly came forward with a proposal that could not be refused. The Council was prepared to lay a pipe to the village a distance of two miles to provide a permanent water supply at a charge of 8d per one thousand gallons. The water was to be had at several draw-off points throughout the village. The last of the old-fashioned cast-iron stand pipes with their domed tops incorporating a lion's head, placed at the side of the road, went out of use in 1918 when a greatly improved water supply from Glenfarg was brought to the village.

Glencraig was slightly ahead of Lochore in developing, and in 1901 a Gothenburg was built at North Glencraig. Two years afterwards in 1903 the United Free Church built a church at Lochcraig, with the Rev. Charles Mason as its minister, to meet the spiritual needs of the people living in the southern half of the village. In the following year the Lochore and Glencraig Nursing Association was established.

98 Crosshill, from the South c.1900

No community, be it ever so young, remains long without some form of sport and in 1905 the Glencraig Juvenile Football Club was formed. The year 1907 saw the formation of the Lochore Golf Club and the opening of a Miners' Institute at Lochore. This was probably due in no small measure to the energy of Mr J. Beveridge, the Manager of Mary Colliery. In this same year a Public Institute was opened at Glencraig under the guidance of William Telfer, Manager of the colliery. A Rechabites' "Tent" was also established this year and the Lochore Star of Hope Lodge of the Independent Order of Good Templars was formed. In 1908 the United Free Church appointed Miss

301

Jessie Glass as mission agent at the Church's Mission Hall held in the former Flockhouse School. In this year a hall was added to the Institute at Lochore and a Coat's Library was opened at Ballingry. The medical practitioners for the district were Doctors Todd, Dixon and Anderson. In 1909 the Lochore and Glencraig Feather Association was formed and James K. Park became Schoolmaster at Ballingry on the death of his father-in-law, William Shaw. Mary A. Dunbar was appointed headmistress at Crosshill Infant's School this year, and Robert Wilson became Manager of Glencraig Colliery and William Lang, Manager of the Mary Colliery, Lochore.

The year 1910 saw many new activities established in the community. The Lochore and Benarty Working Men's Library, the Ballingry Literary Society, the Young Men's Fellowship Association, the "Lochore Castle" Lodge of the Sons of Temperance, the Ballingry Angling Club, the Lochore and Glencraig Darts Association, the Lochore Juvenile Football Club and the Glencraig Rovers Football Club all came into being this year. A Public Hall was opened at Lochore, and Gothenburgs were built at Crosshill and Lochore. A public Hall-cum-Picturedrome was opened at Crosshill under the management of James Preston.

99 Lochore, from the North c.1900

In this year Doctor Anderson left the district and Doctor Sinclair took over his practice. The Lochore and Glencraig Baptist Church was formed and met for worship in Hope Terrace. The Rev. W. H. McDermid was inducted minister of Ballingry Parish following the death of the Rev. David Jamie. Edward Henderson was appointed

302

Missionary of the parish and conducted services at Glencraig and at the Mission Hall, Lochcraig. James Clarke became Manager of Glencraig Colliery. In this year the Tramway service was extended from Lochgelly to Lochore, the fare from Lochore to Dunfermline being 8d.

In 1912 John Henderson became Registrar and Inspector of the poor. In 1913 J. Roden was Manager of the Mary Colliery and in 1914 the Rev. J. Mulherron became parish Priest. In 1917 a Roman Catholic School-cum-Church was built at Crosshill with Miss McCormick as School Mistress. In this same year Miss G. Sorrie was School Mistress in Crosshill Infants School. Other activities included Glencraig Pipe Band, Glencraig Celtic Football Club and Crosshill Hearts Football Club. Quoiting became popular in this year and quoiting grounds were established at Rosewell and at Glencraig. J. Stewart was Manager at the Mary Colliery.

100 *Milton and Wester Crosshill c.1930*

The year 1918 saw another three clubs established. Glencraig Violet Football Club, the Lochore and Crosshill United Football Club and the Glencraig Burns Club. Robert Crawford was appointed Manager at Glencraig Colliery. In 1919 the Ancient Order of Shepherds formed a lodge at Lochcraig, and in 1920 the Ballingry Lodge of Freemasons, the Glencraig Peoples' Picture Palace and the Glencraig branch of the Miners' Union were established.

APPENDIX I

The names of those who were present at the perambulation of the boundaries of Kirkness and Lochore in 1395.

Robert, Earl of Fife and Menteith
Walter, Bishop of St. Andrews
Alexander, Bishop of Caithness
Michael de Ramesay, Lieutenant and Sheriff of Fife
Andrew de Wyntoun, Prior of St. Serfs
Ricardo de Ballingry
Johis de Bosvyle
Roberti de Levygston] Barons of Easter Lochoreshire
Henricus de Arnot
Andreas de Gatmilk
Johannes de Beton
Willelmus Scot de Balweary
Michael de Balfoure
Willelmus de Meldrom
Johonnes de Strivelyn
William de Drumduff
James de Demstartone
John de Glen
John de Balmacankow
Thomas de Karnys
Laurance de Balnavis
Aye (Adam) Jonson
John Andree
Adam Andree
Andrew Duncani
Alexander Hagy
John Hering
Thomas Sibald
John Lassols
Duncan Campbell
Hugo de Ramesay
Alexander Gourlay
Thomas Madoure

APPENDIX II

The Bond as sent out to the Heritors of Fife in 1678.

We the Noblemen, Barons and Heritors of the sheriffdom of Fife underscribing faithfully bind and oblige us that we our wives, bairns, and servants, respectively, shall no ways be present at any conventicle or disorderly meeting, in time coming but shall live orderly in obedience to the law under the pains and penalties contained in the Acts of Parliament thereanent. As also we bind and oblige us, that our haill tenants and cottars respectively, their wives, bairns, and servants, shall likewise abstain and refrain from the said conventicles, and other illegal meetings not authorize by law; and further, that we or they shall not reset, supply or commune with forfeited persons, intercommuned ministers, or vagrant preachers; but do our utmost to apprehend their persons and in case any of them shall contravene the same, we shall take and apprehend any person or persons guilty thereof, and present them to the judge ordinary, that they may be fined and imprisoned therefore, as is provided by the Acts of Parliament made thereanent; otherwise we shall remove them and their families from off our ground; and if we fail therein, we shall be liable to such pains and penalties as the delinquints have incurred by the law, and for the more security, consenting their presints be registered in the book of the Council.

APPENDIX III

Copy of Memorandum of 1867 dealing with the lease of the Lochore minerals during the time of Lady Scott.

Messrs Aytoun, Anderson and Goodall's
Lease of part of Lochore Minerals

The minerals let to Messrs Aytoun, Anderson and Goodall are those under the lands shaded ☐ and ▦ on the Plan.

They are entitled to have surface works upon the lands shaded ☐ but none upon those shaded ▦ except Bores. They may however sink a Pit in the corner of the Horse Park where the Fountain head is. This corner is enclosed with lines on the Plan and is marked A.B.C. This Pit must be filled up in two years.

No minerals are to be worked out below the houses or Steadings nor within one hundred and fifty yards of Lochore House nor within fifty yards of the Offices or any other buildings on the Estate.

They have power to work, win, store and carry away the Minerals, and to sink Pits, erect Engines and other Machinery and put up buildings including houses for Colliers and make Railroads and other Roads, form Reservoirs and Water Runs and Coal Hills.

All works are to be carried on so as to do as little injury as possible to the land and to the houses, fences, woods and crops.

All chimneys are to be of a height to be approved of by the Landlord.

All Railroads and other Roads are to be laid off to the satisfaction of the Landlord and as far as possible must be alongside of the fences and so as not to injure the lands and the farm operations. There are to be no works of any kind within the Woods nor within one hundred yards of them. There are to be no works of any kind above ground within one hundred yards of the farm Steadings or other houses. There are to be no Bores in the Lawn or pleasure grounds at Lochore House nor in the Garden or Office nor in the Gardens or Office of the Steadings or Cottages on the Estate. The Tenants are to sink a proper Pit in order to work the Coal in a place to be approved of by the Landlord and that by 15th May, 1869 at the latest.

No Iron stone is to be removed from the Estate in a raw state without consent of the Landlord.

Colliers houses or other houses and hearths for calcining Iron Stone are only to be erected on lands Shaded ☐ on the Plan and not until the Landlord approves of the site.

Messrs Aytoun & Co. are to pay to the Landlord or to the Landlord's Tenants for all land they take off or damage, and for all damage they cause to houses, walls, fences, wells and water thereof and watering places and Trees, and to the surface of the lands and crops thereon and pasture, and to the woods and Roads.

They are to repair and restore all Drains or anything else damaged by them and to enclose all land broken or taken up by them.

They are also to restore or pay for restoring all fences broken or injured by them and to erect and maintain Gates when required for keeping open the communication between any land they have taken.

They are to enclose all Ponds, Railways, Roads, Hearths for Iron Stone and all other works with a fence four feet high. All Pits not in use are to be enclosed with stone and lime walls five feet high.

They are not to fill up any Pits without consent of the Landlord

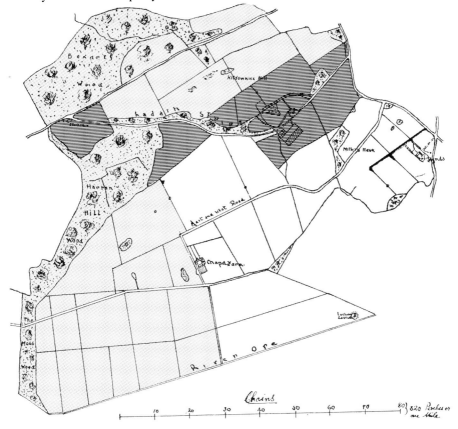

101   LOCHORE MINERALS
Mess.⁴ᵗ NIMMO AND SON 1864.

They are not to use the Avenue to Lochore House, but may use all other Roads, Ponds, Water Runs and Streams but so as not to occasion loss or injury to the Landlord, but they must keep them all in good repair and condition.

All disputes and differences between them and the Tenants on the Estate are to be settled by arbitration as is provided in the Tenants' leases or in the articles of Roup of the Grass Parks and Meadows.

Messrs Nimmo & Sons
Lease of part of Lochore Minerals

The Minerals let to Messrs Nimmo are those under the lands shaded ▦ and ☐ on the Plan.

They are entitled to have surface works upon the lands shaded ☐ but none upon those shaded ▦ except Bores and except also in the East and West Bowhouse Parks where they may have ingoing-eyes but these eyes must be kept below the brow of the banks so as not to be seen from the Avenue. There are to be no Pits nor Engines nor Chimneys in these Parks nor anything that will cause smoke or a nuisance. There may be a hutch way or road from the eyes to the Chapel road but no Coal hills or calcining hearths or any other operations on the surface of the lands.

NOTE: The remainder of this lease is similar to that of Aytoun, Anderson & Goodall above.

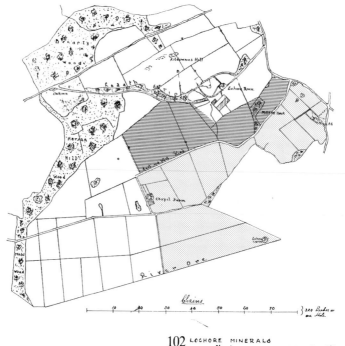

102 LOCHORE MINERALS
Messrs AYTOUN, ANDERSON, AND GOODALL 1867.

APPENDIX IV

Copy of scroll presented to Sir Walter Scott on becoming a member of the Musomanik Society.

THE MUSOMANIK SOCIETY, ANSTRUTHER

BE IT KNOWN TO ALL MEN, by these Presents, that WHEREAS Apollo, the Sovereign Lord of Poetry, hath by particular Predilection, singled us out from the Prosaic Herd of Men, to be the special Vessels of his Illumination, and, in consequence of that Choice, hath, in his high Benignity, shed a generative Ray upon the naturally barren Soil of our Pericraniums, thereby rendering them exceedingly rich and prolific of *Odes, Ballads, Bouts rimés, Acrostics, Pastorals, Epic Poems,* and other *Rhythmical Effusions:*

AND WHEREAS, Deeming it unwise and unprofitable to dissipate the richness and fecundity of our Brains in the vulgar Intercourse with men, We have Associated ourselves into a MUSOMANIK SOCIETY AND CLUB OF RHYMERS, in order to enjoy, by reflection of one another's Fire, the Coruscations of our own festive minds, by that means truly testing, with the heightened gust of Self-Administration, the pleasure of our Poetical existence:

FURTHER, WHEREAS considering, that, Gifted as we are with sharp and penetrating Wisdom, we can easily Discern the Seal of Apollo Stamped upon the Forehead of our Elect Harmonist WALTER SCOTT, WHEREBY it is evident that the Unshorn God Claims HIM for His Own,—

WE, THE VICEGERENT SUBJECTS of the said Apollo in ANSTRUTHER, Numbering that of the Nine Muses, Do Hereby ADMIT, LEGITIMATE, EN-FRANCHISE, AND INAUGURATE the Said WALTER SCOTT Into our MUSOMANIK SOCIETY, BROTHERHOOD, AND CORPS—Freely Bestowing upon Him all its Rights and Privileges; and Granting Him liberty to Rhyme and Scribble in what Shape, Manner, and Degree he Will, whether he be pleased to *Soar in the Epopee, to Sink in the Song,* to *Puzzle in the Riddle,* to *Astonish in the Odes,* or to *Amuse and Make Merry* with the *Bouts rimés.*

GIVEN, SIGNED, SEALED, and NUMBERED at THE HALL OF APOLLO in ANSTRUTHER, the SIXTEENTH day of MARCH, in our Third Year of Grace One Thousand Eight Hundred and Fifteen.
No.37. CHARLES GRAY, *Laureate Chief.* ANDREW JOHNSTON, *Bard.* JAMES DOW, *Songster.* WM. TENNANT, *Recorder.*
L.S. THOMAS WHITE, *Keeper of Seal and Riband.* WILL. COCKBURN, *Treasurer.* MATT. F. CONOLLY, *Sec. and Dipl.* ANDREW G. CARSTAIRS, *Chaplain.* DAVID RODGER, *Warden.*

APPENDIX V

Valuation of several lands in Lochoreshire before the year 1695
(Old Valuation)

Lochead	£1.0	The East Part	
Lochgellie	£3.0	of Lochoreshire	£3.0
Lumfennans	£3.0	Balbedie	£2.0
Pitcairns and Towchits	£6.0	Muirton, Starndy, Pitkenie	
Raith, Glennistoun		and Dundonald	£2.0
and Powguild	£3.0	Cleish-Meldrum	£2.0

Valuation of the lands of Lochoreshire in the year 1695
(New Valuation)

EASTER LOCHORESHIRE		WESTER LOCHORESHIRE OR BARONY OF INCHGALL	
Countess of Rothes	£470.0.0	Sir John Malcolm	£514.0.0
Countess of Wemyss	£280.0.0	Michael Malcolm	£514.0.0
Cardone	£1292.6.8	Balbeady	£668.10.0
Little Balgonie	£601.6.8	Blair	£240.13.4
Balgreigie	£423.0.0	Ballingrie	£156.13.4
Glenistoun	£309.0.0	Countle	£176.13.4
Boghall	£321.0.0	Corshills	£122.0.0
Pitkenny Weemys	£311.13.4	Templeland	£38.0.0
North Strathrudie	£177.0.0	Milntoun	£27.0.0
Easter Bowhill	£227.0.0	Navittie	£153.13.4
Wester Bowhill	£242.6.8	Cartmore	£211.0.0
Mr David Dewar	£592.0.0	Ladath	£130.0.0
Kinninmont	£1122.0.0	Kinninmonth	£123.6.8
Easter Cartmore	£147.0.0	Countess of Rothes	£400.0.0
Powguild	£579.0.0		
Wester Lochgelly	£363.0.0		

APPENDIX VI

POPULATION OF THE PARISH OF BALLINGRY

Year	Number of Persons	
1698	260	34 lived in Balbedie
1700	254	34 lived in Balbedie
1743	389	including 92 fighting men (aged 18-56 years)
1755	464	
1791	220	comprising 55 families
1793	220	
1798	220	
1801	277	
1811	269	
1821	287	
1831	372	
1833	392	
1851	565	91 houses in the parish
1857	568	
1861	736	141 houses in the parish
1871	982	194 families; 173 houses occupied; 11 houses uninhabited; 3 being built
1881	1065	219 families; 178 persons residing in the village of Lochore; 199 houses occupied; 75 houses uninhabited; 70 lived in single-roomed houses; 97 lived in two-roomed houses; 9 reached the age of 65 years; most deaths occurred at 50 years of age; the oldest inhabitant was 85 years of age; 2 spoke gaelic;
1891	2275	410 resided in the village of Lochore

APPENDIX VII

A list of farmers in the barony of Inchgall

BALLINGRY FARM

1763	Mr Crawford
1862	David Cation (farm steward)
1866	Jane Gilmour
c.1918	Grace Robertson

ROSEWELL FARM

1835-1846	Wm. Fowlis (tacksman)
1862	Michael Duncan
1866	Charles Duncan

NAVITIE FARM

1846	David & Adam Beath
1862-1866	Robert Simpson
1885	John Arnott, Jnr
1889	A. L. Liddel
1893	John Robertson

KIRKLANDS FARM

1832-1846	John Wilson
1862-1866	Thomas Wilson
1885-1893	John Paton

HYNDS FARM

1862	David Greig
1866	Thomas Thomson
1869-1899	Lochore & Capeldrae Coal Co.

GLENCRAIG FARM

1866	Robert Henderson

BRIGGHILLS FARM

1866	Thomas Jackson

EAST BLAIR FARM

1837-1846	James Ramsay

WESTER COLQUHALLY FARM

1835-1846	Peter Kinninmonth

EASTER COLQUHALLY FARM

1835-1846	George Kinninmonth
1866	David Kinninmonth

EASTER CARTMORE FARM

1835-1846	David Greig
1866	George Kinninmonth

WESTER CARTMORE FARM

1866	Alexander Greig

CHAPEL FARM

1835	Alexander Christie
1862-1866	John Soutter
1878-1885	David Aitken
1907	John Farmer

LUMPHINNANS FARM

1862	Miss Hogg
1866	George Wilson (farm stewart)
1885	William Drysdale
1893	Hugh Stewart

WESTER BALBEDIE FARM

1835-1846	James Paton
1866-1889	Mrs Ann Paton

WESTFIELD FARM

1893	Laurence & Robert McFarlane

CAPELDRAE FARM

1866	William Mitchell

CRAIGEND FARM

1845-1866	Robert Glass

INCHGALL MILL/FARM

1617	John Hunter
1633	Robert Meldrum
1713	James Black
1794	James Paterson
1832-1846	David Russell
1857	James Brown
1862-1866	William Duncan
1885	W. B. Dick
1893	Janet Drysdale
1900	William Drysdale

APPENDIX VIII

Some unusual place-names in Lochoreshire past—

God-Tour, Cutty-Gates, Gomorah, Flaggis-Pat, Hind-Loup, Penty-Ha', Stand-Still, Tilly-Lum, Ba-field, Glack, Crop-Ha', Hunger-him-out, Sodom, Punnel-Neuk, Coup-Owre, Blink-Bonnie, Hare-Stanes, Satan's Castle, Goat Milk, Bloody-Feet, Mak-im-Rich, White Ha', Pitconmark, Cauld-Back, Puddle-Dub, Shank-o-Navitie, Find-me-out, Spion-Kop, Clerk-Whig, Doll's Park, The Stip, Miller's Neuk, Drumshandry, Cleikum Inn, Dandie Row, Dogtoun, Sillytoun.

The following streets that made up the village of Lochore at the beginning of the present century were associated with Sir Walter Scott. Only the first four streets now remain:

Durward Street, Mannering Street, Ivanhoe Avenue, Abbotsford Road, Waverley Street, Montrose Street, Cumnor Place, Glenallan Street, Peveril Place, St. Ronan's Place, Candlemaker Row, Dumbiedykes, Dandie Row.

INDEX

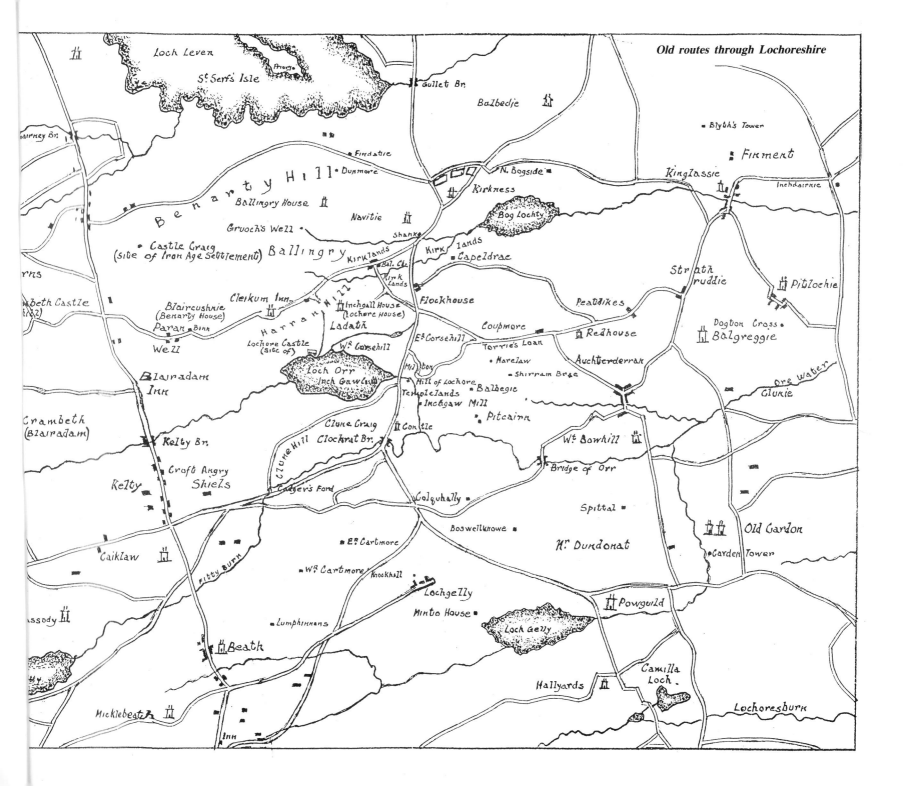

Old routes through Lochoreshire